AF597895

TOWN PLANS IN PLACE AND TIME

Extension Planning and Conservation
in the 1909 Copenhagen International Competition

HÉLÈNE VACHER

TOWN PLANS IN PLACE AND TIME

Extension Planning and Conservation in the 1909 Copenhagen International Competition

HÉLÈNE VACHER

© The Author and Aalborg University Press, 2004

Omslag: Hélène Vacher
Omslagsillustration: Karl Strinz, *Urania*. Detail of the layout plan for the extension of Copenhagen, 1908, scale 1:20.000.
Reproduced by courtesy of the Town Hall Archives, Copenhagen.
Layout: Gitte Thorsted
Tryk: Nørhaven Book, Viborg
ISBN 87-7307-712-7

BOGEN ER UDGIVET AF:
Aalborg Universitetsforlag
Niels Jernes Vej 6B
9220 Aalborg Ø
Tlf. 96 35 71 40 / 96 35 71 41
e-mail: aauf@forlag.aau.dk

CONTENTS

LIST OF FIGURES AND ILLUSTRATIONS VIII
PREFACE IX
ACKNOWLEDGEMENTS X

INTRODUCTION 13

PART I PROFESSIONS AND TOWN PLANNING 19

1 THE MAKING OF GREAT COPENHAGEN 22
Town Planning Competitions and Capital Cities 22
Denmark in the International Movement for Town Planning 24
Town Planning Competition as Civic Experience 28
Planning Great Copenhagen 30
Organising and Holding the Competition 33
The Organisation of the Competition 34
The Jury's Members 37
The Selection of the Entries 40

2 GROUP BIOGRAPHY OF THE NINETEEN ENTRIES 43
'Gefion' 45
'Urania' 45
'⊕' 47
'Tre Træer' 48
'Anno 1977' 49
'Hafnia' 50
'Julemærket for 1908' 51
'Wayland Smed' 52
'Grønne Baand' 53
'Storstad' 54
'For Byen og Borgerne' 55
'Mindre Parker men Parkalléer' 57
'Bella' 57
'Millionbyen' 58
'Københavns Vaaben 1296' 59
'Et Kløverblad' 61
'Stor-Kjøbenhavn' 62

'Richesse oblige' 63
'Axelhus' 64

3 THE COMPETITION, A STAGE IN DISCIPLINES AND PROFESSIONS 65
The Reception of the Competition 65
The International Town Planning Exhibition 65
The Competition in the Light of Newspapers and Professional Journals 68
Alfred Raavad and Charles Schou's Views on the Role of Competitions 72
From Town Plan Design to Physical Planning 74
Competitions and the Professional Movement 75
The Danish Professional Milieu 76
German Surveyors' Enlistment in Planning 80
Sitte's Followers in 1909 85
Engineers in Design Practice 87
'Modernismo' and Planning 88

PART II EXTENSION PLANNING IN THE AGE OF HISTORICISM 91

4 CIVIC ART DESIGN AND THE GREAT CITY 94
Conservation in Town planning
Town Planning's Dimensions 95
The Civic Art Movement and Design 97
Variations on Conservation in Town Plan Design 103
'Urania' 104
'Tre Træer' 106
'Millionbyen' 107
'København Vaaben 1296' 109
'Anno 1977' 109
'Wayland Smed' 111
The Swedish Entries 113
Overview of other Proposals 116

5 CITY FORMS IN DETAIL 118
Karl Strinz's Design 118
Alfred Raavad's Design 120
Incorporating Villages 122
The City's Boundaries and the Fortifications 122
The City's Boundaries and the Connections toward the Lakes 124
The Great City's Macroform and the Treatment of Limits 127
The New Districts' Layouts 129
Raavad's "Midtvejen af park og boulevard beltet" 131

PART III TOWARD THE HISTORIC CITY 141

6 CONSERVING THE CITY, PERCEPTIONS AND STRATEGIES 144
The Debate about Conservation in Europe 1890-1914 144
Vanishing Cities 145
The Place and its Social Dimension 146
The Old city as a Cultural Cradle 147
Municipalism and Conservation 149
Conservation as Professional Expertise 150
About Conservation in a Colonial Set Up 150
From Conservation to Safeguarding Strategies 151
Copenhagen and its Spheres of Transformation 153
Representations of City's Territories 159
Modernity, Practicalities and Hygiene 160
The Picturesque City 162
The City as a Monument 163

7 'OLD COPENHAGEN', FROM SURVEY TO ACTION 173
Conservationists and the 'Old Copenhagen' 173
The Realm of Saturn 174
Architectonics and Harmonics 176
Design in Context 177
Negotiating Conservation 178
The Movement for Conservation 179
Foreningen til Hovedstadens Forskønnelse 181
Østifternes Historisk-Topografiske Selskab 185
Foreningen til gamle Bygningers Bevaring 187

CONCLUSION 191

BIBLIOGRAPHY 198

LIST OF FIGURES AND ILLUSTRATIONS

The Government and Administration of Copenhagen 36
Overwiew over the 1909 Competitions Entries 44
The City Engineer Office 78
Karl Strinz's Design 119
Alfred Raavad's Design 121
Incorporating Villages, Alternative Design Strategies 123
The Old City's Boundaries, Christianshavn's fortifications 125
The City's Boundaries, Connections toward the Lakes 126
The Great City's Macroform, Treatment of Limits 128
New Districts, Alternative Layouts 130
Alfred Raavad, *Midtvejen af park og boulevard beltet* 131
The nineteen Entries according to five Criteria 132
Entry n° 2, *Urania* 133
Entry n° 4, *Tre Træer* 134
Old City's Boundaries in *Tre Træer* 135
Entry n° 15, *Københavns Vaaben 1296* 136
Entry n° 5, *Anno 1977* 137
Entry n° 14, *Millionbyen* 138
Entry n° 8, *Wayland Smed* 139
Spheres of Transformation in the City Centre 155
The Press and the City Skyline 167
Urban Clearance in the Old City 168
Towards the Modern City 169
Great Copenhagen 1900 170
Nybørs or *De Seks Søstre* 171
The Picturesque Copenhagen 172

PREFACE

1908 was an important year for Danish city planning. The ongoing international debate on city planning rested on the late 19th century's intense city development. Cities grew and so did Copenhagen. Around 1900 peasants flocked to Copenhagen. They became workers and moved into the rapidly growing former suburbs, the areas outside the Copenhagen city gates. Copenhagen grew at an unprecedented speed. Those who governed at the City Hall at that time had been far-sighted. The City bought up land also outside the city limit and in 1901-02 a series of rural districts surrounding Copenhagen was incorporated in the Copenhagen government – towns such as Brønshøj, Valby and Husum.

An international city planning movement had emerged and some of the most important works were actually prepared during this period with slum districts, lack of light and air and speculators who instead of creating functional and beautiful cities gained huge profits.

In 1889, Camillo Sitte wrote "Der städte-bau nach seinen künstlerrischen Grundsätzen" and in 1902-04, Ebenezer Howard wrote "City of Tomorrow". In the same period many large European cities such as Vienna (1893), Helsingfors (1899), Helsingborg (1906) and Berlin (1910) arranged competitions on how the rapidly growing cities could be planned to avoid the slum of the 19th century. The same took place in Copenhagen where an international competition on how to plan the incorporated towns was arranged in 1908.

19 projects were submitted – the Germans won with a project made by K. Strinz, which was characterised by the asymmetric and limited squares. The squares were considered areas for the citizens, not for traffic, in fact quite a modern perception. However, it was not the winning project that was implemented, but the Danish project that came in second in the competition.

Historically, other countries have always inspired Copenhagen at times when the City was to expand. As was the case in the seventeenth century when the Dutch planned Christianshavn, and in the eighteenth century when Frederiksstad was on the drawing board. The inspiration came from France. And when the Ørestad was in its initial phase at the end of the twentieth century, the inspiration came from Finland just as the ongoing planning of the Copenhagen Port is greatly influenced by Dutch ideas. This inspiration which Denmark has always benefited by, may well have been at its highest in the early twentieth century when the European city planning became modern. And it is this story that Hélène Vacher with great insight has told in her book and which makes you reflect on how Copenhagen is to develop in the future, when the City is facing major renewals of huge and old industrial areas. Thank you for the inspiration.

Holger Bisgaard
Chief Planner, City of Copenhagen

ACKNOWLEDGEMENTS

The production of this book has passed through many phases in which I incurred many debts. I would like to acknowledge here the many people and the institutions who have in some way or another helped make this book possible and contributed to the research reported in this volume.

First, I would especially like to thank Mr. Caspar Jørgensen who has been generous with his time and has brought his eminently helpful comments to the manuscript. I would like also to express my gratitude to Mr. Kim Dirckinck-Holmfeld, editor of Arkitekten, who has given me the greatest assistance at different times. My heartfelt appreciation goes to Professor Tim Knudsen for keen insight into the significance of my endeavour; also to Professor Jørgen Møller who has been willing to comment the manuscript and to everyone of the Department of Planning at the University of Aalborg who assisted me in various ways. I am particularly indebted to Professors Inge Degn and Helge Gamrath, and to Dr. Ole Degn who have initially supported this project and made the work possible.

In addition, my acknowledgments are due to the Danish Research Council for the Humanities without whose grant the research project could not have been accomplished, and without whose support the book would have been but imperfectly illustrated. My thanks go also to the Department of Languages and Intercultural Studies of the University of Aalborg for the financial assistance to the present publication. I am particularly indebted to Professor Ernst-Ullrich Pinkert who has always devoted time to provide precious guidance and friendly help when needed. Special appreciation goes also to Professor Torben Vestergaard who heads the Department and gave his benevolent assistance on a number of occasions.

Many people, institutions, libraries, and special collections have been drawn upon in the course of my fieldwork that extended over two years. I owe a special debt of gratitude to Mr. Jens Simonsen, at the Plan Directorate of the Municipality of Copenhagen, for the very kind way in which he has invited me consulting the records of Karl Arn Ottosen and other material in his office. I am indebted also to all the people of the City Archives in Copenhagen, and particularly Mr. Torben Ejlersen, for their gracious help and for permitting me to use copies of material in the book. Special appreciation goes to Mr. Bjørn Westerbeek Dahl at the Town Hall Library who provided valuable information; to Mr. Patrick Kragelund at the Library of the Royal Danish Academy of Fine Arts and Mr. Claus M. Smidt, curator of the Architectural Drawings Collection, for having always met my requests; to Mrs. Joyce Svensson at the Town Hall of Copenhagen who was very helpful during my investigations.

I would like to offer my sincere thanks to those from Dansk Byplanlaboratorium, Foreningen til Hovedstadens Forskønnelse, and Foreningen til Gamle Bygningers Bevaring who provided assistance, particularly to Mrs. Vibeke Dalgas, Mrs. Grethe Ilsøe, Mrs. Lene Larsen, Mr. Elith Juul Møller, Mr. Sven Allan Jensen, and Mr. Erik Wassard.

For help with locating information in the various countries represented by the 1909 Competition's entrants, I am indebted to many people. My heartfelt appreciation goes to Professor Sten Gromark, Professor Thomas Hall, Professor Frederik Bedoire, Professor John Ganau, and to Dr. Wolfgang Sonne. Especially helpful was Mr. Arne Wittstrand who kindly sent valuable material.

I would also like to extend my gratitude to the librarians and the archivists who have assisted me during visits to their institutions or given their time to correspond with me: Mr. L. Ploom, Stadsarkivet in Stockholm; Mr. A. L. Vilnon, Stadsarkivet in Malmö; Mr. Söderback, Landsarkivet in Göteborg; Mrs. L. Grønvold, Byarkivet in Oslo; Mr. Ernzerhoff, Stadtarchiv und Stadthistorische Bibliothek, Mrs. Gentz, Geodätische Institut Bibliothek, and Mr. U. Ch. Blortz, Bibliothek für Landbauwissenschaften in Bonn; Mr. Wolfgang Wiedl, Stadtarchiv Wetzlar, Dr. Ballerstedt, Stadtarchiv Magdeburg; D. Weiss, Institut für Geschichte und Theorie der Architektur in Zürich; Dr. Józef Drozd, Archiwum Panstwowe Wroclaw; and Mrs. Ramdell, Form & Design Centre in Malmö.

Finally, I wish to express here my indebtedness to Professor André Grelon whose learned and perceptive insight in historical sociology has stimulated my interest in the history of technical education. I would like also to thank here my colleagues at the Department of Languages and Intercultural Studies of Aalborg University, and those with whom I have been collaborating at the CDHT in Paris and CITERES in Tours for many years: those colleagues have been a source of much encouragement and made various contributions to the development of my ideas. Lastly, my special thanks go to Kirsten Bach Larsen at the Multimedia Department of Aalborg University's Faculty of Humanities for cheerful help with scanning a number of illustrations.

INTRODUCTION

In the early twentieth century Copenhagen gained its present limits by annexing most of its surrounding boroughs. The incorporated districts were then highly rural and did not add much to the population of the capital, but they tripled its area. The large extension of 1901-1902 was thus an important turning point in the Danish capital's physical transformation. Less than 50 years elapsed since the City of Copenhagen had been allowed to expand freely into the large tracks of lands that for a long period had been frozen by the fortifications of the monarch's residence. Whereas the removal of the ring of defences led to an open competition in Vienna in 1858, a similar grand gesture did not materialised in the realm of Denmark. Instead, Copenhagen's extension had been the result of negotiations between the City government and the State's administrations.[1] In this respect, the publication of the programme for an international contest to plan the Danish capital in early 1908 was not only a symbol of forward-looking municipal authorities, but a symbol of the expectations of recapturing the past as well.

This book deals with the international competition for the Copenhagen extension plan held in 1908-1909. It presents a survey of many facets of the event, ranging in perspective from institutional, professional and biographical aspects to design strategies and technical issues in relation to urban form and town plan. In providing a detailed exploration of the competition, the purpose of this book is to draw attention to a significant landmark in the history of Danish town planning, and, more broadly, to suggest that competitions for town planning can provide entrées to a large numbers of aspects of both a discipline and practice over time. The contest was also a forum, which polarised rival views of past and present, and echoed attitudes toward the then existing city whose tangible relics and landscape were identified as both historical marks and cultural heritage. Although the challenge was to convene various assessments of the issues to be faced by a 'Great City' through as many various aesthetic representations of the expansion of the capital with reference to the models of the time – from the garden-city to the compact-blocks town, including the picturesque style or the Beaux-Arts tradition – how to integrate the inherited built forms and landscapes was of chief concern to most of the entries. How town planning had been shaped in convergence with the broad Danish movement for the preservation of nature, cityscape and old buildings in the early years of the twentieth century is another major theme that is discussed in this book.

With a total of nineteen proposals gathering 31 competitors from six different countries, the Copenhagen contest provides a fairly representative sample of the professional milieus involved in the 'technique of town plans' in Denmark and its regional environment in the late nineteenth century and early twentieth centuries. With entrants such as Niels Gellersted, Karl Strinz, Hans Bernoulli or Alfred Raavad, who also submitted to the open international competitions for Great Berlin (1908-1910) or Canberra (1911-1912), the Copenhagen contest had been in the mainstream of the international town planning movement. It ran parallel with others major events such as the opening of the Great Berlin competition, the passing of the 1909 Town-Planning Act in England, and Burnham & Bennett's plan for Chicago the same year. That was soon followed by the international Antwerp competition, the Berlin town-planning congress cum exhibition and the London town planning conference, all in 1910, to name but a few. Other important ral-

1 On this period, see Thomas Hall, *Planning Europe's Capital Cities-Aspects of Nineteenth Century Urban Development*, London, 1997, p.158-167.

lies like the competitions for the new capital of Australia and the Ruhr financial centre in 1912, or the Ghent Exhibition in 1913, marked the climax of this international movement. In this context, Scandinavian cities took similar initiatives, such as Gothenburg in 1901, Hälsingborg in 1906, Trondheim in 1910 as well as Oslo the same year, though the latter competition did not come to fruition. Further East, Helsinki in 1898 and 1901 and Tallinn in 1913 held significant contests as well. In Sweden a 'genuine town planning Act' was enforced in 1907. [2] From the perspective of an international planning movement, which had been sustained by the frequency of close contacts through congresses, exhibitions, and competitions, the Nordic region was well entrenched in this import and export flow of ideas, experiences and planning principles.

***

The Copenhagen competition can be understood as part of an international process of mutual emulation toward the 'Greater city' or the 'metropolis'. It was, however, urged by local and genuine ambition to address the manifold transformations of the city. Between 1873 and 1906, the population of Copenhagen and its neighbouring communes had doubled and almost reached half a million mark. The mid-nineteenth century's royal residence moving at the tempo of the officers' duties and recreations while the guilds beat the rhythm of economic activities were things of the past. In contrast to the long-standing ruin of Christiansborg Palace that burnt to ashes in 1888, the erection of the large Town Hall in 1895-1905, praised abroad for its sophisticated architecture, was a testimony of assertive civic pride. The ruins of the castle in the inner city and the majestic new seat of the City Council on the freshly removed earthworks of the fortifications expressed the important undergoing changes in the social and political life of the kingdom.

A busting and promising modernity was gaining ground with major urban works, including a comprehensive sewage system, a new railways central station and harbour extensions, which accompanied a decisive boost in industrial and commercial activities in the last two decades of the nineteenth century. While Copenhagen gained a strong economic prominence in relation to the other Danish towns, its urban polarities underwent a rapid and significant change. Especially since 1895, the inner city's population had steadily declined, while housing building had mushroomed outside the former line of fortification. This urbanisation was usually depicted as ugly, unhealthy and ill equipped, save for a few residential villas areas. Thus, there were many grounds for the City government to wish to take control of the capital's spatial growth, including the development of the large tracks of land that the municipality had purchased both within and outside its boundaries in the 1890s.

Although the rich literature devoted to Copenhagen and its town planning history often refers to the competition in 1908-1909 and its prize winning plans, the contest has not been thoroughly investigated.[3] As a whole, town-planning competitions have seldom been researched as a subject in their own right, but for a few works with an attendant emphasis on model-founding winning entries.[4] The importance of town planning contests for the planning historiography is, however, outlined in a number of studies, and is in-

2 See Thomas Hall, "Urban planning in Sweden", in T. Hall (ed.), *Planning and Urban Growth in the Nordic Countries*, London, 1991, p.180.

3 Among the major studies on the development of town planning in Denmark, see Arne Gaardmand, *Dansk byplanlægning 1938-1992*, Copenhagen, 1993. Tim Knudsen, *Storbyen Støbes, København mellem kaos og byplan 1840-1917*, Copenhagen, 1988. For a general overview, see Knud Bidstrup, *Ebenezer's disciple, fra dansk byplanlægnings pionertid*, Copenhagen, 1971. Prior to these works two studies should be mentioned for their analysis of the competition, Olaf Forchhammer (red.), *København-De indlemmede Distrikter byplanmæssig Udvikling til 1840*, Copenhagen, 1947, p. 21-30; and Steen Eiler Rasmussen, *København-et bysamfunds særpræg og udvikling gennem tiderne*, Copenhagen,1994, p. 139-149. For a general review on research literature on Scandinavian countries, see Thomas Hall, "Planning history: recent developments in the Nordic countries, with special reference to Sweden", in *Planning Perspectives*, 1994, Vol.9, N. 2, p. 153-179. A broad introduction to the "Romantic" period in the Nordic countries is given by Heleni Porfyriou, "Artistic Urban Design and Cultural Myths: The Garden City Idea in Nordic Countries, 1900-1925", *Planning Perspectives*, 1992, Vol. 7, p. 263-301

4 The work of John W. Reps on Canberra encompasses the bulk of the entries: *Canberra 1912: Plans and Planners of the Australian Capital Competition*, Melbourne, 1997.

creasingly being recognised as a promising field of study that should provide insight into the practice and theory of urban development. This field is also a relevant domain of research in relation to the professional culture of the many occupational groups involved in town planning.[5] The engulfed continent of 'paper towns' can be approached as part of the corpus upon which professional practices have drawn for knowledge, inspiration and identity. 'Virtual cities' also reflect the changing views of professional bodies and social institutions on to the shaping of representations of the city in the course of time. There are thus valuable heritages of urban culture.

There are obvious obstacles to the investigation of such a topic. To begin with, original documentation is a prerequisite, and it should encompass all entries to allow research to uncover the character of a competition and explore the wealth of ideas and techniques, which had been conceived at one time for one place. But usually, the organisers only kept the winning prize entries, which they had paid for. Thus a great many of the other submissions are not easy to be found. Hence studies that have attempted a systematic probe of historical sequences of graphic documents relating to a single city mostly rely on a limited number of entries.

The competition process developed as an important instrument of city management, especially in Central and Northern Europe, since the nineteenth century.[6] It has been suggested that organising competitions played a significant role in establishing the decision making process of planning in which many conflicting interests were entangled. The contests have also been pointed out as an instrument for generating innovations and favouring the diffusion and acceptance of ideas and general guidelines for urban intervention. Competitions were the subject of wide attention, especially through press coverage. In the focus of professional practices contending with each other, competitions provided the circumstances for a strong interplay between professional and administrative bodies. In their heyday, that is about 1880-1914, competitions crystallised public debate and acted as a medium, although always an ephemeral one, for the idea of an urban community through the mirror of a collective challenge centred on the issues of town development and transformation. The dimension of celebration was propitious for the local authorities while they were striving for ambitious schemes and looking for public recognition to perform the role of a mediator for various interests and expectations in relation to new urban rationality and new visions of urbanity all together.

Nonetheless, it has been shown that competitions had been the continuously subjects of heavy and recurrent criticisms.[7] An ill-prepared programme or unclear purposes of the work's assignment, an obscure system of evaluation or an a priori orientation of the jury panels are among the defaults that have been pinpointed. Due to the considerable work input demanded of the participants, the meagre return of the whole exercise, be it in terms of financial compensations or of some kind of contract in relation to the eventual execution, led to a sceptical stand toward this so-called 'challenge of excellence', especially when no execution whatsoever came from it. Another ambiguous character of competitions has been outlined, namely their role in promoting a narrow professional elite, which by being regularly co-opted into the evaluating panels, had been inclined to emphasise its own values and, accordingly pre-emptively discourage the emergence of new ideas, a process in contrast to the very aim of competition.

The Copenhagen and Berlin competitions took place at a time when experiences and competence had

5 In relation to the competitions during the years 1890-1914, it has been remarked that "competitions have been virtually ignored in urban and planning historiography": Peter Breitling, "The role of the competition in the genesis of urban planning: Germany and Austria in the nineteenth century", in Anthony Sutcliffe (ed.), *The Rise of Modern Urban Planning 1800-1914*, London, 1980, p. 31-54: 31. Since then general introductions to planning history have included substantial aspects on competitions, as for instance: Jean Dethier & Alain Guiheux, *La ville, art et architecture en Europe, 1870-1993*, Paris, 1994.

6 See, Anthony Sutcliffe, *Towards the Planned City, Germany, Britain, the United States and France, 1780-1914*, Oxford, 1991, p. 27-35.

7 See Heidede Becker, *Geschichte der Architektur und Städtebauwettbewerbe*, Stuttgart/Berlin/Köln, 1992. Though the book focuses on architectural competitions, it sketches the history of extension competitions in Germany.

accumulated in the field of town-extension planning during the previous decades. One can speak of a momentum in which town planning had matured into a conscious, modern practice and a theorising domain about urban development. After having outlined the importance of competitions in this process, our perspective will focus on how the existing built and non-built environment was assessed within the framework of such a contest. At first sight, a competition for town-extension schemes is oriented towards ideas in relation to the 'modern city'. On the one hand, the participants had to address a growing body of formalised knowledge and know-how about the rational ordering of space through particular functions ranging from circulation, public hygiene, housing schemes to industrial production. On the other hand, it was incumbent on the individual 'artist' to act as an arbitrator of social relations and aesthetic representation of public space when the nostalgia of an idealised lost city was pervasive in the face of the uncertainty of a new city pattern. These two distinct polarities of a contest for town extension were not necessary pitted again each other, yet they referred to two different types of rationality, an instrumental one and a contextual one, which were to be articulated through the technique of design.[8] In addressing the complex ranges of issues in relation to the search for an ordered extending urban space, the participants in the competition had to come to terms with the conceptualisation of the 'Great city', which was implicit in the programme for Copenhagen. How to design such a concept was a central issue for the 'artist', when the two founding historical dimensions of what a city was supposed to be were under strain at the same time.

Up to the end of the nineteenth century in continental Europe, the radius the pedestrian dweller was able to cover in his daily whereabouts roughly gave the territorial limits of the city.[9] The experience of strolling across the city, which was a common literary theme, of the 'flaneur', recalls the scale of the city's space. Accordingly, the sudden change of scale fostered by the pursuit of the 'Great City' was a definite blow to the former equilibrium of the built environment, by which the compact built form gave way to a discontinuous and fragmented territoriality. The second dimension of a great many European cities was intimately linked to the social and cultural sedimentation that had materialised in the built environment during the course of time, in spite of fires and similar disasters. As a whole, the character of each city was in tight relation to the thickness and integrative qualities of these sediments. In contrast, their planned extensions were projected in one-time gesture, but in relation to an existing form, which became the 'inner city' embedded in both a new and alien urban space. Thus, both the spatial and temporal dimensions of what 'ought to be' a city were simultaneously questioned, while the change in scale and in the efficiency of city building determined the circumstances in which the 'Great City' was to be thought of.

In this context, the 'old city' in its broadest extension, including its landscape and natural surroundings, was a corner stone of significant contention. It could be seen as a burden of the past and an obstacle

8 This echoes the distinction between 'formal' and 'material substantive' rationality. However, figures of rationality are fluctuant and multiple according to their domains of application, even more so when articulated in connection with the vocabulary of planning discipline. On Max Weber's concept of rationality, see Julien Freund, *Etudes sur Max Weber*, Paris, 1990. Wordings such as rational, rationality, rationalization have been "catch words" for advocating the reinforcement of planning measures by the early twentieth century. Attempts to articulate both forms of rationality in planning have been numerous. The "rational comprehensive" model is a recent example. On the influence of rationalist epistemologies on planning theories see John Muller, "From survey to strategy: twentieth century developments in western planning method", *Planning Perspectives*, Vol. 7, 1992, p. 125-155. Lilian Anderson has opposed "bureaucratic" or "formal" rationality" to the Sittian and Geddesian methods of planning, see *Mellem byraakrati och Laissez-faire-en studie av Camillo Sittes og Patrick Geddes stadsplaneringsstrategier*, Göteborg, 1989. From a historical standpoint, we shall discuss the tension between the abstract logic of planning, or 'paleo-technocratic' logic, and contextual rationality as it had been developed in the Scandinavian countries during the years 1890-1914.

9 On this aspect see Marc Weil, *La transition urbaine ou le passage de la ville pedestre à la ville motorisée*, Sprimont, 1999. On the changing dimension of space and time by the end of the nineteenth century see Stephen Kern, *The Culture of Time and Space 1880-1918*, London, 1983. On the very category of 'past' and the conflicting values attached to it as a result of Western modernity, see David Lowenthal, *The Past is a Foreign Country*, Cambridge, 1985.

to urban development, as well as a repository of local history and identity and a source of inspiration for national or regional design. In any case, it laid in the horizon of the Great City, especially on the drawing table of the participants in the competition. This brings us to the attempt at exploring how the 'old city', as it was treated by the various entries, represented a *topos* of town planning when it became fully fledged, but before it was consolidated as an autonomous field of practice and a discipline in its own right.[10]

***

The book articulates two broad issues. First, how a town planning competition can be analysed as a structure of communication for conceptual approaches and occupational practices in relation to professional bodies of architects, engineers, surveyors or landscape gardeners, which were confronting views and competence on how to order urban transformation and development. Accordingly, a dynamic could emerge by which urban planning techniques were produced. This process consolidated a specific field with landmarks, which were milestones of common knowledge and experiences' accumulation and circulation. At the same time, competitions were a peculiar situation for mediation between professional bodies and municipal administrations or state agencies, the latter looking for expertise in a new type of controlling and service-providing functions.

The second theme concerns planning as a cultural activity, that is, an activity embedded in historical circumstances. How the Great City concept was designed in relation to the asymmetric Old city concept is the thread we shall follow to identify experience and appreciation of planning in relation to the dimension of aesthetics, in as much as aesthetics encompasses values concerning the 'space of experience', the composition of the shore of memory and of invention.[11]

The first part surveys the organisation and the unfolding of the competition. Each participant is presented on the basis of a biographical note that focuses on his educational background and occupation prior to 1914. The reception of the competition is analysed through the press and professional journals. The second part examines the contributions on the basis of the nineteen entries' graphic documents and memoirs. The design of early 'planners' is addressed with respect to their treatments of existing built and non-built environment in relation to their projects of the extension scheme of Great Copenhagen. A selection of documents is arranged in sets of illustrations intended to compare distinct design's strategies used by the proposals. The third and final part of the book considers the different views of conservation, or preservation, at that time in relation to the discourses and activities of Danish associations concerned with architectural, archaeological and natural heritage. The focus is on how the 'old city' is perceived as a picturesque landscape as well as a historical artefact. The discussion draws on different materials produced from 1890 to 1914, such as records and publications of voluntary societies, professional journals and a selection of contributions addressing the issue of preservation or restoration. All chapters pay attention to the flow of ideas, which circulated at that time between Denmark and its regional environment. The conclusion

10 The Danish association Dansk ByplanLaboratorium was founded in December 1921 to promote studies in town planning and organise seminars for professionals, local politicians and officials of the administrative bodies.

11 The 'Great city' and the 'Old city' have developed as unequal and antithetical terms. Accordingly, the label 'Old city' could be disparaging for its inhabitants at some specific times, according to the territorialisation process in different parts of the city. While the 'Great city' could be associated with the progress of expanding capital cities, the 'Old city' could be seen as a relic from bygone days. Both concepts are asymmetrical in their symbolic resonance, and they differ in every perspective ranging from scale to time accretion within the built forms. In Europe, 'Old' and 'Great' often designated a partially fuzzy entity. Most of the time, the 'Old city' coincided with the central district. In the colonial world, spatial and temporal entities were most often separated. 'Indigenous city' and 'Old city' – or 'walled city' in the British Empire – have coincided in contrast to the 'colonial city' or the modern city. In the colonial world the semantics of territorial units remained stable over a long period of time, while in Europe the meaning ascribed to the words 'Old city' or 'Old district' was open to change and to multiple interpretations. The 'Old city' could be transformed to become a 'City' like in London, but could also become the cradle of national values, and the 'Great' could be interpreted as degenerated product of modernity according to anti-urban ideologies. On the dynamic of asymmetric concepts, see Reinhart Koselleck, *Future past, On the semantic of historical time,* Cambridge Mass., 1985.

explores the changes in the city's territorial identity at the beginning of the twentieth century, and puts into perspective a prevailing trend of 'contextual rationality' in planning at that time.

PART I

PROFESSIONS AND TOWN PLANNING

The three first chapters of this book presents a global picture of the 1909 Copenhagen Competition in order to bring out the relation between modern professions on the making architects, civil engineers and surveyors and the new field of town planning.

In the absence of established training profiles for town-planning activities, competitions had remained since the 1857-58 contest for Vienna privileged platforms for evaluating the credentials of individuals or groups of 'planners'. Together with congresses, exhibitions and specialised literature, they also had an important function as concerns the international circulation of planning experiments. At a time when municipalities were asserting their autonomy in a number of European countries and when the bases of representative democracy were being enlarged, competitions were one of the few open grounds where to formulate and expound general ideas and representations about what a modern city should be.[1]

This first part deals with the organisational and professional side of the Copenhagen Competition, at a time when planning can certainly not be interpreted as a professional field of its own, but merely as a new occupational ground consolidating professions still on the making such as architects, engineers, surveyors and, to a lesser extent, hygienists, landscapers, members of the legal professions, etc.[2] Each of these professions, themselves in the process of establishing their credentials, had their own approaches and theories on urban forms and their own reading of how these forms were produced and should be produced. Sometimes they competed on the drawing boards, but, as it will appear, they also very much collaborated in designing the 'modern city'. Between 1890 and 1914, each of these groups contributed to shaping a new field of knowledge that established its own references as well as body of thinking, and gained in autonomy.

The following chapter surveys the organisational framework of the international competition in relation to urban change. We document more specifically the institutional set up and the composition of the jury. Chapter 2 presents a set of synthetic biographical notes on the competitors. Chapter 3 draws on this comprehensive material to examine the networks developed by professionals and discusses their occupational strategies. As Karl Strinz's entry was the jury's choice and can be rightly seen as a fine example of 'Austro-German' design, we look in some length at the till now little-documented milieu of the German surveyors. This group gained strength in the early years of the twentieth century partly thanks to its specific expertise, an expertise that was particularly relevant to the transformation of urban forms and to conservation approaches. We also consider the educational-

1 Anthony Sutcliffe, "Planning as an International Movement", in Sutcliffe, A. (ed.), *Toward the Planned City, Germany, Britain, The United States and France 1780-1914*, Oxford, Basil Blackwell, 1981, p. 163-201.

2 Following Magali Sarfati Larson we consider professions as, "historically specific forms that establish structural links between relatively high levels of formal education and relatively desirable position". See Magali Sarfati Larson "The formation of professions" in Torstendahl, R. and Burrage, M., The *Formation of Professions, Knowledge, State, and Strategy, London,* 1990, p. 24-50.

cum-training set up that had nurtured the Danish engineers who were involved in planning activities. Lastly, we look at how the competition was received.

The impact of planning competitions on the different professions can be assessed by looking at their attractive potential in the professional milieus and by following up how this professional event was integrated into the general course of individual careers. Concerning the Danish entries, the biographical notes show how attractive the competition was for a rising generation of engineers and architects who had obtained their qualifications in the 1890s. Most of them were to be actively involved in planning, though for a majority of them it remained a secondary focus of interest.

Concerning the international dimension of the competition, the Copenhagen event remained somewhat less international and more distinctly Nordic than other contemporary ones. The Göteborg competition for instance had no less than sixty per cent of foreign entries (mostly Austro-German) compared to forty per cent for Copenhagen, among them only one German entry and none from Austria (in spite of the significant relationships between the Austrian and Danish capitals concerning architecture). Another important character of the Copenhagen contest was the exclusively Danish composition of the jury, at a time when such prominent planners as Joseph Stübben were invited to sit in comparable competitions, e.g. Helsingfor in 1906 or Antwerp in 1910. Concerning Germany, the important national debate about the future of the Copenhagen batteries ring coming to the fore in the 1900s might account for some of the mixed feelings.[3] Concerning Sweden, most of the leading Swedish planners did participate in the competition, though they seem to have approached it only half-heartedly. However this aspect of 'national confinement' should not be overplayed, nor should it be interpreted as a failure. At least five nations were directly or indirectly represented, and the main contemporary schools of urban design were involved: the 'City Beautiful' with Raavad (in a much modified form), the Beaux-Arts tradition with Romeu and different interpretations of the Austro-German current with Strinz and some of the Swedish competitors, not to forget the 'Garden-city' inspired model with Bjerre and Bernoulli. This compares quite favourably with the Berlin competition, which had been well publicised and commented on in the professional press throughout Europe, but which had only three foreign entries out of a total of 27[4] (though it may be pointed out that the Berlin competition was even an almost exclusively Berlin event). For its part, the much-publicised international 1912 Canberra competition did not attract German planners and nearly suffered from an international boycott.

The fact that the award winner of the Copenhagen Competition was German did not crown the success of German 'Städtebau' as such; it rather reflects the increasing professional success of German surveyors in the years 1903 to 1910. The interest of the Prussian surveyor's federation in planning was directly linked to their efforts to obtain a level of qualification that could stand comparison with engineers, which they achieved in the first decade of the twentieth century. From this point of view, the strategy of gaining international recognition in Denmark proved quite a success, at a time when competitions in Germany were dominated by the *Verband deutscher Architekten- und Ingenieurvereine*, founded in 1871. The light cast in Chapter 3 on the professional movement of German surveyors substantiates the pluralistic nature of the early planning milieu this pluralism being understood here in terms of planning theory and design options.

The jury's choice turned out to be a balanced one. On the one hand, it acknowledged the contribution of German Städtebau, even if this was represented by a still little-known professional branch. On the other hand, it comforted the established values of a Danish professional milieu that was in the ascendant, combining complementary aspects of planning in the three first prizes. It also gave a cautious encouragement to

3 The 1909 law on defence decided the abandonment of land fortification. The debate on defence policy has raged during the end of the nineteenth century and partly caused the split of the Venstrereformpartiet in 1905.

4 A French entry by Léon Jaussely and Charles Nicod, an Austrian entry by Siegfried Sitte and a Swiss entry by Hans Bernoulli who was then based in Berlin.

the lone Danish-American runner from the older generation. The competition was to prove a powerful catalyst in the following years, not only for a number of Danish professionals but also for the foreign competitors. Hans Bernoulli, Carl Strinz and all of the Swedish competitors made a strong and long-lasting mark on planning, as independent professionals or as civil servants.

1
THE MAKING OF GREAT COPENHAGEN

1 Town Planning Competitions and Capital Cities

The following chapter deals with the organisation of the 1908-1909 Copenhagen competition. We begin by examining the relationship between the idea of the Great city and the principle of a competition together with the emergence of town planning as a specialised field in Denmark. We then explore the planning environment of the competition, with the burgeoning of urban projects in the Danish capital at the turn of the twentieth century. In this context, we finally present the set-up of the contest.

Of the many outcomes the town-plan competitions had in the last two decades of the nineteenth century that of assessing the complexity of spatial relationships in order to sustain the move toward the Great city had fostered the conditions for a specialised field of studies. The need for comparative experiences at the scale of the 'greater city' induced the interest in the international dimension of city development, which in turn intensified technical and professional exchanges, and nurtured a process of specialization.[1] Before discussing this development in Denmark, we shall consider some aspects of town plan competitions' mechanism.

Our premise is that town-plan competitions in Europe, especially in the period from 1890 to 1914, were important nodal points that catalysed the flux of knowledge on city building. For both city councils and professionals, such tenders gave rise to a swiftly expanding corpus, at a time when town planning had neither quite taken shape nor yet gained academic recognition. In most European countries, town planning only started to be considered as a field in its own right after World War I. In retrospect, capital-city and regional-city competitions can be seen as an pivotal crucible where the experience of extension planning could be accumulated, processed, submitted to critical examination by juries, but also by a more general public, and finally transmitted in time. Competition entries are thus considered in this book as historical products, which can be analysed as such in order to analyse conceptions, designs, graphic styles and know-how that pertain to the planning discipline. Each proposal combines a set of traits, relating to artistic traditions, technical trainings and cultural values, from which arises a synthetic image of what a Great City should be. Moreover entries are also discourses in relation with the setting up of state and municipal institutions that looked to regulating the growth and the transformations of towns.

As historical events, competitions can be traced back to the Renaissance, and in the field of architecture they had been part of the revival of Greco-Roman antiquity. Ever since the Quattrocento, they had been contributed to establishing a distinction between the knowledge of the 'architect' and the 'traditional know-how' of the builder as a craftsman.[2] This apparently remote reference is not purely incidental when one considers the heritage on which town-planning entries were drawing at the end of the nineteenth century, together with the influence archaeological findings and techniques of measurements and drawings had on the academic institution of architec-

1 On the international character of the planning movement, see Anthony Sutcliffe, "Planning as an international movement", in *Towards the planned City, Germany, Britain, The United States and France, 1780-1914*, Oxford, 1981, p. 164-201.

2 See Hélène Lipstad, "Architectural Publications, Competitions, and Exhibitions", in E. Blau & E. Kaufman (ed.), *Architecture and its image, Four Centuries of Architectural Representation*, Cambridge, Massachusetts, 1989, p. 109-137.

ture.[3] By the eighteenth century, competitions had come to play a significant role. They both allowed giving expression to a highly learned type of architectural practice, and extending this practice to the field of urban layout. How ideas had been submitted in relation to embellishment schemes, such as the "Place de la Concorde" in Paris, could be regarded as quasi-competitions. The Empress Catherine II invited architects to compete for an embellishment plan of Saint Petersburg and for the creation of a "Ville toute nouvelle" in 1764. In France, notwithstanding the abolition of the Royal Academy of Architecture in 1793, the competition mechanism remained at the earth of the selection of competence and excellence throughout the Revolutionary period. Indeed the "Concours de l'an II" appears as an important stepping-stone in the renewal of architectural design in relation to evolving programmes and values.[4]

It was not until the nineteenth century that this practice, well established in the fields of arts and architecture –including the arts of the engineer– was developed for urban extension, the Vienna competition in 1858 with its 58 entries being considered as a turning point. It could also be argued that the emulative and cumulative mechanism of extension competition was to play in Central and Northern Europe a decisive role in creating a specialized field of knowledge that was to be known as "Städtebau". By the 1870s German professional associations had set the "rule of the game" for competition practice, and the rapid pace of towns' extensions gave rise to a tremendous amount of thinking within the professional milieus involved in urban transformations. In 1880, the Cologne extension competition, won by the common proposal of Joseph Stübben and Karl Henrici, had set the pattern for a period where was to be established a 'comprehensive urban planning technique' with traffic organisation and the design of public places at its core. In 1893, Vienna's Generalregulierungsplan and Munich's Generalbebauungsplan introduced a new phase in the scale and the issue of planning with the confrontation of alternative strategies.

What was increasingly attempted was to bridge two polarities of town planning. To summarize it briefly: on the one hand, the growing body of increasingly formalised knowledge aiming at a rational ordering of space by assembling distinct functions in relation to circulation, hygiene, industry and trade; on the other hand, the call to take into account the conciliation of private and public interests as well as a representation of civic life, including the building of a cultural heritage for the modern city. To promote the figure of the 'artist' as a mediator of a new and modern urban community, Camillo Sitte and the adepts of his views saw competitions as a strategic tool in checking the monopoly of officials on city development and in stimulating the design of imaginative town plans and city architectonics[5] .

In the introduction we have outlined that town-plan competitions per se remained a generally little studied domain so far. Yet we can relate to capital cities' monographs, which present a state-of-the art approach of some town plan competitions, analysing in great detail the framework of each event, while limiting their scope to awarded entries and with no special attention given to the professional background of participants.[6] Recent literature attempting to describe and analyse planners' carriers is potentially more relevant to our topic provided that it pays particular attention to the involvement of those planners in competitions.[7] Extensive studies have also been carried out by undertaking a careful probe of graphic documents, re-

3 Paul Dufournet, *Architecture, Urbanisme, Paysage – L'apport des modèles antiques dans l'Occident moderne. Continuité, rupture, retour- Extrait des actes du Colloque consacré à l'influence de la Grèce et de Rome sur l'Occident moderne,* Paris, Ecole Normale Supérieure, 14,15, 19 décembre 1975, Paris, 1977.

4 See Werner Szambien, "Les concours de l'an II", in *Les architectes de la liberté 1789*-1799, Paris, 1989, p. 181-202.

5 Camillo Sitte, *Der Städtebau nach seinen künstlerischen grundsätzen*, Vienna, 1922, p.144.

6 See Kurt Mollik, Hermann Reining, Rudolph Wurzer, *Planung und Verwirklichung der Wiener Ringstrassenzone*, Wiesbaden, 1980. This in-depth study of the urban history of Vienna also gives an outstanding analysis of the Viennese competitions of 1857 and 1892. Yet competitions are not in the focus of this work, and non-awarded entries are not included in the analysis. Paris' extension competition of 1919 is analysed in Jean Louis Cohen & André Lortie, *Des fortifs aux périf, Paris, Les seuils de la ville*, Paris, 1992, p. 120-126.

7 Olivier Karnau has documented the importance that competitions field practice had for the work of Joseph Stübben, see: *Hermann Joseph Stübben- Städtebau 1876-1930*, Braunschweig/ Wiesbaden, 1996.

flecting historical sequences of city planning and shedding light on often little-known competitions.[8] Recent work has also involved in-depth studies on the ideological and political background of the iconography in relation to the town plans of 'Great cities' in the 19th and early 20th centuries. Furthermore, planning manifestos and treaties as well as 'ideal plans' or projects provide a rich source of material to see how planners tried to convey values and meanings through widely differing design strategies.[9]

In the German context, planning contests have been analysed as an alternative, or rather as a significant support to direct intervention by local governments or states authorities.[10] They helped buttress the authority of the decision-making process, but also stimulated innovation. They combined democratic debate with inter-professional emulation. All along competitions have been both praised and criticized. Applauded for producing a favourable ground for creative projects. Disallowed as a proper mechanism to provide sound town-plan because of frequently unprepared programmes. Competitions were also disqualified for their weak and often opaque evaluation process, even if German professional organisations were not rejecting the mechanism in principle. As competitions represented a huge investment for professionals, with little direct return to expect for most of entrants, criticisms often focused on the lack of implementation of the schemes that had been submitted to the contests.[11] One consequence of this mechanism of acute selection and 'distinction' was the steady reinforcement of a professional elite through an intensified process of qualification.

1.1 Denmark in the International Movement for Town Planning

Together with the 1910 Berlin and Antwerp competitions, the contest for the 'Great Copenhagen' is part of the wave of international competitions that accompanied a new phase of urban growth and of annexation of city outskirts in the last decade of the nineteenth century. In Central and Northern Europe, following the example set by the Greater Vienna Generalregulierungsplan of 1892-1893, competitions were frequently an opportunity used by professionals to break new ground in planning theory. This had been the case for Eugen Faßbender and Otto Wagner in Vienna in 1893,[12] and for Karl Henrici in Munich the same year to set the path of what subsequently often will be labelled as Sittian planning.[13] It was also to be true with Rudolf Eberstadt, Bruno Mörhing and Richard Petersen's project for 'Great Berlin' in 1910, in which the focus of planning shifted toward a general reflection on housing and city environment.[14]

In the northern part of continental Europe, competitions for town extension, involving as they did extensive professional mobilisation and the scrutiny of the public, played a pivotal role in intensifying the constitution of a new multidisciplinary field, while the development of town planning took other paths elsewhere. In England for instance, the role of urban-housing reformers in dealing with the industrial sub-

8 See Manuel de Torres i Capell, Josep Llobet i Bach and Jaume Puig i Castells, *Inicis de la urbanística municipal de Barcelona: mostra dels fons municipals de plans i projectes d'urbanisme, 1750-1930*, Barcelona, 1986. Also the much comprehensive study: Centre de recherche sur la rénovation urbaine (Préface by André Corboz), *1896-2001, Projet d'urbanisme pour Genève*, Geneva, 2003.

9 The author also gives a listing of town planning competitions during this period: Wolfgang Sonne, *Hauptstadtplanungen 1900-1914. Die Repräsentation des Staates in der Stadt*, Dissertation ETH Nr. 14098, Doktor der technischen Wissenschaften der Eidgenössischen Technischen Hochschule Zürich, 2001.

10 Heidede Becker, *Geschichte der Architektur- und Städtebauwettbewerbe*, Stuttgart, 1992.

11 This was particularly true in the competitions for Munich and Berlin, see H. Becker, *op. cit.*, p. 109-114 & p. 114-132.

12 The work presented in 1893 by the two authors was later to be coined as a major reference for planning theory. See Eugen Faßbender's memoir for Vienna: *Erläuterungen zum Entwurfe eines General-Regulierungsplanes über das gesamte Gemeindegebiet von Wien*, Vienna, 1893.

13 Karl Henrici, *Preisesgekrönter Konkurrenz-Entwurf zu der Stadterweiterung Münchens*, Munich, 1893.

14 Rudolf Eberstadt, Bruno Mörhing, Richard Petersen, *Gross Berlin: ein Programm für die Planung der neuzeitlichen Grossstadt*, Berlin, 1910; see also Joseph Brix, Felix Genzmer, *Hochbahngesellschaft, Grundplan für die Bebauung von Gross-Berlin, mit einem ersten Preise ausgezeichnet*, Berlin, 1911, and Hermann Jansen, *Vorschlag zu einem Grundplan für Gross-Berlin*, Berlin 1909.

urban regions and the implementation of "pilot" garden cities was paramount for the planning discipline. In France, the end of the Haussmannian cycle had brought urban transformations to a standstill and the main developments were often to come from experiences realised overseas.[15]

Copenhagen had already developed a significant tradition of competitions relating to urban transformations prior to the twentieth century. Leaving aside the architectural contests, although they could have a significant impact on the city form, such as the competitions for the Town Hall in 1889-1890 or for Christiansborg Palace in 1904-1906, we should recall that the city, as early as 1848, had organised an international contest for the layout of sewerage and sanitation schemes.[16] In the wake of the declassification of the ring of fortifications in 1856, numerous projects were elaborated, but such proposals were not part of any competition. The final result was to be a compromise between different schemes. Slightly influenced by the Viennese Ring, where Theophilus Hansen (1813-1891) had been one of the leading architects with, among numerous buildings, the design of the Greek styled Reichsrat in the 1870s, the synthesis presented by the architect Ferdinand Meldahl (1827-1908) made room for public buildings, park areas and dense blocks of constructions. In the end, it was approved in 1872 by the municipal council, but not by the city government.[17] The demolition of the fortifications and the implementation of this scheme, slightly revised in 1885, took over two decades.

An important tender took place in 1899 for the organisation of the railway's networks that gathered 22 proposals. The international competition's jury attributed no first prize, and Charles Ambt (1847-1919), by then City Engineer received the second price. Ambt would eventually implement the scheme when becoming general director of the Danish state railways in 1902.[18] By then, other competition projects were in the offing, concerning parks and housing schemes. With the rapid urbanisation of the outskirts of Copenhagen between 1880 and 1900, the surrounding communes having doubled or even tripled their population, the idea of a 'Greater city' came to reflect not only the sharp population increase and the radiating physical growth of the city but also the general notion and cultural representation of what a modern metropolitan area should be.[19] In the book they published in 1907, *Stor-København*, Gnudtzmann and Lind substantiated this general move toward the 'Greater City'. They described and illustrated with a profusion of details and with vivid photographs an emerging urban environment, with the recently built and much internationally commented new Town Hall, but also a wealth of new administrative bodies, modernised fire brigade, medical establishments, electric tramways, telephone cable networks, modernised and extended sewage and the like.[20]

A new terminology

By 1890, the outskirts of Vienna had been incorporated, bringing a threefold increase in territory for the capital of the Habsburgs and sparking the signal for a new competition round that would once again set the tune for many other European towns. Ten years later, Copenhagen was to be engulfed in this general move-

15 On this aspect, see Helene Vacher, *Projection coloniale et ville rationalisée-le rôle de l'espace colonial dans la constitution de l'urbanisme en France, 1900-1931*, Aalborg, 2001.

16 Among the eighteen entries there were eight British proposals, two German, and one French. See Christensen Villads, *København 1840-1857*, Copenhagen 1912, p. 554-567

17 Axel Holm & Kjeld Johansen, *København 1840-1940, Det Københavnske bysamfund og kommunens økonomi*, Copenhagen, 1941, p. 22-23.

18 Jens Vibaek, "Debatten om Københavns 3. Hovedbanegård", *Historiske Meddelelser om København*, 1989, p. 136-169.

19 The population of the communes of Valby, Brønshøj and Sundbyerne raised respectively from 3.240, 3.825, 9.923 to 7.484, 9.964, 22.340 between 1880 and 1901, Frederiksberg commune jumping during the same period from 26.510 to 76.231 inhabitants; Copenhagen counted 234.850 inhabitants in 1880 and 358.091 in 1900, by 1905 its population reached 421.603 inhabitants, including the annexed districts. See Axel Holm and Kjeld Johansen, *København* op.cit., p. 45. For a general overview of the urbanisation process, see Ole Hyldtoft, *Danmark økonomisk historie 1840-1910*, Aarhus, 1999, p. 203-204.

20 See Albert Gnudtzmann & Helmer Lind, *Stor-København, skildringer og billeder af byen og dens liv i vore dage*, Copenhagen and Christiana, 1907. See also this process as understood by A. J. Raavad, *Borgmesterbogen – en bog om dansk byplanlægning*, Copenhagen, 1929, p. 196.

ment of incorporation of the peripheries. The 1901-1902 taking over of the surrounding boroughs, that is Brønshøj, Valby, and Sundbyerne on Amager Island, increased the town's jurisdiction threefold and boosted its population, which merely reached the half-a-million mark as a functional urban entity, including the communes of Frederiksberg and Gentofte that were not part of this reform.[21] Copenhagen's 19th-century urban transformations had taken place through a process that combined international competitions for transportation or technical networks, and municipal services, occasionally outside experts, for the physical side of urban development. The early twentieth century saw the principle of competitions extended to most of continental Europe in correlation to the developing field of planning. In 1910, considering the coming tender for the development of the site of the old railway station, the newspaper *Politiken* highlighted the progress of the town-planning movement in Denmark:

"Naar Kunsten, anvendt paa Gade og Bebyggelsesplaner, atter er ved at komme til sin Ret herhjemme, skyldes dette jo selvfølgelig den stærke Bevægelse paa dette Omraade, som har begyndt at røre sig i de store Kulturcentrer, navnlig Tyskland og England, og som derfra har forplantet sig til andre Lande, endelig ogsaa til os [...] Resultaterne ses nu som sagt ikke alene i de store Lande, men ogsaa i de smaa. Vore Nabolande, Sverige og Norge, er med i Bevægelsen, som ikke lader sig standse."[22]

The same article underlines that there was as yet no word in Danish for the English 'town planning' or the German 'Städtebau'. Though it should be noted that the notion of town planning, or city planning for that matter, was all but of recent use in England. The term was used in the *Garden Cities and Town Planning* periodical in 1904, and town planning was "by late 1906 on the lips of most urban reformers".[23]

In Germany, undoubtedly the pioneering country in this field, the word 'Bebauungsplan' practically dominated after having steadily replacing that of 'Stadt-Erweiterungen'.[24] Giving emphasis to the three-dimensional character of planning activities this term that might be translated by "building plan" was in keeping with the progress of often sophisticated zoning regulations. It had become more frequent in the 1890s to designate the design of town development. In parallel, the word 'Städtebau' conveyed the idea of a specific area of knowledge, rapidly increasing and much more comprehensive than the sole technique of the extension plan. In the professional milieu, this term had become a kind of password after having been used by Camillo Sitte along variants such as 'Stadtbaukunst' in 1889.[25] It was immediately endorsed the following year by Joseph Stübben, who used it as a title for a section of his *Handbuch der Architektur* concerning city building. The term was adopted in 1904 by the magazine *Der Städtebau* and had a long fortune.[26] In France the general word 'aménagement' had been in common usage to designate layout operations. The terms 'tracé régulateur' or 'plan régulateur' with their counterparts 'Reguleringsplan', 'Regulierungsplan', and

21 Copenhagen's area within the fortifications was about 300 hectares and the so-called Old City about 72. Following the integration of surrounding boroughs in 1901-1902, Copenhagen's area within its administrative limits was extended from about 2.350 up to 7.000 hectares, see Olaf Forchhammer, *København fra Bispetid til Borgertid*, Copenhagen, 1947.

22 "In their turn extension plans are acknowledged in our country. This results from a powerful movement, which started in the cultural centres of Germany and England. Important competitions happened in many places. [..] We can see the results non only in the big countries but also in the small ones. Our neighbours in Sweden and Norway are also engulfed in this movement that nothing seems to stop" (our translation), *Politiken*, 28 October1910, article signed by C. Brandstrup.

23 A. Sutcliffe, *Towards the planned...* op. cit, p. 72. The term town planning can be traced back in Australia as early as 1890. Yet the common modern acceptation was used among the professionals appeared in the early twentieth century. For more details, see Anthony D. King, "Town planning, A note on the origins and use of the term", *Planning History Bulletin*, Vol. 4, n. 2, 1982, p. 15-16.

24 This is part of the title of the first full fledged treaty of town planning in Germany: Reinhard Baumeister, *Stadt-Erweiterungen in technischer, baupolizeilicher und wirtschaftlicher Beziehung*, Berlin, 1876.

25 Camillo Sitte, *Der Städtebau...*

26 The first issue of *Der Städtebau*, with the subtitle "für die künstlerische Ausgestaltung der Städte nach ihren wirtschaftlichen, gesundheitlichen und sozialen Grundsätzen", was edited in 1904 by Theodor Goecke (1850-1919) who honoured the memory of Camillo Sitte (1843-1903)by putting his name as joint editor.

'piano regulatore' are rooted in the eighteenth-century notion of 'régularité'. It was especially in use among city surveyors in the post-Haussmannian period. By the turn of the century, one could find the term 'technique des plans de villes' used from time to time by professionals, to designate a specific area of knowledge, while the term 'urbanisme', coined by a geographer in 1910, was almost immediately adopted by the Société française des architectes urbanistes (SFAU) that was formed the following year by a group of architects, most of whom laureates of the "Prix de Rome".[27]

Facing the rapid growth of urbanization by the last decade of the nineteenth century, Denmark's municipal services closely followed developments in urban techniques in the neighbouring countries. In 1888, under the term of 'bebyggelsesplan', Charles Ambt outlined the general principles that should govern the layout and the extension of cities:

"Af disse forskejellige Forhold skal jeg her nærmere omtale Bebyggelsesplanerne, hvis Hovedopgave selvfølgelig bliver at sikre Byen en hensigtsmæssig Udvikling, saaledes at de enkelte Dele kommer til at danne Led i en fælles Organisme. Princippet bliver ved Bebyggelsesplanen at virke præventivt, saaledes at den uindskrænkede Byggefrihed ikke nødsager Kommunen til senere at helbrede de opstaaede Onder ved uforholdsmæssige Offre."[28]

In this text, published one year before Sitte's treatise, Ambt still refers to the French Haussmannian tradition, but mostly draws on German practice linking up explicitly his essay to Baumeister and Stübben's contribution. However, as has been shown in relation to the laying out of streets in the Vestervold district, Sitte's influence was already perceptible in the following years.[29] Important planning events took place during this period at a regional scale, popularising the latest developments of post-1890s German Städtebau. In Schleswig-Holstein, the city of Altona had been through a vigorous process of modernization under Oberbürgermeister Franz Adickes (1846-1915) before his departure for Frankfurt in 1890. The 1890 and 1893 competitions concerning northern and western extensions of Altona contributed to publicise Joseph Stübben's work in its latest form as well as the new style of design introduced by Karl Henrici. It was so again with Flensburg's south and west extension in 1901 and 1903. By that time, the Bebauungsplan type of planning had already reached Sweden, with the Gothenburg 1900-1901 competition producing a new image of the city.

In Denmark, under the key word Gade- og Bebyggelsesplan, the 1908-1909 competition and their entrants were in line with their German counterparts. Prone to theorise, Alfred Raavad refers in his memoir for the competition to Stübben's work as "teoretisk behandling af by-bygningskunsten" (a theoretical treatment of the art of town building). Yet most of the competitors were content with the term Gade- og Bebyggelsesplan. The following year *Arkitekten*, in reference to the London town-planning conference, mentioned a meeting of 'Stadplaner'. 'Byers Planlæggelse', close to the currently used Gadeplanlægning, was also employed.

Differences in the conceptual development of the planning field between countries and the corresponding disparities in vocabulary occasionally proved a source of embarrassment. As the competition's programme was published both in Danish and in French, and interestingly enough not in German, the rendering of Gade- og Bebyggelsesplan was "tracé de plan de constructions et de rues". This literal translation seems to have been mostly interpreted by French architects as a housing scheme. The letters sent to the municipality of Copenhagen were asking for the pro-

27 The Société française des architectes urbanistes was created in 1911. It seems that "Urbanisme" was first used by Pierre Clerget, professor of economic geography in Lyon: "L'urbanisme, étude historique, géographique et économique", *Bulletin de la Société neuchateloise de géographie*, 1910, p. 213-31.

28 "In this context, I shall talk layout plans over. The first task of a layout plan is to ensure an appropriate development of the city whereby its various elements join into one organism. The principle of a layout plan is preventive in nature: it aims at limiting the long-term effects of building activities at random, so that the municipality is not compelled to heal the wounds of excessive damages in the course of time" (our translation): Charles Ambt, "Om Planer til Byers Udvidelse og Bebyggelse", *in Den tekniske Forenings Tidsskrift*, 1888-89, p. 81-90, p. 82.

29 See Caspar Jørgensen, Tim Knudsen & Anders Møller, "Charles Ambt og gadeplanlaegningen i Vestvold kvarter", *Historiske Meddelelser om København*, 1989, p. 85-107.

gramme of "la construction d'un ensemble de maisons", literally "a programme for the building of a group of blocks". However, landscape architect Edouard Redont had a broader understanding of the information published in the French specialised press, as shown by the following expression "plan de systématisation, d'agrandissement et d'embellissement des nouveaux quartiers de la ville de Copenhague" he used in his letter to Copenhagen's authorities.[30] At that time, the *Section d'Hygiène urbaine et rurale* within the foundation Le Musée Social in Paris had just been formed, in January 1908; it was one of the few bodies involved in discussing questions relating to town planning activities in France. Redont was a member of that section between 1915 and 1926 and in the handful of people who founded the above-mentioned SFAU.[31]

Patrick Abercrombie (1879-1957), who then edited the newly founded *Town Planning Review*, understood town planning as "the practical art of constructing a city" and remarked:

"It is only recently that any serious attempt has been made to propound its grammar and syntax, and even when that has been done, there has been a strong inclination to regard the city as an arbitrarily contrived shell into which its population, like the hermit crab, must crawl for protection and adapt itself in a pursuit of a ready-made envelope."[32]

In his view, each country has preferences according to its own "temperament", and develops its particular administrative apparatus, legislative system and artistic sense. Behind the international credo and rhetoric, he believed there was a strong idiosyncrasy in town planning practice linked to the "domination of central bureaucracies", making the development of international exhibitions, congresses and organisations all the more necessary. Those forums would allow for exchange of knowledge to replace what Abercrombie dismissed as "a great deal of loose and hurried study of one nation by another".[33]

1.2 Town Planning Competition as Civic Experience

In continental Europe, the competitions seem to have been the ideal support for direct confrontations and discussions between different design traditions about well-defined projects. This development, however, should not be considered as self-evident historical process. The question then arises why municipal authorities turned to competitions instead of simply calling upon the available municipal technical services or upon commissioned consultants. Why did the Swedish cities of Gothenburg and Hälsingborg decide to organize competitions when Malmö, for example, did not? Narrow municipal know-how nor the rate of urbanization suffice as an explanation, and many more comparative studies together with case studies on specific configurations would be needed in order to shed light on this issue. One can none the less sketch out a few aspects. The choice to go for a competition is supposed to be in relation with the growth of a city. The wave of open competitions, which took place in Germany and in the Nordic countries, can be correlated with a distinct phase of industrialisation and urbanisation, in contrast to England, for example. Thus to acknowledge a new urban complexity could have been a ground for gathering expertise beyond the municipal services.[34] At a time when there were neither academic curriculum nor specific training in the field of town planning, competitions can

30 *Le Bâtiment*, 17 November 1907, 20 February 1908, and 22 March 1908. See the letters sent by French architects to Copenhagen's municipal office, especially the one sent by E. Redont, dated 6 March 1908: Stadsarkivet, Ejendomsdirektorat, sag EJ 1150/1925: "Anmodninger om program".

31 On this aspect, see H. Vacher, *Projection coloniale...* op.cit, p. 72-91.

32 The Town Planning Review was published in 1910 as the journal for the Department of Civic Design at the School of Architecture of the University of Liverpool, see: Patrick Abercrombie, "International contributions to the study of Town Planning and the City Organisation", *Town Planning Review*, Vol 4, n°2, 1913, p. 98-99. On the impact international exchanges have had on the works of municipal services in the Nordic context, see Marjatta Hietala, "La diffusion des innovations: Helsinki 1875-1917", *Genèses*, 10, January 1993, p. 74-89. However, the international dimension of town planning is downplayed by Jean Pierre Saunier, "Changing the city: urban international information and the Lyon municipality, 1900-1940, *Planning Perspectives*, Vol. 14, N. 1,1999, p. 19-48.

33 P. Abercrombie, *International*, op.cit.

34 See A. Sutcliffe, *Toward...* op. cit, p. 29.

be apprehended as the most efficient mechanism for the accumulation and transmission of know-how. But open contests can also be appreciated as public manifestations, in which municipal authorities and leading citizens could show that the city's future was of concern to them. Moreover publicising their quest for the configuration of the 'Great city' was a way to assert their will to be in command of the urban development.

If competitions were not a self-evident choice, the incorporation policies in the end of the nineteenth century and the beginning of the twentieth century were not an inevitable course either. In the case of Berlin, it has been argued that landed interests as well as the Prussian government were opposing the views toward incorporation. In Denmark, the example of Frederiksberg is also a case in point.[35] Frederiksberg commune bordering Copenhagen rejected an early attempt toward incorporation and had become a huge spatial enclave with its autonomous administration within the perimeter of the capital city; it remained so till today. Therefore, considering the social and political transformation that took place in Denmark during this period, we can assume that opening a competition was a significant decision relating to political choices as regards the move toward the 'Great city'.

Copenhagen, long the residence of the monarch, the seat of government ministries, higher learning, commerce, science, and of the arts, came to gather by 1901 close to a fifth of Denmark's entire population. In summer 1901, a year of major political change that gave supremacy to the Parliament by requiring the king to appoint a government having the support of the Folketing (Lower-House), Venstrereformpartiet (Liberal Democratic Reform Party) formed the government, reflecting its overwhelming majority in the Folketing and thereby ending the long rule of conservative forces.[36] This evolution also reflected the rising influence of Socialdemocratiet (the Social Democratic Party) not only in the Folketing but also on several town councils, including that of Copenhagen where Jens Jensen was elected mayor of the powerful Finance Board in the City's government in 1903.[37] This serious setback to the Right, used to running city affairs, caused it to regroup to regain seats with a so-called anti-socialist list. The fear of "gas and water" socialism" had grown in the aftermath of the attempt by Esbjerg's town council to introduce such a programme for the new port city in 1905. The same year saw the formation of Det Radikale Venstre (the Radical Liberal Party) as a split from Venstrereformpartiet. This was perceived as giving new opportunities to the Socialdemocrati to broaden its municipal programme. Although Det Radikale Venstre was small, it had an influential mouthpiece with the daily *Politiken*, founded in 1884. This daily to which collaborated talented writers and arts critics became influential among educated and artistically minded Copenhagen citizens.

The movement for municipal reforms should also be seen in the light of the strengthening of the technical department within the municipal administration during the 1890s. A great number of engineers had been employed to work out large programmes for the city's development with sanitation and transport infrastructures, harbour installations, electric power plant, gas works, telephone installations and the like. Moreover some engineers advocated the development of social housing with the support of the municipality and were instrumental in bringing the 1909 competition to fruition. From a larger, social perspective engineers were striving to assert their so-

35 The case of Frederiksberg is studied by Henning Bro, "Frederiksberg-storbykommunen i hovedstaden", *Historiske Meddelelser om København*, 2001, p. 161-181.

36 Following the defeat that lead to the loss of the duchies of Schleswig and Holstein, the National Liberals lost credibility and their leading position in Danish politics. A conservative turn had occurred giving the Højre (Right) party a firm grip on the government under the leadership of J. B. S. Estrup who hold power from 1875 till 1894. By 1866 Højre representing mainly civil servants and big landowners had succeeded in the revision of the liberal constitution of 1849, in such a way that the Landsting (Upper-House) in consultation with the king could form the government without consulting the Folketing (Lower-House).

37 At that time a Borgmester was elected for a life term. Jens Jensen was elected to the municipal council in 1893 when the parties Venstrereformpartiet and Socialdemokratiet made an alliance to enter the City's government. The pioneering role of Denmark in the field of social housing and its exemplary value for Swedish reformers has been underlined by Mats Deland, *The Social City, Middle-way approaches to housing and suburban governmentality in southern Stockholm 1900-1945*, Stockholm, 2001.

cial status, and this evolution can be seen at the level of the municipal administration of Copenhagen at the turn of the century. At that time the municipal government of Copenhagen was expanded its sphere of activities, and technical competences were needed to control all segments of the city's infrastructure. In this process, engineers could assert their role as actors of change. A town plan competition was therefore a highly significant tribune by calling in professional expertise and demonstrating ambitions to regulate the urban development.

Town plan competitions had another important dimension, which can be approached from two perspectives. From a civic viewpoint, open competitions were in the focus of a great many public activities and exceptional occasions for revealing values and expectations toward the city through representations translated into plans. From a professional outlook, they were rare opportunities to express distinct orientations, cultural and social values, and creativity in relation to the urban forms. Besides, they could be expected to trigger building activities especially in times of recession. After a period of speculative construction, a short but severe economic crisis has hit Copenhagen at the beginning of 1908, which put to a standstill a depressed building industry. Similarly, the organisation of the Berlin competition had been initiated by professional organisations, which were also hoping for a boost in the building sector.

1.3 Planning Great Copenhagen

According to Alfred Raavad, who was active for many years in Chicago, the movement for town planning appeared in Denmark in conjunction with the Nordic Exhibition held in Copenhagen in 1888 – the year when Copenhagen joined the category of "world cities".[38] Trade and industrial activities were at the heart of Raavad's planning concerns. This was to him the constituent force of the 'natural' development of a city. Thus the expansion of port facilities held a central position within Raavad's entry, which envisioned shifting the prevalent north direction of the harbour's development toward the south (see Chapter 4). This was a radical proposal with regard to the options that had been taken by the Port's authorities since the 1870s. Much civil engineering work had been involved in dredging fairways and docks, and the city's marine frontage had been notably modified with digging and filling operations undertaken to deepen the marine channels and to construct wharfs. The main purpose was to retain a share of the seaborne traffic crossing the Øresund (The Sound) channel by adapting to the increasing size of the ships.[39] It was also toward the north of the city that Frihaven was constructed as an attempt to catch part of the transit on the route through the Kiel Canal, built in 1887-1895. Inaugurated in November 1894, the new "Free Port" was extending over 24 hectares with its huge basins and railways station enclosing the city's citadel that had long stand as the northern bastion on the sea. During the same years the city's embankments had been rectified with new bridges connecting to Christianshavn and Amager Island while filling up of shallows had resulted in vast tracks of land made available for industrial development toward south.

Shipbuilding industries and foreign trade had swiftly increased during the last decades of the nineteenth century. The navigation company DFDS is an example of this trend. Created by the tycoon C. F. Tietgen in 1866, Det Forenede Dampskibs Selskab quickly hold the upper hand on Danish firms with its 115 ships of an approximate 139.000 tonnes in 1905, particularly geared toward trans-oceanic traffic. Like DFDS, nearly 63 % of the joint-stock companies had their sieges in the Danish capital.[40] By the beginning of the twentieth century, Copenhagen had caught much of the overseas trade and controlled one third of the volume of exports and more than half of the value of imports, even if the new harbour of Esbjerg had been fast developing with massive export of agricultural products. The revenues linked to the maritime trade

38 A. J. Raavad, *Borgmesterbogen... op. cit.* : "proem"

39 See H. C. V. Møller, "Københanvs Havn", in D. Bruun and al., *Danmark Land og Folk – Historisk-Topografisk – Statistik Haandbog*, Vol. 4, Copenhagen & Christiania, 1922, p. 38-43. See also, A. M. Møller, H. Dethlefsen, H. C. Johansen, *Dansk søfarts historie*, Vol. 5 : *Sejl og damp 1870-1920*, Copenhagen, 1998.

40 See H. C. Jørgensen, "Erhvers- og trafikforhold", in A. Holm, K. Johansen, *København 1840-1940... op. cit.*, p. 165-187.

were ahead of the industrial returns till World War I, stressing the decisive importance of Copenhagen's harbour. Yet the port area was not included in the 1908-1909 competition's programme.

Whether the contest had truly a planning dimension can be a matter of discussion. All the same it can be considered as part of a set of urban design projects concerned with urban development in relation to the city's government. The growth of municipal works is explained in two ways: on one hand it is understood as a response to the requirements of the vigorous process of urbanization associated with the industrialization that ushered the capital in the general European during the 1880s; on the other it is viewed as resulting from the strategies developed by a social category born out of the industrialization process, that of civil engineers. This does not exclude initiatives taken by other social bodies, which however had to be negotiated with the municipal authorities. Thus Tim Knudsen gave a chief role to Charles Ambt, appointed Stadsingeniør (City Engineer) in 1886, in introducing modern town planning to Copenhagen. When Ambt left his post in August 1902 to head the Danish State Railways, his municipal department had a 50 strong staff of employees.

After the railways came under state administration in 1885, Copenhagen's rail network system was markedly enlarged and improved. The idea of extending the existing Central Station was discarded and it was chosen to create a totally new infrastructure. This led to an international competition opened for that purpose on 1 May 1898.[41] The city had wide authority concerning this new infrastructure.[42] We will only note here that Ambt and Johannsen's projects, both members of the jury for the 1908 competition, were awarded prizes. The new Central Station, designed by Heinrich Wenck (1851-1936), was put into service in 1911, and the important trench work required for taking the tracks north through the city was completed in 1917. As a result the development of the site freed by the old station was put on the agenda. Under the heading "Den store Koncurrence" (The Great Competition) the journal *Architekten* presented the programme published by the municipality in July 1910 to open a national competition for the design of the district.[43] This project came in the aftermath of the 1908-1909 competition, and the programme explicitly required from the submissions that the general plan would respect the provisions of the new Copenhagen Bygningslov (Building Code), even though it had not been enacted by the Parliament. The *Illustreret Tidende* weekly chose the title "Det ny Bycentrum" to publish a long article by municipal engineer O.K. Nobel, with drawings of the project he had submitted together with the architects Egil Fischer and Holger Rasmussen, this project having been awarded the first prize.[44] It seems that the mood was still optimistic concerning town planning for the capital in the spring of 1910.

Another aspect of the programme for the 1909 Competition concerns the layout of parks and promenades. The municipality chose to launch another competition, on 25 April 1905, for the design of a large park, Fælledparken, at the same time as it appointed a commission to decide on the use of the land, which the Magistrat had purchased in the outer districts. The initiative gave concrete expression to the debates that had taken place in the town council for a number of years concerning the need for parks. However the situation underwent radical change with the 1901-1902 incorporations, which reduced the global constraints on real estate. There was a wide-ranging consensus concerning the creation of a large park close to the town centre, even among otherwise opposing groups.[45] The powerful property-owners' associations were

41 J. Vibæk, "Debatten"...op. cit., p.136-169. Twenty-two proposals were submitted to the competition; two second prizes were given, one to Charles Ambt and the other to a Danish-Norwegian-German consortium; the third prize went to Frederik Johannsen.

42 In 1911, tramways transportation passed under municipal control. The appointment of Charles Ambt as head of DSB presumably helped for a strong collaboration between the States company and the City's municipal services.

43 "Den store konkurrence", *Architekten*, N. 42, 16 July 1910.

44 O. K. Nobel "Det ny Bycentrum som vi tænker os det", *Illustreret Tidende*, N. 17, 1910, p. 207-211.

45 Tim Knudsen insists on the influence of a strong engineers group, including Frederik Johannsen who after a study tour in the United States of America advocated the role that parks systems for shaping metropolitan areas: *Storbyen* op. cit, p. 156.

pleased with the increased value of their property, the proponents of embellishment were satisfied with the increased cachet and grandeur this would lend the capital, and hygienists were content with the healthy vicinity of a park near densely-populated districts and hospitals. Once the state and the city had agreed on the use to be given to the former Blegdams & Østerfælled practice ground, some 30 ha. were allotted for a park, to also include playgrounds, sports facilities and the possibility of organizing large events such as exhibitions. The park gave a structure to the north-western area of Copenhagen, which had grown rapidly in the 1890s. It also was usefully symmetrical, beyond the lake Sortedam, to the landscaping of the old fortifications, the Botanical Gardens and Østre Park. The jury, which included the mayors J. Jensen and J. Marstrand, as well as M. Nyrop, C. Ambt et E. Glæsel,[46] awarded two 2nd prizes, one to architect and landscaper E. Erstad-Jørgensen, the other to engineers O. K. Nobel and S. Koch, and one 3rd prize to engineer A. Klixbüll and gardener G. Nyeland-Brandt. The following year, the town council adopted the project of a promenade linking this park to Lersø, which it had been decided to develop in 1902.[47] Fælledparken and its facilities were rapidly laid out, from 1908 to 1912, under the management of O.K. Nobel and E. Glæsel.

Toward a new 'Bygningslov'

The faubourgs of Vesterbro, Nørrebro and Østerbro had mushroomed with tenement dwellings, which met with almost universal criticism, be it from aesthetic or hygienist points of view. The proposed alternative was single-family houses with gardens at the back, numerous models of which had been elaborated under the aegis of Lægeforeningen (the Medical Association) after the 1851 cholera epidemic. At the turn of the century, there were indeed few initiatives indeed similar to the "experimental housing" inspired in 1903 by Fr. Johannsen, the chairman of the Telephone Company, to design multi-storey urban housing for low-earners as fully-fledged architectural developments associating economy, hygiene, comfort and aesthetics and opening up on a new vision of town planning and urbanity.[48] The projects submitted for the 1907 architecture competition for the development of the new Islandsbrygge district on Amager showed the difficulty of reconciling the applying building regulations with the design of a new urban fabric for mass housing. Yet it opened the path to the housing programmes that were to be launched at the time of World War I.[49]

In the absence of any obligation compelling a town to draw up a plan, the development of Copenhagen's physical structure was regulated by building codes that had been revised several times during the second half of the nineteenth century. The April 1889 Bygningslov merely gathered multiple layers of easements, by-laws and jurisprudence since 1856.[50] The 1901-1902 annexations had only made this system more cumbersome by adding regulations pertaining to the incorporated territories. The reshaping of Copenhagen's Bygningslov was requested from different quarters, though they had distinct views, especially about prescriptions with regard to expropriation. The Ingeniørforening set up a "committee of experts", the editorial staff of *Arkitekten* published a series of proposals by Den tekniske Forening, and Lægeforeningen added its own committee, with a view to promoting low-density building.[51] In October 1898, the municipal authorities put a commission in charge of preparing a new Bygningslov. City councillor Gustav Philipsen then emphasized that a new building code was to make it

46 *Architekten*, N.1, 1 October 1904; N.34, 20 May 1905.

47 Papers of Karl Arn Ottesen, Plandirektorat, Copenhagen. For a detailed account of the awarded project, see *Architekten*, N. 9, 2 December 1905.

48 Helge Finsen emphasises the pioneering role of Ulrik Plesner in urban housing's architecture with the buildings on Åboulevard in Copenhagen (1896,1898) and those in Frederiksberg (1905) that were financed by a housing association headed by Frederik Johannsen, see: *Arkitekten Ulrik Plesner*, Copenhagen, 1951, p. 17.

49 The competition's awards went to the following architects: Ulrik Plesner & Aage Mathiesen; Egil Fischer; Axel Preisler & Ejnar Ambt; Ejnar Thuren; Povl Baumann & Louis Hygom; Charles Schou; Thorvald Andersen & Christian Borch, see *Architekten*, N. 21, 23 February 1907; N. 22, 2 March 1907; N. 23, 9 March 1907.

50 See Olaf Forchhammer (preface by), *København fra Bispetid til Borgetid*, Copenhagen, 1947, p. 281-290. See also T. Knudsen, *Storbyen...* op.cit. p. 122.

51 *Arkitekten- Tidsskrift for Bygningsvæsen*, N. 260-262, September 1899.

possible to prescribe development plans, not only for Copenhagen but also for the adjoining communes.[52] According to Poul Hertz, Lægeforeningen's dominant figure, the work of the commission was very slow, even too slow, while the committee set up by Ingeniørforeningen submitted a full project in 1902.[53] In 1904, the commission's chairman entrusted the drafting of the municipal project to an engineer from the city's municipal works, Fr. V. Meyer.[54]

But the project took until 1908 to be completed, probably due to the ambitions of some people represented within the City Council that were looking for a planning formula inspired by the so-called Adickes Act applying in Frankfurt-am-Main since 1902. The commission eventually submitted its bulky report on 26 June 1908. After several deliberations, the Council voted a text on 25 November 1908.[55] Apart from new provisions regulating the construction of housing and the plots' land-uses from the point of view of public hygiene, it also allowed drafting a master plan for the entire town area, with zoning provisions, and provided increased scope for public intervention relative to private rights. Moreover it provided for the dissolution of the bygningskommission (commission for constructions) formed in 1856 to control and apply existing regulations, and for giving the City government full authority in this area, with a new ad hoc department. It also laid down the principle of having regulations updated as it became necessary. In the eyes of the editors of the *Politiken* daily, favourable to such new notions, this was not a mere building code but a proper town planning law.[56] When it launched the competition, the City thus trusted that it could rely on a tool allowing it to implement the planning of the capital's extensions.

However, the future was to prove different. To give the municipal project legal force, the procedure required it to be approved by the government and passed by the Rigsdag (Parliament). After a fairly long time spent in the hands of the competent ministry, a revised project, endorsed by the municipal authorities, was submitted to Parliament early 1911. Yet the project was amended to such an extent that the final result produced in 1915 amounted to merely a revision of the 1889 Bygningslov, an outcome far-off the spirit of the 1908 bill.[57]

2 Organising and Holding the Competition

Between 1894 and 1898, Copenhagen's municipality had acquired large areas of land, some 460ha, mainly in Emdrup and Utterslev, in the neighbouring commune of Brønshøj, which had rapidly led it to negotiate the incorporation of this large borough.[58] This land policy was steadily pursued, so that by 1916 the city was the owner of some 1,000ha within its administrative boundaries. On 30 January 1905, Copenhagen's town council set up a commission tasked with submitting a programme for the development of part of these vast surfaces in a residential "cottage style". New neighbourhood schemes were considered for this northwest part of Copenhagen, with parks and promenades, possibly even with working-class housing.

52 This is underlined by K. O. Ottesen in his manuscript: "Den københavnske general- og regionplanlægning i historisk perspectiv", p. 6.

53 P. Hertz, "Fællesudvalgets Forslag til den Byggelov for København", Maanedsskrift for Sundhedspleje, 1908, p. 315-317. For an analysis of the political forces at work in relation to the Building Code project for Copenhagen see, T. Knudsen, *Storbyen... op.cit.*, p. 179-181.

54 Fr. V. Meyer was a graduate of Den Polyteknisk Læreanstalt and a member of Dansk Ingeniørforeningen; he was employed by the Direktorat for Vej- og Kloakanlægene and promoted Afdelingsingeniør 1 October 1905. Gustav Philipsen, member of the municipal council from 1893 to 1904, chaired the commission in charge of the revision of the 1889 Building Code, Fællesudvalg angaaende en Revision af Bygningsloven af 1889; he was elected Rådman (vice-mayor) in 1903.

55 *Politiken*, 27 June 1908 and 26 November 1908.

56 "... ikke blot en Bygningslov, det vil sige en Lov om, hvordan den enkelte bygning skal være, men en Bebyggelseslov, efter hvilken det bliver muligt for Kommunalbestyrelsen at lægge en fast plan for Byens fremtidige Bebyggelse", *Politiken*, 27 October 1908.

57 *Politiken*, 16 February 1915.

58 See Lars Cramer-Petersen, "Brønshøj sogn, indlemmelsen af nordvest", *Historiske Meddelelser om København*, 2001, p. 107-115. See also, "Udvidelsen af København ved Indlemmelse af Brønshøj Sogn", *Arkitekten, Tidskrift for Bygningsvæsen*, n. 251, 14 July 1899.

2.1 The Organisation of the Competition

The commission, which met for the first time on 20 May 1905, comprised mayors Jens Jensen and Jacob Marstrand, rådman (vice-mayor) Hother Hage, and councillors Johannes Rump, Harald Bing, Christian Christiansen, Carl Becker and A. Lorentzen.[59] However, Alexander Foss (1858-1925), an engineer who had become a prominent industrialist in the cement manufacturing process, chairman of Dansk Ingeniørforening till 1907 and member of the Municipal Council (1903-1907) was also attending the first meeting, and the Stadsingeniør was in attendance on 13 November 1906, with H. Hage and C. Becker absent; on 20 September 1907, H. Bing was not attending, but the Stadsarkitekt and the afdelingsingeniør (section engineer) A.C. Karsten were.

In a note of 28 November 1906 to the Stadsingeniør and the Stadsarkitekt, Jens Jensen asked them to prepare a programme for an open competition since the ad-hoc commission resolution had recommended this solution. The preliminary draft required the selection of location for residential, industrial and workers districts in relation to existing railways infrastructure. It was insisted on the fact that all the new streets should be connected to the inner city. Jensen emphasized also that as time was passing the implementation of "en samlet og rationel Plan for Byens Udvidelse" (a general and rational plan for the town's extension) was becoming more and more difficult to realise with landowners left with a free hand.[60] He urged the town council to swiftly move with a programme.

In a memorandum to the town council dated 10 October 1907, the commission recommended drawing up a master plan (gade-og bebbyggelsesplan) for all of Copenhagen's new districts before deciding on the allocation of the sites owned by the commune. Following the example of other cities, it proposed a public competition, adding that it had prepared the programme and drafted a list of the jury, as well as a budget for the prizes.

To draw up the programme, Chief City Engineer J J. Voigt asked the Verband Deutscher Architekten- und Ingenieurvereine (German Association of Societies of Engineers and Architects) for advice. He also turned to the city of Helsinki, who sent him documents used for the 1899 competition, and to Stockholm's municipality, which provided him with the programme for the 1900 Gothenburg competition.[61] A first project was conveyed to the commission on 24 June 1907. The City Architect seems to have played only a modest role in preparing the competition. Friction appears to have occurred between the two heads of departments about the opening of the competition to municipal officials. Unlike the Stadsingeniør, who wanted staff members to be allowed to participate, the Stadsarkitekt wanted them to be excluded out of hand, so as not to discourage private firms—in view of an all too unequal access to information and to existing projects. They also wanted the competition to be open to the "four Nordic countries".[62] It was finally without special deliberation that the town council adopted the commission's conclusions on 28 October 1907, after the Magistrat had approved them on 15 October. At the end of the year, the committee had decided upon the members of the jury.[63] The French journal *Le Bâtiment* immediately printed this news, and in November and December Copenhagen's City Hall received dozens of

59 Note of Fælledsudvalget angaaende den fremtidige Bebyggelse af Københavns communes Jorder i de ydre Distrikter (Commission for the development of the lands owned by the municipality of Copenhagen in the annexed districts) to Borgerrepræsentationen (City's counsellors), 10 October 1907. In the "Forhandlingsprotokol for Fællesudvalg angaaende Bebyggelsen for Kommunens Jorder i de ydre Distrikter" are reported the dates of the meetings with lists of attendance, but there is no report of the content of the meetings: *Ejendomsdirektorat, sag EJ 1150/1925, kas. 3.*

60 Note from Jens Jensen to Stadsingenioren and Stadsarkitekten, dated 28 November 1906: Stadsarkivet, *Stadsingeniørens Direktorat – Byplankontoret, sag 1918/1984 : 977.*

61 Letter dated 4 December 1906 from Verband Deutscher Architekten- und Ingenieure Vereine to Voigt, in which the German association suggests to contact the mayors of Hälsingborg, Götenborg, Pforzheim, Postdam and Landshut; letter dated 5 December 1906 from Helsingfor's (Helsinki) City Engineer to Voigt; letter dated 28 November 1906 from Stockholms Stadsbyggnadschef til Voigt: *Stadsarkivet, Stadsingeniørens Direktorat- Byplankontoret, sag 1918/1984 : 977.*

62 Note signed by the Stadsingeniør and the Stadsarkitekt to Magistratens 2. Afdeling, dated 24 June 1907: idem.

63 The competition committee hold its first meeting on the 3 December 1907.

enquiries.[64] In the following days, the "Librairie centrale d'art et d'architecture" and the "Société des artistes français" wrote to the council for further information.[65]

A limited programme

The programme was finally published on 15 January 1908, and communicated to the press.[66] It opened the competition to "Danes and foreigners", and entries were to be submitted one year later to the day at the latest. It is specified that the City Architect and the City Engineer may not participate. The name of the nine juries is given, as well as that of the bodies that have chosen them: Burgomasters J. Jensen and J. Marstrand, the town councillors P. Gram and J. Rump; the Akademisk Architektforening (Academic Society of Architects) nominees H. Kampmann and M. Nyrop, the Dansk Ingeniørforening represented by C. Ambt and F. Johannsen, and E. Glæsel, chosen, by the Foreningen til Hovedstadens Forskønnelse. (See Chapter 7).

The programme specifies that the jury will award four prizes (of 10,000, 5,000 3,000 and 2,000 crowns), and that it has a budget of 5,000 Danish crowns for buying projects. It also indicates that all the entries will be exhibited after the jury's deliberations, and that the jury will publish a "brief summary of the motives of its decision". The competition is entitled "En Gade- og Bebyggelsesplan for Københavns Kommunes ydre Distrikter", and actually sets a double task. On the one hand, it requires a master plan for Copenhagen's new extensions, to the exclusion both of the city in its pre-1901 boundaries and of its ports, which do not come under the municipality's authority; required are a plan of the main roads and streets, of squares, parks, playgrounds and sports facilities, with the sites of public buildings, as well as the distribution of buildings according to type and function—in effect their overall zoning; this is to include tramways and railways to link to the industrial districts. On the other hand, detailed plans are requested for the land belonging to the municipality, together with perspectives and street profiles.

The work required of the competitors is increased by the request for plans in the scales of 1:10,000 for the general plan and 1:2,000 for the detailed plans. The first scale corresponds to a scheme for a metropolitan area rather than to a real study of a urban layout plan, while the second scale corresponds more to a working plan, and confirms the competition's original motives in giving priority to the development of the city's property.[67]

When the committee-cum-jury met on 19 January 1909, it declared that 19 entries had been submitted, including the last two ones, nos. 18 and 19, that came in from abroad two days after the 15 January deadline.[68] Seeing that the City Hall had received some 50 requests for competition dossiers after its official publication, to be added to the 10 others received earlier than 15 January 1908, more than half of the enquirers had failed to submit a project. Some declared being short of time, sending back the maps and asking for the reimbursement of the 100 crowns required for the dossier: one map on a scale of 1:20,000, two maps on the scale of 1:10,000 giving the plots belonging to the city, seventeen plans to the scale of 1:2,000 with the contours lines "in Danish feet".[69] Most of the en-

64 "La ville de Copenhague met au concours un plan pour la construction d'un ensemble d'immeubles dans les quartiers excentriques. Les architectes étrangers seront admis au même titre que les Danois. Un prix de 10.000 kr., environ 14.000 fr., sera attribué au projet classé premier. Les trois suivants recevront respectivement 5.000, 3.000 et 2.000 kr.": *Le Bâtiment*, 17 November 1907.

65 *Stadsarkivet, Ejendomsdirektorat,* sag EJ 1150/1925, kas. 1.: correspondence.

66 The competition programme has the following title:Program for en offentlige Konkurrence angaaende en Gade- og Bebyggelsesplan for Københavns Kommunes ydre Distrikter. It was sent to the following Danish newspapers and journal – 30 january 1908: Berlinske Tidende, Børsen, Dannebrog, Ekstrabladet, København, Nationaltidende, Politiken, Social Demokraten, Vort land, Architekten, Gartnertidende, Ingeniøren, Teknisk Tidsskrift: *Stadsarkivet, Ejendomsdirektorat, sag EJ 1150/1925, kas. 1.*

67 Tim Knudsen characterised the programme as a guideline for a "town planning scheme", see *Storbyen* op. cit, p. 164-165.

68 Note dated 4 May 1909, *Stadsarkivet, Ejendomsdirektorat, sag EJ 1150/1925 – kas. 2.*

69 The metric system was introduced in Denmark with a law, 4 May 1907, the system becoming compulsory by 1 April 1912. Yet the former, traditional system remained in practice for a very long time. The Stadens økonomikontor delivered 50

The Government and Administration of Copenhagen

Copenhagen had, and still has, a constitution of its own, and the management of its local authorities, which were laid in the Act of the 4th of March 1857, was different from the system for the other "købstader" that were organised by different laws in 1868.

The municipal authorities of Copenhagen were made up of two bodies, *Magistraten* and *Borgerrepræsentationen*, which are usually translated as the City Executive and the City Council. The two bodies shared the power of decision under the control of the Home Affairs ministry to which an appeal was made in case of opposition.

The *Magistrat* consisted of:

The *Overpræsident* (Lord Mayor), the chairman of the executive body was appointed for a life term by the king. Four *Borgermestre* (Mayor/Burgomaster) who were elected for a life term by the City Council each time a mayor was deceased, and who were to be approved by the king. Four *Rådmænd* (Vice-Mayor) were elected for a term of six years by the City Council.

The municipal administration was accordingly made up of four boards, each one headed by a Borgmester. The First Board (Magistratens 1. Afdeling) was in charge of the general administration, the Church's and the education's affairs together with other cultural activities, and it included the local statistics with an office set up in 1883; the Second Board (Magistratens 2. Afdeling) was responsible for the financing and the budget, including the fiscal affairs, and for hospitals; the Third Board (Magistratens 3. Afdeling) was in charge of the relief to the poor and care of the elderly; the Fourth Board was responsible for technical services and public works. Under the 4th Board (Magistratens 4. Afdeling) were the Stadsingeniør, the Stadsarkitekt, the Stadskonduktør and their services. In 1917 a part of the expanding technical services was made up into a new Board. Although the harbour was vital to the town, the port authorities were not under municipal administration.

In the years 1865-1901, the total membership of the Borgerrepræsentation was 36. It was enlarged to 42 members in 1902 (the new six members represented the annexed districts in 1901-1092), and to 55 members in 1913. The 36 Borgerrepræsentanter (local representatives/councillors) were not elected at one time: a sixth of the Council stood for election each year. A restricted franchise limited the participation in the election. With the Act of 20 April 1908, women were entitled the right to participate in the polls and to be elected as well. The required yearly income qualifying one to vote was reduced to 800 Danish crowns. The Council was to be elected as one assembly at one time for a four years term.

The year 1893 saw the election to the town city council of five Liberals and two Social Democrats, and a significant political shift occurred when the Liberals together with the Social Democrats gained the majority in 1898. By 1900, party politics gained ground in the Council. The Social Democrats succeeded in having Jens Jensen elected mayor in 1903, and the Liberals Jacob Marstrand in 1904. With the new electoral system introducing political parties lists in 1908, the Social Democrats held 20 seats in the Council in 1909.

In 1900-1910 the members of the Magistrat were as follows

Overpræsident	C. S. KLEIN (1891-1899) V. OLDENBURG (1900-1910) F. DE JONQUIERES (1911-1924)
Borgmester Mag.1. afdeling	H. TH. DYBDAL (1897-1917)
Borgmester Mag.2. afdeling	L. C. BORUP (1883-1903) J. JENSEN (1903-1924)
Borgmester Mag.3. afdeling	H. A. JACOBI (1891-1909) P.C. KNUDSEN (1909-10) C. F. LEHMANN (1910-1917)
Borgmester Mag.4. afdeling	C.K. ØLLGAARD (1885-1903) J. N. MARSTRAND (1904-1917)
Rådmænd	P. P. GRAM (1910-1923) H. HAGE (1902-1914) K.M. KLAUSEN (1899-1914) P.C. KNUDSEN (1902-1909) J. N. MARSTRAND (1900-1903) G. PHILIPSEN (1904-1925)

Box1

quirers were architects, but there were also engineers and surveyors; most were Danish, but some were Norwegian, Swedish, German and French. The correspondence kept in Copenhagen City Archives includes two letters from New York, one from Barcelona, one from Brussels, to which is to be added, from a batch earlier than the official publication of the programme, a letter from Geneva, one from Amsterdam, one from Antwerp. A Viennese architect P. Paul Brang, who stressed being a former student of Theophilus Hansen, represents Austria-Hungary. It should be noticed that neither England nor Finland were represented in all the requests for the competition's programme.

2.2 The Jury's Members

On 15 January 1908, the municipal authorities made public the names of the jury's members. Among the nine members, four were representatives of the local government of Copenhagen, while four others were chosen by the professional associations Akademisk Architectforeningen and Dansk Ingeniørforeningen and one by Foreningen til Hovedstadens Forskønnelse. Although there was criticism on the fact that a foreign assessor would have been expected in an international competition, the appointed architects and engineers were among the most distinguished among their peers and most were of repute abroad.

This is especially true of Martin Nyrop (1849-1921) who roused strong interest with the timber buildings he designed for the Nordic Exhibition of Industry, Agriculture and Art in Copenhagen in 1888, in which he displayed a new approach to the use of material and colours, as well as a stance for regional traditional styles and craftsmanship. With the design and construction of the new Town Hall of Copenhagen(1892-1905), which is generally considered as his master piece, there is no doubt that he was regarded as a prominent architect at home and abroad. As a leading figure of the so-called National – romantic movement, his artistically innovative and sophisticated buildings, which emphasised constructive quality as well as simplicity of materials, had been widely appreciated in the European professional press at the time of the mounting authority of the "Art and Craft" current over the declining nineteenth century eclecticism. Nyrop received a wealth of honorific distinctions, which included among others a Grand Prix at the Universal Exhibition in Paris in 1900, a membership with the Royal Swedish Academy of Arts in 1901 and with the Royal Institute of British Architects. Nyrop had been the successor of Ferdinand Meldahl as professor at the Academy's school of architecture in 1906, and was the director of the Academy in 1908-1911.[70] He had been a member of Copenhagen's municipal council in 1888-1891. He was much involved in design projects for some quarters of the city, when he was the co-president of the association Foreningen til Hovedstadens Forskønnelse in 1896-1902. One example is his proposal for a regulation plan of Slotsholmen. Nyrop was also a founding member of Foreningen til gamle Bygningers Bevaring, an early member of Østifernes historisk-topografiske Selskab; he was also in the executive committee of the association Bedre Byggeskik founded in 1915. (See Chapter 7).

Hack Kampmann (1856-1920), as was Nyrop the son of a pastor and had a similar training as a craftsman with apprenticeship as a mason (Nyrop as a carpenter) and complementary studies at the technical school. From 1873 to 1878, he studied architecture at Det kongelige Academie for de skønne Kunster (the Royal Academy of Fine Arts' School of Architecture) as Nyrop did in 1870-1876. Kampmann began his career as an assistant for Hans J. Holm and for Ferdinand Meldahl, the former being an advocate of Danish architecture's history and traditions. He received grants from Det Reiersenske Fond, in 1881, and from the Academy in

vouchers of 100 Kroner, corresponding to the amount to be paid for receiving the topographic maps: *Stadsarkivet, Ejendomsdirektorat, sag EJ 1150/1925, kas. 2*: "Anmodninger om program".

70 See Knud Millech, "Nyrop, Martin", *Weilbachs Kunstnerleksikon*, Vol.2., 1949, p. 483-486; Lise Funder, *Arkitekten Martin Nyrop*, Copenhagen,1979; Minna Kragelund, "Martin Nyrop – vor mest dansksindede arkitekt", in M. Kragelund, *Det gode håndværk. Tråden i dansk tradition, Hovedland*, Copenhagen, 2001, p. 38-51; Francis Beckett, *Københavns Rådhus, opført 1893-1905*, Copenhagen, 1908; Egil Skall, "Københavns Rådhus 75 år", *Historiske Meddelelser om København*, 1980, p. 28-58.

1885 and 1886. He was also awarded a second prize by the Academy in 1882, and the first prize in 1884 with a design for a town hall in Copenhagen. He thus embarked on a study tour in 1884-86 in Germany, Italy, as well as in Greece in 1887 together with Carl Jacobsen, a journey on which he executed a number of fine watercolours. For the patron of arts, he designed and built a new villa next to the new brewery and later an extension to the Glyptotek (1901-06). Previously, in 1882-1883, he had studied at the École des Beaux Arts and worked for the architect René Jacques Hermante (1855-1930), who had been a pupil of Joseph Vaudremer, and been awarded the 2nd Grand prix de Rome in 1880. R. J. Hermante was Architecte en chef des bâtiments civils et palais nationaux as well as Architecte en chef de la Ville de Paris.[71] There are some common points in Kampmann's career. He was appointed Inspector of State Buildings for Jutland in 1892 while the city underwent rapid changes. He has designed and built a number of public buildings, especially the Theatre, the Customs and Excise Office, the State Library, the Postal and Telegraph Office, as well as Marselisborg Palace.

Moreover, he also worked, together with C.Ambt, on the extension plan of the city in 1896-1898. Before the competition Kampmann had designed a great many public buildings in other towns of Jutland, in particular in Hjørring, and in 1909 he was responsible for the plan of a model town at the national exhibition in Århus. Kampmann's production developed later in association with younger architects, including his sons, and the Police Head Office in Copenhagen was one of his last works. Kampmann's influence was also significant through his teaching at the Academy's school of architecture in 1908-1918 where he built up the new curriculum of construction, the so-called "Danish class" of the school of architecture.[72] Kampmann was a member of Foreningen til Hovedstadens Forskønnelse, a founding member of Foreningen til gamle Bygningers Bevaring, and an early member of Østifternes historisk-topografiske Selskab, (Society for the historic – topography of the Danish Islands).

Foreningen til Hovedstadens Forskønnelse had chosen Edvard Glæsel (1858-1915) to seat on the Jury. Born in Jutland, near Herning, where his father was employed in the staff of the railways company, De Jyske Jernbaner, Glæsel received his formal education as an horticulturist at the Veterinær- og Landbohøjskole in Copenhagen. He seems to have worked during four years in London before to embark on a study tour in continental Europe, including France, Italy, and Germany. On his return to Copenhagen in 1888, the Royal Gardens Inspector (Kongelig Haveinspektør) H. A. Flindt recommended him for a number of commissions. Among the gardens he designed for manor estates is the park of Vallø's castle, near by Køge, which is regarded as his masterwork. He also produced a number of gardens in Sweden, including the park of the castle in Malmö. For the City of Copenhagen, Glæsel designed the new cemetery of Bispebjerg, and the one called Vestre Kirkegaard, both in the newly annexed districts, as well as the gardens of the new town hall, which means he collaborated with a number of architects, including Hans J. Holm and Martin Nyrop. He was commissioned for the execution of the new city's large park, Fælledparken, in 1905. Glæsel's landscaping of cemeteries especially seems to have had influence at the turn of the century in Northern Europe. He was awarded a gold medal at the exhibition of Düsseldorf in 1902.[73]

In a letter dated 23 September 1907 to Foreningen til Hovedstadens Forskønnelse, Jens Jensen invited the association to propose a member for the jury. On the 29 September, Martin Nyrop wrote to his friend Jens Møller-Jensen, the president of the association, to recommend Glæsel as the best choice because Danish architects had nod specialised in town planning. Furthermore Glæsel worked with Hans J. Holm on a number of schemes of which the design had become a model in Germany. Nyrop concluded: "We can not

71 On J. Hermante, see Jean-Pierre Epron, *Comprendre l'éclectisme*, Paris, 1997, p. 330.

72 See K. Millech, "Kampmann, Hack", *Weilbachs Kunstnerleksikon*, Vol. 2, 1949, pp. 100-111; Kay Fisker, *Arkitekten, Professor Hack Kampmanns rejsebreve og skitser*, Copenhagen, 1946; Jørgen Fink, "Byens rum", in I. Gejl (red.), *Århus – byens historie 1870-1945*, Vol. 3, Århus, 1998, p. 26-53.

73 See *Gartner-Tidende- organ for Alm. Dansk Gartnerforening*, N. 25, 24 June 1915, pp. 144-147; Axel Lange, "Glæsel, Fritz Edvard", *Dansk biografisk leksikon*, Vol. 8, 1936, pp. 183-4.; *Architekten*, N. 39, 26 June 1915, p. 378.

find a better person than Glæsel for the jury". Architect A. Clemmensen also wrote to Møller-Jensen on 2 October asking him to support Glæsel on behalf of Akademisk Architektforening: "He is well known and in high esteem among the architects". [74]

Another distinguished figure to seat in the jury was Charles Ambt (1847-1919) who, together with Frederik Johannsen was nominated by Dansk Ingeniørforening. Ambt, son of a glazier, was born in Copenhagen where he spent all his life. He oined Den Polytekniske Læreanstalt in 1863, graduated in 1868 and began his career as an engineer with the Port's Administration at the time of the construction of Knippelbro. In 1869 he joined the staff of the City's Public Works (Brolægnings & Vejvæsen) until he was appointed City Chief Engineer in 1886, a position he held until he took over as Director of the Danish State Railways in 1902. As already mentioned, Ambt was involved in the main infrastructure works of Copenhagen from the time when the town expanded out of its fortifications until the annexation of the surrounding districts, and under many respects he left his mark on the planning of the capital. Ambt who was a member of the executive committee of Dansk Ingeniørforening since its foundation became its fourth president in 1901 till 1904.[75] He was also in the advisory commission of Foreningen til Hovedstadens Forskønnelse between 1894-1910. (See Chapter 7)

Frederik Johannsen (1855-1934) was a driving force in the creation of the Association in 1892 and was part of its executive committee until 1896 when he came into dissent with his peers by advocating a broader right of admission. Johannsen, who was the son of an army officer, studied at Det Polyteknisk Læreansalt in 1872-1877 and began his career by working for the constructor Niels Andersen in 1879-80. He was then successively hired by the Engineers corps and the Public Works of the municipality of Copenhagen (Brolægnings & Vejvæsen). In 1881-1884 he worked in railways construction for the State-owned Sjællandske Jernbaneselskab and in 1886-1888 the Engineers corps for the fortifications works, north of Copenhagen, again employed him. From 1888 he worked as an independent contractor, often in partnership with other contractors like P. Madsen or Gluud, and was involved in construction works for harbours, like the Freeport of Copenhagen, railways and fortifications. In 1903 Johannsen was appointed general director of Kjøbenhavns Telefon-Aktieselskab, a company in which the state was the main shareholder, where he stayed until his retirement. In 1896-1906 he was a member of the municipal corporation of Frederiksberg, and was much involved in the construction of the local tramways company in 1897. Johannsen, a member of the newly established Industriråd (Federation of Danish Industries) in 1910, is generally regarded as an important figure that promoted enterprise culture among the engineers. Johannsen was a member of numerous boards and technical commissions and eventually became the president of Dansk Ingeniørforening in 1916-1920.[76]

Two council members, Peder Pedersen Gram (1850-1923) and Johannes Christian Magnus Rump (1861-1932) represented the municipality of Copenhagen. They had very little in common. P. P. Gram, a son of a fisherman, was born in Jutland and had worked most of his life as a bricklayer (muresvend) in Copenhagen where to he moved as a young man. In 1886 he started his own building firm and was rapidly successful in the trade. He held an important position in the masons' guild (Murerlavet) of Copenhagen. He is known for having built Frihavn's Church as well as Esaja Church, which both were designed by Thorvald Jørgensen, and a great many terraced houses for the Arbejdernes Byggeforening. He was elected to Copenhagen's municipal council in 1904 on the so-called antisocialist list and became Rådmand (vice major) for the 3rd board of the town administration in 1910.[77]

Johannes Rump (1861-1932) had a very different

74 Landsarkivet for Sjælland, Lolland-Falster & Bornholm, Records of Foreningen til Hovedstadens Forskønnelse, Behandlede sager, N.11, "De ydre Distrikters Bebyggelse": correspondence.

75 P. Vinding, "Ambt, Georg, Christian, Charles", *Dansk biografisk leksikon*, Vol. 1. 1932, p. 269-272.

76 P. Vinding, "Johannsen, Frederik (Frits)", *Dansk biografisk leksikon*, Vol. 12. 1937, pp. 16-21; A. Hannover (red.), *Dansk Civil Ingeniørstat*, Copenhague, 1942, p. 21-22.

77 P. Stavnstrup, "Gram, Peder Pedersen, *Dansk biografisk leksikon*, Vol. 8, 1936, p. 274-275.

background. He was the son of a government officer, who had been a member of the Parliament and Minister of Justice. Rump received his education at the Sorø Akademi before he studied engineering at Den Polytekniske Læreanstalt where he graduated in 1886. Rump began his career as a constructing engineer with the tramways company Strandvejens Dampsporvejsselskab in 1886-1887 before joining the Public Works Department of the City of Copenhagen (Brolægnings- og Vejvæsen) in 1887. The following year he moved to the City Engineer's department, which he served until 1890. That year he established his own engineering office and specialised in sanitary works. In 1900 he was elected to Copenhagen's municipal council and was part of the Social Democrats group in 1903, where he became the spokesman for technical issues. In 1911 Rump was member of the Port Authorities council and by 1914 member of its board. This wealthy landowner was especially known as an art connoisseur whose collection of painting was outstanding. In 1900-1922, he was a member of the board of Albertina Award in 1900-1922, one of Carl Jacobsen's foundations, and a trustee for the Thorvaldsen's Museum in 1916 and the Ny Carlsberg Glyptotek in 1925.[78]

The other representatives of the municipal authorities were Jens Jensen (1859-1928) and Jacob Nicolaj Marstrand (1848-1935). Respectively, burgomaster of the 2nd Magistratens Afdeling, and of the 4th Magistratens Afdeling, the board in charge of technical works. Jens Jensen is generally regarded as a main figure of the Social Democratic party and of the Labour Union. He was elected to the municipal council in 1893, the year when the Liberals and the Social Democrats joined forces to enter the city government, and succeeded Borup as burgomaster of the 2nd Magistratens Afdeling (Finance Board) in 1903. In 1895 he had been elected to the Folketing. J. Jensen was to become Overpræsident in 1924. Originally from Funen, he apprenticed to a building painter and soon engaged himself in politics. He moved to Copenhagen in 1879 and by 1884 he was fully devoted to trade unions activities. He took part in a number of workers' congresses abroad and by the turn of the century he was a well-established figure in the socialist reformist movement. During his tenure within the Magistrat of Copenhagen, he promoted building activities and housing policies, and was certainly a leading force in opening the competition which took place in the aftermath of a deep crisis, following the bankruptcy of main credit and banking institutions in 1908; the building sector after a decade of booming activities had come to a standstill.[79]

Jacob Marstrand had been elected to the municipal council in the same political move as Jensen, but in the Liberal's group. He had hoped to study engineering, however because of a sudden adversity in his family he eventually entered the baker's trade, where he was successful enough to hand over his business over to his son in 1904. In 1900 he was rådman (vice-burgomaster) for the 4th Board of the municipality, which he became burgomaster of in January 1904. He was at the head of the technical engineering services, which were in constant expansion during those years up until 1917. Marstrand was part of the Grundtvigian movement and the president of the Grundtvigs – Kirken Komite as well as president of Foreningen for Højskolens Fremme.[80] He wrote a few books, which includes his memoirs in which there is no mention of the competition.[81]

2.3 Selecting the Entries

The jury met on 12 February, later on 3, 17 and 21 April and finally on 4 May 1909 to deliberate on the entries. No minutes were taken. The only remaining document is a printed four-page memorandum dated 4 May, a public report on the jury's work. It states that two municipal officers have been asked to examine the 261 plans and nineteen outlines that are to be exhibited in the Town Hall for the juries to be able to consult at leisure. It does not mention the relief plan attested by a receipt dated 21 January 1909 and men-

78 L. Swane, "Rump, Johannes Christian Magnus", *Dansk biografisk leksikon*, Vol. 12. 1982, p. 472.

79 O. Bertolt, "Jensen, Jens", *Dansk biografisk leksikon*, Vol. 11, 1937, pp. 452-457.

80 H. Gammelgaard, "Marstrand, Jacob Nicolaj", *Dansk biografisk leksikon*, Vol. 9. 1981, p. 436-437.

81 Jacob Marstrand, *Tilbageblik gennem et langt Liv*, Copenhagen, 1928.

tioned in the outline of entry no. 15 awarded the 3rd prize to which it is enclosed.[82] It also states that a "printed summary of the contents of each project" has been submitted to each of the juries. This consists of three pages organised under a series of headings, probably prepared by the City Engineer's board, that are intended to allow evaluating the project.[83] The headings correspond to the points of the programme, and have to be filled out with the appropriate comments prior to submitting to the jury. It can be noted that the first heading gives rise to the fullest outlines. It concerns the highways, and in particular the radial and the circular roads. The heading for the types of constructions is also substantial, while the others are far sketchier. (See, Box Evaluation Model).

The juries were given a formula that had been established by the services of the City Engineer. The City Architect has presumably been involved at some stage in the conception of this guidelines. The duplicated formula were then filled up for each entry and bound together into booklets that were given to the juries, so they each had a kind of memo for the nineteen entries on which they could note their comments. Unfortunately, there is only one such memo with anonymous hand-written annotations kept with the records of the Competition. On the one hand, the criteria chosen are developing the competition's programme, hereby helping the jury to evaluate according to the guidelines, which the working committee had opted for together with the Council and the Magistrat. On the other hand, they provide a sort of pre- evaluation that the juries could not ignore. The formula has four headings (A, B, C, and D), which are divided into a number of sub headings, and it ends with a table intended to allow a resume of the appreciation. It appears that the first heading "Hovedgader" (main thoroughfares) is clearly the one, which presents most of the descriptive comments. For the next headings, "Bebyggelse" (constructions), "Parker" (parks) and "Stranden Benyttelse" (development of the sea shore) the comments are far less developed, especially for the last one, while the last heading "særlige Bemærkninger" (special remarks) is most often left empty.

According to the printed report, the juries state that they have unanimously judged project no. 2, "Urania", to be the best, followed by projects no. 4, 5 and 15. They add that they found it "difficult" to grade the latter.[84] It is said that during the 3 April 1909 meeting the jury ruled out the entries, 3, 6, 7, 9, 10, 12, 14, 16, and 19. The next meeting of 17 April 1909 was spend discussing the entries, 1, 2, 4, 5, but we are not informed of any decision.[85] During the next meeting held on 21 April, with Hack Kampmann in absentia, entries 2, 4, 5 and 15 were finally selected for a price and it was also decided to purchase entry number 8. We found trace of a vote, probably on 4 May since the final order of prizes is mentioned. As this is the only document giving us an idea of the respective choices of the nine juries, we reproduce this data here.[86]

Vote of the jury, 4 may 1909

Nyrop	Ambt	Gram	Rump	Glæsel	Johannsen	Marstrand	Kampmann	Jensen	Proposal
3	2	1	2	2	1	1	2	2	No. 4
1	1	3	3	1	3	2	3	3	No. 5
2	3	2	1	3	2	3	1	1	No. 15

82 Letter to Simon Koch, kontorchef for Magistratens 2. afdeling), 21 January 1909, *Stadsarkivet, Ejendomsdirektorat, sag EJ 1150/1925, kas.1.*

83 The complete files are kept in the City's Planning Office in Copenhagen, where we have consulted them.

84 Printed note dated 4 May 1909, *Stadsarkivet, Ejendomsdirektorat, sag EJ 1150/1925, kas.1*

85 "The projects n.1, n. 2, n. 4 and n. 5 have been discussed at the meeting, 17 April 1909": Forhandlingsprotokol for Fællesudvalg angaaende Bebyggelsen for Kommunens Jorder i de ydre Distrikter, *Stadsarkivet, Ejendomsdirektorat, sag EJ 1150/1925, kas.3.*

86 *Stadsarkivet, Ejendomsdirektorat, sag EJ 1150/1925, kas.1.*

We understand this as giving the respective ranking (1st, 2nd, 3rd) that jury's member awarded to each of the 3 projects here. This would mean that:

Project no. 4, " Tre Træer ", finally awarded the 2nd prize, obtained three 1st choices (Gram, Johannsen, Marstrand), five 2nd choices (Ambt, Rump, Glæsel, Kampmann, Jensen) and one 3rd choice (Nyrop).

Project no. 15, "Københavns Vaaben 1296", awarded the 3rd prize, obtained three 1st choices (Rump, Kampmann, Jensen), three 2nd choices (Nyrop, Gram, Johannsen) and three 3rd choices (Ambt, Glæsel, Marstrand).

Project no. 5, "Anno 1977", awarded the 4th prize, obtained three 1st choices (Nyrop, Ambt, Glæsel), one 2nd choice (Marstrand) and five 3rd choices (Gram, Rump, Johannsen, Kampmann, Jensen).

Project no. 8, "Weyland Smed", was bought for an amount of 1,500 crowns.

The report gives practically no clue as to the criteria for the selection of the projects or for the prizes they were awarded. The purchase of the "Weyland Smed" project is justified by the "original ideas and interesting suggestions" presented by Raavad in his outline, in spite of the fact that the plans "do not meet the essential requirements, while going way beyond what could be practically implemented." Only the first prize gives rise to a few remarks: featuring "good transport links, as most of the other proposals", the project stands out by "the carefully thought-out design of the road network and by the quality of the crossroads for the main streets", as well as by its study of an extensive network of railway lines. A few reservations are noted, regretting that the city's maritime location has not been sufficiently taken into account, especially for the Kalvebod parks opening out onto the beach, and "the street perspectives did not find favour with the jury".[87] Following the competition, the municipality had the general plans of the four prize-winning projects and that of the purchased one published as an appendix to the volume gathering the minutes of the town council for the year 1909, without any further comment.[88]

The jury's handling of the competition was criticised in different quarters. The journal *Architektur* published a much critical comment questioning the programme as well as the jury's choice (See Chapter 3). On 13 May the Danish newspaper *Politken* published a letter signed by three architects, U. Plesner, E. Fischer, and L. Hygom and engineer K. I. Einersen in which the jury is criticised for having failed to deliver a public statement of the arguments for the evaluation of the entries, winning and not winning alike. They insisted on the fact that this was part of the conditions specified in the initial programme.[89] It seems that the professional milieu was at large disappointed by the jury's code of conduct. Pålhman for instance criticised the lack of report from the jury and the lack of compensation for interesting projects.[90] On 8 May 1909, F. Johannsen forwarded to Mayor Jensen a letter from P. V. Jensen Klint arguing in favour of distributing the remaining sum of 3500 Kroner earmarked for the non-awarded price. Klint suggest dividing the sum into small amounts of 500 Kroner, each to be given to promising, young architects as a token of encouragement.[91] Finally, these scattered elements seems to indicate that a group of young Danish professionals evolving around the group of Den Fri Architektforening had been rather disappointed in their hope of getting some reward for their contribution. Their expectations were echoed by senior architects, such as P. V. Jensen Klint and Carl Brummer, pointing out in particular the quality of the project "Bella" that was not selected by the jury. (See Chapter 3).

87 Printed note dated 4 May 1909, idem.

88 Tillæg til Københavns Borgerrepræsentanters Forhandlinger, Copenhagen, 1910.

89 See the article "Den kommunale konkurrence om gadeplaner", *Politiken,* 13 May1901.

90 Letter of Påhlman to Jens Jensen, not dated, together with a stencil copy of a letter dated 20 October 1909 with about the same content: *Stadsarkivet, Ejendomsdirektorat, Hovedjournalsager, Sag EJ 1150/1925, kas. 1.*

91 Letter, dated 8 May 1909, written by Frederik Johannsen to Jens Jensen, with a joined letter from P. V. Jensen Klint, not dated, Idem.

2

GROUP BIOGRAPHY OF THE NINETEEN ENTRIES

This chapter aims at presenting a group – biography, in the sense that it displays a collective, but individual biography of the 31 participants to the 1909 Competition. The criteria that have been chosen to elaborate the biographical notices intend to identify the constants and the variables among the data for the whole group with respect to their social origin, education and professional occupation. The purpose is to explore the figure of a town plan designer in the early twentieth century.

This group-biography is arranged in 19 units, which refer to each entry. Thus the participants in the Competition are listed as the entries' authors according to the numbers assigned to their submissions after arrival in Copenhagen's Town Hall in January 1909. This number was marked on each material received by the municipality, including the receipts issued for the return of the 100 Danish crowns, which had been paid by the participants in order to receive the set op maps and the programme. The nineteen captions at the beginning of each unit show the entry's number, the motto of the project and the name of the authors of the project at the time of the Competition.

The units are organized in the following manner. First, they account for eventual prize and premium and the documents located in Copenhagen Town Hall Archives (Københavns Stadsarkiv), including the Collection of maps and drawings (Kort- og Tegningssamlingen). All the memoirs attached to the plans and drawings have been identified, except for the entry "Gefion". Second, the units focus on the biographical data. The place of birth and father's occupation, when known, are indicated. Special attention is given to the professional education of the competitors, including their affiliation to professional associations: Dansk Ingeniørforeningen (The Danish Association of Civil Engineers), set up in 1892 to protect the interests of the graduates of Den Polytekniske Læreanstalt (The Technical College), and Akademisk Architektforening (The Academic Association of Architects) formally founded in 1879 to meet the needs of the architects who studied at Det kongelige Academie for de skønne Kunster (the Royal Academy of Fine Arts) (See Chapter 3). Although a number of entrants had a long and sometimes very successful career, we concentrate on the period of the Competition and do not give much detail for years after 1918. The addresses of the competitors are known, but are not given here.

Third, entrants' membership of the following associations is systematically reported: Foreningen til Hovedstadens Forskønnelse (The Society for the Beautification of the Capital) and Foreningen til gamle Bygningers Bevaring (The Society for the Protection of Ancient Buildings).

Finally, a list of the sources and a selection of the competitor's works, which have been consulted, complete each biographical notice. The references of the archives' records are listed in the book's general bibliography. The main reference books used for biographical data are here mentioned:

M. Bodelsen, P. Engelstoft (red.), Weilbachs Kunstnerleksikon, Copenhagen, Aschehoug Dansk Forlag, 3 vol., 1947, 1949, 1952.

S. Hartmann (red.), Dansk Kunstnerleksikon Weilbach, Copenhagen, Rosinante, 9 vol., 2000.

P. Engelstoft (red.), Dansk biografisk leksikon, Copenhagen, Schultz Forlag, 1933-1944.

S. Cedergreen Bech (red.), Dansk biografisk leksikon, Copenhagen, Gyldendal, 1979-1984.

Dansk Civil- og Akademiingeniørstat, 1971 – biografiske oplysninger om kandidater fra Danmarks tekniske højskole og Danmarks Ingeniørakademie (1829-1968), Copenhagen, Dansk Ingeniørforening og Krak, 1971.

R. Jespersen (red.), Biografiske Oplysninger angaa-

The 1909 Competition's Entries

ENTRIES	AUTHORS	COUNTRIES
1. Gefion	H. ELLIOT, eng. A. E. PÅHLMAN, eng.	Sweden
2. Urania (1st pr.)	K.STRINZ, surveyor	Germany
3. "⊕"	V. AHLMANN, arch.	Denmark
4. Tre Træer (2nd pr.)	A.BJERRE, eng.	Denmark
5. Anno 1977 (4th pr.)	O. K. NOBEL, eng. H. RASMUSSEN, arch.	Denmark
6. Hafnia	E.W.BJERKNES, eng-surveyor.	Norway
7. Julemærket for 1908	E. FRÖLICH, eng. A. BRANDT KLIXBÜLL, eng.	Denmark
8. Wayland Smed (selected)	A. J. ROEWADE, arch-eng.	United-States of America
9. Grønne Baand	H.BERNOULLI, arch.	Germany
10. Storstad	A. RIIS, eng. H. V. CHRISTENSEN, eng.	Denmark
11. For Byen og Borgerne	N.O. GELLERSTED, eng. E. BÜLOW-HÜBE, eng.	Sweden
12. Mindre Parker men Parkalléer	R. ERSLEV, eng.	Denmark
13. Bellla	K. I. EINERSEN, eng. L. HYGOM, arch. C. MANICUS-HANSEN, eng.	Denmark
14. Millionbyen	E. FISCHER, arch.	Denmark
15. Københavns Vaaben 1296 (3rd pr.)	U. PLESNER, arch. A. LANGELAND-MATHIESEN, arch. M. FRANDSEN, eng. A. HANSEN, landscape gardener	Denmark
16. Et kløverblad	V. CLAUSEN, arch.	Denmark
17. Stor-Kjøbenhavn	F. SUNDBÄRG, arch. A. LILIENBERG, eng.	Sweden
18. Richesse oblige	P. O. HALLMAN, arch. F. W. BERGER, eng.	Sweden
19. Axelhus	F. ROMEU I RIBOT, arch.	Spain

Box 2 The nineteen entries are listed according to the numbers assigned by the Competition's committee; the names of the entrants and their countries of residence are given at the time of the Competition.

ende Den Polytekniske Læreanstalts Kandidater 1829-1929, Copenhagen, Dansk Ingeniørforening, 1930.

A. Hannover (red.), Dansk civilingeniørstat 1942. Biografiske om Polytekniske kandidater 1829-1941, Copenhagen, C. A. Reitzels Forlag – Axel Sandal, 1942.

Danmarks kommunale Forvaltning, Den kommunale Forvaltning, Indenrigsministeriet, Københavns Kommune, Frederiksbergs Kommune, Copenhagen, Selskabet Vort Samfund, 1929.

Krak, Vejviser for København og Omegn, Gade- og Husregister, Copenhagen, 1908.

H. Weitemeyer (red.), Trap – Kongeriget Danmark, Vol. 1 – Indledende Beskrivelse af Danmark, Kjøbenhavn og Frederiksberg, Copenhagen, G. E. C. Gad, 1906.

Entry n° 1, motto "Gefion" – H. Elliot & A. E. Påhlman

Documentation in Copenhagen Town Hall Archives:

The photographic plate of the general plan (oversigtsplan); the photographic version of the general plan in Gengivelser af Konkurrenceprojekter vedrørende Københavns ydre Distrikter, 1909.

Hans O. Elliot (?, ?), engineer
August Emmanuel Påhlman (?,?), engineer

Hans O. Elliot and August Emmanuel Påhlman were both Swedish civil engineers. In 1909 they also sent a common proposal entitled "Södra Bergen" to the competition for the planning of Katarinatrakten, in Stockholm, which was bought for 1.500 Swedish crowns.

In the correspondence kept with the records of the competition, there are four letters sent by Påhlman to the Mayor J. Jensen. They probably met on 10 May 1909 with the result that Påhlman could hope for his project to be bought by the municipality. In a telegram sent on 21 May 1909, he is asking if the project Gefion could be bought as it has been suggested, and for how much, in a minute dated 22 May, J. Jensen notified that no answer can be given before the Council's meeting of 27 May. In a long letter, with no date, sent by Påhlman to the Mayor, a number of arguments are put forward to emphasise the strength of the project. On this occasion, Påhlman added to his signature: "Civilingeniör, Stadsplaneingeniör i Stockholms stads lantegendomsnämnd (civil engineer, town plan engineer in the board of Stockholm's municipal estates). He develops a comparison between his proposal and the winning entry "Urania" with respect to the projected ring railway, and to the distribution of high and low density built areas. He also underlines a number of ideas in his project, which are common to the entries "Wayland Smed", the civic centres, and "København Vaaben 1296", the location of public buildings or parks on municipal tracks of land, as well as original suggestions for road extensions in comparison to other designs. In his concluding remark, he insists on the input of work and money that is necessary to design the project. With his letter he sent a press cutting, "Den kommunale Konkurrence om Gadeplaner".

The careers of Påhlman and of Elliot have not yet been documented. According to Hans Bjur, Påhlman was town engineer when he sat in the Working Committee for the preparation of the Swedish national exhibition in Gothenburg, 1923.

Påhlman signed the article, "Städernas fästighetsbilnung och mätningsväsen", published in Svenska Stadsförbundets Tidskrift in 1919. He was also co-author, with H. Helberg, of a topographic map of Stockholm (1:8000) edited by the Generalstabens litografiska Anstalt, Stockholm, in 1917-1927.

Sources:

H. Bjur, Stadsplanering kring 1900 – med exempel från Göteborg och Albert Lilienbergs versamhet. Göteborg, 1984, p. 54; "Katarinatraktens ordnande", Arkitektur och Dekorativ Konst, 1910, p. 1-13; Copenhagen, Stadsarkivet: Ejendomsdirektorat, Hovedjournalsager, Sag EJ 1150/1925, kassette1: correspondance; Libris Catalogue on line.

Entry n° 2, motto "Urania" – K. Strinz

Winning entry: 1st prize with a premium of 10.000 Danish crowns.

Documentation in Copenhagen Town Hall Archives:

Memorandum to the proposal "Urania", seventeen pages (handwritten in Danish).

Original drawings: oversigtsplan (general plan) in a set of four pieces, scale 1:10.000; five oversigts planer (general plans), scale 1:20.000, with various colour nuances; seven 'detaille' (land use plans), scale 1:2.000; seven grundtegninger (detailed plans), each one with a perspective drawing (water coloured) depicting monumental buildings such as churches, square or a boulevard, as well as villas' quarter with a park; one profile of a monumental suspension bridge, scale 1:1.000; a series of section drawings of thoroughfares: eleven with a tramway line, eight avenues with trees, six residential streets, scale 1:200.

A copy of the memorandum and of the general plan in Beskrivelser til de fire præmierede og det indkøbte konkurrence–projekt angaaende bebyggelsen af Københavns ydre distrikter, Tillæg til Københavns Borgerrepræsentanters Forhandlinger fra den 1. April 1909 til den 29. Marts 1910, p. 1-12.

Photographic version of the general plan in Gengivelser af Konkurrenceprojekter vedrørende Københavns ydre Distrikter, 1909.

Karl Strinz (1869 – 1942), land surveyor

Strinz was born in Köln-am-Rhein 11 June 1869, the son of an evangelist schoolmaster. He completed his education in Köln's Realgymnasium (grammar school) and obtained his final examination, Abitur, in 1887. Strinz decided to enter the profession of land surveying and worked for a couple of years at the Prussian railway administration in Köln before joining the formal surveyor's education at the Königlichen jPreussischen Landwirtschaftlischen Akademie (The Royal Academy of Agriculture) of Poppelsdorf (Bonn) in 1890. He successfully passed, with a good marking, the state's examination of licensed surveyors, in June 1892. In November 1891 he was employed as Landmesser by the Prussian railway administration in Köln, which he served until January 1895 with a nine months interruption for military duties. With the best recommendations from the lstate's railway direction, Strinz applied for the position of Stadtgeometer (City's Surveyor) in the city of Düren in December 1895, and entered this new service in February 1896. He held this position until 1902 when he sent his candidature, dated 21 April, for the position of Leiter des städtische Vermessungsamt (chief of the city's cadastre) to the city of Bonn and he was appointed "Stadsgeometer" in Bonn in September 1902. For reasons, which are unknown to us, he applied for the position of Vermessungs- Direktor in the city of Magdeburg to which he moved in early 1913. From that date up to 1934, he served as director of the city's cadastre and he died in Magdeburg 29 November 1942.

Strinz was very active in the professional organisation of German surveyors, and in his brief obituary he is said to have had a good reputation among his peers. In July 1903, he participated in the German surveyors' congress in Dresden and, from 1905 onwards, he often wrote technical articles for the organisation's journal Zeitschrift für Vermessungswesen. He became especially involved in the union of the municipal surveyors, Verein preussischer Landmesser im Kommunaldienst, and a note signed by Bonn's Oberbürgmeister allowing Strinz to join the general assembly of that association in Erfurt, July 1908, tells us Strinz then acted as the secretary of the executive committee. He held that responsibility until the general reorganisation of the surveyors' professional bodies that took place in Germany after the First World War. Strinz was also part of the movement for promoting the surveyors in municipal town planning by asking for their representation in the official commissions. He participated to a number of public competitions. For his proposal "Mens agitat molem", he was awarded the 4th prize in the competition for the eastern extension of Manheim in 1907. In the year of Copenhagen's competition, he received the first prize together with the Stadtbaumeister of Düren, Dauer, with their entry "Sterntor" to the contest hold in Bonn for the design of reclaimed land from the Sterntor military barracks. Strinz also submitted a project, entry number 20 "Ne quid nimis", to Great Berlin's competition in 1909, as well as he participated in the competitions held in Breslau (Wroclaw) and in Wetzlar in the 1920s. At the Wetzlar competition (1924-1925), Strinz's entry "Erst wäg's, dann wags" was not awarded a prize but the jury recommended to buy the project. While in charge of the cadastre in Bonn and in Magdeburg, Strinz was also involved in the design of the town development of both cities. He wrote many articles, especially on land use topics often on the surveyors calculation methods, and in 1919 he also gave lectures at the town planning seminar organised by J. Brix et F. Genzmer at the Technische Hochschule in Berlin.

Sources:

Bonns Stadtarchiv, PA 1957/2080/D; Information provided by the Municipality of Wetzlar; Information provided by the Stadarchiv, Landeshaupstadt Magdeburg (Magdeburg City's Archives); Zeitschrift für Vermessungswesen – Deutscher Verein für Vermessungswesen, 1943, Heft 3, 15 March, p. 48; Der Städtebau, 1908, Tafel 75; W. Sonne,"Ideen für die Grossstaadt: der Wettbewerb Gross-Berlin 1910", in T. Sheer, J.-P. Keihues, P. Kahlfeldt (ed.), Stadt der Architektur – Architektur der Stadt: Berlin 1900-2000, Berlin: Verlagsbuchhandluing Beuermann Gmbh, 2000, p. 67-77.

Selected writings by Strinz:

"Die gesetzliche Regelung der Baulandumlegung", Der Städtebau, 1905, p. 135-138; "Die günstigste Form und Tiefe der Baublöcke in wirtschaftlicher Beziehung", Der Städtebau, 1907, p. 38-40, 46-50, 52-60; "Die Weitermittlung der Baugrundstücke und die Umlegung solcher Grundstücke auf Grund ihres Wertverhältnisses", Zeitschrift für Vermessungswesen, 1905, p.201-211, 225-239; "Zur Umgestaltung des Vereinswesens", Zeitschrift für Vermessungswesen, 1919, p. 395-402; "Die historische Entwicklung des Siedlungsgedankens", Zeitschrift für Vermessungswesen, 1920, p. 674-682.

Entry n° 3, motto "⊕" – V. Ahlmann

Documentation in Copenhagen Town Hall Archives:

Memorandum to the proposal marked with "+", five pages (handwritten).

Original drawings: one general plan (overisgtsplan) in a set of four pieces, scale 1:10.000; a set of nine detailed plans, scale 1:2000; one perspective drawing with the site plan of a group of buildings.

Photographic version of the general plan in Gengivelser af Konkurrenceprojekter vedrørende Københavns ydre Distrikter, 1909.

Hans Vilhelm Ahlmann (1852-1928), architect

Ahlmann was born in Scania, south of Sweden, the son of a landowner. He served an apprenticeship as a carpenter in Copenhagen and followed courses at Den Tekniske Selskabs Skole (The School of the Technical Society) where he qualified in 1869 for admittance to the School of Architecture at Det kongelige Academie for de skønne Kunster (the Royal Academy of Fine Arts). In 1870-76 he studied architecture and began his professional career by working a number of years for the architect Hermann Baagøe Storck (1839-1922) and later for the architect Johan Daniel Herholdt (1818-1902). In those years he became involved with restoration works of churches. He eventually opened his own practice in 1885 in Århus, where he also taught construction at the local technical school. In 1902 he settled in Copenhagen and he became a member of Det særlige Kirkesyn (The Inspection of churches' buildings) in 1905. Ahlmann, a skilful draughtsman, was involved in the systematic survey drawings of old churches in Denmark and a number of his drawings were published in various books, including the portfolio series of Tegninger af Ældre Nordisk Architektur (1871-1919). A great many of his commissions were for restoring churches, especially in North Jutland, and also timber framed buildings (e.g. Næstved). He designed and built a number of public buildings, including new churches in Frederikshavn (1897) and Holstebro (1907), the technical school of Næstved (1884) and many office buildings. Ahlmann was awarded the 2nd prize in the 1901 competition for a church in Vejle; the 1st prize in the 1907 competition for the design of model housing for state's employees and the 3rd prize in the 1908 competition for the design and construction of a church in Rønne.

Ahlmann was a member of Akademisk Architektforening as well as of Foreningen til Hovedstadens Forskønnelse and Foreningen til Gamle Bygningners Bevaring.

Sources:

Weilbachs Kunstnerleksikon, vol. I, 1947; Weilbach, Dansk Kunstnerleksikon, vol. 1, 1994, p. 44-45; Arkitekten, 1928, n. 22, p. 136; Det kongelige Danske Kunstakademiets bibliotek- Arkitektur samlinger.

Entry n° 4, motto "Tre Træer" – A. Bjerre

Winning entry that was awarded the 2nd prize with a premium of 5.000 Danish crowns.

Documentation in Copenhagen Town Hall Archives:

Memorandum to the proposal "Tre træer", 30 pages (typewritten), with an annexe: map's section of the northern area of Copenhagen on which is drawn the main thoroughfare towards Lyngby and Dyrhaven.

Original drawings: oversigtplan (general plan) in a set of four pieces, scale 1:10.000; a set of eight detailed plans, scale 1:2.000 .

A copy of the memorandum and of the general plan in: Beskrivelser til de fire præmierede og det indkøbte konkurrence-projekt angaaende bebyggelsen af Københavns ydre distrikter, Tillæg til Københavns Borgerrepræsentanters Forhandlinger fra den 1. April 1909 til den 29. Marts 1910, p. 13-40.

Photographic version of the general plan in Gengivelser af Konkurrenceprojekter vedrørende Københavns ydre Distrikter, 1909.

Aage Bjerre (1868-1954), engineer

A. Bjerre was born near Lillerød, north of Sjælland, the son of a landowner and wine merchant. From 1885 he studied at Den Polytekniske Læreanstalt, Copenhagen and received his civil engineer degree (candidat polytechnices) in 1891. That same year in March, he was employed by the municipality of Copenhagen in the Brolægnings- & Vejvæsen (the office of roads and bridges). He rose quickly in the technical administration and was appointed section's engineer in January 1894. From June 1897 to January 1898, he was briefly under the department for Vandforsyningen (water supply), before joining the services of the Stadsingeniør (City Engineer) in February 1898. In January 1907, he was appointed afdelingsingeniør (division's engineer). In March 1927, he was nominated Stadsingeniør at the head of the Stadsingeniøren Direktorat (City Engineer's Directorate) and was especially in charge of the town plan department until he retired in April 1936.

Bjerre was an active member of Dansk Ingeniørforeningen for which he served as secretary and librarian in 1895-1896. He was also a member of Selskabet for Sundhedsplejen (The Society for Hygiene) and of the redaction of the Society's journal, Maanedsskrift for Sundhedspleje, in 1905-1909, and of the Society's executive committee in 1915. In 1907 he became a member of the Royal Sanitary Institute in London. In 1913-1914, Bjerre was a Danish delegate to the Commission permanente d'assainissement et de salubrité de l'habitation, and after the First World War, to the Council of the International Federation for Housing and Town Planning. Bjerre was one of the founding members of the Dansk Byplanlaboratorium (Danish Town Planning Laboratory) in 1921.

With a special interest in sanitary issues, Bjerre turned towards town planning through his involvement in municipal works. He was engaged in the preparation for a new building code for Copenhagen that paved the way towards a master plan for the whole city. He gave a great number of lectures during the 1910s for meetings of Grundejerforeninger (Landowners' associations) in order to arouse an understanding of town planning and to develop collaboration with the municipal authorities. He was advocating the ideas of the garden city with large municipal ownership to provide individual housing for small incomes, and he was a member of the board of Arbejdernes Byggeforening (the Workers' Building Society) in 1917-1923. He was also involved in technical education as a censor for Den Polytekniske Læreanstalt (1917-1923) and as president of the Lyngby technical school's board (1921-1926). After the war and especially from 1927 onwards, when he was Stadsingeniør, Bjerre was a leading force in preparing the planning schemes for Copenhagen and its region. He wrote many articles, usually short ones, dealing with sanitary topics and planning issues for various periodicals. Prior to the competition for Copenhagen, his proposal together with the engineer G. Jochimsen for the sewage system of Gentofte, north of Copenhagen, was awarded the first prize in 1907.

Sources:

P. Vinding, "Bjerre, Aage", Dansk biografisk leksikon, 2nd ed., Vol 3, 1934, p. 169-70; S. Jensen, "Bjerre, Aage", Dansk biografisk leksikon, 3rd ed., Vol. 2, 1979, p. 183; P. Vedel, "A.Bjerre", Ingeniøren, 27 March 1954, p. 303; C. Schou, "Den nye Stadsingeniør", Bygmesteren, 1927, p.31; O. Forchhammer, "Stadsingeniør A. Bjerre", Stads og Haveingeniøren, Copenhagen, 1936, p.86-87; J. Kristensen (red.) Dansk Ingeniørforening gennem 50 Aar, 1892.1942, Copenhagen, 1942, p.41; A. Hannover (red.) Dansk Civil Ingeniørstat, Copenhagen, 1942, p.54-55.

Selected articles by Bjerre:

"Hustanken i Stockholm", Maanedsskrift for Sundhedspleje, Year 1908, p. 96-98; "Gadeplan for en Del af Enskede ved Stockholm", Maanedsskrift for Sundhedspleje, Year 1908, p. 349-350; "Forslag til afskærende Ledninger og Vand-klosetters Indførelse i Aarhus", Maanedsskrift for Sundhedspleje, Year 1909, p. 83-90; "Havebyer ude og Hjemme", Gads Danske Magasin – Dansk Tidsskrift, 1910-1911, p. 255-264; "Byplaner", Maanedsskrift for Sundhedspleje, Year 1917, p. 133-165.

Entry n° 5, motto "Anno 1977" – O. K. Nobel & H. Rasmussen

Winning entry that was awarded the 4th prize with a premium of 2.000 crowns.

Documentation in Copenhagen Town Hall Archives:

A copy of the memorandum and of the general plan in: Beskrivelser til de fire præmierede og det indkøbte konkurrence-projekt angaaende bebyggelsen af Københavns ydre distrikter, Tillæg til Københavns Borgerrepræsentanters Forhandlinger fra den 1. April 1909 til den 29. Marts 1910, p. 47-73; Photographic version of the general plan in Gengivelser af Konkurrenceprojekter vedrørende Københavns ydre Distrikter, 1909.

Ove Kruse Nobel (1868-1916), engineer

O. K. Nobel, the son of a retailer, was born in the small town of Grenaa in Jutland on the Kattegat sea, where he received his education (secondary school). He entered the Katedralskole in Århus where he got his student examination with first-class results. Subsequently he received his "candidatus philosophiæ" diploma in 1887. From 1886 to 1893 he studied engineering at Den Polytekniske Læreanstalt. Immediately after having earned his degree in civil engineering with the highest distinction in 1893, he worked for a couple of months in the mechanical firm of Ludvig Launds in Copenhagen. In March the same year Nobel joined the staff of the municipality of Copenhagen and was employed as assistant engineer in the City Engineer's office, which was then under the supervision of Charles Ambt. From 1896 Nobel was in charge of the new scheme for the town's sewage outflow, an engineering work of which the design and description was published in 1903 by the city's authority. In November 1902, he was promoted chief engineer for the newly established division (afdelingsingeniør), which had responsibility for the development of the sewage infrastructure in the districts that had been integrated in Copenhagen's boundaries. Nobel's involvement in the shaping of Great Copenhagen was not confined to the underground networks. Together with his colleague engineer Sven Koch he won the second prize in the 1905 competition for designing Fælledparken; subsequently he was commissioned to implement the sport facilities of the park. Together with the architects Egil Fischer and Holger Rasmussen he won the first prize in the 1911 competition for the layout of the former railways station's area. Moreover, he wrote for the influential weekly Illustreret Tidende (January 1910, n°17) a long article presenting their project for what was thought of to become the new city centre. Before his untimely death, Nobel designed his last scheme together with Rasmussen; it was a regulation plan for the fortifications of Christianshavn (see the following entrant Rasmussen).

In the 1910s O. K. Nobel was member of a number of commissions for the design of municipal sewage, as well as a consultant for the sewage outlet in Kristiania (Oslo). He belonged to the Ingeniørforening and was a member of its executive committee (1901-07); he was also a member of Foreningen til Hovedstadens Forskønnelse. In 1911 he received the Danish Order of the Dannebrog.

Sources:

Dansk biografisk leksikon, bind 17, 1939, p.227-9.; J. Voigt, "Afdelingsingeniør O.K.Nobel", Ingeniøren, 1916, n° 53; H. Rasmussen, "Afdelingsingeniør (1904-1916) O.K. Nobel", Arkitekten, 1916, n° 40; J. Kristensen, Dansk Ingeniørforening gennem 50 Aar, Copenhagen, 1942, p. 180; Forskønnelsen, 1916, p. 52.

Niels Holger Rasmussen (1871-1952), architect
Rasmussen was born in the city of Slagelse in Zeeland, the son of an iron founder. In his hometown he completed his carpenter's apprenticeship in 1890, which included a tour in England and Scotland in 1887. His training was supplemented by regular courses at Den Tekniske Selskabs Skole in Copenhagen. From November 1892 to January 1898, he received his training as an architect at Det kongelige Academie for de skønne Kunster. During this period he successively worked in the offices of two influent architects in Copenhagen, Vilhelm Klein and Martin Nyrop, and from 1894 until 1903 he was also employed by the City's architect Ludwig Fenger. Rasmussen won a number of prizes, which included the Larsen's award in 1896, the Neuhausens premium in 1899 and the Academy's minor gold medal in 1903 together with travel grants. He was thus able to journey first in Germany in 1896 and later in Italy, Greece and Turkey in 1904-05. In 1905 he spent about eight months in Lindos on the island of Rhodes drawing on the archaeological site, which a Danish team had been excavating and surveying since 1902. Back in Copenhagen he was again employed at the City's architect office and became afdelingsarkitektchef (division's architect) in 1918, a position he held until he retired in 1941. Rasmussen won many prizes in competitions for architectural designs and his drawings were displayed in a number of exhibitions including the Charlottenborg Salon in 1899, 1902-04, 1906-07, the national exposition of Århus in 1909, and Stockholm's exhibition in 1918. He built housings for the railway employees, schools and a number of villas as well as the Free Masons Lodge premises in Copenhagen.

He was awarded a number of prizes in extension-planning competitions which were organised by municipalities: together with the engineer J. T. Lundbye for the plan of the southern district of Frederiksberg in 1899; together with J. T. Lundbye and the enginner A. E. Lund for the plan of an extension of Bergen in 1900; with A. E. Lund he won the first prize for the extension of the city of Randers in 1910, and a new first prize with the architects Egil Fischer and Holger Rasmussen for the lay out of the former railways station's area in Copenhagen in 1911. He was commissioned by the Voldkommitte (the Christianshavn fortifications committee) to prepare a plan for the regulation of Christianshavn and the planning of the adjacent area on Amager in 1913. For the professional journal Architekten he gave a series of articles entitled "Moderne Byplanlæggelse og Boligreform in England" (modern town-planning and housing's reform in England) published in 1912. His involvement in town planning continued after the First World War and he was a member of the constitutive assembly of the Dansk Byplanlaboratorium in November1921. Rasmussen was a member of Foreningen af 3. Dec. 1892 and of the Akademisk Architektforening; he was the editor of the journal Architekten in 1911-1916. He was also a member of Foreningen til gamle Bygningers Bevaring and of Foreningen til Hovedstadens Forskønnelse.

Sources:
Weilbachs Kunstnerleksikon, Copenhagen, Vol.3, 1952, p.20-21; Weilbach Dansk Kunstnerleksikon, vol. 7, 1998, p. 32-33; K. Varming, V. Lorenzen, Dansk Arkitektur gennem 20 Aar 1892-1912. Copenhagen, 1912, p. 104; Arkitekten Ugehæfte, 1953, p. 55; K. Millech, K. Fisker, Danske arkitekturstrømninger 1850-1950, Copenhagen, 1951, p. 262, 281; K. Dirckinck Holmfeld (red.), Arkitekten 100 år, Copenhagen, 1998, p. 22-23; H. E. Glahn (red.), Opmaalinger, Foreningen af 3. Dec. 1892, Copenhagen, 1992, p. 125, 143-151; Det kongelige Kunstakademi Bibliotek- Arkitektur samlinger.

Entry n° 6, motto "Hafnia" – E. Bjerknes

Documentation in Copenhagen Town Hall Archives:

Memorandum to the proposal entitled "Hafnia", seventeen pages (hand written).

No original designs but for one sketch of a workers' housing scheme with park and playground, scale 1: 2000

Photographic version of the general plan in Gengivelser af Konkurrenceprojekter vedrørende Københavns ydre Distrikter, 1909.

Ernst Wilhelm Bjerknes (1865-1955), engineer and land surveyor
Bjerknes was born in Kristiania (renamed as Oslo in 1924), the son of a professor. He received his education in building engineering at Kristiania tekniske Skole (Technical School) where he graduated in 1887, and completed his studies by attending courses at the High Technical School of Berlin where he got a degree in 1891. He began working as assistant engineer in Statens Veivesen and Statens Jernbaneanlæg (National Road and Railway Construction) in1891-1897. He was then employed in Kristiania's Opmålingsvesen (the City's Surveying Department) and was appointed Regulereingssjef (town surveyor) in 1903 – a position he kept until 1905 (1906?). In 1904, the municipality gave him a grant for studying town planning in Germany, Switzerland and Austria. During the years 1905 (1906?) – 1908, he was Secretary of the Regulation-Town Planning Commission in Kristiania, and in 1907 he made the layout plan for the new industrial area near Oslo. In 1908 he started his own private practice as consulting engineer: Ingeniør & Konsulent M.N.I.A.F., and it is in this quality that he submitted his proposal to the competition for Copenhagen's extension. Although he left Kristiania town administration he kept a significant influence on town planning development in Norway as a member of many juries in public competitions, including the ones in Trondheim, Berlevåg, Drammen, Tønsberg, Skien, Hamar and Oslo. In 1908-1913, Bjerknes was a member of the Board of the Norsk Polyteknisk Forening (the Polytechnical Society) and a member for life of Den Norske Ingeniørforening.

Sources:
Information from Byarkivet (City Archives), Oslo; Norsk Kunstner Leksikon, Oslo: Universitetsforlaget, 1982, bind 1, p. 231-32

Writings by E. Bjerknes:
Articles about town planning in Teknisk Ugeblad: 1905, p. 148, 160, 458; 1906, p. 82, 105, 117; Med ski, velosiped og skissebok, Oslo, 1943; Barndom og ungdom, Oslo, 1945; Map of Nordmarken and Sörkedalen -for skilöbere og turister (skier and tourists) (1:30.000), 1890, Trondheim.

Entry n° 7, motto "Julemærket for 1908" – E. Fröhlich & A. Klixbüll

Documentation in Copenhagen Town Hall Archives:

Memorandum to the proposal marked with a stamp like image on which is written "Julemærke-Sanatoriet", (ten pages (typewritten)).

Original designs: general plan in a set of four pieces, scale 1:10.000 (oversigtsplans); six detailed plans, scale 1: 2.000; one longitudinal section.

Photographic version of the general plan in Gengivelser af Konkurrenceprojekter vedrørende Københavns ydre Distrikter, 1909.

Emil Frederik Fröhlich (Frøhlich) (1872-1951), engineer
Fröhlich was born in Snertinge, the son of a chemist. After secondary schooling and with the degree opening to higher education he studied civil engineering at Den Polytekniske Læreanstalt in Copenhagen where he graduated in 1899. He worked a couple of months for the landinspektør (chartered surveyor) Møller in Lyngby nearby Copenhagen, then in Kalundborg for the engineer F. L. H. Jensen. In September 1899 he was employed as an assistant engineer in the office of the City Engineer (Stadsingeniør) within the municipal administration of Copenhagen and in 1907 he was appointed engineer. Under the reorganization of the urban technical services of the municipality in 1925, he joined the new Byplanafdeling (the town plan's division) within the Stadsingeniørdirektorat (the City engineer's directorate).

Sources:
Dansk Civil- og Akademiingeniørstat, 1971 – biografiske oplysninger om kandidater fra Danmarks tekniske højskole og Danmarks Ingeniørakademie (1829-1968), 1971; Biografiske Oplysninger angaaende Den Polytekniske Læreanstalts Kandidater (1829-1929), 1930.

Aage Læssøe Brandt Klixbüll (1875-1950), engineer
A. L. B. Klixbüll was born in Hjørring, North Jutland, and the son of a manufacturer. After ordinary schooling, which he completed in 1891, he studied drawing at Det Tekniske Selskabs Skole in Copenhagen. Later he followed the curriculum of the Statens Tegnelærer

(Official teachers of drawing). He worked as a foreman on the building site of the railway between Aarhus and the small town Hammel and a couple of months in 1893 for the Stadsingeniør Ambt in Copenhagen, who was busy with a competition's project for the "Banegaardsforholdene" (the railway station's system). In 1900, Klixbüll was eventually employed by the municipality as a draughtsman within the office of the Stadsingeniør. He was promoted fuldmægtig (head of section) in 1920, but without the rank of engineer. He taught the evening classes of drawing in Den Tekniske Selskabs Skole since 1903. Before submitting his proposal to the competition for Copenhagen, he had, together with the then handelsgartner (horticulturalist) G. Nyeland Brandt, won the 3rd prize in 1905 for the creation of a park, Fælledparken, with sport facilities on the Blegdamsfælled and Østerfælled (common lands of the City of Copenhagen). In 1912, his proposal "2 Fugle" was awarded a 4th prize at the competition for designing an extension plan of Aalborg (konkurrencen on en bebyggelsesplan for Aalborg kommunes jorder). Klixbüll probably died in 1950: his name ceased to appear in the Kraks Vejviser (Copenhagen's directory) in 1951.

Sources:
Danmarks kommunale forvaltning- den kommunale forvaltning, Indenrigsministeriet, Københavns Kommune, Frederiksberg Kommune, 1929, p. 231; Architekten, 1905, p. 95, 1912, p. 48-50; Uddrag af Aalborg Byraads forhandlinger for 1912-1913, 1913, Tillæg n. VII, p. 26-27; Københavns Borgerrepræsentanters Forhandlinger, Copenhagen, 1907, p. 48: Kraks Vejviser from 1915 to 1952.

Entry n° 8, motto "Wayland Smed" – A. J. Roewade

Not a winning prize, but the jury decided to select the project with a premium of 1.500 Danish crowns.

Documentation in Copenhagen Town Hall Archives:
Memorandum to the proposal entitled "En kort Beskrivelse over Wayland Smeds – Plan for Bebyggelsen af Kjöbenhavns ydre distrikter." 37 pages (handwritten), including drawings and photographs, with two appendices: a detailed plan of Utterslev Bysogn, and a longitudinal profile of a street, "længdeprofil af Söborg allee".

Original designs: one plan "Forslag til Havneplan for Kjøbenhavn", scale 1: 20.000; one general plan in a set of four pieces, scale 1:10.000; one plan "Forslag til boulevard plan for Kjøbenhavn", scale 1: 20.000; one plan "Midtvejen: af park og boulevard beltet", scale 1: 8.000; a set of fifteen detailed plans, scale 1:2.000.

A copy of the memorandum without the drawings in Beskrivelser til de fire præmierede og det indkøbte konkurrence–projekt angaaende bebyggelsen af Københavns ydre distrikter, Tillæg til Københavns Borgerrepræsentanters Forhandlinger fra den 1. April 1909 til den 29. Marts 1910, p. 75-109.

Photographic version of the general plan in Gengivelser af Konkurrenceprojekter vedrørende Københavns ydre Distrikter, 1909.

Alfred Jensen Raavad (1848-1933), architect and engineer
Alfred Jensen was born in a village, Raadvad, north of Copenhagen, the son of a mason. When he settled in the capital, he found convenient to add the name of his birth place to his family's name in order to distinguish himself from the many homonyms and, later, while living in Chicago, he "Americanised" his surname in Roewade. On the letter he sent with his submission to Copenhagen's competition is written: Alfred J. Roewade, Consulting Engineer – Civic Designer, New York Representative K. Roewade.

Raavad was apprenticed in woodcarving as well as in masonry by working for his father and completed his education at the Tekniske Institut, which became Den Tekniske Selskabs Skole in 1876. He worked as a draughtsman for the stucco master Christian Berg as well as for the architects Leth and J. A. Stillemann before making a long journey and presumably occasional works in Germany, Autria, Belgium and France. Back in Copenhagen in 1876, Raavad went into partnership with August Johansen in order to practice architecture and they built a number of blocks of flats in Copenhagen. However, they went bankrupt and Raavad, at the age of forty-two, sailed with his family to Philadelphia in April 1890. He was presumably hoping to find work with the preparation of the Universal Exhibition of Chicago in a period when Danes emigrated en masse to America – about 10.000 in 1890. At the time, Raavad had already written a great deal for the various Danish newspapers, and he had also been much involved in launching a national campaign for the construction of the new military fortifications around Copenhagen with the periodical Fædrelandets Forsvar, which he edited in 1885-1889. In the meantime he had drawn up a general plan for Copenhagen in 1886. In Chicago, Raavad was first shortly employed as a draughtsman in the Engineering Department of the Bureau of Construction of the World's Columbia Exposition, which design and works Daniel Burnham directed. During all the years he lived in the United States until his return to Denmark in 1914, Raavad worked for various employers as an engineer or as an architect. Moreover, he wrote as a freelance journalist for various papers or journals, and also gave lectures on town planning at meetings of the Scandinavian Engineering Society, of which he was one of the founding members since its inception in 1891. He designed a number of proposals, such as plans for commercial harbour development in Chicago and in Milwaukee, but without being commissioned, and he submitted a project in the competition for Canberra in 1912 (entry n° 74) that was not selected.

Back in Copenhagen, Raavad was co-opted by the Akademisk Architectforening on the ground of his proposal for the 1909 Competition that M. Nyrop supported, and his series of articles published in Architekten. Raavad, who set up his own consultancy office in association with the architect Sven J. Risom, designed a number of plans for the development of Copenhagen's harbour, which were exhibited – in particular at the Gothenburg Exhibition in 1923. At the end of his life, Raavad succeeded in getting his "rational conception of town planning" published in 1929 by the Akademisk Arkitektforening with the title: Borgmesterbogen- En Bog om Dansk Byplanlægning.

Sources:

E. Fischer, "Alfred J. Råvad", Arkitekten, n°16, 1933, p.73-75; H. H. Madsen, Chicago-København. Alfred Råvads univers, Copenhagen, 1990; K. Millech, "Råvad, Alfred Christian Ludvig Jensen", Weilbachs Kunstnerleksikon, Vol. 3, 1952, p. 8-9; J. W. Reps, Canberra 1912, Melbourne, 1997, p. 186, 213, 357-363.

Selected writings by A.J. Raavad

Forslag til anlæg af en arbejderforstad ved Kjøbenhavn, Copenhagen, 1887; "Beton og Bygningskunst", *Architekten*, N. 25, 20 March 1909, p. 282-285; "Architekten som sociolog" a series of thematic articles (functional layout of a house, maritime routes, town plans, harbours, etc.) marked with the successive letters of the alphabet, published in *Architekten*, Vol. XII, 1909- 1910, Vol. XIII, 1910-1911, Vol. XIV, 1911-1912, Vol. XV, 1912-1913; Borgmesterbogen – En bog om dansk Byplanlægning, For Embedsmænd under Stat og By, Folkerepræsentanter, Ingeniører og Arkitekter samt skattydende Borgere (gående, ridende og kørende; sejlende og flyvende), Copenhagen, Arkitektforening, 1929.

Entry n° 9, motto "Grönne Baand" – H. Bernoulli

Documentation in Copenhagen Town Hall Archives:

Memorandum to the proposal "Grönne baand", five pages (hand written).

Photographic version of the general plan in Gengivelser af Konkurrenceprojekter vedrørende Københavns ydre Distrikter, 1909.

Unfortunatly there is no documentation concerning Bernoulli's work for the Copenhagen competition in the Bernoulli holdings at the GTA Archives in Zurich.

Hans Bernoulli (1876-1959), architect

Bernoulli was born in Basel and came from a famous mathematicians family. After failing to complete secondary schooling and a short lived commercial education, he studied building design at the Gewerbeschule in Basel and architecture at the Technischen Hochschule in Munich, 1897-98, where he also worked for a while for his professor, the architect Friedrich von Thiersch. He completed his formation at the Technischen Hochschule in Karlsruhe in 1900 and at the Technischen Hochschule in Darmstadt where he worked for the architect F. Pützer in 1901. He travelled extensively in Germany, Holland, England, Italy and visited Wien, Paris and Copenhagen in 1902. He settled in Berlin and worked a while for the architects Hart and Lesser before running his own architectural office in partnership with Louis Rinkel in 1903-1912. During this period he built a number of commercial and housing buildings as well as villas near Berlin, and he was also commissioned to design town plans for Grieshein (near Frankfurt-a-M.), Plauen district of Dresden, Nuhnen (near Frankfurt-a-O) and the Falkenberg "garden-city" in the vicinity of Berlin. He also sent a number of projects for town plan competitions: Saarbrücken and Kattowitz (1905), Mannheim (1908). In 1907-09 he was assistant to the professors Joseph Brix (1859-1943) and Felix Genzmer (1856-1929) in the town-planning seminar at the Technischen Hochschule in Berlin, before being the assistant to the professor Franz Seeck at the Kunstgewerbemuseum. In the journal Gartenstadt (1911), he published a piece on the land reform issue as a corner stone for the 'new city', a topic that became central in his practical work. In 1912 he went back to his homeland where he developed his carrier as town planner. After being the chief architect of a building firm in Basel (1912-1918), he opened his own drawing office. His contribution to town planning has been significant through his lectures at the Polyteknikum of Zurich (from 1913 onwards and professor in 1920 until he was dismissed in 1939 on political grounds). Bernoulli made numerous designs of urban districts and workers housing estates, and wrote a great many articles as well as books on town planning. He is considered as an architect cum – theorist of town planning.

Sources:

K. and M.Nägelin-Gschwind, Hans Bernoulli. Architekt und Städtebauer. Basel / Boston / Berlin, 1995; E. C. Lanza, P. Marti, "Braillard und Bernoulli als Städtebauer", Werk, Bauen + Wohnen, nr. 5, 1995, p 60-65; Archithese, vol.11, no 6, 1981 (a special issue on Hans Bernoulli); M. Jauslin, "Hans Bernoulli", in I. Rucki, D. Huber (hrsg.), Architektenlexikon der Schweiz 19./20. Jhr., 1998, p.51-53: W. Schmid, Hans Bernoulli, Städtebauer – Politiker, Weltbürger. Schaffhausen, 1974; U. Jehle-Schulte Strathaus, M. Stegmann (Hrsg.) Hans Bernoulli – Aus den Skizzenbüchern / Arkitekturmuseum Basel, Basel / Boston / Berlin, GTA-Archiv, ETH – Hönggerberg, Zürich, 1996.

Entry n° 10, motto "Storstad" – A. Riis & H. V. Christensen

Documentation in Copenhagen Town Hall Archives:

Memorandum to the proposal "STORSTAD", eight pages (typewritten).

No original drawings; a photographic plate of the general plan; photographic version of the general plan in Gengivelser af Konkurrenceprojekter vedrørende Københavns ydre Distrikter, 1909.

Axel Marius Riis (1881-1948), engineer
A. M. Riis was born in Copenhagen, the son of a bookbinder. After Præliminæreksamen (schooling's exam) in 1897, he served an apprenticeship as a draughtsman at the engineering office of Evald Fenger. In 1899 he entered Den Polytekniske Læreanstalt and received his degree in civil engineering with specialisation in building in 1904. He was immediately employed as an assistant engineer by Copenhagen's municipal administration in the Direktorat for Vej- og Kloakanlæg (Roads and Sewage utilities' Directorate). In April 1907 he was appointed town engineer and building inspector by the municipality of Søllerød, north of Copenhagen, where he served nineteen years. When the Ministry of Transport and Public Works opened the Dansk Vejlaboratorium in 1928, Riis became the chief engineer of the new research centre for roads and transports, a position he held until his accidental death while sailing on the ship "Kjøbenhavn" that was sunk by a mine in June 11th 1948. He wrote a great many articles for technical journals including Teknisk Tidsskrift, Ingeniøren, Maanedsblad for Sundhedspleje, and from 1922 onwards he was the editor of Stads- og Havneingeniøren, the organ of the engineers' union employed by the municipal and port authorities. He was also a member of Akademiet for de Tekniske Videnskaber (the Danish Academy of technical sciences), and the secretary of the Danish branch of the Nordisk Vejteknisk Forbund. His peers in Denmark as well as in the

other Scandinavian countries regarded him as a specialist of repute in the techniques of road construction.

Sources:
Dansk Civil- og Akademiingeniørstat, 1971; Biografiske Oplysninger angaaende Den Polytekniske Læreanstalts Kandidater 1829-1929,1930, p. 240; Ingeniøren, 1948, N. 32, p.441-42.

Selected writings by A. Riis:
"Hovedtrafiklinier i Københavns Region", Stads- og Havneingeniøren, 1927, p. 59-66; "Københavns byplanmæssige Forhold", Stads- og Havneingeniøren, 1933, p. 88-89.

Harald Vestergaard Christensen / Rygner (1878-1965), engineer
H. V. Christensen, who took the name of Rygner in 1915, was born in Copenhagen, the son of a bank accountant. He received his education at the Metropolitanskole (grammar school in Copenhagen) where he took Studentereksamen (formal examination for admittance to the University) in 1897. He entered Den Polytekniske Læreanstalt and received the civil engineer degree with specialisation in building in 1902. That same year he worked a couple of months as assistant engineer for Copenhagen's Vandværk (municipal water works), before being employed as engineer for the water installations of Lyngby-Taarbæk borough, immediately north of Copenhagen. In 1904-1907 he held the position of town engineer and building inspector for both the boroughs of Lyngby-Taarbæek and Søllerød. In April 1907 he was appointed town engineer and building inspector in the municipality of Lyngby where he served ten years. He won prizes for his works on roads and traffic's betterment in 1913 and 1915, and was awarded the second prize at the competition for the town plan of Hirstals in 1919. In 1917, he moved to Odense to become Stadsingeniør (City Engineer), a position he held until his retirement in 1948.

He wrote a number of articles for technical journals, as well as longer pieces, especially on housing issues. In 1911-1920 he was a member of the editorial board of the journal Månedsskrift for Sundhedspleje. He was involved in the Danish technical education as a member of both the Svendeprøvekommission (Commission for apprentices' qualification) in Lyngby (1910-1917) and the examination board of Den Polytekniske Læreanstalt (from 1921 onwards). He was also influential with the professional bodies as a member of the boards of Stads- og Havneingeniørforeningen (1911-1929) and of Dansk Ingeniørforeningen for the section of roads and railways (1917-1934).

Sources:
Dansk Civil- og Akademiingeniørstat, 1971, p. 785; Biografiske Oplysninger angaaende Den Polytekniske Læreanstalts Kandidater (1829-1929), 1930, p.214.

Entry n° 11, motto "For Byen og Borgerne" – N. Gellersted & E. Bülow Hübe

Documentation in Copenhagen Town Hall Archives:

Memorandum to the proposal "For byen og borgerne", 25 pages (typewritten).

Original plans: oversigtplan (general plan) in a set of four pieces, scale 1: 10.000; detailed plans, scale 1:2.000 and section drawings.

Photographic version of the general plan in Gengivelser af Konkurrenceprojekter vedrørende Københavns ydre Distrikter, 1909.

In 1934, N. Gellersted answering to the request of Copenhagen's town engineer A. Bjerre agreed to give his documents relating to the competition to the Municipal Archives in Copenhagen, cf. Stadsarkivet, Stadsing. Dir., Byplankontoret, BP sager 1918-1984 / Sag 977: correspondence.

Nils Otto Gellerstedt (1875-1961), engineer
Gellersted was born in Örebro, a main railway junction town in Sweden, and the son of a schoolmaster. He got his education in his hometown and entered Chalmers Tekniska Läreanstalt (Technical Institute) in Gothenburg where he studied in 1894-1898. He obtained his degree in civil engineering with specialisation in väg- och vattenbyggnadskonst (road and hydraulic building). From 1899 Gellersted was employed at the Stads Byggnadskontor (Public Works

office) of Stockholm until in 1902, he established his own consulting agency: Kommunaltekniska Byrån – civilingeniör Nils Gellersted, which he ran until 1945. His office became involved in a great many urban projects and was commissioned for the topographic surveys and for the plans of about a hundred of towns or town districts in Sweden. Gellersted held important positions in the planning development of his country as a member of Stockholm's Railway Commission in 1909-1920, of the Transportation Commission for Stockholm, and of Stadsplanekommisionen (the Town planning Commission) in Stockholm (1909-22).

He was the author of numerous projects for public contests, which included a second prize (together with the architect Torben Grut) in the competition for Gothenburg in 1901, a first prize (together with the architect A. Bergman) in the competition for Hälsingborg in 1906, a second prize (together with the architect Lars I. Wahlman) for both the planning of Katarinatrakten in Stockholm in 1909 and for the plan of Trondheim in 1910. Gellerstedt's entry in the Canberra competition in 1912 (together with Ivan Lindgren and Hugo de Rietz) was the third choice of the minority judge. He was responsible for preparing master plans or partial plans for about one hundred cities in Sweden including Aksersund, Falun, Falkenberg, Hudiksvall, Lidingö, Linköping, Nora, Sollefteå Sundsvall, Söderhamm, Varberg and Östersund.

He served as a member of several competitions' juries, including the competition for the quarters of Bergen after the great fire in 1917.

Gellersted wrote a number of articles in technical journals on planning and bridge construction. He is regarded as one of the pioneers of city planning in the early decades of the 20th century.

Sources:

G. Sidenbladh, Planering for Stockholm 1923-1950. Stockholm/Uppsala, 1981; T. Hall, Urban planning in Sweden, in T. Hall (ed.) Planning and Urban Growth in the Nordic Countries. London, 1991, p.167-242; T. Paulsson, Den glömda staden – Svensk stadsplanering under 1900-talets början med särskild hänsyn till Stockholm. Idéhistoria, teori och praktik, Stockholm, 1959, p. 82-84; J. W. Reps, Canberra 1912, Melbourne, 1997, p. 188-191,215-218, 303-304; Svenska män och kvinnor, Stockholm, vol.3, 1946, p. 42, Arkitektur och Dekorativ Konst, 1906; Der Städtebau, 1906.

Erik Bülow Hübe (1879-1963), engineer

E. Bülow Hübe was born in Göteborg, the son of a building contractor. As Gellersted, he studied engineering at Chalmers tekniska Läreanstalt, with specialisation in both väg- och vattenbyggnadskonst (road and hydraulic building) and husbyggnad (house building), where he graduated in 1898. He completed his education in architecture during two years at the Eidgenössische Polytechnikum in Zürich (1898-1900). In 1900-1904 he worked for the Stads Byggnadskontor (Public Works office) of Gothenburg, as well as in Malmö for the Stadsingenjörskontor (Town Engineer's office) and for the firm Kockums Mekaniska Verstad. During six years (1904-1910) Bülow Hübe was employed by Nils Gellersted's engineering office in Stockholm and collaborated to the proposal, which was awarded the second prize in the competition for the design of Katarinatrakten area in 1910. He started his own consulting practice in town planning in 1911. He was commissioned for preparing the plans for a number of cities, including Eslöv, Herrljunga, and Broby, and also for designing parks and villas. During the 1910s he also worked for the development of Saltsjöbadan near Stockholm. In 1921, when the city was undergoing a fast development, Bülow Hübe was appointed Stadsingenjör (City engineer) in Malmö. Until his retirement in 1946, he was responsible for a great many schemes in that city, including among others the new residential areas of Rostorp and Friluftstaden, as well as the lay out of Pildammsparken. E. Bülow-Hübe was a member of a number of juries in public competitions and lectured in town planning at the Royal Technical College of Stockholm.

Sources:

We are especially indebted to architect Arne Wittstrand for the information he communicated about Erik Bülow Hübe, including a copy of the curriculum vitae E. Bülow Hübe sent to the Royal Academy of Agricultural Sciences in 1946; S.E. Rasmussen, "Erik Bülow-Hübes Malmö", Byggmästaren, 1959, p. 161-171; T. Tykesson, B. Magnusson Staaf, C. Hansson, A. Reisnert, K. Brunnberg, (red.), Guide till Malmös arkitektur, Stockholm, 2001.

Entry n° 12, motto "Mindre Parker men Parkalléer" – R. Erslev

Documentation in Copenhagen Town Hall Archives:

Memorandum to the proposal "Mindre Parker men Parkalléer", seven pages (handwritten).

No original drawings.

Photographic version of the general plan in Gengivelser af Konkurrenceprojekter vedrørende Københavns ydre Distrikter, 1909.

Rolf Aage Erslev (1881-1954), engineer

R. A. Erslev was born 21 February 1881 in Copenhagen. His father was a head archivist. He was apprenticed in mechanics in the electromechanical firm Titan Ltd in Copenhagen and passed his secondary school examination in Sloman's school. He completed his education in mechanical engineering at the Tekniske Selskabs Skole (Technical School) in 1902 and worked at Titan A/S the next year. In 1904 Erslev went to Switzerland and worked for the company of F. Martini manufacturing automobiles in St-Blaise. He spent about one year with Martini (F. Martini & Co was sold in 1906) and returned to Copenhagen end of 1905 to start his own consultant office. During the years 1908-1911, he wrote a number of articles on urban transport schemes for the technical journal Ingeniøren and also for Der Städtebau. However, it seems his office was not successful enough, and in 1911 he was employed as an engineer by the Carlsberg breweries. He rose up in that company and became the manager (driftsinspektør) of the mineral waters department sometime during the 1920s.

Erslev was neither a member of Dansk Ingeniørforening nor of Ingeniør – og konstruktørsammenslutning. However, Erslev was a member of Foreningen til Hovedstadens Forskønnelse. Erslev probably died in 1954: his name ceased to appear in the Kraks Vejviser (Copenhagen's directory) in 1955.

Sources:

Danske Ingeniører fra Teknika, 1945, p. 276; Danske Teknika og deres Dimmittender gennem 50 Aar, 1931, p.114; C. Jacobsen (red.) Dansk Brygger-stat, bind 2, 1935, p. 217. Forskønnelsen, 1923, p. 88; Kraks Vejviser from 1915 to 1960.

Selected writings by R. Erslev:

"Boulevardbanen", Ingeniøren, 1908, p.11; "To forslag vedr. Københavns Jernbaneordning", Ingeniøren, 1908, p. 246-50, 270; "Gross-Kopenhagen", Der Städtebau, 1910, 10. Hefte, p.116-118; "Vesterbro Passage – Gaderegulering", Ingeniøren 1911, p. 462-64 & 524; Trafiklinier: Stor-København 1910-1940. Kritik og Forslag – med 9 planer og 14 billeder, Copenhagen, 1909, 29 pages.

Entry n° 13, motto "Bella" – K. I. Einersen, L. Hygom & C. Manicus-Hansen

Documents in Copenhagen Town Hall Archives

Memorandum to the proposal "BELLA-", six pages (typewritten)

No original drawings.

Photographic version of the general plan in Gengivelser af Konkurrenceprojekter vedrørende Københavns ydre Distrikter, 1909.

Karlo Immanuel Einersen (1882-1958), engineer

Einersen was born in Copenhagen, the son of a captain and ship constructor. He entered Den Polytekniske Læreanstalt in 1899 and graduated as construction engineer in 1904. From February 1904 to the end of March 1910, Einersen was employed as assistant engineer in the 3rd section of the Direktorat for Vej- og Kloakanlæg (directorate for roads and sewage utilities) of Copenhagen's municipality, which is the same service where Manicus-Hansen worked. He was a founding member of the municipal engineers' union and a member of its first executive committee in May 1907. On 1 April 1910 he got a permanent position as municipal engineer (4th grade) in the same service, where he served nine years. After the War, he established a consulting engineering firm in Copenhagen.

Sources:

Dansk Civil- og Akademiingeniørstat, 1971 Copenhagen, 1971; Biografiske Oplysninger angaaende Den Polytekniske Læreanstalts Kandidater 1829-1929, Copenhagen, 1930, p. 236. J. Kristensen, (red.), Dansk

Ingeniørforening gennem 50 Aar, 1892-1942, Copenhagen, 1942, p. 149-151.

Louis Hygom (1879-1950), architect
Born in Copenhagen, L. Hygom was the son of a physician employed by the municipality (kommunelæge). He was apprenticed as a mason, a training he completed in 1899, and he attended Det Tekniske Selskabs Skole to be qualified for admittance to the School of architecture at Det kongelige Academie for de skønne Kunster. His architectural studies at the Academy were short: 1905-1907. He joined the dissident group of students who looked outside the "Temple" for their training and he was one of the founding members of Den Fri Architektforening (The Free Architects Society) in 1909. Hygom gained his experience by working for various architects, including P. V. Jensen-Klint, Axel Preisler, Ulrik Plesner, and he was employed for a while by the Stadsarkitekt (City architect) Ludvig Fenger. As Plesner, he chose England as a destination for studying architecture. In 1912, Hygom started his own practice and designed a number of villas before being commissioned for the building of blocks of flats. Prior to the Copenhagen's competition, he submitted, together with Povl Baumann, the project entitled "De solvendte Arbejderhuse" to the competition, which was organized for the new quarter of Islands Brygge in 1907. The proposal was awarded the 4th prize. After the War, he joined Den Akademisk Architektforening and became a member of the executive committee in 1921. At the time of the Copenhagen's competition Hygom is not listed as a member of Foreningen til gamle Bygningers Bevaring nor as one of the members of Foreningen til Hovestadens Forskønnelse.

Sources:
N. D. Olsen, "Den Fri Architektforening", Architectura-10, 1988, p. 84-132; A. Cock-Hausen, "Louis Hygom in memoriam", Arkitekten, Ugehefte, 1950, p. 24; Weilbach Dansk Kunstnerleksikon, Vol 3, 1995, p. 436-437; collection of drawings at Det kongelige Kunstakademi – Arkitektur samling.

Carl Hans Theodor Manicus-Hansen (1877-1960), engineer
Manicus-Hansen was born in Copenhagen, the son of a wholesale merchant. He received his education at the Metropolitanskole (grammar school) in Copenhagen, which he completed in 1896. He entered Den Polytekniske Læreanstalt and was in the same promotion as H. V. Christensen (see Entry n.10) when he received the civil engineer degree with specialisation in building in 1902. He worked a few months for the Stadsingeniør (city engineer) of Silkeborg in Jutland before being employed in September 1902 as assistant engineer by the municipality of Copenhagen in the 3rd section of the Direktorat for Vej- og kloakanlæg (directorate for road construction and sewage system). On 1 January 1907, he was promoted to the rank of engineer (4th grade). He made his entire career within this department and became section's engineer in 1937.

Sources:
Dansk Civil- og Akademiingeniørstat, 1971 – biografiske oplysninger om kandidater fra Danmarks tekniske højskole og Danmarks Ingeniørakademi (1829-1968). Copenhagen, 1971; Biografiske Oplysninger angaaende Den Polytekniske Læreanstalts Kandidater 1829-1929, Copenhagen, 1930, p.216.

Entry n° 14, motto "Millionbyen" – E. Fischer

Documentation in Copenhagen Town Hall Archives:
Memorandum to the proposal "Millionbyen", four pages (typewritten).
No original drawings.
Photographic version of the general plan in Gengivelser af Konkurrenceprojekter vedrørende Københavns ydre Distrikter, 1909.

Egil Fischer (1878-1963), architect and painter
Fisher was born in Copenhagen, the son of a landscape painter, and became a talented artist who exhibited his paintings at Charlottenborg on several occasions. Fischer was formally trained as a mason and completed his education at Det Tekniske Selskabs Skole in 1897. There is no indication that Fischer was a regular student of the Royal Academy of Fine Art's School of Architecture. During the years 1897-1904,

he worked as a draughtsman for Martin Nyrop, as well as for Martin Borch, and he was in a position to tour Germany and Italy in 1901-1902 and again in 1904-05. M. Nyrop together with V. Schmidt and K. Varming recommended Fisher in November 1908 for membership of Akademisk Architektforening but without apparent success, and Fisher joined for a short while Den Fri Arkitektforening. He eventually entered Akademisk Architectforening in 1922. Prior to the competition in 1908, Fischer had received a number of prizes in public competitions, including a second prize for the development of a new district of Odense in 1901, a second prize for a block of buildings on Grønningen, Copenhagen, in 1906 and another second prize for the building of the new quarter Islands Brygge in 1907. With his proposal for housings (villa-type) in the developing area of Marselisborg in Aarhus, he was awarded the first prize. During the years 1909-1912, Fisher was employed by the Stadsarkitekt (City Architect) of Copenhagen to work on the town plan, and the proposal he submitted together with H. Rasmussen and O. K. Nobel for the design of the area of the ancient railway station was awarded the first prize in 1911. It seems, however, that Fisher met strong opposition within the municipality. In the opinion of G. Philipsen, who was Rådmand (vice-mayor) with the 4th Department of the City government in 1904-1925, Fischer was a stubborn idealist who gave little consideration to all the aspects of a situation (quoted in Arkitekten, year 1963, p. 223). Fischer also voiced strong criticism against the proposal for a new building by-law for Copenhagen that the municipal authorities handed out in 1908. In his article "Byggelov kontra Byggekunst" (Buildind code against architecture) published in 1911, Fischer disqualified the principle of provisions regulating aesthetics and architecture, and the same year he was seated in the commission that was set up to work out an other proposal for the building by-law. After the First World War, a period where he went into art and antique trade, Fischer was much involved in the subsequent works for a planning legislation, especially as president of the ad hoc commission set up by Akademisk Arkitektforening in December 1929, and he wrote extensively on these issues. He developed his consulting practice as a town planner with emphasis on conservation schemes together with his architect's studio. His scheme for Dragør (south of Amager) can be viewed as one of the first comprehensive planning designs for the safeguard of an entire town in Denmark, as well as an innovative endeavour in relation to the conservation policies undertaken throughout Europe in the late 1940s.

Fischer had been a member of Den Fri Arkitektforening and of the Akademisk Arkitektforening. He was a member of Foreningen til Hovedstadens Forskønnelse as well as a member of Foreningen til gamle Bygningers Bevaring from the onset.

Sources:

V. Villadsen, "Ficher, Egil", Dansk biografiske Leksikon, Vol. 4, 3rd ed., 1979, p. 416-417; H. F., "Fischer, Egil", Weilbachs Kunstnerleksikon, Vol. 1, 1947, p. 315-316; Arkitekten, 1963, p. 223; Fischer's Records at Det kongelige Kunstakademi – Arkitektur samling.

Selected publications by E. Fischer:

"Det ny Bycentrum", Forskønnelsen, n. 2, 1911, p. 17-23; "Byggelov contra byggekunst", Forskønnelsen, n.6, 1911, p. 85-95; "Byplanlægningens love", in O. Asmussen, (red.), København, som den er og som den burde være, Copenhagen, 1914.,p. 43-77; "HøjBrokonkurrencen", Arkitekten, 1926, p. 185-196; "Fredninssagen", Arkitekten, 1926, p. 201-208.

"Regulering, sanering og censuring", Forskønnelsen, 1938, n. 1, p. 7-9; "Magistratsenevælde under den nye byggelov", Arkitekten, n. 46, 1938, p. 205-207; Byggelovgivningen.Uddrag af Akademisk Arkitektsforenings Forslag til en Lands-Byggelov, sammenholdt med den nye Byggelov for Københavnn, Copenhagen, 1939.

Entry n° 15, motto "Københavns Vaaben 1296" – U. Plesner, A. Mathiesen, M. Frandsen & A. Hansen

Winning entry: the 3rd prize with a premium of 3.000 Danish crowns.

Documentation in Copenhagen Town Hall Archives:

Memorandum to the proposal "København Vaaben 1296", four pages (typewritten).

Original drawings: one detailed plan (1:2.000) ; the profile of one street with one site plan for a group of buildings.

A copy of the memorandum and of the general plan in: Beskrivelser til de fire præmierede og det indkøbte konkurrence-projekt angaaende bebyggelsen af Københavns ydre distrikter, Tillæg til Københavns Borgerrepræsentanters Forhandlinger fra den 1april 1909 til den 29. Marts 1910, p. 41-45.

Photographic version of the general plan in Gengivelser af Konkurrenceprojekter vedrørende Københavns ydre Distrikter, 1909.

Ulrik Plesner (1861-1933), architect
Plesner was born on the west coast of Jutland, the son of a clergyman. He followed regular schooling and a short apprenticeship in masonry before studying at Den Tekniske Selskabs Skole in Copenhagen. He entered the so-called preliminary class of Det kongelige Academie for de skønne Kunster in 1880 and completed his architectural studies in January 1893. During those years he worked as a draughtsman for Hans J. Holm (1835-1916) as well as for H. B. Storch (1839-1922). According to H. Finsen, Plesner's production was especially significant for having generated a new approach to the conception of housing buildings among Danish architects. His earliest major work was the design and the construction of the housing blocks on Aaboulevarden (n. 16-18), Copenhagen, in 1898, which were followed by a great many others, especially in Frederiksberg (see, A.H. Langeland-Mathiesen). At the turn of the century, he was a much praised architect, however, also much criticized for his original production with strong forms, often non customary replicable ground plan, and with a style deeply rooted in the domestic building culture. Plesner was also known to "have put aside everything he had learnt from the Academy" and was therefore solicited by the group of young architects who in 1903 were looking for an alternative to the teaching of the Academy (they founded Fri Architektforeningen in 1909). Since 1892, Plesner had developed close links with the artists community of Skagen, the small fishing place in the north of Jutland which had become a fashionable summer resort for painters in the 1880s. Here he built a great many buildings, especially at the end of his career when he settled there. Plesner was a member of the Academy's council in 1911-1929 and was a honorary member of the Akademisk Arkitekforening in 1931. He was also a member of Foreningen til gamle Bygningers Bevaring and a member of the executive committee of Foreningen til Hovedstadens Forskønnelse in 1911-1918.

Sources:
K. Millech, "Plesner, Ulrik, Adolph", Weilbachs Kunstnerleksikon, Vol.2, 1949, p.592-94; H. Finsen, Arkitekten Ulrik Plesner, Copenhagen, 1951; C. Schiøtz, "Ulrik Plesner", Arkitekten, n. 48, Vol. 35, 1933, p 221-22; Collection of drawings and watercolours at the Kunstakademiets Bibliotek, Samlingen af Arkitekturtegninger.

Aage Henrik Langeland-Mathiesen (1868-1933), architect
Also known as Aage H. Mathiesen, he was born in Aarhus, the son of a building inspector. Mathiesen was apprenticed to carpentry and masonry and completed his training at Den Tekniske Selskabs Skole before going on to study architecture at Det Kongelige Academie for de skønne Kunster. After completing all the works required for architect acknowledged by the Academy in January 1895, he worked for the architects H. B. Storch and Axel Berg. In 1897 he received a grant from the Academy as well as the Neuhausens Prize. He assisted O. V. Koch (1852-1902) in survey drawing of old churches in 1894 and 1898 and contributed to the works of the National Museum with surveys and investigations of ruins. His knowledge in historical buildings supported his fine restoration works of manors like Kongegaard in Korsør and Steensgaard near by Fåborg on Fyn. Prior to the competition, Mathiesen had developed his own practice with a number of apartment buildings in Copenhagen. The block he built at the corner of Østerbanegade and Trondhejms Plads is considered as one of the few examples of Jugendstil in Denmark. In the years 1906-1910, Mathiesen often worked in collaboration with Ulrik Plesner for complexes of housing buildings in Frederiksberg (Danasvej 22, 24; Danasplads 10-20; Vodroffsvej 37-43, etc.), as well as for the design and the realisation of Studenterforeningen (The Students' Association) premises in Copenhagen, which was awarded a first architectural prize in 1909. Together

they also designed a project for a new quarter of Islands Brygge that won the 2nd prize in 1907. Mathiesen, who had travelled extensively all around the world, was also known for his keen interest in the then new sport of car racing. He was a member of Foreningen til gamle Bygningers Bevaring and of Østifternes historisk-topografiske Selskab.

Sources:
K. Millech, "Langeland-Mathiesen, Henrik Aage", Weilbachs Kunstnerleksikon, Vol.2, Copenhagen, 1949, p.216-217; V. Jørgensen, "Aage Langeland-Mathiesen", Arkitekten, n. 28, 1933, Vol. 35, p. 122; Collection of drawings and watercolours at the Kunstakademiets Bibliotek, Samlingen af Arkitekturtegninger.

Selected publications:
"Passage gennem Rundetaarn", Architekten, n.12, 15 March 1901, Vol 3., p. 151-152; (in collaboration with C. Axel Jensen) "Bremerholms Admirasgaard udenfor gamle Østerport", Fra Arkiv og Museum, Vol 1., 1899, p. 191-207; Det kongelige kjøbenhavnske Skydeselskab og danske Broderskab (2 vol.), Copenhagen, 1934.

Marius Frandsen (1872-1952), engineer
Frandsen was born in Aarhus, the son of a retailer. He studied at the Metropolitanskole where he graduated in 1891 and he received his diploma of Candidatus philosophiæ in 1892. From 1891 to 1898, he studied engineering at Den Polytekniske Læreanstalt. Immediately after having earned his civil engineer's degree, he worked a couple of months for the new Tramways Company of Frederiksberg (Frederiksberg Sporvejs- og Elektricitets Aktieselskab). In May 1898, he was employed as assistant engineer in the office of the City engineer in Frederiksberg and in April 1900 he was engaged as engineer with the municipal administration. Frandsen started his own consulting engineering office in November 1903, which became the Frandsen & Meyer engineering firm in 1926. At some time he was the president of the locally powerful association of landlords in that city, Frederiksbergs Grundejerforening, and as such he prepared a plan in 1907 to propose a solution for the much-disputed street opening through the park of Frederiksberg castle. Frandsen was a member of Dansk Ingeniørforening, which he represented in the committee set up in 1916 for the renewal of Prinsensgade in the inner city of Copenhagen.

Sources:
Dansk Civil- og Akademiingeniørstat, 1971 – biografiske oplysninger om kandidater fra Danmarks tekniske højskole og Danmarks Ingeniørakademi (1829-1968), Copenhagen, 1971; Oplysninger angaaende Den Polytekniske Læreanstalts Kandidater 1829-1929, Copenhagen, 1930, p. 175; Den Tekniske Forenings Tidskrift, Year 1910, p. 89; Vilhelm Malling, København i søgelyset, noget af et puslespil, Copenhagen, 1960, p. 23-27; Forskønnelsen, 1916, p. 72.

Aage Hansen (?-1936), landscape gardener
In 1915, Aage Hansen was a member of Den Almindelige Danske Gartnerforening (Danish Market Gardens' Association) and was living in Copenhagen (Engtoftvej 1, Vesterbro). Unfortunately the career of Aage Hansen has not yet been identified. A. Hansen probably died in 1936: his name is not listed in Kraks Vejviser in 1937.

Source:
Gartner-Tidende, Year 1915; Kraks Vejviser from 1915 to 1940.

Entry n° 16, motto "Et Kløverblad" – V. Clausen

Documentation in Copenhagen Town Hall Archives:

Memorandum to the proposal with the design of a trefoil leaves (et Kløverblad) as motto, three pages (handwritten).

Original drawings: general plan (1:10.000); a set of fifteen detailed plans (1:2000); two streets sections.

Photographic version of the general plan in Gengivelser af Konkurrenceprojekter vedrørende Københavns ydre Distrikter, 1909.

Vilhelm Clausen (1880-1919), architect
Born December 27th 1880, V. Clausen was trained as an architect at Det Kongelige Academie for de skønne Kunster. According to his obituary in Arkitekten, he

was planning to open his own practice when he suddenly passed away. He seems not to have enjoyed a wide public recognition although the few who knew him could trust his skills and commitment to his work. He worked for a number of architects, especially for Kristoffer Nyrop Varming (1865-1936) and was also lecturing in construction drawing at Den Polytekniske Læreanstalt. He acted as secretary of the committee of Akademisk Architektforeningen during eight years and was called as a member of the editorial board of the journal from January 1910 to assist the editor K. Varming. He continued co-editorship with Holger Rasmussen, who took the direction of the journal in October 1911. When Rasmussen resigned at the end of September 1916, Clausen took the whole editorial job until Vilhelm Lorenzen was chosen to lead Architekten in February 1917. Clausen left the journal in august 1918, presumably due to bad health.

Clausen was a member of Akademisk Architectforeningen and of Foreningen til Hovedstadens Forskønnelse.

Sources:
K. Varming, "Architekt Vilhelm Clausen", Architekten, 1919, nº 21, p. 165-166; Arkitekten, 10.12.1948, p. 20; K. Dirckinck Holmfeld (red.), Arkitekten 100 år, Copenhagen, 1998, p. 20-30.

Entry n° 17, motto "Stor-Kjøbenhavn" – F. Sundbärg & A. Lilienberg

Documentation in Copenhagen Town Hall Archives:

Memorandum to the proposal "Stor-Kjøbenhavn", 49 pages (type written, German language).

Photographic version of the general plan in Gengivelser af Konkurrenceprojekter vedrørende Københavns ydre Distrikter, 1909.

Johan Fredrik Sundbärg (1860-1913), architect
Sundbärg was born in Leksand, Darlana. He attended the Royal College of Technology (Kungliga Tekniska Högskolan), Stockholm and later the Architectural School of The Academy of Fine Arts (Konstakademien). He held the position of city architect (stadsarkitekt) first in Jönköping (1891-1900) and from 1901 onwards in Landskrona, where he stayed until his death in 1913. Besides a great many commissions for public buildings he collaborated on several occasions with Per. O. Hallman, especially for the competition in Gothenburg in 1901 where their project "Natur och Konst" was awarded the 1st prize. Published in 1897, his article "Om stadsplaner – med särskild hänsyn till svenska förhållanden", presents the principles to be followed in order to design town plans with respect of the local conditions, be it the topography, the natural environment or the ancient cities centres, has probably much contributed in introducing the ideas of Camillo Sitte in Sweden.

In a letter dated May 15 to Koch, the chief clerk of Magistratens 2nd Afdeling (the Finance board of the City's administration), Martin Nyrop wrote on behalf of F. Sundbärg: he requests the municipality to return the three deposits paid by F. Sundbärg, A. Lilienberg, and the firm Vattenbyggnadsbyrån. These were all involved in the project "Stor Kjöbenhavn", which Nyrop had believed to be a German proposal. A note, signed by Albert Lilienberg, Fredrik Sundbärg and Carl Semler confirms that Aktiebolaget Vattenbyggnadsbyrån was involved in the proposal "Stor-Kjøbenhavn". This consulting firm limited by shares was based in Stockholm and specialised in electrical works and hydraulic infrastructures, and on its behalf the engineer Carl Semler, Captain Ingemar Petersson and Professor J. G. Richert worked for the project.

Sources:
Svenska Konstnärer – biografisk Handbok, Stockholm, 1974; E. Eriksson, "Intenational Impulses and National Tradition", in C. Caldenby, J. Lindvall, W. Wang (ed.) 20th-Century Architecture Sweden, Munich &New York, 1998, p. 19-45; H. O. Andersson, F. Bedoire, Svensk arkitektur: ritningar 1640-1970, Stockholm, 1986; Stadsarkivet, Ejendomsdirektorat, Sag EJ 1150/1925, kassette 2: correspondence.

Selected writing by F. Sundbärg:
"Om stadsplaner – med särskild hänsyn till svenska förhållanden", Ord och Bild, 1897, p. 147-160; 193-213.

Albert Lilienberg (1879-1967), engineer
Lilienberg was born in Ronneby, the son of a magistrate. He attended the Royal College of Technology (Kungliga Tekniska Högskolan) where he graduated in 1903 as civil engineer.

He worked in Per O. Hallman's architectural office (1903-1904) and travelled in Germany and in the USA, Chicago especially. He lectured for a while at the technical school of Norrköping (1905) before working for the technical services of the city of Halmstad and for the City engineer's office in Malmö (1907). He became the City engineer of Gothenburg in 1907, a position he held until 1927 when he succeeded Per O. Hallman at the head of the Town Building and Planning administration of Stockholm (Stadsbyggnadsdirektör). He retired in 1944.

His career as a town planner started with his proposal to the competition for the plan of Hälsingborg, 1906, which did not get a winning prize but was bought. He became a leading debater on town planning issues as well as a prominent figure in physical town planning from the 1910s onwards. He attended most of the town planning congresses, including the one held in London 1910, and he was the chief organizer of the national exhibition held in Gothenburg in 1923 that hosted an international town planning congress. That year, he participated in the Congrès international d'Urbanisme et d'Hygiène municipale held in Strasbourg. Lilienberg would later chair the town planning convents in New York (1925) and in London (1935). Besides his master plan for Gothenburg and the urban development of the new districts of the city in the 1910s- 1920s, he designed plans for a great number of Swedish towns. He also lectured in town planning at Chalmers Technical Institute in Gothenburg, and chaired the local branch of the Technical Society in 1916-17 and 1924-25.

Sources:

H. Bjur, Stadsplanering Kring 1900, med exempel från Göteborg och Albert Lilienbergs verksamhet. Göteborg, 1984; Svensk biografiskt Lexicon, Stockholm 1977-1999, Vol. 2.

Arkitektur och dekorativ konst- organ för svenska teknologföreningens afd. för husbyggnadskonst; Svenska Konstnärer – biografisk Handbok, Stockholm, 1974; English Catalogue of the International Cities and Town Planning Exhibition, Jubilee Exhibition Gothenburg, 1923.

Entry n° 18, motto "Richesse oblige" – F. W. Berger & P. O. Hallman

Documentation in Copenhagen Town Hall Archives:

Memorandum to the proposal "Richesse oblige", two pages (type written).

Photographic version of the general plan in Gengivelser af Konkurrenceprojekter vedrørende Københavns ydre Distrikter, 1909.

Per Olof Hallman (1869-1941), architect
Hallman was born in Ödeshög, Östergötland and attended the Royal College of Technology (Kungliga Tekniska Högskolan), Stockholm and later the Architectural School of the Academy of Fine Arts (Konstakademiens arkitektskola). After he graduated in 1893, he spent one year in Berlin. He was assistant architect at the Public Works Office of the City of Stockholm in 1894, appointed architect in the öfverintendentsämbetet in 1906 and vice city architect in 1913. He was awarded Sweden first academic post in the planning field (stadsbyggnadskonst) in 1897 at the Royal College of Technology where he lectured until 1932. In 1909, he became a member of the Town planning Commission set up that same year, and presided over the City town planning office of Stockholm in 1922-1927. He is considered to have dominated Swedish town planning in the 1910s. Hallman executed plans for a great many Swedish towns and new districts including Kiruna, 1900, Lärkstaden, Enskede and Tellusborg (1907), Röda Bergen (1909) and Helgalunde (1916). He participated to a number of town planning competitions and obtained many winning prizes in Sweden, Finland and Norway (Helsingfors, Tammerfors, Trondheim, Krisitiania, Trolhättan, Norrköping, Drammen, Tönsberg, etc.) which included a 1st prize, together with Fredrik Sundbärg, for the town plan for Gothenburg in 1901. He wrote a great many articles and essays on town planning issues and joined the town planning convents in London (1910) and Gand (1913).

Sources:
H. Bjur, Stadsplanering kring 1900 – med exempel från Göteborg och Albert Lilienbergs verksamhet, Gothenburg, 1984 ; T. Hall, "Urban Planning in Sweden", in T. Hall, Planning and urban Growth in the Nordic Countries, 1991, p. 167-246 ; A.-L. Löfquist, Per Olof Hallman, 1869-1941, Förgrundsgestalt för estetiskt stadsbyggande i Sverige, Stockholm Universitet 1991; T. Paulsson, Den glömda staden – Svensk stadsplanering under 1900-talets början med särskild hänsyn till Stockholm. Idéhistoria, teori och praktik, Stockholm, 1959; Svenska Konstnärer – Biografisk Handbok, Stockholm, 1974.

Selected writings by Per O. Hallman:
"Principerna för anläggandet eller utvidgandet af en stad eller stadsdel", Förhandlingerna vid Nordiska Teknikermötet i Stockholm, Stockholm, 1898, p. 170-74; Kortfattad beskriftning öfver Stockholms byggnadsförenings verksamhet i under de förta femtion åren, Stockholm, 1898; "De nya stadsplaneidéerna", Arkitekten, Meddelelser for Akademisk Arkitektforening, 1901, p. 287-292; "Tysk nutida stadsanläggningskonst. Studier från utstillingen i Dresden", Teknisk Tidskrift avdelningen för Arkitektur och Dekorativ konst, 1903; Stockholm and town-planning: a short introductory survey, Stockholm, 1911; Plantering å gårdor inom kvarter i Stad: inledning till diskussion ur lag-, byggnadsstage- och byggnadsordningssynspunkt, Stockholm, 1912.

The career of F.W. Berger, civil engineer, has not yet been identified.

Entry n° 19, motto "Axelhus" – F. Romeu

Documentation in Copenhagen Town Hall Archives:

Memorandum to the proposal "Axelhus", nine pages (handwritten, French).

Photographic version of the general plan in Gengivelser af Konkurrenceprojekter vedrørende Københavns ydre Distrikter, 1909.

Ferran Romeu i Ribot (1862-1943), architect
F. Romeu i Ribot, born in Barcelona, studied architecture at the Escola d'Arquitectura (Barcelona School of architecture) and obtained the title of architect in 1887. In 1899, he started lecturing at the same school where he was later appointed professor. As an architect he designed a number of buildings in his town. He also had a strong interest in town planning and his entry in the competition for the extension of Barcelona in 1905 won the 2nd prize, as did his proposal to the competition for the plan of Lleida in 1921. He was also responsible, together with the architect Ezequiel Porcel for the master plan of Barcelona in 1917, and he drew the plan for the development (Reforma) of the historic city centre in 1914 together with the "Modernist" architects Lluis Domènech i Montaner and Josep Puig i Cadafalch.

Sources:
J. Ganau, "Town Planning and Conservationist policies in the Historic City Centre of Barcelona, 1860-1930", Planning History, vol. 19, n. 2/3, 1997, p. 23-31; Diccionario Biografico de Artistas de Cataluña, dir. por J.F. Ráfols, t. 2, 1952, Barcelona, Editorial Milla, p. 479.

3

THE COMPETITION, A STAGE IN DISCIPLINES AND PROFESSIONS

1 The Reception of the Competition

On 6 May 1909, the exhibition of the projects in the town hall's room of ceremonies was opened to journalists, and the following day all the plans and drawings were exhibited for one week in the building's large lobby. *Absalon*, the municipal employees' journal, reported on the exhibition as follows:

"Som rimeligt er, har denne Udstilling vakt ganske usædvanlig Interesse i Arkitekt- og Ingeniørkredse. I hvilken Grad det samme kan siges for det store Publikums Vedkommende, er mindre klart".[1]

At first, the impact of the competition on the general public – as seen through the press – and on the professional milieu seems to have been of little significance. The Danish press only modestly reported on the competition. The professional journals printed some extensive reports, but without much discussing any issue. For the reasons already mentioned, the international professional journals that had announced the competition were almost silent. Above all, even at the national level, the competition seems to have sunk rapidly into oblivion, being only mentioned sparsely in the following years. The winning projects were included in the material presented by Copenhagen's municipality at the Danish National Exhibition that took place in Aarhus in the summer of 1909, and were not displayed since.[2]

Diverse factors were responsible for this relative neglect. At the national level, it can be assumed that the wide interest aroused by the opening on 18 May 1909 of the Aarhus National Exhibition, which almost coincided with the announcement of the competition results, probably overshadowed the Copenhagen event. With its strong focus on architecture and on spectacular exhibits, the manifestation in the second largest city of Denmark was widely reported on in the press and the professional journals. At the international level, it could be envisaged that a surveyor being awarded the first prize resulted in a semiconscious "conspiracy of silence", except, obviously, in the journals of the German surveyors. This is not a gratuitous assumption when considering the general boycott of the 1911 International Canberra Competition, which resulted in the non-participation of most of the best-known German, English and American planners.

But a closer examination shows a more complex and contrasted picture. This chapter explores the reception of the competition by examining, respectively, how its results have been accounted for in town planning exhibitions and congresses, and which coverage the press and professional journals gave.

1.1 The International Town Planning Exhibition

The international town planning movement did take a genuine interest in the Copenhagen competition, and this is well attested by the correspondences between Werner Hegemann, Raymond Unwin, and Co-

1 "The exhibition aroused lively interest among architects and engineers. It is more difficult to appreciate how much the general public was concerned "(Our translation) in *Absalon*, n. 142, 1. June 1909, p. 140.

2 Note from Magistratens 2. Afdeling to the Stadsingeniør and the Stadsarkitekt, dated 2 June 1909: "The plans that were awarded a prize as well as the plan, which was bought by the municipality (...) will be displayed at Aarhus Exhibition during one month from the 1 June up to the 1 August 1909" (our translation), *Stadsarkivet, Ejendomsdirektorat,EJ 1150/ 1925.*

penhagen authorities.[3] Taking advantage of the Great-Berlin competition, a large exhibition was organised to give the widest possible publicity to the results of the contest, using the debates about the entries as a springboard to make town planning better known in all European cities. Werner Hegemann (1881-1936), who had been instrumental in bringing to fruition the 1909 Boston and New York exhibitions, was responsible for the organisation of 'Die allgemeine Städtebau-Ausstellung', held in Charlottenburg's Fine Art Academy in May and June 1910.[4] The exhibition was planned as the momentum of a travelling exhibition across European countries, which was successively invited at Antwerp, Düsseldorf and London.[5] In this context, Hegemann wrote to the municipal authorities of Copenhagen and requested the awarded entries of the 1909 Competition. However, he met, to his dismay, a strong reluctance from the City officials. At that time, the technical services of the Danish capital were designing an overall plan on the basis of the winning projects and the municipal engineer in charge, Aage Bjerre, who had been awarded the second prize, wanted to keep all the plans at his disposal. In his view, it was simply not possible to finalise an extension plan within the planned timing of the exhibition, and he did not wish to be deprived of the awarded plans during the entire duration of the Berlin exhibition. Besides, the duplication of the plans would be a very costly affair.[6] The exchange of notes between the technical office and the City government shows that working out the municipal plan was more desirable than displaying the competition's winning entries in Berlin. To be represented in the German capital nonetheless, the municipal authorities then chose to send recent urban projects, namely the plans of Fælledparken, the new central park designed by O. K. Nobel and E. Glæsel, the layouts of two new cemeteries, a fountain design, and an urban renewal project in the inner city.[7] As we shall see in more details, this streets-widening project received negative appreciation by T. Goecke. (See Chapter 7).

All this material was first exhibited in Berlin, then in Düsseldorf between 5 August and 25 September 1910. It then went to London on the occasion of the Town Planning Conference held between 10 and 15 October 1910. The following year this tour was extended to Zurich, where a 'Städtebau-Ausstellung' was held in February and March 1911.[8] When the City Architect Wright notified the municipal administration about the documentation the City had lent abroad in March 1911, he confirmed all the plans and photographs had come back, save for the plan on urban clearance in the old town and some material lent to Zurich.[9]

It is difficult to find a single explanation for this apparent choice not to invest in the international movement for town planning. One possible reason could be that sending around the winning plans of the 1909 Competition not only consumed much of Copenhagen municipal staff's energy, but also drained

3 *Arkitektur*, n. 7, July 1909, p. 99.

4 Die Ausstellung für Städtebau und städtische Kunst in New York, 3-16 May 1909.

5 "The great international Town Planning Exhibitions held during the year 1910 in Berlin, Dusseldorf, and London have afforded opportunities for studying comparatively the town-planning work of all the great countries of the world (...). (It) drew attention to the remarkable difference in the character of the town-planning work as carried out in different countries." Raymond Unwin, *Town Planning in Practice – An Introduction to the Art of deigning Cities and Suburbs*, London, 1912, p. xiii.

6 *Stadsarkivet, Ejendomsdirektorat, EJ 1150/1925*: letter dated 13.01.1910 from Kirschner, Oberbürgmeister, Berlin; letter dated 15.01.1910 from Bjerre and letter dated 31.01.1910 from Voigt and Wright to Magistratens 2. Afdeling; letters from Hegemann to the Magistrat dated 11 and 16 February 1910; 8 and 15 April 1910.

7 *Stadsarkivet, Ejendomsdirektorat, EJ 1150/1925*: note dated 16 February 1910 from the Stadsingeniør and the Stadsarkitekt to Magistratens 2. Afdeling, with the description of the material sent to the Städtebau-Austellung in Berlin: Fælledparken (2 plans and 2 drawings, Vestre cemetery (1 plan and 1 photograph), Bispebjerg cemetery (1 plan and 1 photograph), Gefion fountain (2 plans, 1 section, and 1 photograph), the urban renewal of the unhealthy districts in the inner city (1 plan, 1 section, and 1 photograph). This was reproduced in Werner Hegemann (ed.), *Der Städtebau nach den Ergebenissen der allgemeinen Stätebau-Ausstellung in Berlin, 1910*, Berlin, 2 vol., 1911-1913, vol. 2, p. 298 & p. 367.

8 *Schweizerische Bauzeitung*, 28 January 1911. A town planning exhibition was also held in Frankfurt/Main from the 15 January to the 15 February 1911 presenting in particular Hegemann's collection on American and English town planning .

9 *Stadsarkiv, Ejendomsdirektorat, EJ 1150/1925*: letter, dated 13 March 1911, from the Stadsarkitekt to Magistrat, 2. Afdeling

its finances, when the capital was hardly recovering from the short but severe 1908 crisis. Another possible explanation could be that Copenhagen municipality wanted first to assert its action in favour of social hygiene and limited beautification schemes, when a new building code for the capital was under discussion. Such an orientation was also in tune in to the collective work on sanitation improvement for Copenhagen, including a contribution by Aage Bjerre on "Staderweiterung, Bauordnung und Parkanlagen" (town extension, building code and park layout), which was published in German in 1907.[10] A few years later, the call of the "Danish committee for Denmark's participation in the International Hygiene Exhibition in Dresden", received the support of Copenhagen municipal authorities for funding a Danish delegation.[11] The event of 1911 was comprised of a dozen sections, each of these subdivided into several themes, and the material sent by Copenhagen, including the clearance scheme for the old city, was integrated into the subsection on *Städtebau* chaired by Joseph Stübben. Yet no Danes were present in this group that gathered leading figures in the field of city building; the Danish delegates flocked to the sub-section on school hygiene group and to the section devoted to the history of hygiene.[12]

Denmark's projection abroad

Danish professionals were involved fairly actively in the transfer of urban techniques, as attested by their contributions to the Nordic Technique Congress of 1897 held in Stockholm, and, more significantly, by the organisation of the Copenhagen Congress of Technique and Hygiene in 1903.[13] But they much less participated in the build-up of town planning or Städtebau as an international movement. What seems like a policy of restraint from the main events and arenas dedicated to questions of urban development was occasionally interpreted as a very negative singularity. For instance, Vilhelm Lorenzen, who was an influential advocate of town planning in Denmark, much resented the absence of any official Danish delegate to the International Congress of Architects held in Vienna in 1908. In the report he gave to *Architekten*, Lorenzen mocked Denmark's pusillanimity in not paying any attention to the event in the "city of Theophilus Hansen" and to the meeting of "Kulturstaterne" (the Nations of high culture). He criticized both the petty attitude of the official authorities and the behaviour of professional milieu that was poorly interested in the propagation of Danish national culture, all of which resulted in the conspicuous absence of Denmark in the international exhibition of architecture. By contrast, he emphasised Sweden's effort, which proved the "civilised world" that Scandinavian people were not anymore living as "cavemen".[14] This strong statement, which was published at the time of Copenhagen competition, seems to be highly rhetorical aiming at what we might call a selective propagation of Danish achievements. Olaf Schmidt, the Danish delegate to the Paris International Hygiene Housing Congress of 1904, expressed the specificity of the Danish situation regarding international contribution by declaring to the audience:

"Les grands pays ont le devoir de faire les expériences, les petits pays ont le devoir de suivre et d'exploiter les résultats des travaux qui ne peuvent être entrepris que dans les grands milieux."[15]

10 Dr. Th. Weyl (Hrsg.), *Die Assanierung von København*, Leipzig, 1921. The contributors were A. Berg, A. Bjerre, St. Friis, H.V.S. Gredsted, P. Heiberg, P. Hertz, E.M. Hoff, F. Levison, H. Neergaard, K.M. Nielsen, H.A. Nielsen, Vilh. Nohr, F. Öllgaard, N.P. Schierbeck, F. Tobiesen, and A. Ulrik.

11 Letter, dated 26 April 1910, from Dr. C.J. Salomonsen, president of the committee, to the Mayor J. Jensen, *Stadsarkivet, Ejendomsdirektorat, EJ 1150/1925.*

12 R. Unwin, P. Geddes, F. Adickes, R. Baumeister, T. Goecke, J. Brix, F. Genzmer, and E. Henard were among the 54 participants in the town planning section of the congress, see Internationale Hygiene Ausstellung, Dresden 1911 – Vorsitzende und Mitglieder der wissenschaftlichen Gruppen.

13 See A.G.V. Petersen (ed.), *Beretning om Tekniske og Hygiejniske Kongress i Kjøbenhavn den 24-27 Juni 1903*, Copenhagen, 1904. Also W. Hoffsted (ed.), *Förhandlingarna vid nordiska teknikkermötet i Stockholm den 15-19 Juni 1897*, Stockholm, 1898.

14 Vilhelm Lorenzen "Indtryk fra Architektkongressen i Wien", *Architekten*, 20 June 1908, p. 436.

15 "The great countries should carry on experiments, while the small ones should follow and exploit the outcomes of the works that can only be undertaken in large environments" (our translation): *Congrès international d'assainissement et de salubrité de l'habitation, Paris, 1-8 novembre 1904*, Paris,

Accordingly, resources should be concentrated on assimilation and adaptation of innovations, while efforts at exporting ideas should only be undertaken selectively.

Within this context, it should be stressed that the Copenhagen competition did not aim, in contrast to the Berlin one, to project the capital city as a political and cultural centre on the continental level. While Alfred Raavad's proposal aimed at projecting the port city on the international seaborne trade, the other Danish entries envisaged Copenhagen on the regional level. Raavad singled himself out with a vision of a Nordic metropolis, which was probably much coloured by his experience of Chicago. While Danish officials attended a number of international planning meetings at that time, and were well aware of the state of the art, the municipality of Copenhagen did not try to capitalise from the achievements of the competition on the international scene. By putting forward technical and financial reasons to decline the lending out of its materials to the General Secretary of the Berlin exhibition, the municipal authorities did not strive to promote a specific discourse on town planning.

In the following years, the page was swiftly turned. The competition was not a topic in the Ghent International Congress and Exhibition of 1913, where the Mayors Jensen and Marstand together with Trap represented Copenhagen City.[16] Neither was it recalled in major post-war planning events: the Gothenburg International Cities and Town planning Exhibition held in 1923 and the Congrès international d'urbanisme et d'hygiène municipale held in Strasbourg the same year.[17] French surveyor and town-planner René Danger noted that Denmark exhibited in Strasbourg "de vieux plans dans la manière du XVIIIème siècle, tous très curieux et très attrayants."[18] In Gothenburg, a large part of the materials displayed by the Danish committee was indeed devoted to urban history.[19] Yet these also encompassed urban development projects, such as the "centralization-decentralization scheme" for the capital region by Charles J. Schou, the design by Steen E. Rasmussen and Knud H. Christiansen for the new town of Hirtshals, Alfred Raavad's new harbour project for Copenhagen. Emphasis was given to housing projects, ranging from the terraced houses (rækkehuse) in Hellerup to the cluster of housing estates on Bispebjerg around P.V. Jensen Klint's church in commemoration of Grundtvig. In contrast, little emerged from the 1909 Competition period, save for Rasmussen and Fischer's project of 1910 to develop the site of the former railway station and the design of Fælledparken. While the Danish exhibition in Gothenburg was dominated by urban-history documents referring to the 17th and 18th centuries, suggesting the anchoring of town planning in classicism, the jump into contemporary town and housing schemes ignored the 1909 Competition.

1.2 The Competition in the Light of Newspapers and Professional Journals

The daily papers reported about the competition to insist on the exceptional character and on the historical

1905, p. 706-07. Dan Ch. Christensen addresses this question in relation to the dynamics between the circulation of innovations and the development of institutions in Denmark, see *Det Moderne Projekt, Teknik & Kultur i Danmark-Norge 1750-1814-1850*, Copenhagen,1996.

16 *Premier Congrès International et Exposition Comparée des Villes*, Bruxelles, Union Internationale des Villes, 1913.

17 See *International cities and town planning exhibition, Jubilee exhibition Gothenburg, Sweden 1923*, Gothenbourg,1923. Also Societé Française des Urbanismes, *Oú en est l'urbanisme en France et à l'étranger?*, Paris, 1923. Anthon Karsten, then City Engineer, and the surveyor Kai Hendriksen represented Copenhagen in the meeting in Strasbourg.

18 "Old plans in the eighteenth-century style, all very curious and attractive" (Our translation), in *Le Journal des Géomètres-experts français*, 1923, p. 414. Charles J. Schou also commented that the Danish exhibition of historical town plans was among the most successful displays: *Meddelelser udsent af Dansk Byplanlaboratorium*, vol.1, nr. 3, 1923, p. 4. V. Lorenzen, who was part of the Danish Committee, was probably instrumental in giving this overtone to the Danish contribution.

19 The Danish Town Planning Laboratory organised the Danish contribution to the Gothenburg exhibition. Though its aim was to "perform systematic work" to solve the issues of the growth of towns and to promote practical realisation, town history played a pivotal role, at least for some of the founding members of the institution like Vilhelm Lorenzen. The members of the Danish committee for the Gothenburg exhibition are given in: *Den Internationale Stadsplansudstilling – den Nordiske Afdeling, Danmark, Katalog*, Gothenburg, 1923, p. 3-4.

significance of the event for the capital of Denmark. On 5 May, the liberal daily *Politiken* published the result of the competition and announced that "numerous visitors" were expected to visit the exhibition in the Town Hall. The conservative *Berlingske* underlined the huge work input of the competitors and stressed that the public was not yet given access to the exhibition. The following day, the press pointed to its readers they had to wait one more day to see the plans for the capital. Later on, *Politiken* praised the Magistrat's enlightened decision to go for a competition as a happy departure from the 19th-century liberal policy of selling land to developers. Despite the overall approbation of a move that gathered a host of ideas, the editor further pondered upon the practical use of all these plans:

"Størstedelen af de vidtspændende Projekter til et omformet Stor-Kjøbenhavn, der nu er udstillede i Raadhushallen, er af en saaden Beskaffenhed, at de, der har udtænkt dem, næppe vil opleve at se dem virkeliggjorte. Selv om man fraregner de mest fantastiske blandt Planerne, vil deres Udførelse koste Hundreder af Millioner. Det er Fremtidsmusik, og som saadan maa det bedømmes."[20]

The daily press also published a long piece written by the architect Carl Brummer (1864-1953), which is by far the most detailed and informed article, giving an overall survey of the entries.[21] At the turn of the century, Brummer had built a number of villas, among which some were held in repute, including the one located on Svanemøllevej built in 1904, a fine interpretation of the Neo-baroque style joining a sense of proportion with an imaginative type of Arts and Crafts handling of details.[22] In veiled terms, the architect criticised the evaluation of the jury and especially the lack of transparent criteria for such an evaluation. In his view the attribution of the first prize is not well founded. He agreed that Strinz's plan was deemed comprehensive, carefully adapted to the existing layout, and successful to distribute built masses and high-density housing. Nonetheless he estimated that the east-west links were too weak, and the circular railway in a too reach from the city-centre. Regarding the green belt drawn by Strinz to mark the limits of the extensions, Brummer was not convinced of its utility. Bjerre's plan is described as thoughtful and "professional", in spite of stiffness in the handling of the road network and a lack of originality in detail plans. Brummer especially praised Plesner and Mathiesen's proposal that included a relief plan of the new city; he valued the design of the street layout, with a north-south orientation giving maximum sunlight to the housing and the arrangement of picturesque views, but he thought the distribution of the built masses was not very sound in comparison with other prize-winning projects. Nobel and Rasmussen's entry is mainly mentioned for its imaginative ideas concerning the street layout. Brummer also considered entries that were not selected. Hygom and Einersen's project is mentioned as regards the streets layout, and one can note genuine sympathy for the nascent movement of Den Fri Architektforening. Praise is also given to the original solution put forward in Fisher's entry in order to deflect the traffic away from the inner city (See Chapter 5). Finally Brummer underlines the competitors' massive work input and rebukes the municipality for not having used the whole amount that was earmarked for non-awarded projects.

Both *Politiken* and *Social-Demokraten* paid tribute to Raavad's project for its innovative features. *Politiken* especially emphasises his unfailing interest in his homeland while depicting his vision of tomorrow Copenhagen that will soon be full of motor cars, equipped with rapid electric mass-transportation systems, and geared up to the tempo of a big American city.[23] Some of Raavad's more cosmetic ideas, such as a panoramic restaurant belvedere at the top of a wa-

20 "Most of the thrilling proposals for Great Copenhagen, which are presented in the town hall, were not really conceived by their authors to be realised as such. Although the most fantastic projects were put aside, it will cost hundreds of millions to implement the proposals. They rather ought to be evaluated in their own terms, as the music of the future." (Our translation): *Politiken*, 10 May1909.

21 Carl Brummer, "Kjøbenhavns ydre bebyggelse-konkurrencen om Gadeplaner", *Berlingske politiske og Avertissementstidende*, 13 May 1909.

22 See *Weilbach, Dansk Kunstnerleksikon*, Vol. 1, 1994, p. 414-416. The drawings of the villas built are kept in Kunstakademiets Bibliotek, Samlingen af Arkitekturtegninger, with the reference 491 A 9083 / 9084.

23 "Den dansk-amerikanske Arkitekt Roewade", *Politiken*, 6 May 1909.

ter tower, or a new Tivoli at Brønshøj, also got strong attention from the columnist. Besides, the full-fledged protection of Utterslev village and the landscaping of natural features are noted, as well as the proposal for new, but costly harbour facilities. Raavad's critical posture toward the discharge of sewage at sea and his views on a decentralised administration of the new urban districts seem to have contributed to arousing the interest of the press. Raavad was the only competitor to whom *Social-Demokraten* devoted a biographical note, which sketches the figure of the prodigal son who escaped near-misery through hard work and training before a success story in America as a specialist in metallic high-rise structures.[24] The paper also comments Strinz's entry, praising the good street network in his general plan, and pays special attention to a residential scheme in Brønshøj by describing at length a perspective with tower-belvederes, staircases in landscaped gardens and fountains.[25]

'Blending of imagination and technique'

The professional journals reviewed the event in more depth. We give here only a summary of their general comments on the competition. Observations on particular aspects of various projects are dealt with in more detail in the next chapter.

Both *Architekten* and *Maanededsskrift for Sundhedspleje* reported extensively, while *Ingeniøren* mainly focused on two proposals: Bjerre's project and Nobel & Rasmussen's project.[26] Yet *Ingeniøren* none the less merely reproduced the documents as the competitors wrote them. *Arkitekt-Foreningens Tidsskrift*, the journal of the non-academic architects, acknowledged the difficulty in making a balanced review of such a wealth of projects and briefly described the main features of the prize-winning entries, while observing there were a number of valuable ideas in some non-awarded entries as well.[27] *Absalon*, the municipal employees' journal, chose to publish short abstracts of the awarded projects, which are characterised as a blending of "imagination and technique". The periodical singled out the project "Bella" among the non- winning entries because of its quality; two of the three authors had been active in the set-up of the municipal engineers' union.[28]

The Swedish journal *Arkitektur* took a critical stand on various dimensions of the competition.[29] First, the journal objects to the preparation of the contest: the data were insufficient for a project of this scale, and required documents would have necessitated the involvement of more official departments than the municipal ones. A second observation concerns the lack of focus of the task: the competitors had to spread their efforts over detailed urban development plans on one hand and over a general plan on the other, the scale of the later not allowing an accurate treatment for a master plan; thus two competitions should have been organised to meet the expectations of the municipality. Third, the journal is critical of the organisation and work of the jury: the award panel was exclusively Danish, comprised a minority of qualified technicians, and its decisions should have been explained and made public. Finally, it is pointed out that the budget earmarked for non-awarded projects was not entirely allocated. Beyond this set of distinct but conjoined critics, there lurked a much deeper frustration from the general assessment of the competition. None of the Swedish planners who participated was awarded a distinction, and there were hardly any comment on their works in the Danish press, compared with projects such as "Wayland Smed" or "Bella". Altogether, the Swedish professional organ thought the competition did not comply with the prerequisites for a genuine international contest, which was a ground for prejudice against leading Swedish planners. The exclusively Danish panel that was in charge of evaluating the entries also offers a possible understanding of the silence from the German journals on the competition.

24 *Social-Demokraten*, 9 May 1909

25 *Social-Demokraten*, 7 May 1909

26 "De præmierede projekter til gade- og bebyggelsesplan for København ydre distrikter". *Ingeniøren*, 19 June 1909, p.213-228.

27 "Konkurrencen om gadeplaner i Københavns ydre distrikter", *Arkitekt-Foreningens Tidsskrift*, 22 May 1909, p. 161-162.

28 "Udstillingen af Konkurrenceprojekter til bebyggelse af Københavns indlemmede distrikter", *Absalon*, 1 June 1909, p.140-144.

29 *Arkitektur*, nº 7, 1907, p. 99.

Let us return now to the Danish professionals' point of views. *Architekten* published in two successive issues the analysis of Rolf Schroeder (1872-1948) who had initially considered participating in the competition. This architect was then known to be associated to the National Romanticism's school with his design of Grundtvig's House that was just built (1906-1908) as a reminder of the Palazzo Vecchio in Florence.[30] He was also oriented towards town planning and was to be awarded the first prize for his entry entitled "for the future generation", worked out together with Fr. Wagner, in the competition for Aalborg's extension in 1912. Later he became a member of Danish Town Planning laboratory's plenary assembly while he worked for housing schemes funded by a State's agency. In contrast to most other commentators who expressed their doubts about the well-founded choice of the winning entry, Schroeder strongly maintained the "unquestionable" pre-eminence of Strinz's proposal, though he agreed with the widespread criticism of the perspective drawings. With this concession to his fellow architects apart, Schroeder praised the design of the general plan, and commented Strinz's method of design to demonstrate how forms and patterns of street networks can be combined to create variety and differentiation. It is apparent that Schroeder was committed to the development of understanding of a rather sophisticated and meticulous plan design, which informed his subsequent work for the Aalborg competition.

Schroeder was also very positive about Nobel and Rasmussen's entry that displayed technical soundness as well as a thorough analysis of both spatial and aesthetic conditions. Likewise he valued Plesner and Mathiesen's work: a talented piece with special attention for housing schemes, in spite of the distribution of built masses. Raavad's entry is acknowledged for its wealth of ideas, but judged somewhat "vehement" in its propelling of Copenhagen in the direction of a "world city"; the harbour installations were definitely over-scaled for the town. Schroeder viewed Bjerre's entry as a sound, professional synthesis of the municipal projects that were under way, though he pointed out rigidity in the handling of the road network and a difficulty in the management of the spatial dimensions of the plan, a defect due to a lack of collaboration with architects. In fine, the project is assessed, in not so veiled terms, as too constricted by the existing relations with the surrounding communes – in other words, being too well informed proved an impediment to imagination.

Largely drawing on the booklets of the competitors, the journal of *Selskabet for Sundhedsplejne* (the Society for Hygiene) focused on the award-winning entries. The approach is, however, quite different here, in the sense that the detailed drawings are given maximum attention by the journal publishing some of the projected housing schemes. Strinz's plan receives good marks for its spatial comprehensiveness, but is criticised for its lack of precision with zoning. Bjerre's plan naturally finds particular favour with this comment that takes the opposite point of view of Schroeder:

> "Det er en med sikker Haand udtænkt rational Plan, under hvis Udarbejdelse Fantasien ikke har faaet Lov at digte Æventyr om Anlæg og Grundudnyttelse, som Virkeligheden ikke vil kunne godkende."[31]

The distribution of densities and the provision of land for housing schemes are especially appreciated; the design of Brønshøj neighbourhood is given as an example for a well-balanced repartition of different housing types. The Plesner & Mathiesen project, with its emphasis on a strict north-south orientation and compact housing blocks, is noted for its formal research and possible picturesque effects arising from simple combinations of volumes. Once more, the Nobel & Rasmussen project is praised for its careful study of the housing question and its proposal for adapting the traditional type of provincial housing to the capital city, i.e. rows of one or two-storey houses with contiguous back gardens providing for large, green and healthy open space.

30 "Gadeplanerne", *Architekten*, 5 June 1909, pp.41-58, and 12 June 1909, p. 424-6. On Rolf Schroeder, see Weilbach, *Dansk Kunstnerleksikon*, Vol. 7, 1998, p. 357-358. The drawings of the building are kept in Kunstakademiets Bibliotek, Samlingen af Arkitekturtegninger, with the reference RS 431, A 9211 a-m.

31 "It is a rational plan that a sure hand draw; here no indulgence in fantasy with free reins to dictate adventurous dispositions or land-uses, all of which the real world can not cope with." (Our translation): *Maanedsskrift for Sundhedspleje*, vol. 1908-1909, p. 134.

While acknowledging the significant efforts made by the participants to the competition in producing a comprehensive plan for Great Copenhagen, the journal of the Hygienists is critical of the high built density option that is predominant in many entries. The magazine deplores a too strong focus on three housing types, namely 'closed housing', 'half-closed' housing and villas, to the detriment of individual family housing, or "spread housing", which could be developed as 'natural extension' of the town. Social housing should be the corner stone Copenhagen's development, according to the Society for Hygiene, which hoped to have its say during the implementation phase.

1.3 Alfred Raavad and Charles Schou's Views on the Role of Competitions

Thinking about town-plans' competitions as an efficient mechanism for the accumulation and transmission of know-how in the planning discipline, we already suggested that they could be considered as a significant matrix for producing and spreading innovations by engaging in professional emulation.

By the turn of the twentieth century, extension-planning competitions had much in common with architectural contests that were partly rooted in the 18th-century academic tradition of city embellishment with schemes that often included the layout of the surroundings of monumental buildings, the design of large parks and sometimes of new residential quarters. The movement of extension-planning competitions launched in continental Europe in the second half of the nineteenth, with Vienna as the epicentre, largely drew on this huge substratum. This era of continental competitions saw a rapid accumulation of a wealth of knowledge and know-how, a fertile soil for new professional specialisation, while the design's dimension and skill of the design remained the decisive and distinctive criterion for 'city builders' as well as a privileged cultural medium.[32] At the turn of the twentieth century, the Austro-German Sittian trend of Städtebau reactivated this 'tradition'. Yet there were other movements with different orientations that also wanted to develop a renaissance of the academic tradition through the Grand Manner type of design.

The Austro-German current, with emphasis on the enclosure of spaces, on both the continuity and diversity of built forms, and on rules about adaptation, localism and complexity, was strongly rooted in an internalised, individualistic approach of planning stimulated by competitions' emulation. Planning was considered by Camillo Sitte and most of his followers – whatever their inclinations – as an internal dialogue between the Städtebauer and his work-in-process. Thus, the planner could emerge as a medium for social communities whose cultural values had been eroded beyond reparation by the transition to industrial modernity. However, the movement for extension-planning competitions, like paying the price of its success, run out of steam in the years before the First World War. New issues had also come to the forefront, as shown in the Berlin competition and the London Town Planning conference in 1910, leading city building towards a scientific approach of urban space.

What was then to be the role of competitions? Two Danish planners, Alfred Raavad and Charles Schou, gave their opinion on this matter, listing the pros and cons in detail. Their comments are particularly relevant for us as both were part of the early Danish planning movement, and hence directly connected to the 1909 event. Alfred Raavad addressed the issue in *Borgmesterbogen*.[33] Raavad stresses the contradictions that can arise between planning as a disciplinary field and the process of competition as such. He begins with the general fact that programmes are decided upon by the authorities in charge, whose viewpoint are largely determined according to quite practical constraints. Programmes therefore fail to analyse a city as a dynamic whole, and this ipso facto restricts their prospective dimension. Besides, there are two distinct agendas in a competition, two "town councils" wrote Raavad, the one of the organisers and of the jury, which may not coincide; thus, planners can be caught, to the point of paralysis, between the expectations of those

32 A thorough analysis of the transformation of the eighteenth-century tradition of design is given by Daniel Wieczorek, *Camillo Sitte et les débuts de l'urbanisme moderne*, Bruxelles, 1981.

33 Alfred J. Raavad, *Borgmesterbogen, op. cit.*, p. 208-210.

who designed the programmes on the one hand, and the values of the members of the evaluation panel on the other. Furthermore, the competition system is caught in a series of crises, which affect the quality of designs in the long run. Another issue is specific to the international dimension of competitions. How can foreign planners put forward adequate solutions without being fully cognisant of the complex and often implicit realities of a location they have not prior knowledge of? International contest run the risk of being "insipid" with proposals "alien to the cultural and aesthetic conditions" of the place.[34] This concern may reflect Raavad's strong 'cultural nationalism', which manifested itself throughout his works and writings; it may also mean a call for a methodical localism cum realism.

Raavad did not put forward clear proposals for reforming the system; he nonetheless remained definitely in favour of planning competitions and suggested some ways out of the crises. First, the programme and the rules applying to the final evaluation should be harmonised as much as possible, to give the planner maximum autonomy in his work. Second, he pleaded for more openness, suggesting a public exhibition of the plans before the jury's decision, a procedure that would allow the planner to defend his ideas and the public to be involved in the process. Finally, he emphasised the transactional and communicative dimension of a competition: the jury's decision ought not intend to penalise anyone, rather it should aim at the fruition of new values and ideas.

The architect Charles Schou (1884-1974) also gave his views in the article "Land, By og Byplanlægning" (land, city and town planning) published in 1924, a year after his treaty about town planning, *Om Bybygninsgskunst*, came out.[35] Schou did not participate in the 1909 Competition, but he was actively involved in planning activities as a participant in the London Town Planning Conference, as the winner of the second prize in the 1912 Aalborg competition, as the architect of the garden-city of Vigerslev, and as a leading, founding member of the Danish Town Planning Laboratory.[36] Schou first emphasises the difference in approach that had developed between Anglo-Saxon planning and the continental tradition, with English cities relying more on experienced professional consultants. He considers competitions as a transitional historical phenomenon, to be explained by the lack of a planning milieu sufficiently established to provide municipalities with planners of proven competence. His critical approach of competitions chiefly concerns the dimension of the programmes, which infers there is a difference in kind between a well-defined architectural programme and 'urban' programme.

Schou sees surveys as essential in planning understood as a process whereas competitions are aiming at a final result with a minor role given to comprehensive enquiries. Thus, he considers competitions cannot bring about useful planning solutions, while they are very costly and time-consuming processes. Instead, he believes that cities should select professionals by organising public invitations to tender; possibly organising closed, or restricted competitions between tenders in case of remaining doubts about their competence. However, he does not wholly exclude public competitions as contests of ideas, and he recommends that organisers carefully define their objectives in the preliminary phase and state clearly the purpose of a competition: to gather and select ideas, to obtain guide-lines plans, or to select and contract the right planners.

Although Raavad and Schou are from different generations and hail from distinct intellectual, professional and cultural backgrounds, they share some common views on competitions. Thus, they acknowledge the tremendous effort required of competitors and the organisers' responsibility in clearly defining "the rules of the game". They both point to the purpose of programmes, and to the limits to what can be expected of a competition, as, in general, plans soon become outdated. In spite of such criticism, both are ready to

34 *Idem*, p. 210

35 Charles J. Schou, *Om Bybygninsgskunst- Indledningsforedrag til Bybygnings Studier*, Copenhagen, 1923; "Land, By og Byplanlægning", *Meddelelser udsendt af Dansk Byplanlaboratorium*, Vol.1, n°2, September 1924, p. 10-22, esp. p. 16.

36 On this plan see, "Konkurrencen om en vej og bebyggelsesplan for Aalborg", *Architekten*, 26 October 1912, p. 33-46. Schou was associated with Frederik Nielsen and Thorvald Engqvist.

acknowledge competitions as a privileged opportunity for stimulating the emergence of ideas and values about the city, and finally as part of a civic and cultural exercise that can contribute to the development of a democratic urban community. Nonetheless an internalised mode of planning seems to permeate Raavad's discourse, which emphasises the charismatic character of the planner, whose "science" and imagination – both dimensions are linked according to Raavad – enable him to project a synthetic, holistic knowledge of the city in the future. In contrast, Schou conceived planning as an ongoing process that requires meticulous work, and as a form of regulative system constantly amended by planners.

1.4 From Town Plan Design to Physical Planning

Another explanation for the fact that the 1909 Competition sank into oblivion could pertain to the simultaneous attempt to pass a bill for a new Copenhagen's by-law. In 1912, there was not much hope the municipal proposal will be accepted, and in 1915 the whole project was abandoned. Without an appropriate Building Act that would entail planning provisions, of which use could town plans projects be in the hands of the municipal administration?

In November 1909 the Magistrat requested the Stadsingeniør to prepare, in collaboration with the Stadsarkitekt, a plan for the extensions of Copenhagen, while the bill was pending. A few years later, the development of the tracks of land owned by the municipality came back to the forefront. In this context, the mission given to the Stadsingeniør to bring about a comprehensive plan was quickly entangled in a mass of contradictions. On the ground, any achievement in following the plan directives would rest on sensitive and reasonable negotiations between the office of the town engineer, the town council, the city government and the various landowners to say the least. It is neither within the scope of the present study to investigate the urbanisation process after 1909 nor to assess the practical implementation of a town plan in the aftermath of the competition. We limit our comment to some insight into the perception of the main actor in charge of the town plan, that is, the City Engineer's office.

In April 1942, a note from the City Engineer to the 4th Board of the City government presents an evaluation of the outcome of the competition.[37] The note refers to the report about the urban development of the incorporated districts, which had been handed out by the City Engineer's department in January 1942, "*København – de indlemmede Distrikter byplanmæssig Udvikling, 1901-1941*". [38] In October, the same year, a new report came out from the same office, which presented a proposal for the planning of those very areas, "*København – de indlemmede distrikter – Forslag til Byplan*".

In the January report, there is a chapter about the competition with the title "Konkurrencen 1908-09 om en Gade- og Bebyggelsesplan", and the note explicitly refers to this section. It sketches the decision's process which led to the competition, as well as the main outlines of the wining entries and of the Egil Fischer's project; it synthesises the proposals in regard to the main thoroughfares, the parks and promenades, the distribution of various types of housing and concludes on the general value of the competition. It also mentions that although the town plans that the municipality had paid for could not be entirely used they could nonetheless give directions, and Strinz' plan provided the guidelines for assessing the various building and street projects, which were dealt with by the municipal technical department.[39]

The above-mentioned note reports a series of implemented schemes, which the ad hoc division of the City Engineer's office had carried out on the basis of the awarded projects, first of all Strinz' plan. Between

37 Olaf Forchhammer (1881-1964) was City Engineer in 1936-1951; he had been employed by the municipality in 1907, just before the competition.

38 The note from Stadsingeniørens Direktorat to Magistratens 4. Afdeling is dated 8 April 1942 and titled: "Bebyggelsesplan af 1909 om Københavns ydre distrikter", *Stadsarkivet, Stadsingeniørens Direktorat, Byplankontoret /Alm. Adm./ BP-sager, 1918-1984/ 977, minute BP 636.* The report is prefaced by Olaf Forchhammer, see *København. De indlemmede Distrikter byplanmæssig Udvikling 1901-1941*, Copenhagen, Stadsingeniørens Direktorat, 1942.

39 *København. De indlemmede Distrikter byplanmæssig Udvikling 1901-1941* I, op. cit., p. 29-30. It should be stressed that this book's chapter (p. 21-30) is the main source of the few comments about the competition, which have been published until now.

October 1909 and October 1919, twenty such occurrences are given, fifteen of them before the war. A significant shift took place in the early 1920s; by that time, Strinz's plan ceased to be used as a guideline for the technical office that Aage Bjerre supervised until 1936:

"Det synes dog at man i Begyndelsen af 20-erne er bleven klar over at 'Urania' ikke fortsat kunde danne Grundlag for Byplanens Udvikling, og derefter har man, hvor Forholdene har muliggjort det, gennemført andre og almindeligvis de klarere og fastere Linier i Planen".[40]

The note assumes that new conceptions were taking over the ones that Strinz's plan encompassed, and the realisations to come were more in line with Bjerre's ideas than with the project that once was chosen to be the scheme to be followed.

2 Competitions and the Professional Movement

For civil servants and members of the liberal professions alike a competition for a town master plan was generally the result of a rather exceptional juncture. Such a work was offering ample opportunity for theoreticians or practitioners to display their abilities that are seldom noticed in their usual practice. They could formulate a synthetic and relatively widely readable document, which suggests the broad lines of a programme aiming at helping mastering the development of the built environment. Furthermore, their endeavour was widely acknowledged to be one contribution to a complex task calling for a wide range of skills. In short, a competition could be a tribune enhancing professional status, especially for relatively young architects or engineers as Påhlman expressed it:

"Jag ämnar söka en befattning i Sverige, och som relativt ung ingenjör torde endast deltagandet i denna tävlan vara en förtjänst".[41]

But the Stadtbauer or city-builder was dependent on his professional grounding and identity as engineer, architect, or surveyor, which education, peers' group affiliation and occupation delineated. Thus their activities in planning can be understood as a means to foster one's promotion within one's field of profession. Yet, and how contingent a professional career could be, a 'new expertise' could lead not only to shifting perceptions, values and practices, but also to shifting professional orientations.[42] To be sure, there were rivalries opposing in particular engineers and architects and their respective professional bodies within the planning field at the beginning of the twentieth century. Yet a more complex picture arises, as we shall see, from the 1909 Competition in which collaboration between professions is a significant trait. Among the nineteen entries, seven were presented by engineers, five by architects and five others by groupings of diverse capabilities.

Projects designed by adding various professional skills to each other, so that the combination could be more effective to address the scope of a planning task, were not uncommon in the Nordic countries or in Germany in the early twentieth century, and some consulting firms were formed and developed in this respect. In Germany, the role of the Verband Deutscher Architekten –und Ingenieurvereine, a powerful professional organisation grouping civil engineers and architects, in spearheading a debate about the "shap-

40 "In the beginning of the 1920's, it was considered that Urania could not be the guideline for the development of the town plan anymore; since then other directive lines have been implemented, whenever it was possible, which were in general clearer and more rigid"(our translation),*see Stadsingeniørens Direktorat til Magistratens 4.* Afdeling, note of 8 April 1942, p. 4.

41 "… I am thinking to apply for a position in Sweden, and as a young engineer my participation to the competition (for Copenhagen) should be an asset" (our translation). Letter written by the civil engineer A.E. Påhlman, who participated to the 1909 Competition, to Jens Jensen, dated 20 October 1909: Stadsarkivet, Ejendomsdirektorat, sag 1925/1150, kas. 1.

42 Planning further developed as a specialization rather as a full fledged profession on its own. On this question see the discussion by Magali Sarfati Larson, "Emblem and Exception: The Historical Definition of the Architect's Professional Role", in J. R. Blau, M. La Gory, J. Pipkin, *Professionals and Urban Form*, Albany, 1983, p. 49-86.

ing of towns" has already been asserted.[43] Similarly, the lively discussion on town planning that took place in Austria and Switzerland in the 1890s can be considered in the light of the complementary relationships between architecture and civil engineering as developed by both the associations Österreichischen Ingenieur -und Architektenverein and Schweizerischer Ingenieur -und Architektenverein. This type of bond partly rested on common training in civil engineering and in architecture within higher polytechnic learning institutions. Furthermore, architecture should be considered in relation to the respective position and significance of the fine arts academies and to the craftsmen organisations according to the various countries of Europe. In respect to those short comments, we only stress here that the idea of designing a town or a town extension according to 'artistic principles' could be embraced by professionals from different backgrounds and horizons still in the early years of the twentieth century.

2.1 The Danish Professional Milieu

The eighteen Danish entrants were almost equally divided between ten engineers and seven architects, and a landscape gardener was the single representative of his profession. Among the ten Danish entries, architects defended three, engineers four (two alone and two grouped), and groups including architects and engineers three. The majority of the competitors were confirmed practitioners such as Ulrich Plesner reaching the apex of his career as a leading figure of the Neo Danish Baroque style. His entry mobilised the largest array of competence and was the only one to present a city-model. A number of architects of the younger generation, who were founding members or closely associated to Den Fri Architektforening (the Free Association of Architects) founded in spring 1909 participated in the competition. None of their entries were selected, but it is apparent that some of these projects became a clear buster in some careers. The competition also played an important role in the career of the engineer A. Bjerre who was distinguished by the second prize, while many comments of the Danish press stressed he should have been awarded the first prize.

43 This association is Verband Deutscher Architekten- und Ingenieurvereine: see A. Sutcliffe, *Toward the planned. op. cit.*, p. 23-24.

Strengthening Networks of Engineers

All the engineers who competed, except two, had taken their degree (candidat polytechnices) at Den Polytekniske Læreanstalt. This higher-education institution had greatly increased its intake after the mid-1890s, turning out 534 engineers between 1896 and 1905, more than half of which specialised as building engineers.[44] These eight engineers were also members of the Dansk Ingeniørforening, the association formed by Den Polytekniske Læreanstalt in 1892 to represent civil engineers and almost 700 strong in 1905.[45] Like A. Bjerre, O. K. Nobel and M. Frandsen, who were awarded a prize in the competition, many civil engineers who had graduated from Den Polytekniske Læreanstalt found employment in the municipal works, which were in a phase of rapid growth in the last decade of the nineteenth century: while only 22 engineers were heading municipal works for the whole country in 1901, their number had almost doubled in 1910, and at the time of the competition Copenhagen alone employed about 100 engineers, half of whom at least were civil servants.[46] This technical corps organised itself with the creation in 1901 of the Stads- og Havneingeniørforeningen (Association of City and Port Engineers), a branch of Dansk Ingeniørforeningen, but also as an union with the Kommunale Ingeniørforbund (the Union of Municipal Engineers), founded in May 1907 in Copenhagen. On the first executive committee of the trade union sat K. I. Einersen, who together with L. Hygom and G. Manicus-Hansen had submitted the entry "Bella".[47]

The municipal works at the turn of the century had two main departments, Direktoratet for Vej-og Kloak-

44 According to the statistics of *Dansk Civil- og Akademiingeniørstat*, Copenhagen, 1971.

45 *Dansk Ingeniørforening gennem 50 Aar 1892-1942*, 1942, p. 45.

46 Idem, p. 150.

47 Dansk Ingeniørforeningen did not welcome the new union, Københavns kommunale Ingeniørforbund, *Ibid*, p.150.

anlægge (the Roads and Sewage Directorate), and Stadsingeniørembedet (the City Engineer's Office) in which the winners A. Bjerre, O. K. Nobel, as well as other entrants were working. From 1897 to 1925, both units were successively reorganised, significantly increasing their staff to cope, in a first phase with the development of the new urban areas reclaimed from the fortifications, the construction of new streets, a comprehensive network of railways and railway stations, a general sewage system and the development of harbours installations, especially Frihaven. With the taking over of the whole of Brønshøj commune and of the main part of Hvidovre borough as well as Sundbyerene on Amager Island, both technical units for the city of Copenhagen further expanded until they were merged into one large department, the Stadsingeniørens Direktorat, at the head of which A. Bjerre was appointed in 1927 (See Box 3). At the time of the competition, A. Bjerre was chief engineer of Afdeling A, where E.F. Fröhlich and A.L.B. Klixbüll were also working, while O.K. Nobel was chief engineer of Afdeling B in the department of the Stadsingeniør. Two other entrants, K. J. Einersen and C. H. T. Manicus-Hansen, belonged to the third Department of Direktoratet for Vej- & Kloakanlæg. Two other engineers were at the head of the municipal works of the communes Lyngby-Taarbæk and Søllerød, immediately north of Copenhagen.

Such an overwhelming representation of the municipal works in the competition led to inevitable criticism. In January 1909, the day before the deadline for submitting the projects, the journal *Architekten*, following up an article printed in the daily *Berlingske Tidende* on 30 November 1908, entered into an argument with A.C. Karsten, afdelings ingeniør (section engineer). *Architekten* pointed out that the section engineer was perfectly informed as well as in control of the plans and projects underway in the City engineer's Office, and thus of what the town council expects, and consequently would be the best placed to obtain a prize. The journal asked: Should an "insider" such as a chief municipal engineer be allowed to compete? Does this not discourage those who would be interested in submitting their own project but lack the right connections to obtain precious knowledge?[48]

48 *Architekten*, 9 January 1909, p. 153-154.

On this ground the academic body of architects hoped to discourage municipal engineers to participate into the competition. Though A. C. Karsten eventually wrote to *Architekten* he will not participate, he emphasized that it was only from lack of time and not because he agreed on the principles stated by the architects' organ.[49] In the end, two municipal section engineers did submit entries, being awarded the 2nd and the 4th prizes.

Architects and Masters Builders

Three architects were associated with award-winning entries: H. Rasmussen, U. Plesner and A. Langeland-Mathiesen; they were members of the Akademisk Architektforening, which in 1905 had a membership of 162. Since 1879, the association was representing the architects who had been trained at the Academy of Fine Arts and successfully passed a number of tests.

In 1898, a period of intensive construction activity, to distinguish themselves from the run-of-the-mill craftsmen, builders or contractors, the first issue of *Meddelelser fra Akademisk Architektforening*, was published concurrently with the journal *Arkitekten-Tidsskrift for Bygningsvæsen*.[50] In 1901, the two journals agreed to merge under the title *Architekten*, but the rift opened up again in April 1908 with the publication of *Arkitekt-Foreningens Tidsskrift*, the organ of the architects who were not alumni of the Academy.[51]

The extremely lively debates on the training of architects throughout the first two decades of the twentieth century evolved around the relevance of the instruction in construction techniques given by Den Tekniske Selskabs Skole in relation to the Academy's training. A regulation from April 1888 had linked the two formations, the former one being a preliminary to the second.[52] The traditional training of architects rested on an apprenticeship in a crafts trade, such as

49 *Architekten*, 30 January 1909, p. 199.

50 See Kim Dircking Holmfeld (red.) *Arkitekten 100 År*, Copenhagen, 1998, p. 2-8.

51 In 1929, the architectural profession had stabilised; its journal was published under the new title *Arkitekten*.

52 See Knud Millech, "Arkitekturskolens Historie efter 1904", in A. Marcus (red.) *Det kongelige Akademi for de skønne Kunster 1904-1954*, Copenhagen, 1954, p. 382.

The City Engineer Office

The so-called Municipal Act of 4. March 1857 introduced a new system of local government for Copenhagen together with a municipal administration to decide upon works, which were previously under the authority of the state government. Magistratens 4. Afdeling (the Fourth Department of the City government) was created at that time, and the Stadsingeniørembedet (the City Engineer Office) together with the Inspektorat for brolægnings- og vejvæsenet (the Inspection of roads and bridges) were placed under its direction. The City Engineer was supervising the planning and the execution of technical works.

In April 1897, both the Inspektorat for Brolægnings-og Vejvæsenet and the Stadsingeniørembedet were re-organised and the Inspektorat for Brolægnings-og Vejvæsenet was transformed into the Direktorat for Vej-og Kloakanlæg (Directorate of roads and sewage utilities):

Direktorat for Vej-og Kloakanlæg
Direktorats kontor: bogholder m.v; sporveje og busser
1. Ingeniørafdeling: bygge- og spildevand sager
2. Ingeniørafdeling: anlæg af gader, veje, parker, broer, kloaker

Stadsingeniørembedet
Stadsingeniørens kontor: projekter af kloaker, veje, udstyknings sager
1. Ingeniørafdeling: øvrige anlæg og visse offentlige bygninger.
2. Ingeniørafdeling: ingeniørarbejder ved visse offentlige bygninger

With the annexation in 1901-1902, both the departments were significantly enlarged. The number of engineers, including assistant engineers, is given for the year 1909:

Direktorat for Vej- og Kloakanlæg
Direktør: O. M. Didrichsen (01.09.1905)
Direktorats kontor:
1. Afdeling (1909: 8 eng.)
2. Afdeling (1909: 6 eng.)
3. Afdeling (1909: 5 eng.)
4. Afdeling (1909: 3 eng.)

Stadsgartner

Stadsingeniørembedet
Stadsingeniør: J. J. Voigt (01.08.1902)
Stadinsgeniørens kontor:
Afdeling A (1909: 6 eng.)
Afdeling B (jan.1909: 7 eng., dec.: 11 eng)
Afdeling C (1909: 10 eng.)

The fifth Department (Magistratens 5. Afdeling) was established in March 1917 to administrate the water supplies, the electricity and gas utilities and the public transports.

In 1925, the Direktorat for Vej- og Klokanlæg and Stadsingeniørembedet were melted into one department: **Stadsingeniørens Direktorat:**
Under the new directorate were the following divisions: Byplanafdelingen; Byggesagsafdelingen; Vejafdeling – indre By; Vejafdeling – ydre By; Kloak- og Broafdeling; Materialafdeling; Stadsgartnerafdeling; Vejinspektion; Bogholderi.

Box 3 *Sources:* Bygge-og Teknikforvaltningen, Plandirektorat: Records of Karl Arn Ottesen; Ingeniøren, n° 76, 21 September 1912

carpentry or masonry, together with a curriculum in drawing, mathematics, physics, chemistry, which technical schools provided, especially Den Tekniske Selskabs Skole in Copenhagen.[53] It was usually after this training that aspiring architects entered the Academy's School of Architecture. When this institution eventually opened its own technical school for construction (bygningstekniske skole) in October 1908, projects to reform teaching of architecture came in the forefront, aiming at the emancipation of architecture from this tradition.[54]

There was, however, a lively interest in the Danish "byggeskik", as exemplified by an architect such as Ulrik Plesner, the author of the project that was awarded the 3rd prize. While many minds were dedicated to the renaissance of the training of bygmester (master builders), first of all P.V. Jensen-Klint (himself formed as an engineer at Den Polytekniske Læreanstalt), another trend was looking for a specific art of the architect and a renewal of the teaching of design in the academic curriculum, until then based on the study of styles and of perspective. Architects were faced with a number of issues relating to the new modes of construction, emerging out of industrialisation and the associated new materials, out of innovations induced by the technical systems that were changing the design of habitations, out of new types of buildings, including the production of cheap urban housing, and out of the arrival of new actors among contracting authorities.

The debates over the training of architects also overlapped with others concerning construction and stylistic approaches. *Architekten* published a letter of a student architect who explained at length why was founded a "free school of architecture" in 1902. Some students were rejecting most of all the "doctrinal" education of the Academy and believed that young architects should be allowed to choose and study other styles than those of Roman and Greek Antiquity.[55] Above all, they demanded to be exempted from drawing sketches on subjects pertaining no relations with architecture. Rather, they should work freely on architectural projects, particularly on modern housing buildings. It is in this context that in 1902-1903 a handful of young students left the benches of the Academy to look for an alternative training. In 1909, they formed Den Fri Architektforening. This movement is reminiscent of the 1883 Kunsternes Frie Studieskole, which was set up by young artists in protest against the Academy's conservative teaching. The Fri Architektforening did not grow beyond a small group of 24, and the experience was relatively short-lived, ending in 1919 when its leader, Povl Baumann, eventually joined the Akademisk Architektforening. The young architect Louis Hygom, who worked for the "Bella" entry, was a member of this group throughout, from 1902 to 1919. Egil Fisher, who submitted the "Millionbyen" project, was also involved, though apparently only for a very short while.

The 1908 edition of the *Krak-Kjøbenhavns Vejviser* directory lists 351 architects in Copenhagen, the town where most of the profession were concentrated. Among them, less than half (154) were recognised by the Academy.[56] The City architect Office was quite small in comparison to the one of the City engineer, though the municipality had started a large programme of construction of public buildings, schools especially, from the 1890s. The opportunities for being employed by the municipalities were limited and few architects found appointment, Niels Holger Rasmussen for example. It was then important for the architects to be involved with associations like the Foreningen til Hovedstadens Forskønnelse and the Foreningen til Gamle Bygningers Bevaring, which can be viewed as essential bridges in that period between

53 For an overview see Hélène Vacher "L'enseignement technique et l'émergence du génie civil au Danemark au 19e siècle", in M. Eftermova (ed.), *Livre du Cinquantenaire de la Faculté d'Electricité de L'Université Technique de Prague*, Paris/Prague, 2003, p. 48-71.

54 Between 1912 and 1918, students who graduated from the technical schools were required to pass an entrance examination before attending the Academy School of architecture.

55 See the article "Om Architektuddannelse", *Architekten*, 23 January 1904. About Den Fri Architekforening, see Nina Dahlman Olsen, "Den Fri Arkitektforening", *Architectura-10*, Copenhagen, 1988, p.84-132.

56 In the Directory's professional section, pp. 998-1000, architects are listed by names and indexed with an asterisk when holding a certificate from the Academy of Fine Arts. Engineers outnumber architects, while chartered surveyors are in a small number: 45 in Copenhagen and one only outside the capital (in Esbjerg), p. 1175.

the civil servants of both central and local authorities and the civil society (See Chapter 7). They constituted social bodies that could channel and support professional strategies.[57] All of the Danish architects who participated in the competition were members of the above-mentioned associations, with the exception of L. Hygom, whose name is not on the lists of either Foreningen til Hovedstadens Forskønnelse or of Foreningen til Gamle Bygningers Bevaring at that time, but who worked for the City architect for a while. The Danish entrants were residents of Copenhagen or of localities in the vicinity. Among the 52 requests for the competition dossier, none were sent from other parts of Denmark. In most respects, the competition was a Copenhagen's affair.

2.2 German Surveyors' Enlistment in Planning

Though it is not in the scope of this book to discuss the question of professions in detail, we explore the German surveyors milieu at some length. The very fact that the surveyor Strinz was awarded the winning prize grounds our choice. But it should also be stressed that there is very little literature concerning surveyors in relation to early twentieth-century town planning. For assessing the specific characters of Strinz's contribution to a strong planning paradigm, which shall be analysed in Chapter 4, the professional context of this German surveyor needs to be presented. In contrast we shall only briefly deal with the other foreign planners, especially the Swedish ones, whose works and environments have been already well researched.

Among the nineteen entries, eight were foreign ones in as much Raavad's contribution can to some extent be considered as a foreign entry. Among these, Karl Strinz's prize-winning entry is remarkable both for being the only German project and because Strinz was the only surveyor among the competitors. Strinz's success can be appreciated in the light of the achievements of a second wave of German planning between 1890 and 1910 that was closely observed all over Europe, especially in the Scandinavian countries, and assimilated to the prosperity and dynamism of the then new rising continental empire. Yet Strinz's presence in this contest, mostly ignored by German planners in comparison to a significant number of French architects who showed interest even though they eventually did not participate, is related to a more specific professional context. Though Strinz in his endeavour had no doubt counted on the aura of German planning, his motive most probably had to do with the corporate swift move the German land surveyors made towards municipal planning in the first decade of the century.

Leiter des städtischen Vermessungsamt (Head of the survey office) in Bonn from 1902 up to 1912, Strinz could use the term Stadt Geometer (City Surveyor) in his letters to the Magistrate of Copenhagen in 1908 and 1909. During those same years he was the secretary of the Verein- preussischer Landmesser im Kommunaldienst (the Union of Land Surveyors in local service in Prussia), and it was in this capacity he signed the petition to the Prussian administration for the opening of lectures in town planning for surveyors at both the Landwirtshaftliche Hochschule in Berlin and the Landwirtschafliche Akademie in Bonn-Poppelsdorf.[58] A regular member of the Deutscher Geometer-Verein (the German Union of Geometers), founded at the end of 1871, Strinz wrote many articles for the union's organ, *Zeitschrift für Vermessungswesen*, and was also an early collaborator of *Der Städtebau*.

57 See Lars Bo Kaspersen, "Associationalism – some reflections on the Danish Society, paper given at the ECPR Joint Session", Torino, March 2002. Ola Wetterberg underlines the changes that took place in relation to building conservation in Sweden in the early twentieth century, when philanthropic voluntary associations became more oriented toward political strategies. Those associations grouped many architects, conservationists and historians striving to assert their professional expertise with respect to the official bodies, see *Monumentt och Miljö*, Gothenburg, 1992.

58 Three other surveyors unions of Prussia co-signed the petition: Verein der Vermessungsbeamten der preussischen Landwirtschaftlichen Verwaltung, Rheinische – Westfaliche Landmesser Verein, Vereinigung selbständiger in Preussen vereidete Landmesser zu Berlin; See Verbands-Zeitschrift – Preussicher Landmesservereine in den Provinzen Schlesien und Posen und des Vereins der Vermessungsbeamten der Preussischen Landwirtschatlichen Verwaltung, Heft 7, 1 June 1908, p. 247-251.

Through his writings and his activities within unions of surveyors both at the level of the Prussian kingdom and of the German Empire, he significantly contributed to raising the interest of his colleagues in planning questions.

An Ascending Professional Movement

In the first ten years of the twentieth century, surveyors, that is "Landmesser", "Stadtgeometer" or "Katastergeometer", gained some headway in town planning competitions by winning a number of prizes, such as in Erfurt (1897, 2nd prize), Linden near Hanover (1901, 3rd prize), Freiberg in Saxony (1903, 1st and 3rd prizes), Postdam (1904, 1st prize), St Johann a.d. Saar (1905, 1st prize) and Pforzheim (1907, 1st and 3rd prizes).[59] There were also other minor successes in Stolpe-Berlin (1908), Eisenach-Johannistal (1909) and Saarbrücken-Triller (1909). Strinz successfully competed for the eastern extension of Mannheim in 1907. In 1909, his achievement in Copenhagen was comforted by an equal success for the laying out of the area of a former military cantonment in Bonn.[60] The same year, C. Würcker, a surveyor in Cuxhaven, was equally successful in winning the 1st prize in Danzig-Schellmüh competition.[61]

Numerous articles in the professional press addressing the specific approach of surveyors in planning reflect this wave of surveyor-led town extension schemes. The book *Der Landmesser im Städtebau* published in 1901 was an illustration of the aspiration of the surveyors' professional body to be reckoned with. The preface to the second revised edition of the book asserts both the competence and the professional rights of the Vermessungsingenieur, engineer-surveyor, alongside any other "cadets" of town planning, thanks to their achievements in a host of public town plan competitions.[62] It also argued that the scope of Städtebau, particularly city extension development, entails an ample field for specialised professional activities. Accordingly, the traffic, first of all urban railways, together with water and gas supply and sewerage works, are the domain of the engineer; the artistic dimension pertains to the architect, while the surveyor has to do with the appropriate use of the land, the "Örtlichkeit" (the place), the economic activities in general and the careful adjustment to property lines. Abendroth's treatise is similar in its practical orientation and systematic presentation of planning topics to the work of Stübben.[63] The purpose of Abendroth's book is to offer a comprehensive approach to the laying out and the implementation of extension plans, which are in the focus of the city surveyor's activities. His work introduces surveyors to the "modern town planning concept" as it has been especially developed by R. Baumeister in the aftermath of the Prussian Law of 2 July 1875, but also by E. Schmitt, J. Stübben, J. Röttinger, K. Henrici, C. Sitte, and T. Goecke among others. *Der Landmesser im Städtebau* restrains its ambition to present various models and detailed practical principles, including aesthetic ones, for the laying out of a plan. Many aspects are considered from the technical, the economic, and the administrative points of view in relation to municipal urban planning, such as land use policy and land properties registries. A detailed index, together with the Prussian laws and regulations at that time underline the practical purpose of the book meant for the surveyor, civil servant or not, whose practice is engaged in urban land development. Our systematic survey of the journal *Zeitschrift für Vermessungswesen* shows that it gave a large coverage of the debates and studies relating to urban and planning questions, especially in the years 1906-1912. Numerous articles concerning the specific contribution surveyors could bring to the field of planning were published during this period. Competitions, exhibitions, and publications were extensively reviewed, as were the developments in the field of pro-

59 Idem.

60 Strinz in association with Dauer, Düren's Stadtbaumeister, participated in the competition for the planning of the area, which was formerly occupied by the military cantonment Sterntor, and their project was awarded the first prize in 1909, see R. Schultze, "Der Wettbewerb um den Bebauungsplan des ehemaligen Sterntorkasernengeländes zu Bonn", *Der Städtebau,* 1909.

61 See Plähn, "Architekten und Landmesser, Zum Bebauungsplan von Gross Berlin", *Zeitschrift für Vermessungswesen,* 1 August 1910, p. 592-595.

62 Alfred Abendroth, *Der Landmesser im Städtebau. Praktisches Handbuch zur sachgemäßen Erledigung der landmesserischen Geschäfte im Gemeindedienst.* Berlin, 1909, p. VII.

63 See Oliver Karnau, *Hermann Josef Stübben – Städtebau 1876-1930,* Wiesbaden,1996, p. 80

fessional training.[64] This points out a vigorous effort to promote the professional identity of surveyors in the field of urban planning, both from an internal and external perspective.

The Surveyors' Practice and Town Planning

At the end of the nineteenth century, the great move of cadastral survey and assessment linked to territorial expansion, especially in East Prussia, and to the agricultural reform, was completed at large, and by the 1880s the ad hoc administrations had ceased to enrol surveyors.[65] In contrast, the state and the municipalities' administrations had taken over increased responsibilities to promote and to cope with industrialised services, from the railways to the urban infrastructures, providing new opportunities for those with professional and technical qualifications. In the view of the surveyors' federation, improved education with a level of qualification that would compare favourably with engineers was an important goal to achieve for gaining access to an increasingly industrial and urbanised environment. The two major Prussian educational institutions in Berlin and Bonn, which were preparing for the state's examination in surveying entitling the "Landmesser" to enter the civil service or to practice freely, with their acts carrying official value, were answerable to the Ministry of Agriculture.[66] This training, in spite of courses being given in geodesy from 1880, was, however, not recognised as on equal footing with the Institutes of Technology that were allowed to deliver the doctors' degrees from 1899 onward. In this context, the Surveyors federation's strategy clearly aimed at extending the legitimacy of surveyors' practice. The *Zeitschrift für Vermessungswesen* drew attention to the career prospects for surveyors in city administrations thanks to the developing field of town planning and to the need for accurate topographical as well as for conciliation of the interest of land properties while preparing an urban development project.[67]

However, surveyors had to fight their case to participate as peers in planning matters with already well entrenched "Baumeister", engineers and architects. To this effect they tirelessly developed several type of arguments. The first was that the surveyor is by far the best informed about topographical as well as cadastral details, and that plans can be made effective only if details are sufficiently precise and up to date. The second argument proceeds from the first one: through his practice, the surveyor develops an intimate knowledge of the place; he is the best informed about natural and geographic conditions, land-tenure and parcelling traditions. Implicit is the idea that topography in its larger sense remains the cornerstone of planning, with architecture being de facto a secondary aspect. In those years German surveyors were also attentive to the raising movement for the "Denkmalpflege", willing to preserve monuments and historical buildings. They argued that historical built environment is not evenly distributed in space, and that groups of old trees, ponds, watercourses, hills, rocks, etc. could also have an "historic" character and deserve special care and attention, since they constitute a whole environment that can come under the concept of "Natur-Denkmal". "Natur-Denkmäler" are therefore a kind of territorial starting point that can be found basically everywhere and used to advantage when encompassed in the planning process.[68] The third argument concerns the central function of planning as a technique for mediating between private and public interests. The surveyors' offensive came at a time when the costs of development schemes were closely taken into account by the officials in charge of city treasuries. The dominance of landed interests, an only emerging comprehensive legislation, and active

64 Our probe concerns especially the journal *Zeitschrift für Vermessungswesen,* between the years 1904 -1912.

65 By German, we refer to the area of the German Empire (1871-1918). But the great variety in the status, professional education and organization of the land surveyors among the states of the German Empire ought to be stressed.

66 These schools were the Königliche Landwirtschaftliche Hochschule in Berlin and the Königliche Landwirtshaftliche Akademie, in Bonn-Poppelsdorf. The first institution was allowed to deliver the Doctor's degree in1918, while the second one became a Hochschule in 1919 only.

67 See in particular Bolck, "Der Geometer im Städtebau, insbesondere die Bearbeitung der Bebauungspläne durch den Landmesser, *Zeitschrift für Vermessungswesen,* 1906, 11 December, p.916-928.

68 See Bornhofen, "Erhaltung landschaftlicher Schönheiten bei der Bearbeitung von Fluchtlinienplänen", *Zeitschrift für Vermessungswesen,* 15 July 1904, p. 408-413.

speculation often combined to bring the planning process to a standstill. At the same time, planning and the extension of municipal activities were, at the turn of the century, more and more widely accepted in an effort to rein on private interests and to maintain social stability. At this juncture, surveyors came to apply and develop the new provisions for "Umlegung" (land consolidation), and the techniques designed to improve land-use efficiency—the City's Council of Frankfurt had adopted provisions for "Umlegung" in 1902. On this occasion, Franz Adickes, then head of the municipal council of that city, had been particularly praised by the Deutscher Geometer Verein for having introduced the statutory participation of the surveyors in the commissions in charge of the town plan.[69] Finally, it was put forward that the surveyor was both technically and culturally equipped to make the most of the cultural-social-economic setting enshrined in spatiality, with the more or less clearly spelt-out implication that engineers were too ensconced in the problematic of infrastructure, reducing cities to a system of networks, and architects too obsessed with the creation of three-dimensional superstructures.

Historicity and 'Umlegung'

Strinz significantly contributed to the debates and proposals revolving around the transformation of land use, at a time when the movement for land reform and the "Gartenstadtgesellschaft" (1902) aimed at solving the housing question. His expertise in the technicalities of "Zusammenlegung"— in particular in estimating the effect of replotting and of creation of public space on land value, and the assessment of optimum plot size relative to location—was noted by his colleagues and probably had a much larger audience through his articles on that topic in the journal *Der Städtebau*.[70] Strinz characterised the German planning of the years 1872 to 1890 as dominated by what he called "monumental Städtebau". According to him, this monumental type of planning did not give its full due to the specificity of each location and had favoured high speculation, endangering the financial balance of municipalities and contributing significantly to housing shortages. He therefore presented the second wave of Städtebau as closely linked to a strong social demand for decent working-class housing with access to cultural, educational and health amenities, and to a new vision of living closer to nature, with plenty of air and of light.[71] It is from this perspective that Karl Strinz's involvement in the planning debate has also to be appreciated.

A possible explanation of the dilemma for surveyors is the following. Sitte's approach to the historicity of land use and to the traditional patterns of human settlement could be a powerful argument to justify a larger call in town planning on the expertise of surveyors. On the other hand Sitte and especially his followers made no mystery of their project to give a central role to the architects, the masters of the three-dimensional approach—therefore implicitly or explicitly sidelining surveyors. However, it was even worse when Sitte himself opposed the "Zusammenlegung" process, precisely when it had become the surveyors' main argument for being involved in town planning. Theodor Goecke published in *Der Städtebau* an article by Sitte explaining that land consolidation schemes were not such an advisable thing after all and concluding that streets should adapt to existing parcelling and not the other way round.[72] This was followed by Stübben's critical article on "Städtebau plan, Enteignung und Umlegung", arguing that such a complex approach to planning and design would practically bring the implantation of any plan to a complete standstill.[73]

69 See Block, op. cit. Franz Adickes (1846-1915) was Oberbürgermeister (Lord Mayor)of Frankfurt a. M. from 1891 to 1912, and the City's law, Gesetz betrefend die Umlegung von Gründstücken, from 28 July 1902, attached to his name, has been the model for framing similar legislation in Prussia.

70 See K. Strinz, "Die gesetzliche Regelung der Baulandumlegung", *Der Städtebau*, 1905, p. 135-138, and "Die günstigste Form und Tiefe der Baublöcke in wirtschaftlicher Beziehung", *Der Städtebau*, 1907, pp. 38-40, 46-50, 59-62.

71 See K. Strinz, "Die historische Entwicklung des Siedlungsgedankens", *Zeitschrift für Vermessungswesen*, 15 October 1920, p. 674-682.

72 Camillo Sitte died on 16 November 1903, and the first issue of *Der Stätdtebau* was published in January 1904. See Camillo Sitte, "Enteignungsgesetz und Lageplan" *Der Städtebau*, 1904, p 5-8, p. 17-19, p. 35-39.

73 Joseph Stübben, "Stadtbauplan, Enteignung und Umlegung", *Der Städtebau*, 1904, p. 127-130.

Strinz entered the debate at that stage and was to be instrumental in attempting to elaborate a compromise position. Strinz accepted Sitte's criticism of "Umlegung" as well founded, and even displayed case studies as examples.[74] Not only could land consolidation be useless or unjust for some owners, it could also bring back the schematic tendency widely condemned in former planning practice. Strinz was nonetheless critical of a systematic rejection of consolidation schemes, seeing land consolidation as a necessity in extension planning and as an improvement in spatial distribution without necessarily modifying the traditional patterns and "Stimmung" (atmosphere) of the place.[75] For him, the surveyors' key expertise was in finding the middle ground between existing parcelling and transformational choices, their technical capacity being a guarantee against unsuitable patterns and parcelling sizes, and at the same time fully taking account of the morphogenesis of the place.

Through his writings and his career, Strinz illustrates the swift development of the modern town planning municipal movement in the first decade of the twentieth century. Appointed in Düren in 1895, he belongs to the first wave of town surveyors that emerged in the Rhineland and in Westphalia in 1880-1890. By 1906, there were some 30 head-surveyors and 200 land surveyors in Prussia's municipalities.[76] His success in several competitions as well as his numerous publications made him an important mouthpiece of the profession. At this point, when leading architects of the Sittian current were trying to exclude surveyors from planning, or more precisely to restrict them to the role of mere "providers of survey drawings", the competitions constituted a major issue for the profession. The polemic went open, particularly when Hermann Jansen (1865-1945), editor of *Der Baumeister* and winner of the Greater Berlin competition, made surveyors historically responsible for all the mis- planning in the capital of the Reich. The *Zeitschrift für Vermessungswesen* had already replied several times to this type of arguments, pointing out that there were "Baumeister" and not surveyors who used to be in charge of topographical plans that mostly turned out to be useless because of their inaccuracy.[77] In the later case of Berlin, the topographical documents drawn up in 1876 were of uncontested quality, however the surveyors had not been involved in the planning project.[78] Concerning Jansen's plan, the *Zeitschrift für Vermessungswesen* balanced Strinz's plan for Copenhagen favourably, including its careful study of urban peripheral railways, with the Jansen's beautiful but prohibitively costly project for Berlin.[79] Nothing was said of Strinz's project for Berlin. The polemic raged on during the following years.[80] The threat of a boycott of the Canberra competition by Australian architects, endorsed by sections of the German professional bodies, was to be another bone of contention in the pre-war period.[81] If Strinz's entry for the Berlin competition had been practically ignored in Germany, his "Urania" entry in Copenhagen was a stepping stone in the offensive of the German surveyors in the period from 1903 to 1910 to be accepted as equal players in the planning process. By giving lectures in 1919 at the seminar on town planning, which Joseph Brix and Felix Genzmer had established at the Berlin Technische Hochschule, Strinz was closed to his aim embodied in the petition of 1908.[82]

74 K. Strinz, "Die gesetziche Regelung der Baulandumlegung", op. cit.

75 This was developed in parallel to the above article in K. Strinz, "Die Weitermittlung der Baugrundstücke und die Umlegung solcher Grundstücke auf Grund ihres Wertverhältnisses", *Zeitschrift für Vermessungswesen*, 1 April 1905, p. 201-211 & 11 April 1905, p. 225-239.

76 *Zeitschrift für Vermessungswesen*, 1906, 15 October, p. 920.

77 Block, *Der Geometer… op.cit.*, p. 926.

78 For the full argument concerning also the former Hobrecht project, see Hempel " Die Schönheit der Landschaft und Liebe zur Heimat", *Zeitschrift für Vermessungswesen*, 11 July 1910, p. 532-538.

79 Idem.

80 See Meincke, "Landmesser und Stadterweiterung", *Zeitschrift für Vermessungswesen*, 21 April 1911, p.348-350.

81 The Australian jury grouped an architect, an engineer and a surveyor alike: Arnemann, "Architekten und Landmesser", *Zeitschrift für Vermessungswesen*, 1 March 1912, p. 191-195.

82 We identified two conferences entitled, Die Beschaffung der Planunterlagen für Bebauungs-und Fluchtlinienplänen, and, Vermessungstechnischen Aufgaben bei der Durchführung des Stadtbaupläne.

2.3 Sitte's Followers in 1909

Hans Bernoulli

The Swiss architect from Basel, who had followed an architectural education in Munich, Karlsruhe and Darmstad, had been living and working in Berlin since 1902, where he set up his firm with Louis Rinkel in 1903.[83] It is in this context, that he decided to take part in the Copenhagen competition. It seems that Sitte's work had already influenced him at the time. He had helped his fellow Swiss student, later archaeologist and architect, Camille Martin (1877-1928), to translate *Der Städtebau*.[84] It is known that Martin's almost complete "reinvention" of Sitte's book through translation contributed to the perception of the Austrian architect as a "medievalist planner" among francophone professionals. But Bernoulli architectural work does not seems to land much concession to a historicist leaning. His early production was rather in tune with what was then termed in Switzerland as "traditional master-builder architecture", including some strong rural accents. This trend can be seen in his first garden-city projects in Berlin, Potsdam, and Frankfurt. However, this middling traditionalism, also influenced by Hermann Muthesius (1861-1927), soon receded in regard to his interest in classicism and some form of metropolitan architecture. In Berlin he elaborated a sober and modernist architecture, as illustrated by several projects for rental and commercial housing.[85] While Bernoulli was an assistant at the Brix and Genzmer's seminar at Charlottenburg from 1907 to 1909, where Sitte's influence still prevailed at that time, he developed a strong interest for the movement for social housing, an interest he maintained throughout his career. He wrote a number of articles published in *Der Städtebau* and in *Gartenstadt*, in particular the article "Die neue Stadt", where he exposed his views about urban reforms and the social and cultural purpose of the garden-city concept.[86]

The participation of Hans Bernoulli in the Copenhagen competition is quite notable considering the low level of publicity about this event in the German professional press, surveyors excluded. But, in the lack of any information in relation to his entry, the circumstances of his participation can only be surmised.[87] Some authors mention a study tour by Bernoulli in Copenhagen around 1901[88], and the inventory of his sketchbooks confirms his passage in Stralsund, Copenhagen and Rostock in 1908-1909.[89] After his arrival in Berlin, Bernoulli took part in many competitions involving architectural projects. However, his first participation in a town-extension scheme seems to have been in 1907, for the eastern extension of Mannheim, with Karl Strinz being among the competitors. Again, like Strinz, he went on to enter the Copenhagen and Berlin competitions in the following years. In that sense one can say that, together with his participation in the Brix-Genzmer seminar, the Copenhagen competition represented for Bernoulli the beginning of a career marked by a close connection between social reform and architectural and planning problematic.

Per Olaf Hallman

The Swedish architect is credited with having early introduced German-type planning to Sweden, namely the works of Joseph Stübben and Camillo Sitte.[90] His

83 See Manfred Jauslin, " Hans Bernoulli", in I. Ruck & D. Huber, *Architekten lexikon der Schweiz 19/20 Jhr*, 1998, p. 51-53. Also Werner Schmid, *Hans Bernoulli, Städtbauer-Politiker, Weltbürger*, Schaffhausen, 1974.

84 This is reported by G.R. & C. Collins, *Camillo Sitte. op. cit.*, p. 133. It should be noted that Martin and Bernoulli wrote much later: *L'Urbanisme en Suisse*, Neuchatel, 1929.

85 Klaus K. Weber "Hans Bernoulli in Berlin (1902-1912)", *Archithèse*, (6), November /December 1981, p. 10-12.

86 Hans Bernoulli: "Die neue Stadt", in *Gartenstadt, Mitteilungen der deutschen Gartenstadtgesellschaft*, 1911, p.109.

87 For an extensive account of Bernoulli's works see Karl und Maya Nägelind-Gschwind, *Hans Bernoulli. Architekt und Städtebauer*, Basel, 1995. However, Bernoulli's entry to the Copenhagen competition is not mentioned. Likewise, there are no records in the GTA Archives of Zurich with respect to Bernoulli's participation in the Copenhagen competition.

88 M. Jauslin, "Hans Bernoulli" op.cit.

89 Ulrike Jehle-Schulte Strathaus und Markus Stegmann, *Hans Bernoulli-Aus den skizzenbüchern, Architekturmuseum Basel*, Basel, 1996, p. 125-139.

90 For a general introduction see Thomas Hall, "Urban Planning in Sweden", in T.Hall (ed.), *Planning and Urban growth in the Nordic Countries*, London,1991, p. 176-187. See also the interpretation of Bjorn Linn, "Sitte secondo una pro-

early career epitomises the swiftness of the diffusion-cum-adaptation of Sitte's ideas. There were only a couple of years between Hallman's post-graduate year spent in Berlin (1893) and his study-trip report on new planning tendencies in Europe (1895). His communication about the principles of town layouts to the Nordic Technique Congress, held in 1897, was widely commented in the Swedish press for having strongly emphasised the 'modern planning ideas' as developed by Stübben, Sitte and Henrici in order to criticise the prevalent practice at home. While presenting the advantages and drawbacks of different types of layouts (radial, triangular, etc.), he pleaded for a close collaboration between architects and engineers, and went on discussing the production of urban monumentality in relation to open space in reference to the new literature of the 'German school' by quoting E. Genzmer. He also discussed the conservation of old buildings of historic interest, and showed sketches of the "old Stockholm" to illustrate that the restructuring of old districts need not necessarily entail pulling down old structures.[91] Hallman's intervention came at the time when a new radical proposal for regulating and clearing the core city of Stockholm (Gamla Stan) was put forward by the City's administration. But the issue aroused a vivid opposition calling for the respect of the 'historic city'.[92] In relation to the Gothenburg competition, the Danish journal *Architekten* published an article by Hallman in 1901 that presented a synthesis of his views on planning, with which we come in some details.[93]

The article approaches planning as a surveying and a resource-mobilisation problem and calls for distinguishing old methods of planning from new ones. Constituting potential assets as they do, topography, landmarks, existing built and non-built elements ought to be given their full due in the plan. It is assumed that all that is artificial entails a cost: therefore artificiality must be methodically reduced, and a proper study of the contour lines of a topographical map can drastically reduce earthworks. Natural vegetation should also be integrated in the layout of new parks, thus securing the immediate presence of old trees. Geological configurations should also be duly assessed and taken into account to avoid mistakes in the location of buildings or roads. Hallman claimed that this "new planning" was coming to the fore. Old planning was simplistic and schematic, Westeras being quoted as example, in contrast to new plans established by Professor E. Jacobssons, a successful attempt at restoring complexity, and by City-engineer A. Nilsson for Malmö, taking full account of the natural environment. It followed from all this that old built structures should be preserved and transmitted, for they reflect a time where building was an "art of building".

In fact, as we shall see closer in the following chapters, these ideas are not particularly "Sittian". By far, the main emphasis concerns what we might call "environmental conservation", paving the way for an early junction with the garden-city movement that was emerging in Sweden by that time. However, references to Sitte do stand in the background as general guidelines concerning the problem of "monumentality" in town planning. Hallman then warns against the danger of agoraphobia when designing large squares, insists on problems of scaling in built forms and on the advisability of grouping cluster of monuments. In 1901 Hallman together with Fredrik Sundbärg had won the first prize with their entry named "Natur och Kunst" (nature and art) at the competition for the extension of Gothenburg. In 1907, the Gamla Enskede project, an urban development scheme south of Stockholm, applied the principles of landscaped adaptive design, adjusted to "bared land". Such a project of a garden suburb was applauded by Raymond Unwin, one of the founding fathers of the garden-city concept, and published in *Der Städtebau*.[94] It was widely commented in Scandinavia, A. Bjerre writing a laudatory report

spettiva svedese" in Guido Zucconi (ed.), *Camillo Sitte e i suoi interpreti,* Milano,1992, p.184-191.

91 Per O.Hallman, "Principerna för anläggandet eller utvidgandet af en stad eller stadsdel", *Förhandlingarna vid Nordiska Teknikermötet i Stockholm, 15-19 juni 1897,* Stockholm, 1898, p. 170-174.

92 On this issue and the shift in attitudes toward Gamla Stan, see Gösta Selling, *Hur Gamla stan överlevde,* Stockholm, 1973, especially p. 45-72.

93 P. O. Hallman, "De nya stadsplaneideerna föredrag vid gefle teknikermöte 1901" , *Architekten,* 15 August 1901, p. 287-292.

94 On this project see Heleni Porfyriou, "Artistic urban design and cultural myths: the garden city idea in Nordic countries, 1900-1925", *Planning Perspectives,* (7) , 1992, pp. 263-301, esp. p. 271-272.

in *Maanedsskrift for Sundhdspleje* in 1908. Although Hallman was not among the winners, his participation seven years later in the Copenhagen competition—this time worked out with the collaboration of engineers—came as his position as a leading planner was already well established; in 1909 he was town planning adviser to the Stockholm's town plan commission established the same year.

Fredrik Sundbärg

The career of this Swedish architect is closely parallel to Hallman's in articulating the rising influence of professional planners with the new Austrian – German syllabus of planning. His article about town plans history published in the magazine *Ord och Bild* in 1897 is a thorough introduction to Sitte's principles with a wealth of examples, also taken from Nordic countries. Article's references also include Karl Henrici's plans for Dessau and Munich and J. Stübben's *Der Städtebau.* Bearing witness to the development of the new trends in Sweden, Sundbärg refers to Per Hallman, to Gustav Lindgren's proposal for the old city of Stockholm, to Eugen Thorburn's project for Gothenburg, and to the writers Georg Nordensvan and Ellen Fries. Sundbärg concentrates on Sitte's aesthetic principles of urban architectonics. But he also considers conservation as such, calling for a stop to ongoing campaigns of destruction, in particular the medieval city walls of Visby. For him new planning methods ought to be developed through "friluftsarbate" ("outdoor work"), and encompass all dimensions of culture and not only legal and administrative procedures.[95] It is apparent that Hallman and Sundbärg decisively contributed to inflect the orientation of Nordic planning between 1894 and 1897, at a time when industrial cities were undergoing rapid extension in Scandinavia, and they successfully demonstrated the value of the new paradigms in their 1901 Gothenburg entry.

It should be stressed that both architects prepared their Copenhagen entries in collaboration with engineers. As has been demonstrated for Sweden, engineers together with surveyors were by far the strongest professional group involved in planning.[96] The new paradigms for planning, reinforcing the need for a three-dimensional approach of urban space, helped in the last years of the nineteenth to give credibility to the commitment of architects for a better city, moving away from wild industrialisation and urban development. But engineers also embraced the news ideas, questioning the former methods used to generate city forms, and were ready to integrate them into their own planning practice.

2.4 Engineers in Design Practice

For the "Stor-Kjøbenhavn" project, Sundbärg associated himself with engineer Albert Lilienberg who had previously worked in Hallman's firm, and been involved with the city-planning board of Chicago and Philadelphia before becoming chief city engineer in Gothenburg in 1907.[97] Lilienberg's input in the design of infrastructure networks can be strongly felt in the Copenhagen entry (See Chapter 4). This little-noted event in his biography, as well as his participation in the 1910 London Town Planning conference were nonetheless important stepping stones for his career, before he became one of the main mouthpieces of the Swedish planning profession.

How swiftly the new planning paradigms were taken up can also be observed in the entries designed by Gellersted and Hübe. Gellersted & Bergman's award-winning entry for Hälsingbor in 1906 had been applauded by Th. Goecke and singled out by *Architektur*

95 Frederik Sundbärg, "Om stadsplaner med särskild hänsyn till svenska förhållanden", *Ord och Bild*, 1897, p.145-160 & 193-213.

96 During the years 1850-1910, engineers and surveyors accounted for more than two-third of the professionals involved in town planning, and the surveyors might has been underestimated: See Thomas Hall, *Planning... op.cit.*, p. 184.

97 Stadsarkivet, Ejendomsdirektorat, sag EJ 1150 /1925: letter from M. Nyrop to Magistratens 2. Afdeling, dated 15 May 1909: " Fredrik Sundbärg, who participated in the competition visitedme. He is City architect in Lanskrona. He worked on the proposal "Stor-Kjøbenhavn", which I believed was a German project, in collaboration with Lilienberg, City engineer in Gothenburg..." (our translation). For a biography of A. Lilienberg, see I. Hasselgréen, G. Sidenbladh, "Lillienberg, Albert", in E. Grill og Lager-Kromnow (red.) *Svensk biografiskt Lexikon*, Stockholm, 1977-79, p. 775-79.

och Dekorativ Kunst as a specific example of the progress of new planning ideas in the Nordic countries.[98]

The case of Bjerknes is another good example of this evolution. With the support of Christiana's City Council, he had travelled extensively in 1904 to study what we have called Austro-German town planning. In 1907, he made a second study trip to examine the layout of industrial districts in Germany. By then he had became an advocate of the "modern German town planning principles" in a series of articles and lectures in 1905-1906. He was a staunch supporter of Sitte's ideas and of Henrici's planning options for Munich, strongly criticising the municipal planning options for Kristiana (Oslo), on aesthetic as well as economic grounds. His participation in the Copenhagen competition coincided with his departure from the town planning commission of Kristiana City. He then started his own engineering firm of consultant, and was to exert important influence on planning in Norway, participating in competitions' juries and in numerous urban projects.

By 1900, the ability to articulate new types of design practice was comforting professional credentials for architects and engineers alike. However, this "Austro-German" influence was soon merged with other trends, like Frederick Law Olmsted's type of landscaping, the eighteen-century tradition of picturesque gardens, the nineteen-century experiments of "green" company towns. By 1905, the garden-city idiom was being adapted to the physical and social environment of Nordic countries. The landscaping design, where the importance of built forms and stylistic questions gradually receded behind the arrangement of hill slopes, parks, plantations, the integration of lakes and open spaces, was a safer ground for civil engineers. Gellerstedt's near success for Canberra in 1912 clearly shows this evolution. The Austrian-German model was no more the sole reference for Swedish planners in the 1910s, engineers or architects. Even the plans of Hallman could feature a "slightly stereotyped picturesque".[99] Thus, the Austrian-German type of planning could be seen as having been in the focus of attention in the Nordic countries between 1893 and 1900 with an implementation phase from 1901 till 1908, after which other paradigms prevailed even if some flagrance of the years of "romantic planning" remained in plans for many years after the First World War. In comparison with drawings more committed to the Civic Art stream in the Copenhagen competition, the Swedish entries did not emphasised a much strong and comprehensive conservation paradigm. Besides the already mentioned Danish-Swedish rivalry, this may also explain the relatively poor results reached by prime Swedish planners in the 1909 Competition.

2.5 'Modernismo' and Planning

The architect Ferran Romeu belonged to the Catalan 'Modernismo' trend, a local version of Art Nouveau with nationalist overtones. He was close to architect, art historian and politician Josep Puig i Cadafalch (1869-1956), a leading figure with Antoni Gaudi and Lluis Domenech i Montaner of the "Art Nouveau" movement. In 1913, Romeu was involved with Luis Domènech and Cadafalq in a project aiming at improving access to the old city of Barcelona, which advised an "organic layout" of the main connecting street to respect the monumental and archaeological value of the site.[100] In 1917, Cadafalq was named President of the regional government of Catalonia, and Romeu was commissioned with his colleagues E. Porcel and F. Falqués to modify and prepare the implementation of the "Plano General de Urbanization de Barcelona".

Before Romeu submitted his proposal at the Copenhagen competition, he had been awarded the second prize in the international competition for the extension of Barcelona, won by Léon Jaussely in 1905.[101] It should be stressed that his approach and

98 See *Der Städtebau*, 1906, pp. 43-46 and *Arkitektur och Dekorativ Konst*, 1906.

99 According to Thomas Hall, "Urban Planning in Sweden", *op.cit.*, p. 193.

100 See Joan Ganau, "Town Planning and Conservationist Policies in the Historic City Centre of Barcelona (1860-1930)", *Planning History*, Vol. 19, n. 2/3, 1997, p. 23-31.

101 On this project, see Manuel de Torres i Capell, "Barcelona: planning problems and practices in the Jaussely era, 1900-1930", *Planning Perspective*, (7), 1992, p. 211-233. The contribution of the Jaussely project to early urbanism is also discussed by O. Soubeyran, "L'écologie urbaine de Jaussely

design could not have been more alien to the prevailing Nordic conception of the time. Though Romeu was to be involved in other important planning projects, his participation in the Copenhagen competition seems to have been unique in regard to international contests.[102]

ou la maïeutique du milieu", in V. Berdoulay & O.Soubeyran, *L'Ecologie urbaine et l'urbanisme-Aux fondements des enjeux actuels,* Paris, 2002, p. 147-176.

102 See Thomas Hall, "Urban Planning in Sweden", *op.cit.*, pp. 184-185. Also, Hans Bjur, *Stadplanering kring 1900 med exempel från Göteborg och Albert Lilienbergs verksamhet,* Göteborg,1984.

PART II

EXTENSION PLANNING IN THE AGE OF HISTORICISM

The two following chapters consider the 1909 Competition for the greater Copenhagen from the unique standpoint of the design strategy put forward by planners. More specifically, we will consider the design methods developed by competitors in order to achieve an equilibrium between the existing urban area and the new, projected environment.

The strategies for building 'the modern city' and the devices employed to preserve its existing core as well as to retain elements of its inherited surroundings have not developed as two worlds apart. Chapter 4 analyses the efforts undertaken by planners in developing an integrated and dynamic relationship between two polarities of planning: transformation and creation on the one hand, and conservation and integration on the other.[1] The main focus here is to investigate how the will to safeguard the built environment informs early twentieth century planners' design. We do so by analysing the graphic and written documents of the entries to the Competition. Chapter 5 concentrates exclusively on complementary comments on the bases of a selection of graphic documents assembled in thematic sets.

Until recently, the importance of graphic documents to study the development of planning has been neglected for different reasons. Firstly, as already noted, archives barely leave us with a complete set of plans. This tends to reinforce the award bias whereby interesting entries are supposedly the winning ones. This bias gives an oversimplified picture of planning ideas and doctrines according to set of 'successful' plans. Secondly, within the field of planning itself, the status of design and of plans — understood as representations of a projected territory — has been constantly declining. After World War II, planning has been more and more understood as a continuous process and as a framework for decision-making within a general strategy de-linked from any doctrine of physical formal embodiment. It is only fairly recently that the role of urban design began to be reasserted as a disciplinary field within which 'urban projects' could be elaborated; a rejuvenated urban morphology being eventually mobilised as an exploratory tool.[2] Thirdly, the syndrome of the 'award bias' has combined with the relatively falling status of design within planning, to produce another kind of distortion. It is implicitly inferred that the distance between the plan

1 We link conservation with the purpose of integrating, using, and eventually enhancing historic buildings, group of buildings and sites. A large room is accordingly open to creation. By preservation we refer to the option of maintaining a historic structure, or artefact, as it currently stands in all respects whatever its stage of decay. Within cities, 'segments' can sometimes be preserved, but the city as such could only be 'conserved' or, more rightly formulated, 'safeguarded'. For an in-depth discussion on the issue see Peter J. Larkham, *Conservation and the city,* London and N.Y., 1996, p.15-59. On alternative versions of conservation according to urban cultures see Anthony M. Tung, *Preserving the World's great cities-The destruction and renewal of the historic metropolis,* New York, 2001.

2 For instance, some authors define the urban project as a possible instrument to articulate the distinct scales of the city and of architecture, and the strength of the project relies on urban and contextual conventions. See David Mangin and Philippe Panerai, *Projet Urbain*, Marseille, 1999.

and its physical implementation would be the ultimate testing ground to judge the quality of the plan. The same rationale can be turned the other way round, the rare conformity of implementation schemes with up-stream projects being the proof of the failure of an 'out-dated' phase of planning doctrines.

The point here is not to negate the changing status of design as an auxiliary technique within the planning discipline. On the contrary, our aim is to 'historicize' towns plans as techniques of representation conveying knowledge and ideas about an evolving urban fabric. For most of the early planners, town plans were not the simple translation of architectural drawings. The change of scale inferred by the shift from plot scale to city scale was precisely the neuralgic centre whereby different professions came to claim their key expertise. Therefore, the role played by urban design within the field of planning needs to be put into the proper perspective. One can interpret plans as "complex objects".[3] They present simultaneously a combination of form proposals bounded in locality, the fragmented reflections of ideal models and finally the fixed image, the representation of a possible and advisable political and social consensus on a given city. The modelling of this object might be quite differently structured according to the institutional context in which the plan is produced. Plans could be designed by the technical services of the municipalities, elaborated by contracted consultants, or resulting from a national or international competition. In the latter case, the complexity of the object remains. The plans were still a 'fixed image' whereby planners acted as mediators trying to reflect some of the expectations more less articulated within the urban community. However, this intervened in a specific context whereby competitors ought to have maximised the effect of the tremendous work effort they invested in making a plan. This general framework tended to favour seductive moves relaying on the adaptation of ideal models likely to gather wide acknowledgement, notwithstanding the concocting of subtler long-term strategies, whereby plans could first and foremost expressed theoretical standpoints.

The two following chapters assess the unfolding of a course within town planning which might be brought under the umbrella of 'Civic Art Design', the aim of which was also linked to the development of an integrated strategy of planning incorporating strong elements of conservation. Our purpose is essentially to address planners' creativity in relation to urban conservation and more largely to the idea of ' urban continuity'.[4]

The presence of a strong 'conservation paradigm' in most of the entries seems at first largely verified. Of course, jury members such as Martin Nyrop or Hack Kampmann who had been leading figures of the 'national romantic' movement could not but be sympathetic to those orientations partly formulated in the competition programme. Those architects had contributed much, perhaps not in quantity but in quality, in shaping the post-international Beaux-Art stream in Denmark. They were receptive to plans expressing the uniqueness of place, searching for the continuity of system of meaning and paying respect to authenticity and aesthetic wholeness.

Most of the entries suggest the pervading influence of a trend committed to ethical as well as aesthetic values grounded in the continuity of cultural 'heritage'. A great deal of effort was put into sustaining these values and translating them into design proposals. However, beyond this common ground we have seen a wide plurality of approaches. The frequent allusion to the dominance of the 'Sittian' school is indicative of a line of thought. Yet we shall see that it does not give sufficient account of the complexity of urban design of the time. In the third part of this book we will insist on the fact that Sitte's ideas and principles

3 On this aspect, see André Lortie, "Dessins de villes et destins de plans", *Quels Desseins pour les villes, De quelques objets de planification pour l'urbanisme de l'entre-deux-guerres*, Paris, Dossiers TTS, Ministère de l'Equipement, du Logement et des Transports, n° 20/21, 1992, p. 285-293.

4 Looking for 'urban continuity' can be broadly defined as a conscious effort to take into account existing site and built environment in elaborating the urban project. This also comprehends both the maintenance and the ongoing change of the built environment. History of urban development can be approached as a succession of waves of continuity and rupture. 'Continuity' does not describe a particular formal way of producing, or for that matter conserving the city. It rather indicates a chief paradigm of planners who chose to handle the relationship between 'form' and 'time'. See Marcel Roncayolo, *Lecture de villes, formes et temps*, Paris, 2002.

had a complex and rapidly evolving relation with extension planning. His contributions were soon filtered and developed into systems by 'disciples'. In the meantime segments of those ideas were integrated into mainstream planning discipline. In fine, parts of the remaining message were transferred into an already prevalent design style, often pertaining a much closer relation with eighteenth-century picturesque and Arcadian cultural tradition than with the criteria put forward by the 'urban' and even 'mineral'-inclined Camillo Sitte. Therefore we propose using the umbrella of Civic Art to refer to an early trend, which had consciously decided to take into account, but not necessarily to privilege, this dimension of planning and to integrate it in its design. We shall acknowledge at least three types of orientation.

The 'conservationist' tendency looked for a kind of formal continuity between inherited forms and newly built environment. The 'middle range' tendency leaned toward a compromise between these guidelines and 'modern' requirements. If existing forms should make their way into the future, they ought to be, nevertheless, transformed and modelled according to contemporaneous needs. It seems that this trend of planners perceived their contemporary time as a period of transition toward modernity. The 'preservationist' inclination acknowledged the irreversibility of modernity together with its disgraces and promises. Therefore they put a high value on knowing the past and on transmitting a heritage, which should be pragmatically and theoretically defined and educate the goals of this modernity. In line with the post–Viollet-le-Duc rationale for restoration, they were opposed to 'creative' aspects of conservation that transformed inherited artefacts as well as landscapes. This typology grounded in the analysis of the plans of the 1909 Competition is only indicative and might not encompass all the variety of orientations within Civic Art design. Moreover, each tendency is seldom expressed as a comprehensive strategy. Various elements pertaining to different orientations can be combined, thus generating a wealth of highly differentiated projects.

4

CIVIC ART DESIGN AND THE GREAT CITY

1 Conservation in Town Planning

Importantly, planning cannot be thought of as a theory or practice that developed in a linear manner.[1] Rather, it should be considered a highly complex and contradictory social activity embedded in time, place and symbolic representations. Design attempts which have not been realised should therefore be not only considered a part of urban and planning history but also as significant testimonies of diverging views on what might be a 'Great city'. Plans are the partial achievements of professions striving to forge a cultural image of an emerging city.

The 1908 Copenhagen Competition has given rise to a number of comments. They refer to the finalists of the Competition and their designs, while the entries submitted by the other competitors have only rarely been discussed or even mentioned. The complete list of the entries had actually never been published since the Competition was held, not even in 1909. This book often refers to the few works that have discussed the Competition, and it is therefore of relevance to specify the general scope of these studies in relation to the present contribution.

Officers of the municipality made the first comprehensive analysis. Engineer Olaf Forchhammer, head of the Stadsingeniørens Direktorat in 1936-1951, made an evaluation of the planning of Copenhagen from 1901 onwards, as we already mentioned. In order to draw guidelines for the coming developments after the Second World War, Forchhammer found it opportune to assess the outcomes of the Competition in relation to the schemes that were implemented in the 1910-1930s. One chapter in the book, published by his office in 1942, reviews the four-awarded entries and takes into account the creative features in the submissions of Alfred J. Raavad and Egil Fischer.[2] The famous planner and architect Steen Eiler Rasmussen made the next important reference to the Competition, in the 1960s. In his souvenirs, Rasmussen refers to Bjerre's endeavour to implement a circular ring of large boulevards in "Haussmann's grand manner", as well as to the abandonment of large parts of Strinz's project, especially a ring railway line linking the districts on the periphery. At a time of renewed interest for conservation schemes, Rasmussen payed close attention to the proposal that E. Fischer had put forward in order to deflect the traffic from the 'old city' toward the place called Jarmers Tårn. The other projects are, however, little discussed.[3] In his seminal study on the social, economical and political conditions in which town planning developed in Denmark at the end of the nineteenth century, Tim Knudsen discusses the changes that took place in 1900-1910 with the Competition as an illustration. According to Knudsen, it was a time when the architects attacked the gridiron planning together with the engineers' competence and entrenched power in the municipality. With the different styles of urban design, it was a contention for supremacy over professional control of the emerging field of town planning. While underlining the delicate political momentum that allowed the first breakthrough of planning ideas in Denmark, Knudsen set forth the limits of the whole exercise that

1 For a discussion about conceptual and instrumental development of planning, see Raphaël Fischler, "Toward a genealogy of planning: zoning and the Welfare State", *Planning Perspectives*, Vol. 13 (4), 1998, p. 389-410.

2 Olaf Forchhammer (Preface), *De indlemmede Distrikter byplanmæssige Udvikling 1901-1941*, Copenhagen, 1942, p. 21-30.

3 Steen E. Rasmussen, *København – et bysamfunds særpræg og udvikling gennem tiderne*, Copenhagen, 1994 (first ed. 1969), p. 139-143.

is the Competition. He also points to the mixed feelings that the contemporaries had concerning the idea of "Great Cities", which presumably did not allow the most innovative schemes to take sufficient social grounding for being implemented.[4] Bo Larsson and Ole Thomassen, in their study on "Urban Planning in Denmark", do mention the 1909 competition as a significant moment of town planning in Denmark. To them it was a time when a diffuse ideal of planning opposed "dense high-rise urban development", and they cite Strinz's plan, explaining that it was in line with the ideas of Camillo Sitte.[5] In the series of the *Byatlas*, which presents a great number of Danish cities with focus on morphological analysis and conservation, one volume is devoted to Copenhagen. The authors refer to the Competition to underline some particular urban forms of the present capital. They cite Bjerre's project to explain the localisation of industries on the east coast of Amager, along Sydhavn, and in Valby; they also mention Strinz's design to point to the "sinuous layout", which is a characteristic of some residential districts in Vigerslev and Utterslev, and they state:

"Flere af de mere fremsynede idéer fra forslagene f.eks. en forstads ringbane, blev aldrig gennemført, men på trods heraf må det konkluderes, at denne første store, internationalt udskrevne konkurrence for byens omegn har haft afgørende betydning for dens fysisk strukturer."[6]

The following paragraphs discuss attempts made by planners to address the then prevalent views on town extension in order to shape contemporary urban development and at the same time to make sense of the inherited fabric.

4 Tim Knudsen, *Storbyen støbes – København mellem kaos og byplan 1840-1917*, Copenhagen, 1988, p. 415-436.

5 Bo Larsson and Ole Thomassen, "Urban planning in Denmark", in Thomas Hall (ed.), *Planning and urban growth in the Nordic Countries*, London, New York, 1991, p. 7-59, esp.17-18.

6 "Most of the far-sighted proposals like a suburban ring railways were never implemented. Yet, one must say that the first significant international competition, which was organised for the neighbourhood of the city, have had great importance for the city's structure", in Jensen H. Toft (red.), *Byatlas København – bevaringsværdier i byer og bygninger, Skov- og Naturstyrelsen, kontoret for bybevaring*, Copenhagen, 1996, p. 68-69.

1.1 Town Planning's Dimensions

Coinciding with the second industrial revolution and the perceived inadequacy of social and spatial conditions in the burgeoning urban fabric the world over, town planning developed as a practice aimed at integrating recently developed technical fields, such as urban engineering, with social sciences and design education and training.[7] The aim of what was gradually becoming more and more an applied discipline was to effect a 'rational' ordering of space. The main problems identified were the manifold consequences of rapid urban growth, e.g. sanitation problems, inadequate transportation and housing and the poor condition of public facilities. Both the professional milieu concretely involved in city building activities and the technical and architectural teaching institutions came to accept the legitimacy of this specific field of study. Even so, its all-encompassing and empirical character, and its distinctly heterogeneous intellectual grounding, for a long time prevented town planning from achieving a strong academic position. Town-planning institutes devoted to the field were being developed on the eve of the First World War. These few trailblazers created an early and strong impulse. In Europe however, full institutional recognition was largely postponed to the inter-war period.[8]

The rising legitimacy of planners arose, in the ethical sphere, from the professed aim to realise the 'public good' and, in the technical – economic sphere, from the wish to optimise resources. Obviously, there were and still are many divergent interpretations of the very

7 Town planning is distinct from ancestral plan layout techniques by its effort for reflexivity and for creating a multidisciplinary field. For a general discussion, See Françoise Choay, *La règle et le modèle, sur la théorie de l'architecture et de l'urbanisme*, Paris, 1980.

8 Joseph Brix and Felix Genzmer organised a seminar on Städtebau in 1907 at the Technischen Hochschule in Charlottenburg. The conferences were published by 1920. The Department of Civic Design was set up in 1909 at the School of architecture, University of Liverpool. with the sponsorship of W. Lever. Raymond Unwin's conferences started in 1912 at Birmingham University. In France several attempts were made before World War I. L'École des Hautes Etudes Urbaines was created in 1919 and integrated to Paris University in 1924. In Italy, the first chair of "urbanistica" was created in 1921.

content of these ethical and technical frameworks. Ideally, the two spheres should be optimally balanced. In fact, the intention was that they would converge naturally, thus securing the full legitimacy of the planner's occupational field. But in practice, this construct was liable to fall apart for any number of reasons, among which were the planners' capabilities or inclination, or municipal authorities favouring one sphere over the other.

Early town planning can be described as being founded and developed on the basis of three main underlying dimensions. Obtaining the widest possible legitimacy was directly linked to the mastering of a comprehensive strategy of intervention based on these overlapping and interacting dimensions, each of which contributed to the continuous modelling of the social and spatial layout of the city.

The first dimension could be described as the dimension that envisions the city as "Stor By" (Great city). That is, it is concerned with the city's efforts to achieve a position of prominence in the face of regional or even international competition to attract productive industries and commercial development. During the period considered, there was a strong link between the nation-state building process and the metropolitan building process, leading to what might be called the "networked city".[9] At the design level, this dimension presupposed the production of innovative devices aimed at enhancing the circulation network and transportation facilities, sometimes inducing the production of new civil-engineering type of infrastructure.[10] The development of steel and reinforced-concrete construction provided a large range of options to develop what some planners called the "city machine"[11], and some of the engineers participating in the Copenhagen competition were actors of the then developing field of urban engineering.

The second dimension, a pivotal concern for planning, addresses the balance between social and spatial forms, a balance in which zoning might be employed as a regulatory tool in order to organise a relative specialisation of spaces and to intervene in city density and shape. Here the production of innovative housing design adapted to the aims of the planner's strategy and/or of the city authorities' policy was a key issue. Nevertheless, within the period considered here, planners' attitudes toward zoning were rather disparate, going the full range from obsessive concern for the prescription of specialised spaces to strong misgivings about a possible socially "divided city". The different interpretations of zoning techniques ascribed to by those early planners deserve a special chapter of its own.[12] Suffice it to say in the present context that this future cornerstone of town-planning practice was the subject of greatly varying degrees of attention and sophistication among planners.

We will mainly addresses what we call the 'third dimension', that is to say the way of dealing with the 'static' role of the inherited city and, more generally, the existing spatial environment. That domain was soon understood to be a specific field of intervention, a potential reserve of countervailing force to the continuous voluntary or 'spontaneous' reshaping of the city.[13] In the Scandinavian countries, studies have shown that planners chose to implement this field in their current practice early in the century.[14] Among the tools a planner had at his disposal, 'conservation' was frequently acknowledged as an efficient social and

9 Joel Tarr, Gabriel Dupuy, *Technology and the rise of the networked city in Europe and America*, Philadelphia, 1988.

10 For instance, Henri Prost (1874-1959) designed a "Belvèdere": a huge concrete platform connecting rail, water and land transport lines in his submission, "Golden Ring", to the Antwerp competition. See Hélène Vacher, "Henri Prost: the colonial experience", *Nordic Journal of Architectural Research*, Vol.9, N. 3, 1996, pp. 67-80.

11 Léon Jaussely, a founding member of the Société française des Architectes Urbanistes, was the most vocal advocate of the theory of the 'city machine' in France. In 1910, his entry to the Berlin competition (in collaboration with Charles Nicod) strongly emphasised the organisation of mass transit lines. His views were developed during the General Congress of Civil Engineering held in Paris in 1918. See Hélène Vacher, "Building the Modern City – Planners and Planning Expertise at the École spéciale des travaux publics" (1898-1939), *Planning Perspectives*, Vol. 17 (1), 2002, p. 41-60, esp. 47-49.

12 See Raphaël Fischler, "Toward a genealogy. op. cit.

13 See Kristiana Hartmann, "Städtebau um 1900, Romantische Visionen oder pragmatische Aspekte", in Cord Meckseper and Harald Siebenmorgen (Hrsg.), *Die Alte Stadt: Denkmal oder Lebensraum? Die Sicht der mittelalterlichen Stadtarchitektur in 19 und 2O. Jahrhundert*, Göttingen, 1985, p. 90-113.

14 See Ola Wetterberg, *Monument och miljö. Perspektiv på det tidiga 1900-talets byggnadsvärd i Sverige*. Gothenburg, 1992.

spatial harmonising tool that could counteract the disruptive forces of modernity and help balance the first two dimensions considered.

In a different historical setting—the French colonial context—the concern for the global conservation of the 'historic city' found expression in the first decade of the century.(See Chapter 6). Henceforth, the dream of disconnecting fragments of time-space entities was realised to a certain extent.[15]

In Europe, the feeling of closure of time-space fragments was exceptional. Generally the struggle to occupy a high-density built centre did prevail. However, some municipal officials and planners did conceptualise the possible conservation of the 'historic city' by the first decade of the century. They started to elaborate planning theories and modi operandi about conservation in relation to city as a whole. (See Part III).

The following paragraph will assess the unfolding of a current within planning that might be brought under the umbrella of 'Civic Art design', the aim of which was also the development of an integrated strategy that incorporated strong elements of conservation.

1.2 The Civic Art Movement and Design

This paragraph about Civic Art should be considered together with the chapter 6, which focuses more precisely on planning strategies developed in relation to the 'old city'. In order to address how what we have called "the third dimension" of planning was incorporated into some of the competition entries, it is necessary first to present the movement of 'Art Public' in Europe and to clarify the notion of 'Civic Art' as well.

By using the term of Civic Art we underline that convergent methods and common references, both implicit and explicit, characterise a number of entries in the 1908 Competition. Civic Art, as an early planning movement with influence at the time, effectively pervades most of the submissions to the Copenhagen competition, including the Danish ones.

In relation to the Art Public movement, A. Sutcliffe drew attention to the relatively rapid shift from a European movement, centred primarily around a preservationist tendency, towards a more global, urban approach aimed at integrating new trends in urban design, particularly "Arts and Crafts ideas of creative design".[16] He insists on the puzzling accretion of meetings and wide-ranging types of influences through which some ideas of urban planning managed to make their way.

Under the Belgian aegis, the Art Public congresses had, between 1898 and 1910, become a common platform of exchange for professionals in Europe and the United States. The movement also enlisted a sizeable corps of non-specialists, writers, artists and academics interested in urban affairs. By 1909, *L'Art Public*, the official journal of the Institut international d'Art Public, could number as its collaborators people of widely different backgrounds. Personalities involved in planning—a small minority—came from a fairly large spectrum.[17] Mainly revolving around Belgium, the movement was wide open to international influences, with the German-Austrian inspired Städtebau enjoying a prominent influence. Major findings of the second-generation Städtebau also having developed quite independently of the Wallonian milieu involved in planning activity soon appeared in close complicity in their urban diagnoses and remedies as well. The nucleus of Belgian founders of the movement displayed a high receptivity to the Austro-German message. Art Public Congresses were a forum for ideas and strategies geared towards the conservation of the city core as well as to the promotion of aesthetics and

15 On this aspect of conservation introduced by the French 1912 Protectorate over Morocco see Hélène Vacher, *Projection coloniale et ville rationalisée – le rôle de l'espace colonial dans la constitution de l'urbanisme en France, 1900-1931*, Aalborg, 2001, p. 139-145.

16 Anthony Sutcliffe, "Planning as an International Movement", in A. Sutcliffe, *Towards the Planned City, Germany, Britain, The United States and France, 1780-1914*, Oxford, 1981, p.163-201, esp.170-171.

17 Among such personalities were, Dr Cornelius Gürlitt (Dresden), Bruno Mörhring (Berlin), Siegfried Sitte, (Vienna), D.H Burnham (Chicago), Olmsted Brothers, (Brooklyn), etc.

Planners were in clear minority behind notables and art critics. The permanent council of the Institut International d'Art Public was formed by Belgian personalities. Victor Horta was among the sixteen members of the permanent council. See, *L'Art Public*, Revue de l'Institut International d'Art Public, N° VII&VIII, December 1909.

cultural values in keeping with an assumed idea of urban continuity. Accordingly, the first section of the 1910 Congress addressed such program topics as: "Conservation of city, districts and monuments of the past", "the profaning character of advertising on the historic physiognomy of cities", "the ethics for conserving monuments", etc.[18] In addition to this strong focus on urbanity, culture and aesthetics—part of a multi-faceted struggle against "urban ugliness"—the congresses addressed many other issues, such as the development of a "nationally" rooted "builder culture". On can concludes: "The aesthetics concerns of the Public Art congresses proved too restrictive to allow the incorporation of the complete planning idea...".[19]

While acknowledging the influential network created by this movement, Marcel Smets has discussed its "limited potential", emphasising the untimely withdrawal of Charles Buls.[20] Buls had apparently been quite annoyed by the self-promoting interest and the relative amateurism that characterised the leadership. However, it could be argued that the Art Public movement managed to secure and sustain the co-operation of such first-rank personalities as Joseph Stübben, Bruno Möhring, J.C.N. Forestier, Siegfried Sitte, D.H. Burnham and the Olmsted brothers, etc., during the first decade of the twentieth century.

More than the heterogeneity that informed its approach to design and its underlying doctrines, the growing rifts created by the international character of the movement and the increasingly substantialist search for "national character" proved detrimental to its development. In 1905 for instance, the third Annual Congress _ called for the "renovation of national tradition" and railed against "all that is forced and sterile within the cosmopolite manners". Finally, "a return to the national traditions" was called for, and even "ethnological traditions" were looked to, not "to copy but to innovate".[21]

18 Idem, p. 10 –11.

19 Idem.

20 Marcel Smets, *Charles Buls, Les principes de l'art urbain*, Brussels, 1995, p. 145-148.

21 "Rénover partout les traditions nationales"; "faire tomber tout ce qu'il y a de forcé et de stérile dans les conventions cosmopolites", *IIIe Congrès d'Art Public, Rapport et comptes-rendus, Liège 15-21 septembre 1905*, Brussels, 1905, p. 8.

Already on the decline by 1910, with a wealth of parallel events taking place in London and Berlin, the movement had almost vanished in the aftermath of the First World War.[22] In Paris, during the war, an ephemeral Superior School of Art Public was founded around a nucleus of Belgian refugees, with the support of prominent French planners.[23] As a movement however, in the post-war years the Art Public movement for the main part did not extent beyond its strongholds of Geneva and Lausanne in French-speaking Switzerland. Only in this country did the Société d'Art Public, the French-speaking Swiss version of the German Heimatschutz movement, succeed in developing to such a level that it maintained some influence on city affairs during the following decades.[24]

This brief overview highlights some of the contradictions and ambiguities that proved to be hindrances for the ultimate development of an Art Public movement, while summarising some features that united its otherwise different branches.

22 It could be argued that the 1913 International Congress held in Ghent reflected the contribution of the Art Public movement and that is true to a certain extent, conservation being still a prized topic of the Congress. However, the focus and the institutional set up surrounding the movement, including the personalities heading it, announced a major shift. J. Jensen and M. Marstrand represented Copenhagen and Denmark at the congress. See *Premier Congrès International et Exposition Comparée des villes, Organisé sous le Haut Patronage et avec le Concours de la Ville de Gand à l'occasion de l'Exposition Universelle en cette Ville, 1913*, Brussels, 1913.

23 On the founding of this school, Vacher, H., "Building... op. cit, p. 41-59, esp. 50-51.

24 The Société d'Art Public, section genévoise de la Ligue pour la conservation de la Suisse pittoresque (Heimatschutz) was active between 1907 and 1951. It was formed shortly after the set up of the Commission d'Art Public in August 1901. The Society aimed at encouraging the conservation "of everything of some kind of artistic, picturesque or historic value" within the city and the canton of Geneva, but also "to elaborate, examine and realise projects aiming at beautifying Geneva". See *Statuts de la Société d'Art Public*, Genève, Imp. "La Tribune de Genève", 1908, p. 2-3. This Society had the ambition to function as a lobby but also as a council of enlightened citizens. On the long run its influence remained marginal despite a sustained interest for urban and planning questions. The permanence of the Swiss movement might give an insight into the undeveloped potentialities of the Belgian movement that was weakened by personal rivalries and the consequences of the First World War.

Diffusion and Dilution of 'Sittian principles'

First and foremost, this movement's main source of inspiration remained Austrian and German. In investigating Camillo Sitte's influence on the town planning movement, Collins mentions that his contemporaries interpreted Sitte's works as *Raumkunst* (spatial art) and the making of the city as a *Gesamtkunstwerk* (total work of art).[25] Within the Art Public movement, the "post-Sittian" German planners certainly found a receptive platform. Yet Sitte's influence was much diluted and filtered through different kinds of *aggiornamentos*. By the beginning of the century, the image of the Viennese master was often 'Stübbenized' or 'medievalised.[26] Sitte's *Der Städtebau* had been instrumental in taking the transition between the pre-industrial city and the modern urbanisation to task, and, broadly speaking, in studying 'what went wrong' with industrial modernity and 'why and how it went wrong'. His approach was to be particularly successful in central and northern Europe, where the rapid pace of urbanisation has caused a spectacular debasement of rural culture.[27] Through planning practice, Sitte further investigated what could be done to correct the disruptive effects of industrial modernity. Albeit essentially operating on small towns, he did display his ability to translate some of its principles into actual layout.[28] By the turn of the century, the movement's followers redoubled efforts to develop an 'adaptive' technique of the layout of city peripheries. Nevertheless, through this process of the diffusion of so-called 'Sittian' ideas in extension planning competitions, initial planning issues had became partially blurred and even distorted. One result of the distortion gave rise to the specious and much commented-on debate between "the straight and the crooked lines".[29] Even if stylistic anecdotes and 'picturesque' eccentricities had clouded with confusion some of the central issues raised by Sitte within a few years, some of his design principles had managed to make their way unscathed. Fragments of Sitte's ideas became part of the repertoire of 'middle range' planners, such as J. Stübben. This prolific planner had incorporated—in fact as early as 1892-94 in his winning entry for the Vienna competition—some aspects of 'Sittian' urban aesthetic. At the same time he explicitly refused to accept it as a general framework for design.[30]

Some of these ideas were summarised during the 1905 Brussels Congress. One of many proposals advised subordinating public work schemes to aesthetic control, elaborating preliminary studies to avoid designing streets that were too uniform, too straight, too long, and suppress the fad for star-shaped squares, that had proved totally inefficient as concerns the flow of traffic. Moreover, others ideas that had come into practice in many German cities were added, for example: encouraging not only architects, but also artists and landowners, to study the "picturesque beauties"; carrying out extensive and scientific inventories of old buildings, using modern techniques such as photogrammetry, etc.; and taking the preservation of historic monuments into consideration when applying street lines schemes, etc.[31]

Second, the movement was informed by a measured anti-academic inclination, with an implicit critique of the predominant beaux-arts traditions, more or less associated with an 'international style'. At the 1905 Congress, Buls had strongly voiced his opinion, saying that it was during 'sterile periods' that acad-

25 George R. Collins and Christiane Crasemann Collins, *Camillo Sitte and the Birth of Modern City Planning*, London, 1965, p. 51-52.

26 Idem, p. 89.

27 On the hypothesis of a "Sittian geography" of planning, see Anthony Sutcliffe, "la diffusione delle teorie sittiane: un'ipotesi per definirne lo sfondo" in G. Zucconi (ed.), *Camillo Sitte e i suoi interpreti*, Milan, 1992, p. 99-108.

28 Among the main projects were, Ljubljana, Marienberg, Marienthal Olmütz, Ostrava, Reichenberg, and G. R. Collins, *Camillo. op.cit.* p. 113-114.

29 It is well established that C. Sitte did not favour the "crooked line", but short and straight streets, this being in line with his leaning toward the Baroque design. However, *Der Städtebau* places emphasis on three-dimensional relations and does not aim at codifying a catalogue of urban forms.

30 For instance, Sitte criticised Stübben for having plagiarise Henrici's Munich plan in his entry for the Vienna 1892 Competition. See, G. R. Collins, *Camillo... op. cit.*, p. 84. See also Brian K. Ladd, "Urban aesthetics and the discovery of the urban fabric in the turn of the century Germany", *Planning Perspectives*, 1987, N. 2, p. 270-286. However, Smets insists upon Buls's influence on Stübben: M. Smets, *Charles Buls. op. cit., p.161.*

31 See *IIIe Congrès d'Art Public... op. cit.*

emies and schools 'crystallised constructive knowledge in mathematical formulas'.[32] Consequently, this current sought most of its inspiration in late Gothic, Renaissance or 'vernacular regional' constructive traditions. References to aesthetics as well as ethics betray nostalgia for the values and crafts of the medieval commune. A strong commitment was made favouring the renewal of drawing training at school, as well as the study of building tradition and crafts through the development of applied arts. Consequently, many followers of this movement turned their back on the 'urban art' as understood by the '*Embellissement*' tradition inherited from the French eighteenth century. However, Art Public should not be summarily equated with "Gothic historicism" or "neo-medievalism". Early on, authors like Werner Hegemann pointed out that Sitte had devoted much more attention to medieval layout than to the study of Antiquity, Renaissance and the Baroque. Hegemann and Peet's book, *The American Vitruvius: an Architects' Handbook of Civic Art*, published in 1922, displays a wide plurality of orientation in planning.[33] The French Beaux-Art reference had been a cornerstone for the overseas planning main stream, which was also involved, albeit marginally, in the Art Public Congresses. Leading American planning personalities, such as the Olmsted brothers or Daniel H. Burnham, had laid down their names as collaborators of *L'Art Public*. However, overseas planning was itself far from being unified in stylistic attitude. Olmsted's picturesque landscape tradition was much at variance with Beaux-Art influence and 'dilated' American neo-classicism—a hallmark of the City Beautiful movement, certainly not to be confused itself with the baroque tradition of central and southern Europe.[34]

Returning to our point, neither the anti-academic leanings of the movement nor its proclivity to 'national' or 'ethnic' traditions and a vernacular building culture as opposed to the international character and centralist and Absolutist origin of classicism in planning should be interpreted as a permanent dogma. Rather, these tendencies were indicative of the general ethos and aesthetic and cultural values shared by numerous professionals involved in this movement. Though the postulate behoves the substantiation that only further investigations in the training process of professionals can bring, it may be that this anti-academic inclination was also strongly stimulated by the influence of non-academically trained architects and of master builders making efforts to cope with the nascent building industry.[35] This tension was particularly perceptible in non-core countries of Europe, where pre-industrial social relations offered much resistance during the nineteenth century, particularly in the building sector.[36]

A third uniting characteristic of the Civic Art current was that it exhibited a deep concern for the existing site in the broadest sense, as this physical product was the receptacle of sensory experience and correlated accrued meanings. Particularly in the Nordic countries, but also for instance in German-speaking Switzerland, the 'natural' landscape was also considered as part of the product of national culture. Accordingly, the preservation of ordinary buildings and clusters of houses was prized, as these represented an inexhaustible mine of inspiration for the ongoing construction of identities.

If we move beyond this broad sketch that sums up a few characteristics of this movement, its heterogeneous character and, at times, contradictory nature

32 *Idem*, Charles Buls's intervention was titled "Le nationalisme dans l'art", p. 2.

33 Werner Hegemann & Elbert Peets, *The American Vitruvius: an Architects' Handbook of Civic Art*, New York, 1922.

34 On the role and influence of F. L. Olmsted on the City Beautiful, cf. William H. Wilson, *The City Beautiful movement*, Baltimore & London, 1989.

35 This anti-academic leaning was in line with the anti French Beaux-Art tradition, the later being associated with the 'international style'. In non-core countries like Denmark, Switzerland and Belgium, a growing convergence between the current engaged in the development of "industrial arts" or "applied arts", and a "retrospective" approach toward building style can be observed. In the case of Denmark, the strong academic tradition in architecture and the pervading influence of 'neo-classical' international style should be taken into account to characterise such an approach; see Knud Millech og Kay Fisker, *Danske arkitekturstrømninger 1850-1950*, Copenhagen, 1951.

36 C. E. Schorske wrote in relation to Camillo Sitte's father:"For contemporary English reformers such as Ruskin and Morris, revival of the dead artisan and craft culture was the issue. In backward Austria, the issue was not revival but survival. The preservation of an artisan society, still alive but mortally threatened": Carl E. Schorske, *Fin de siècle Vienna, Politics and Culture*, Cambridge, 1981, p. 65.

in relation to the emerging discipline of town planning would soon be exposed. This current was especially much stretched between two tendencies: on the one side the will to oppose a widely identified counter model to Academism. On the other a naturalistic sensibility looking for authenticity freed from any stylistic formalism while deeply rooted in cultural history and historical constructive knowledge. Nevertheless, we shall see that Civic Art, as an informal school of design did still exert a strong influence on the aforementioned third dimension of planning.

Regarding Scandinavia, we should note that the cities of Aarhus, Bergen, Gothenburg and Stockholm were represented in the 1905 Art Public Congress in Brussels when the Institut International d'Art Public was founded. Grundhoig, a librarian from Aarhus, was the lone participant from Denmark, when Sweden sent a sizeable group of architects, engineers, artists and personalities.[37] Among the issues in debate were Charles Buls and Pr. Cloquet's planning strategies in relation to old urban centres. The journal *Architekten* reported this discussion in the aftermath of the 1906 International Architects' Congress in London.[38] Unlike Sweden, Denmark was little involved formally in the Art Public movement. However the topics and questionings of this movement were at the heart of the problematic of leading professionals in Denmark, and were also reflected in the activity of organisations such as Foreningen til Hovedstadens Forskønnelse. (See Chapter 7)

'Grand Manner' and Craftsmanship

The term of Civic Art has been frequently adopted to describe the unfolding of the 'Sittian' approach to planning. However, the term of 'Romantic planning' has been used alongside Civic Art to describe a pre-World War I planning preoccupied with artistic purpose and generally informed by the National Romantic culture. The converging aspects and the cognate meaning of English Civic Art, Art Urbain and Art Public, and finally American Civic Art itself, closely associated with the City Beautiful movement, has been recently discussed.[39] While acknowledging "specific approaches", J. Luques insists upon "evident similarities". Theses might be ensconced in the sharp dividing line established between the social and public nature of Civic Art, and the 'private' significance assigned to architecture. At the risk of oversimplifying matters: Civic Art would stop short at the façade, leaving the inner organisation of the building untouched. However, the historical content of each notion, and in particular the positioning of German planning, is outside our scope here, as a whole range of 'Sittian' disciples, surveyors as well as architects were actively involved in the housing reform movement. Meanwhile, the central purpose of this study is to elucidate the final victory of the Modern Movement over Civic Art. This victory is directly related to the former movement's ability to provide a strategic transformational role for architecture. The risk of de-historicisation of the disciplinary process might prove a hindrance to the rendering of the complexity of theoretical position within early town–planning, particularly as the two movements did not develop simultaneously. However, the hypothesis concerning the mechanism of historic bifurcation of the theory of architecture in relation to Civic Art is particularly fruitful. What the author calls the "cost of victory" of the Modern Movement is analysed in terms of the growing abstraction of external space, renewed formalism and finally the general impoverishment of the built environment— precisely the difficulties that the Civic Art current had tried to tackle. From this point of view, Civic Art would have failed to deliver a coherent formula linking architecture and planning.[40]

Before proceeding further, we should insist on the

37 See, *IIIe Congrès International de l'Art Public*… op. cit. Denmark was praised for the educative character of its "Free air museum" in Lyngby. See H. Lageman, "Les musées de plein air en Scandinavie", *L'Art Public*, N° VII & VIII December 1909, p. 31-42.

38 See the series of articles published in *Architekten*, N. 22, N. 23, N. 24, 2, 9, 16 March 1907, p. 222-224; p. 230-232; and p. 240-244.

39 See Jose Luque "Architecture and Town Planning: Uninterrupted Dialogue; the Birth of the Two First Urban Tradition", *Planning History*, Vol. 24 (2 & 3), 2002, p. 35-42.

40 The status of architecture within Civic Art is further discussed in the third part of this book. Most Civic Art 'planners' were fully engaged in the study of urban continuity, from the scale of housing to the scale of city as attested by the works of Strinz, Plesner, and Rasmussen for the 1909 Competition.

fact that the term Civic Art may be just about meaningless if not used with due prudence.[41] The phrases 'Civic Art' and 'Civic Design' were catchwords of the Anglo-American movement for urban reform at the turn of the century, after having been introduced by the English pioneers of urban planning. Charles M. Robinson's writings, which were to become a cornerstone of early American planning, made it a central reference, Civic Art being defined as: "this art, which serves so many social ends, [is] municipal in the sense of communal".[42] Robinson's approach in terms of urban design was pluralistic. He saw the Civic Art movement as "truly international" and his book drew largely upon the "public architecture" of Europe.[43]

Raymond Unwin, in his work *Town Planning in Practice, An Introduction to the Art of Designing Cities and Suburbs*, endeavoured to merge the Howardian project with some of the most notable contributions of the fast developing continental tradition, among which the thematic of "centre and enclosed place" was to be given a considerable attention.[44] However, William H. Lever sponsored the opening of a "Civic Design" course geared towards America. This was accompanied by a renewed enthusiasm for classicism in design, as interpreted through American professionals, who had motivated the decision of opening a course at the "Liverpool School of Architecture [resembling] the Ecole des Beaux Arts at Paris". Announcing of the creation of chair of Civic Design, *The Builder* was highly dismissive of the "craftsmanship theory" and denounced quite vehemently the "accidental picturesque".[45] In-depth studies also show that W.H. Lever and Charles Reilly's Liverpool Civic Design initiative deliberately turned their back on the "Civic" as well as the "Arts and Crafts" English tradition rooted in Christian socialism and utopianism.[46]

As a result, Civic Art became a notion only loosely connected with its original content—that is a community-based approach to urban culture and an Arts and Crafts type of design, with strong emphasis on vernacular or 'bürgerlich' constructive knowledge. The somehow diverted label became a loosely defined notion called upon to build a transatlantic bridge. Here monumental architecture inspired by the academic technique of composition came to play a central role.

The term Civic Art became emblematic for a whole generation of international planners. For instance, in direct relation to this study, Alfred J. Roewade (following here his Americanised spelling) presented himself in 1908 for the Copenhagen competition as a "Consulting Engineer and Civic Designer". The notion's ambiguity could be further illustrated by the already mentioned first edition of Hegeman and Peet's treaty, in which the chapter dedicated to the "Modern revival of Civic Art" was an accurate synthesis of Sitte's theories. But, as already mentioned, the book paid a large tribute to the American City Beautiful neo-classicist current as well.[47]

To sum up this point, while one can establish a strong semantic, historical and formal relation between Civic Art and Art Public, both terms involving a political meaning and a specific approach to art understood as a social expression of the urban community, no simple equivalence can be made from a historical standpoint. One must certainly acknowledge the societal-political and cultural content of both notions, in parallel to the more neutral concept of town planning as well as the nearly scientific pretension of French "urbanisme" as a new disciplinary field.[48] It remains

41 G. R. Collins, *Camillo Sitte… op. cit.*, referred to the ambiguity of this notion. H. Porfyriou used this term to describe the progress of 'Sittian theories' in the Nordic countries: Heleni Porfyriou, "Artistic Urban Design and Cultural Myths: The Garden City Idea in Nordic Countries, 1900-1925", *Planning Perspectives* Vol. 7 (3), 1992, p. 263-301.

42 See Charles Mulford Robinson, *Modern Civic Art, or the City Made Beautiful,* New York and London, 1904, p.26.

43 Idem, p. 22 & p. III respectively.

44 Raymond Unwin, *Town planning in practice, an introduction to the art of designing cities and suburbs*, London, 1911 (first ed. 1909), esp., p. 175-234.

45 See *The Builder*, N. 95, 12 December 1908. The shift in design strategy for Port Sunlight has been analysed by A. A. Sutcliffe, *"Planning as… op. cit."*, p. 181-184.

46 On the watering away of the Arts and Crafts style of design, see Christopher Crouch *Design culture in Liverpool School of Architecture*, Liverpool, 2002. Peter Richmond, *Marketing Modernisms: The Architecture and Influence of Charles Reilly*, Liverpool, 2001, provides a detailed account on the development of a neo-classical current in Liverpool intimately linked to the planning movement in America.

47 Werner Hegemann and Elbert Peets, *The American… op. cit.*

48 We should note the cautious wording of some authors. For instance, C. R. Robinson, Modern… op. cit., p. 34, mentions attempts "to formulate a sort of science of city-building".

that each of these notions should be used with caution. These designations may be misleading if they are not each time put in their proper historical and geographical setting. In this study, we essentially refer to the continental tradition of Eastern and Northern Europe, as emulated by Sitte and his 'interpreters', also described here as Austro-German planners[49].

This school had developed and formalised its approach to design on the basis of a thorough study of urban layout starting with antiquity and covering the late Gothic, Renaissance and Baroque periods. This could be drawn upon for a wide variety of designs. Moreover, there should be emphasised – and this is particularly relevant concerning Sitte and his followers – the degree of kinship between the late Gothic tradition, fond of tormented and plentiful forms and inspired by the play of curve and countercurve, and the constant search of the Baroque artistes for enclosedness, 'surprise effects' and passion expressed through the dynamic of tortuous, convoluted and crooked lines.[50]

2 Variations on Conservation in Town Plans Design

To evaluate the potential of the Civic Art approach, we shall examine its influence on the designs put forward in entries to the Copenhagen competition. Of the nineteen projects submitted, we have selected six plans for a detailed study. However, we shall also consider the main traits of all the proposals, especially the Swedish ones regrouped for a closer look. The main criterion used for selection was the strong focus given by some projects to the 'third dimension in planning'. However we have also considered some planners' long-term contributions to the question of conservation, and taken other innovative characteristics included in their proposals into account. The following part of this book will explore, in parallel to this analysis focusing on extension planning, the strengthening of the conservation movement in relation to the transformations happening within the city centre, examining the relationship between these two occurrences. Here we shall focus on the main aspects of the conservation approach in relation to extension planning. It should be emphasised that we have examined the non-awarded entries' designs on the basis of the black and white photographs, which has been taken at the time of the competition. Hence we have been missing part of the coloured information in relation to the allocation of specialised areas. Moreover, detailed plans and perspective drawings had not been photographed by the municipal services.

The elements that have been retained to analyse entries can be split into two groups of questions. The first group addresses the strategy adopted in the various entries in relation to existing spaces. We will consider the connecting devices imagined by planners to link the city centre to the new districts, with a consideration of the various proposals concerning the crossing of the centre. This must allow us to examine not only solutions adopted for the handling of the contact zone between the old and the new city, but also policies concerning feeders and ring roads. The second set of considerations within the new districts revolves around choices made with regard to existing land pattern and road systems. Meanwhile, the third set of issues has to do with the policy towards existing villages and forms that would, in time, be built. Fourthly, at issue is also the attitude toward existing topography (levelling aspects), the policy concerning 'open space' and/or 'natural space'. And a final consideration is the relation between the old and the imminent city skyline.

The second group of questions essentially addresses

49 This current may be more appropriately characterised as "south German" since its influence was weak in Prussia. Strinz's views on design reflect a relative equilibrium between the much typified 'historicised' design as applied by Karl Henrici among others, and the 'realistic' version of the 'post- 1890' design of Joseph Stübben. Strinz, who was trained and worked in the Rhineland, had a first hand experience of the 'Sittian' method of design. However, the Rhineland was administratively part of Prussia, and the professional movement (in which Strinz was much active) was organised accordingly. It should be noticed that the 'Sittian school' of design was sidelined at the Berlin Competition in 1910 (even Brix and Genzmer's entry was little 'Sittian'). Hoever, this school of design was much alive in northern regions of Germany as in Hamburg, Altona, or Flensburg..

50 On Gothic and Baroque 'connivance' see Victor Louis Tapié, *Baroque et Classicisme*, Paris, 1980.

the method by which new urban spaces were produced. Factors such as choice of buildings types and, accordingly, of cluster density, scales of volumes, suggestions of architectonic models, but also treatment of the new city limits and projection of the urban macro-form all play a part. Concerning architecture, the evidence provided by archives remains limited. But for Strinz, there is little evidence of the perspective drawings and architectural plans of the awarded entries in archives. However, few scattered archives – sometimes unexpected one's as in the case of Ahlmann, authorise from time to time to risk some broad remarks.

We analyse the conceptual framework of architecture as oscillating between historicism and traditionalism. "Transitional architecture" might also be used as a broad category encompassing various forms of eclecticism or a form of mild modernism. By 'historicism' we mean knowledge and imitation of ancient architectures. This position is fundamentally distinct from 'traditionalism', which does not acknowledge the rupture of industrial modernity and which strives for continuous creative and innovative renewal within an acknowledged framework of building convention and practice. Eclecticism should not be confused with 'historicism', as eclecticism is essentially a process of selection and merging of techniques and formal architectonic characters. However, 'historicist' standpoints are almost impossible to maintain at a significant urban scale. Therefore historicist positions are symbolic statements. 'Historicist' architects or engineers articulate their practice on a thorough constructive knowledge that can also be mobilised toward innovations. Confronted to the anachronism of the programme, they invariably tend to evolve toward eclecticism. Therefore 'historicist' positions translated into design display a tendency to be transformed in the course of time.[51]

We shall finally examine the proposals put forward by the different entries in relation to the search for 'urban historical continuity'. The memoirs accompanying the drawing plans should also provide some indication of planners' motives in relation to conservation. In the subsequent paragraphs, selected plans are analysed, and in this process most of the queries summed up above are posed to each of them. The memoirs accompanying the plans are of unequal quality and often do not do justice to the excellence of the plans themselves.

51 On eclectic architecture see Jean Pierre, Epron, *Comprendre l'éclectisme*, Paris, 1997. We refer to the term 'traditionalism' as to the search of constructive historical continuity and cultural identity. For an in depth study see Giorgio Pigafetta and Ilaria Abbondandolo, *Architecture traditionaliste, Les théories et les oeuvres*, Sprimont, 1997.

2.1 "Urania"

The jury praised Karl Strinz's project (named after Tycho Brahe's Uraniaborg) for its skilful mastery of design practice and its attention to detail. At first glance, his plan is remarkable from the point of view of the quality of its design. The handling of detail of parcelling is meticulous, and only minimal inflections of lanes and land patterns are used to generate the new streets network. This unique method is reflected in the graphic sharpness of the drawing style were the much diversified size and shape of ground plans of buildings of special interest are moulded after the inherited features of the 'rural' paths and roads. On the general plan implantation of blocks figuring public buildings are used to highlight the directional growth lines of urbanisation. It is assumed that by regrouping contiguous land plots generally maintained within the limits of existing lanes, one may be able to achieve the formation of blocks of buildings in keeping with the original two-dimensional plane then conveying a sense of spatial continuity. This method of 'fitting buildings' that we could call 'generative cohesive' is supposed to prevent the formation of accidental vacuums around new clusters and to produce a non-artificial inexhaustible diversity.

The plans attempts to create a new city boundary based on a line of marshlands, ponds and lakes connected by an almost continuous network of serpentine pedestrian alleys forming a green belt (See Chapter 5, Figure 6C). This is even repeated, albeit in a lighter mode, with the soft integration of Sundby district on Amager, a region treated by most of the other competitors as a land open to continuous urban expansion.

Within that boundary, existing villages or existing road connections are to be used to generate urban centres. They are conceived as high-density nuclei with their "sluttet bebyggelse" (closed building type), surrounded by ring of "aaben bebyggelse"(open building type) and by a third ring of villas. Some of the nuclei close to the boundary are "snail shaped", or inward looking (toward the city centre). They represent an invitation to swift residential urbanisation. This system, which is employed on the periphery where urban block types of building are placed along new streets connecting different nuclei, is almost invariably based on the old road network with but a few alterations made to facilitate secondary connections. In a few places, particularly Amager Island, where old networks were almost non-existent, Strinz relied upon a similar pattern, a design of gentle curves, to generate new centres. The planned street network derives closely from the existing one. Mannerist forms are absent. This method of design resulted in a series of squares of varying size and shape according to the "turbinplatsen" pattern.

The perspective drawings presented along with this submission may be described as 'free historicist' architecture, which is only vaguely reminiscent of 'local' architecture (See, Chapter 5,1A & 1B). Here, the skill of the surveyor displays far less virtuosity. While an exploration of the "picturesque" effect is its focal point, the intention is to reflect the bourgeois aesthetic and the ethos of a flourishing city. But this technique might also be interpreted as a method to differentiate space and to make the directional lines of urbanisation clearly perceptible. Historicist architecture with towers, domes and spires was also seen as a straightforward means to provide a general system of orientation defaulting in most nineteenth century suburbs. The form taken by the city core was perpetuated in the proposed southern fortification of Christianshavn, though a much more diluted form, a park, was opted for. This intermediate solution reflected the choice adopted between 1872 and 1885, in which a park layout replaced the northern fortifications that had been dismantled in 1856.[52]

Strinz's memoir is essentially descriptive, successively presenting the main thoroughfares, the squares, the parks and sport facilities and finally the building types.[53] Zoning is little diversified, with residential units distributed along the parks. Emphasis is put, instead, on the mixing and general geographical distribution of construction types. Thoroughfares that link the city to new urban nuclei are used as vectors of dense urbanisation.

The plan also pays attention to the study of a comprehensive circular-railway mass-transit system. Though it was criticised for being laid out on the outer periphery, it is carefully designed to serve the outer districts evenly, both on the fringes and in the 'contact' zone toward the centre. This is quite original, as most others mass-transit systems concentrate almost exclusively on radial linkages. Another character of this serpentine railways line is it's landscaping with slopped earthwork and trenches to be integrated into the landscaped edge of the city.

The ring is completed with a 42-meter-high suspension bridge linking the Kastellet to Amage. This engineering project made a strong impression on the commentators. Emphasis put on ring linkage of the suburbs is therefore reinforced by the strong historicist inspiration of the bridge seen as the symbolic gate of the new city. The ring attempts to create a new city boundary based on a line of marshlands, ponds and lakes connected by an almost continuous network of serpentine pedestrian alleys forming a green belt. This is even repeated, albeit in a lighter mode, with the soft integration of the Sundby district on Amager Island, an area treated by most of the other competitors as land available for continuous urban expansion. (See also Chapter 5).

On the whole, the strong point of the plan designed by Karl Strinz is its ability to combine high-density nuclei on top ground with low-density and natural landscaped network on low ground, and then conveying the feeling of evenly distributed and homogeneous "parcels" of urbanity. Concerning the core, we should remark that the crossing of the city expressed graphically on the plan despite the fact that this aspect is not a part of the programme. Three bridges connect the southern and northern parts of the old

52 On these projects, see Axel Holm and Kjeld Johansen, *København 1840-1940, Det Københavnske Bysamfund og Kommunens økonomi*, Copenhagen, 1941, p.16-23.

53 *Beskrivelser til de fire præmierede og det indkøbte konkurrence – projekt angaaende bebyggelsens af Københavns ydre distrikter, Tillæg til Københavns Borgerrepræsentanters Forhandlinger fra den 1. April 1909 til den 29. Marts 1910*, Copenhagen, 1910, p. 1-12.

city. Street-widening schemes are not indicated, and the crossing of the centre is led through the twisted Købmagergade leading to Slothsholmsgade.

The combination of 'technical' and 'artistic' skill in the handling of city form and topographical detail received very favourable professional comment at the time, particularly by architect Rolf Schroeder.[54] In contrast, the *Maanedsskrift for Sundhedspleje* regretted the lack of detail concerning population density. Even if not expressed in a straightforward manner, the hygienist journal was only half-heartedly endorsed the high-density buildings of the urban nuclei.

A key point of Strinz's design consists in maintaining a strong inter-connexion between urbanised nuclei retaining the qualities of density and diversity. Natural and artificial inherited patterns are generally conserved. Extension planning proceeds through duplication of urban nuclei by following existing plot structures and road networks. Low-density housing is to be articulated on the periphery of urban nuclei. Modern facilities and infrastructures are immersed in the general landscaping of the project. Historicist architectonic contributes to homogenise the overall plan.

2.2 "Tre Træer"

This entry symbolises the continuity of the "Garden city" with the three towers of the city's coat of arms. The project presented by the municipal engineer, which won the second prize, was quite different from "Urania" with regard to method in that it placed a strong emphasis on zoning, with decreasing density toward the outer ring. Far less importance was placed on details, in particular topographical fine points. In his memoir, Bjerre started with a direct reference to the garden city 'theory' and 'ideal', and underscored the advisability of maintaining low density in the new districts, and, along that line, preserving "the rural character of the place".[55] The belief is that architectonic extravagance and "grand-manner" effects would be out of place here.

This project was later used as a guideline by the municipality's technical services, with the circumstantial addition of some of Strinz's ideas. Bjerre also utilised the old road network as a basic canvas, in conformity with the jury's advice. However, the sense of using the networked patterns in a generative way is lacking. A few urban layout schemes are indicated on the plan. They heavily betray some gaucheries in the design style. An example of this is the two-pronged fork device near Rødkilde, where the attempt to create some forms of monumentality quite fails.

Yet the notion of delimiting the new urban areas is still present. He proposed a tree-lined avenue linking the main park that surrounds the city. The relative attractiveness of this green and blue city boundary – also more elusive than the corresponding element in the Strinz project – seems to favour low densities in the 'in-between' districts. While no precise instructions are given in the memoir for the actual layout forms within the zones, a few valuable points can be ascertained. The author is critical of the so-called "picturesque effect" -e.g. arbitrarily curved streets- and insists on the necessity of a layout that would facilitate clear orientation, as in the "old Copenhagen". Moreover, Bjerre devotes considerable attention to the skyline of the proposed new districts. Areas with relatively high building density should be restricted to the hills and residential villas situated on the lowland. High-density type buildings should also follow the main arterial roads. These particularities of zoning made it realistic to combine some of the aspects of Strinz and Bjerre's plans.

However, Strinz's strategy was far more systematic in creating densely built urban units that punctuate a landscaped low-density terrain in a regular pattern. According to Bjerre, this device would help create aesthetic contrasts in a country characterised by its soft topography. With regard to the city core, Bjerre's scheme adhered to a coherent "delimiting" approach. To the north, he considered that the tree-lined boulevard already in existence could be sufficient to protect the city from disruptive connections with the extension zone. To the south, his plan preserved the existing fortifications and moats almost without exception, and reinforces this line with a tree-lined boul-

54 See Rolf Schroeder, "Gadeplanerne", *Architekten*, 12 June 1909, p. 425. See also our analysis in Chapter 3.

55 "Nærværende Projekt søger derfor at bevare et Skær af landlig Karakter over den vordende Bebyggelse i de nye Distrikter", *Beskrivelser til de fire præmierede og det indkøbte konkurrence… op. cit.* p. 13.

evard bordering a green belt. Bjerre emphasised the "important role of Christianshavn in the history of the city" and even insisted on conserving the atmosphere of the place, complete with its cherry trees.[56]

A classical quadrant device, opening up Christianshavn to the surrounding Amager districts, is the only alteration to the fortification line proposed by the Bjerre project (see 4B). Furthermore, the engineer's determination to protect the city core from disruptive forces is underlined by the conspicuous absence of new intra-core connections, the bridges between the two main entities being included in the external ring system. The memoir accompanying Bjerre's project recommended that all industrial activities be removed from the inner core. He also called for improved access to a long city embankment for public leisure, and his park on Kalvebod Strand received much positive comments.

2.3 "Millionbyen"

Though it did not receive any special recognition, this significant Danish entry, which focuses on the protection of the city core, is worth mentioning. Egil Fischer's project, termed "Millionbyen" (a population of one million was expected by 1950), belonged to the series of projects that placed great emphasis on zoning. The general idea was that density should decline toward the periphery, the same principle being applied to each new centre. His plan clearly shows a green belt combining blue and green spaces, which also form a new city edge. These should be conceived as comprising housing districts with their own public and commercial facilities, low-density housing and parks forming a natural edge for each district. We should note that no mention is made of existing villages in the booklet, but the drawing plan indicates a relative permanence of these places.

Fischer's contribution was later heralded for its originality by leading Danish planners.[57] Having worked for the architects at the head of the 'national romantic' movement – Martin Nyrop and Martin Borch among others – Fischer had already won accolades as an architect, and was to become, for a short while, a member of the *Den Frie Architektforening*. He opens his memoir by proclaiming one of his main aims:

> "For at bevare Byens historisk og arkitektonisk værdifulde Dele for Neddrivning af Hensyn til Trafikken, ledes denne udenom den gamle Bys snævre Gader…".[58]

Thus, Fischer systematically avoided any encroachment on the heart of the city. His plan only partially utilised the existing radial highways, instead proposing a northern transverse axis to channel part of the traffic pressure to the district beyond the lakes and then to the "Jarmers tower" junction, thus driving the pressure tangentially towards the city core. He also recommended building a tunnel at Tolboden to organise a northern link with Christianshavn. It is worth noting that he suggested constructing a bridge joining Christianshavn between Nyhavn and Grönlandske Handel, thus prolonging the Gothersgade axial road. However this was to be conceived as an intra-urban connection that linked Christianshavn, often described as a "provincial district" (see Part III), to the city life, and of course not as a trans-urban thoroughfare.

The outer district plan was mainly a zoning plan. Fischer provided the jury with very little layout details. In general he insisted on the separation of pedestrian circulation from road traffic, suggesting parallel pathways. In the years to come, he was to develop much further the idea of separating types and forms of circulation networks in relation to speed of movement, to intensity of traffic and to functions.[59] A scheme of 'red' thoroughfare and 'green' alleys was to be consequently developed for the city.

Not unlike Alfred Raavad, Fischer deliberately ex-

56 "Volden har spillet en saa fremtrædende Rolle i Byens Historie", *Idem*, p. 23.

57 See Olaf Forchammer, *København… op. cit.*, p. 28 and Steen Eiler Rasmussen, *København – et bysamfunds… op. cit.*, p. 141-142.

58 "To protect the historic and architectural heritage from being destroyed by traffic, the latter must be channelled outside the narrow lanes of the old city." (Our translation): Stadsarkivet, Stadsingeniørens Direktorat, Byplankontoret – BP sager 1918-1984, Sag 977: memoir *Millionbyen*, 4 p.

59 The principle of hierarchy of urban network is explained in great details by Egil Fischer, "Byplanlægningens Love", in O. Asmussen, *Kjøbenhavn, som den er og som den burde være*, 1914, p. 56-74.

ceeded competition guidelines by including in his proposal plans for the construction of a new southern industrial harbour beyond the Christianshavn fortifications. His strategy here was to facilitate a quick exit from the city via the northern, valued, residential district and leading rapidly toward the much prized open countryside and woods. It was also intended to split passenger and commercial traffic. In this way, passenger traffic was to be confined to the north. The connection between the northern and southern part of the city could be kept essentially peripheral to the core with the construction of the Kastellet tunnel. Not only did Fischer believe that the city core should be protected from heavy traffic, but he also believed that it should be free of buildings surrounded by hectic activity: hospitals, army barracks, private schools and the like. In 1907, Fischer had been involved in a privately funded project aimed at bringing about a partial renovation of the southwest portion of the Christianshavn bastion. The project consisted of creating a double opening onto Amager to revitalise a depressed district.[60] First, a double-lane entry was drawn between two southern bastions, which were preserved, and further north, a trivium-like form was created to provide access to Amager and lend a classical look to the inner district. It is noteworthy that Fischer returned to this early, comprehensive strategy of conservation in the Millionbyen project, though in a slightly watered-down version (See, Chapter 5, 4 D). While the memoir does not describe the layout of the extension zone in detail, he makes his stand on adaptive design in the respect that he advocates employing existing levelling for the design of secondary streets and lanes.

Fischer wrote extensively about his town-planning conceptions in the following years. In an article on "Fredningssagen" (The Matter of Preservation) published in 1926 in *Architekten* in which he made explicit references to his 1909 entry, together with his early involvement with the *Foreningen til Gamle Bygningers Bevaring*. While his article is written in the perspective of the Law on the Protection of Natural Sites, he stresses his ideas about planning in relation to the safeguarding of cities.[61] Quoting as examples cities such as Ribe, Visby, Rothenburg, etc., he highlights the importance of the effect of wholeness of the urban fabric. He then introduces the notion of "critical moment", that is when a specific interference (such as the building of a railway station) creates new pressures on the existing urban fabric. He sees the best reply in the complete disconnection of modern and old facilities, or at least in sufficient spatial provision to avoid direct pressure.

When one is left with fragmented pieces of dilapidated clusters, displacement and re-erection can be chosen as the last-resort solution if this is done with sufficient know-how, Lillehammer, Skansen, Bygdø and Lyngby being given as well-managed examples.

As a general safeguarding policy, he puts forward a three-pronged strategy. First the avoidance of traffic pressure on the old city fabric by way of any kind of spatial device, the 1909 "Millionbyen" being a key reference in this regard. Second the drafting of a building law including a compensatory density mechanism according to locations, taking especially into account the relation between built forms and open spaces. Such a law could then give a framework within which to operate the 'green alleys' idea, giving Copenhagen an alternative landscaped network. In the framework of the same expected new building law, Fischer set forth a third recommendation: abandon the urban-clearance approach for the old Copenhagen. He advised intervening prudently, similarly to the "diradamento" method inaugurated by Giovannoni (See Chapter 6), while not giving any precise reference. He also believed that one could even if need be resort to street-opening schemes through city blocks without endangering the consistency of existing urban fabric. His strategy, summarily sketched here, was to partly rely on the conservation law passed in 1918. As an active member of the *Bevaring*, Egil Fischer had been an articulate proponent of such a law since 1907 (See Chapter 7). All along his general philosophy and desire had been to progressively incorporate the principle of the safeguard of the city, in all its historic, artistic, and cultural aspects, into the public sphere policy.

60 On this project see V. Malling, *Rundt i Byen-Lidt stof til efter tanke*, Copenhagen 1959, p. 41-43.

61 Egil Fischer, "Fredningssagen", *Architekten*, 1926, p. 201-208.

2.4 "København Vaaben 1296"

Two of the leading architects of those years, Ulrik Plesner and Aage Langeland Mathiesen, in collaboration with an engineer and a landscape designer, obtained the third prize for their "Arms of Copenhagen". Plesner and Mathiesen were among the main proponents of the neo-Baroque style in Denmark.[62] At the time of the competition, this style was steadily supplanting or, to put it better, prolonging National Romanticism. National Romanticism was mostly confined to the production of a few high-quality public buildings. After having acquired a first-hand experience of the neo-vernacular vocabulary in England, Plesner blended "Arts and Crafts" type of design with Nordic stylistic references. This provided a remarkable, coherent, practical repertoire to shape the built environment. Plesner and Mathiesen's memoir is only descriptive. The fact that an impressive relief plan and detailed drawings, today missing, were also provided as part of the entry makes a systematic comparison of this project with other awarded designs difficult.[63]

The plan combines a network of radials and a carefully studied "spider-net" system comprising six ring roads. To make the most of sunshine, streets are systematically oriented along a north-south axis—with the ensuing consequence that less attention is given to the existing topography and inherited road layout. In comparison with the projects discussed above, the inner grid of the district displays much more rigidity, and short, curved secondary streets convey a feeling of artificiality. Generally speaking, emphasis is placed on the density of housing blocks. However the strategy followed is exactly the opposite of the one followed in Strinz's and Bjerre's plan: The low-rise buildings are located on high ground and the high-rise on low ground. Unfortunately, except for a few sketched perspectives on small vignettes, most of the architectural drawings of this bronze medallist have disappeared from the archives. The vignettes depicting the squares of Valby and Vigerslev suggest a pleasant semi-rural, atmosphere. A significant part of the interest aroused by this contribution may have been concentrated in the detailed study of housing, the entry striving to attain the same innovative heights as the schemes produced for the 1907 Island Brygge Competition.

A site plan published in the *Maannedsskrift for Sundhedspleje* shows the pursuit of this research with the design of "closed", almost regular blocks, managing for a wide variety of resting places and playgrounds, and a lot of visually contrasted effects.[64] Likewise, the authors' allusion to the "Dutch picturesque" and the canal aesthetics in their plans for the Kalvebod area are noteworthy.[65] The plan does not suggest a further extension of the city, and no continuous ring belt is designed. As mentioned by the *Sundhedspleje*, the thoroughfares tend to converge toward few outer points.

However, this somewhat unfamiliar layout reflects the participants' wish to take into account the new ring of batteries planned during the 1885–1894 period, which could implied some restrictions on the location of the exit/entrance points of the capital. "København Vaaben 1296" is an original project, with a strong effort—in spite of providing for detached housing and low-density areas—to maintain a dense fabric conveying quite an urban character. This project demonstrates a strong attachment to the volumetric and stylistic homogeneity of the townscape.

With regard to the city core, the plans left the old fortification belt nearly intact, with a special provision for a park on Amager facing the fortification ring.

2.5 "Anno 1977"

The fourth prize-winning entry, referring to the fact that the population was expected to reach 1,250,000 by 1977, came from engineer O. K. Nobel and architect H. Rasmussen.

The 1909 competition proved rather successful for O. K. Nobel. In fact it was an "in-between event" that

62 Knud Millech, Kaj Fisker, *Danske. op.cit*, p. 253-259. On Plesner's contribution to housing architecture see Helge Finsen, *Arkitekten Ulrik Plesner*, Copenhagen, 1951.

63 Despite renewed diligent efforts of the Town Hall staff, it has been to this day impossible to locate this relief plan. For the memoir see, Beskrivelser til de fire præmierede og det inkøbte konkurrence – projekt angaaende bebyggelsens af Københavns ydre distrikter op. cit., p. 41-45.

64 See "Konkurrencen om Gade-og Bebyggelsesplan for Københavns ydre Distrikter", *Maanedsskrift for Sundhedspleje*, Vol 1908-1909, p. 131-152, esp.140-144.

65 *Idem.*

came after his second prize in the 1906 Fælledparken Competition and just before his first prize of 1910, with associates E. Fischer and H. Rasmussen, for the layout of the old railway station site. Both competitions were key events in the transformation of Copenhagen in the early twentieth-century.

The pair took a contrary stance to other competitors on several important issues; not being satisfied in their memoir with mere descriptions, they made comments about the options they proposed.[66] For instance, "Anno 1977" devoted very little attention to the new limits of the city. In fact, the "belt" idea is conspicuously absent, with little circular linkage or road linkage between the new districts. The emphasis is rather placed on expeditious railway transportation and the possibility of developing a subterranean and/or aerial network.

The extension layout of the road network was designed to protect "the larger part of existing gardens and plantations".[67] It was also pointed out that small open spaces are not really attractive, and that one should concentrate on large parks instead and ensures that they are disturbed by non-pedestrian traffic. The plan places such a park south of Amager, a district most often given over to open urbanisation by the other projects.

The duo's entry is characterised by relatively high building density along main arteries, though it advised, in general, favouring low building density. In addition to existing models within the Construction Law, the authors suggested adding a model ascribed with the "old Danish art of building"[68]: two-story homes and rows of abutting houses with back-gardens added. This type of layout, providing for numerous enclosed gardens benefiting from each other, is said to have been modelled after the provincial "købstad" (market town) tradition. This low-density construction also allows for the creation of interesting street profiles, with sudden openings on the "closes" or inner gardens. Also not explicit, this type of scheme is somewhat reminiscent of Camillo Sitte's observations on the "Großstadtgrün" problematic: the rejection of indiscriminate use of vegetation within the city and the idea of "innerer Gartenkern". Rasmussen and Nobel raise objections against the systematic plantation of trees, especially for the network of secondary streets. Other pieces of advice prove the attachment of Nobel and Rasmussen to the idea of urban continuity and atmosphere. More generally, the authors criticise the indiscriminate laying out of wide streets, which they deem unnecessarily expensive and boring. The authors also strongly feel that most of the existing naturally curved village streets should be preserved (Utterslev, Vigerslev and Emdrupsoen providing appropriate examples). Along a similar line, Rolf Schroeder also noted with satisfaction that Rasmussen and Nobel strove to preserve some traditional buildings, such as timber-framed farmhouses. After inclusion in the city they should be provided with a proper setting. Similarly the existing natural landscape and curiosities were to be preserved as much as possible.

The author noted the good collaboration between the architect and the engineer, the subtleties and refinement of most of the proposal, a sense of space and aesthetics in direct relation to the actual site, not restricted to the graphic effect to be seen on the plan.[69]

With regard to the city core, the plan remains cautious, not presenting any special connection. The authors are the only competitors to openly regret the demolitions of city's fortifications that took place in the late nineteenth century and the beginning of twentieth century [70]. In addition, they roundly rejected the stereotyped landscaping strategy adopted by that time. Consequently, they believed that "whatever remained, must be conserved",[71] and their plan provides for only two new connections between Christianshavn and Amager, discretely designed through two bastions. With a slightly dismissive attitude towards the common repertoire of contemporary planners, they remark that "modern districts and decorative parks can be found by the hundreds around the world",[72] while

66 *Beskrivelser til de fire præmierede og det inkøbte konkurrence... op. cit.*, p. 47-72.

67 *Idem.*

68 *Ibidem.*

69 Rolf Schroeder, "Gadeplanerne", *Architekten*, 5 June 1909, p. 416-418.

70 The last remains of the fortifications Østervold were destroyed by 1912; despite an active campaign, the attempts to preserve these landmarks proved unsuccessful. See, "Forslag til Østervolds Bevarelse", *Forskønnelsen*, 1912, N. 4 , p. 49-52.

71 *Idem.*

72 *Ibidem.*

the fortification site, rendered so memorably by the Norwegian painter Thaulow, still emanated a strong feeling of uniqueness. This entry very much echoes Nicolaus Lützhoft's and Peter Johansen appeals to safeguard the valuable historic and cultural aspects of Copenhagen city. (See Chapter 7).

The indirect impact that may have competitions and well articulated entries on physical planning is illustrated by the course of events concerning the fortifications of Christianshaven in the following years. The association *Foreningen til Hovedstadens Forskønnelse* got increasingly involved in general planning issues concerning the Capital city. The destiny of Christianshavns fortifications did then appeared as a topic likely to mobilise a sizeable group of citizens with the perspective of recovering large areas for public use from the army, which had planned to cease these lands. It was argued that in the hand of the municipality this would create a highly attractive leisure ground not only for the Copenhageners, but also for the inhabitants of the relatively depressed districts of Christianshaven and Sundbyerne. To this effect a Committee for the fortifications was created in summer 1913, with the backing of a number of personalities, including Bering Liisberg, and received the support of the City government. This led to the decision of preparing a plan, which would encompass the conservation of fortifications as well as the development of neighbouring areas on Amager, and the task was given to H. Rasmussen and O. K. Nobel. The campaign for the preservation of the fortifications was successful enough to collect the means for some restoration works and the design of a park on the southern part of the enceinte. In summer 1916, the committee could hold a feast to celebrate the first step of the fortifications' restoration. The project's plan was ready by 1915. Its design was a handy combination of the awarded entries of 1909, integrating the suppleness of Urania's layout, the provision for English type of 'closes' as well as play grounds and gardens aiming at reinforcing the 'ring feature'.[73]

73 For an account of this project together with the plans, see "Kristianshavns Volds Bevarelse, Forskønnelsesforeningens plan til voldens regulering", *Forskønnelsen*, 1916, N. 3-4, p. 41-50. In 1915, the restoration of the enceinte and the landscaping was entrusted to the architects Erik Erstad-Jørgensen and Kai Gottlob.

2.6 "Wayland Smed"

Weyland Smed, or Wayland the Smith, was a mythological figure in Germany and in Scandinavia. He had become a byword for the art of the smith and the forging of supernatural objects.[74] Such a reference is not surprising in as much many of Raavad's works show a keen interest in Nordic folk culture.

Raavad's project is probably one of the most atypical plans among the Danish entries. In fact, its somewhat provocative design made such an impression on the jury that the municipality decided to purchase the plan. Raavad's "policy of graphism" should be underlined here, standing as it does antipodal to the type of drawing in Strinz's plan. Raavad's plan presents itself as a "sketch", which alternates with the sharpness of the drawings provided for few new urban nuclei and "empty territory" left to further development with but a few indications of transportation lines. The contrast between the rigidity of the few geometrically designed districts—in keeping with heavy engineering work—and the informal suppleness of the suggested traffic lines conveys a dynamic vision of the city that sets Raavad's style worlds apart from other entries. The written document is also most imaginative, including photographs and sketches depicting the way of life of city folk as well as forms of urban leisure.[75] Raavad presented himself officially as a "consulting engineer and civic designer". He had presented in the same year 1908 a series of articles on the subject of "the architect as sociologist", published in *Arkitekten* (See, Chapter 2).

His plan constituted an imaginative mixture, a free interpretation and blending of European and American features. In his memoir, Raavad made explicit references to Stübben and Sitte, while in the same breath admonishing against too superficial a reading of their writings. Raavad's design was simultaneously informed by a search for Danishness, a quest for roots that was forcefully expressed in his often convoluted and visionary discourse. At first, he seems to prioritise what we have described as the first dimension of planning,

74 According to legend, he could not refuse any commission, no matter how impossible the task, once he had been offered a payment.

75 *Beskrivelser til de fire præmierede og det inkøbte konkurrence... op. cit.*, p. 75-109.

energetically promoting Copenhagen as an important maritime hub for an international sea route. However, he goes on to consider the other dimensions thoughtfully, particularly the relationship between the 'old' and the 'new'.

Raavad strongly advocated the shifting of a substantial part of transoceanic traffic between Europe and America. He repeatedly argued that the northern route toward America was the shortest and that Greenland could provide a convenient station. Accordingly Copenhagen, situated at the mouth of the Baltic, could be promoted as a major Northern European harbour.

In his proposal, the macro-form of the city is transformed drastically by the creation of a Øresund channel deflecting part of the navigation away from the city. Raavad aims at catching the traffic by getting a proper ship's draught to lay the foundation for the construction of large-scale harbour installations and industrial districts in southwestern Copenhagen (See Chapter 5, 4 E). However, fascinating as this aspect of harbour engineering might have been, he was criticised for being out of touch with the economic reality of the city. It is worth noting that he was to insist again at the end of the First World War on the necessity of modernising the port facilities of Copenhagen, giving an extensive report on the question of harbour utilities in a column in *Architekten.*

His plan of 1909 would have diminished trans-urban naval traffic and would have, concentrated most new industries to the south.

Raavad also aimed at changing the relationship between the city and the sea. For him, as a seaport, the Danish capital was decidedly introverted. He was convinced that Copenhagen should be developed as a summer seaside resort for the leisure and health benefit of its inhabitants, and accordingly, he designed a park and beach complex facing Christianshavn, while the opening of the proposed channel would have put part of Christianshavn's bastions in close contact to the open sea.

The drawing plan is almost silent concerning the core of the city; connections between the new districts and the city centre are only sketched out, leaving one to assume that they follow the existing street network. As Amager would be further cut off from Christianshavn by the digging of the canal, subterranean linkages are proposed.

Raavad made his views more explicit a few years later in *Architekten.*[76] Ravaad's thinking in matters of planning often proceeds through a mixture of provocative, paradoxical and purposely digressive statements converging toward a balanced final argument. In an article on "geometric streets plans", he acknowledges the value and inheritance of the European pre-industrial street plans, while leaving large room for transformation. He explicitly deplored the demolishing of Copenhagen's gates. In parallel he went on mocking the excesses of the German school, with its love for "fantastic irregularities". For him, such a practice of random imitation, falling not far short of forgery, only debased the value of authentic ancient buildings and other evidence of the past. He went on even more vehemently about arbitrary relocations and copies of historic remains (also see infra). Concerning the built fabric of inner Copenhagen, he deplored the inconsiderate lengthening of streets. Moreover, he declared that if "vandalism was the chosen path", and then streets should be straight and short and allow for gardens. At the same time he suggested the maintenance of old street lines patterns. That modernity should also allow for a quantum of "vandalism" was made perfectly clear a few year later in another article concerning the transformation of Knippelsbro in order to upgrade port installations.[77]

With regard to the extension, only outlines were suggested, with landscaping devices and sketches of new urban nuclei repeating quite an ingenious, if slightly obsessive, pattern of clusters or groups of housing, which incorporates inner pathways almost isolated from transit traffic (see 2A). Furthermore, according to the proposal, the "natural environment" of marshes, woods and meadows which made up the city boundary would be maintained and, if need be, reinforced by planting dark conifers. With respect to the extension zone, Raavad stressed the crucial importance in his eyes of the "understanding and development of existing topography".[78] He mocked the then

76 The article "Geometriske Gadeplaner" is part of the series titled "Architekten som sociolog"; *Architekten*, N. 21, 24 February 1912, p. 239-242.

77 The article is part of the series, "Havn og Industri som elementer af byplanen"; *Architekten*, N. 23, 9 March 1918, p. 216-218.

78 *Beskrivelser til de fire præmierede og det inkøbte konkurrence... op. cit.*, p. 98

current "Nordic tradition" of grouping rural buildings in a picturesque manner in open-air museums, when rural villages throughout the country were being dismantled. In other words, Raavad probably took the clearest stance on this issue, maintaining that existing surrounding villages belonged to Copenhagen's "historic heritage", and should not only be preserved but also "naturally" developed, in harmony with their surroundings. This stance seems to have made a strong impression on contemporary observers. Architect Poul Holsøe (1873-1966) (who had a leading role in creating the "Tegnehjælp" (design assistance group) at the initiative of the *Akademisk Architectforening* between 1908-1912 and was later to play a leading role in Denmark's conservation movement) underlined in the *Gads danske Magasin* the positive and original contribution of Raavad's extension scheme concerning the villages.[79] In the same vein was his suggestion to preserve or to re-establish the ancient toponymy. Finally, he advised that a decentralised administrative model should be employed in the peripheries, taking its cue from the London borough system. Eleven 'civic-centres' should be modelled on the Old Danish villages with a central square and a symbolic "ting" (See Figure 2B). He laid great stress on the fact that each unit should be conceived from this decentralised perspective, allowing for a real diversity of the suburban area.

It can be noted that Raavad's entry for the competition of 1912 for the Australian capital shows reuses one of the basic housing-block cluster already to be found in his Copenhagen 1909 entry (See Chapter 5, 2A). Ravaad's Canberra entry relies on the combination of three grid layers, orthogonal, transversal and octagonal, which with more little good fortune fits in with its "meandering gade" system. This grid is geometrically articulated around a horseshoe-shaped "acropolis" opening onto a monumental perspective passing over across the river and through to the cathedral. It should be worth undertaking a systematic comparison of the discrepancies occurring between Raavad's Copenhagen and Canberra plans, and also Gellerstedt's plan for the two cities. The two city competitions give us the chance to evaluate the adjustment of planner know-how for planning a 'colonial city' or planning the extension and transformation of an existing one. Suffice it here to say, that Gellersted exercise consist in translating some of the principles of European Civic Art to a bare land with a radio-concentric non-geometric plan and an intricate pattern of enclosed spaces combining all sorts of forms. Contrarily, Raavad's plan for Canberra combines what is essentially a geometrical layout with a strong focus on the study of hydraulic engineering work, which was a security issue in relation to the risk of flooding in the case of Canberra.

Raavad's entry for Canberra shows much less of the dynamic relationship illustrated in his Copenhagen entry, where he successfully managed to balance preservation concerns with city development. In the meantime it can be said that his Canberra entry hold positively a comparison with much of the geometrical layout exercises offered during this competition. In particular it allows for some conciliation between neighbourhoods of relatively closed units with their inner service lanes and multidirectional inter- and trans-urban traffic network. As we have shown with Civic Art, the City Beautiful label should be used very prudently, such caution applying in general, as the movement is far from homogeneous in its manifestations, but even more so concerning Raavad, for another set of reasons.

It should be underlined that Raavad's type of design for Canberra shares more relationship with an imaginative and innovative interpretation of engineers' know-how in layout design as accumulated throughout the nineteenth century, than with the academic references which form the main matrix of 'City Beautiful'. This is particularly visible when he makes every attempt to articulate monumentality and axial patterns with his grid layout, trapezoidal and nodular forms completely alien to the neo-classical type of design.

2.7 The Swedish Entries

Leading Swedish planners credited with having introduced the "Sittian" school into the Nordic countries were also among the competitors. Their works were

79 Poul Holsøe, "Fra Kjøbenhavnske torve og gader", *Gads Dansk Magasin*, 1910-1911, p. 281-289, p. 282. Holsøe was a member of *Det særlige Bygningssyn* from 1918 to 1943.

somehow dissimilar from the projects described above. Yet they display a wide variety of approaches indicative of professionals who may be described as having been under the influence of the Civic Art current of design.

"Stor Kjøbenhavn"

F. Sundbärg's project, on which he was seconded by Lillienberg, (the later just embarking on a prolific career), is one good example. In his short memoir, Sundbärg described "great cities" as those shaped by forces that should be harnessed to avoid the development of contradictory impulses.[80] He believed – in the sense that infrastructure network comprises relatively immovable objects, producing enduring constraints – that maximum attention should be given in the Copenhagen plan to railways and ports and ad hoc industrial facilities, which would then forge the very foundation of the new city, command the road systems and shape the main characteristics of the district. Thus, Sündbarg's plan presents a holistic image of an industrial city, integrating to the north and to the south port facilities and detailing the points of railways and road connections. The city is thereby approached as a systemic unit at all levels, and the author also insists upon the desirability of a "system" linking "natural spaces".

In his proposal, Sündbärg would preserve the whole of the core city as well as the fortifications for "their historic value"[81] and, in effect, his plan displays a city centre which main thoroughfares are left essentially untouched.

However, as the city centre was being progressively dedicated to commercial and business activities, Sundbärg conceded that enlargement might, in many cases, be justified if it were to lead to easier access to the centre. With respect to the periphery, the plan is virtually filled out completely. This "big city" proposal combined segments allying curved ring roads with engulfed axial patterns, reminiscent of Baroque design. Moreover, an unmistakable similarity with Strinz's methods of drawing is there as well, with a strong emphasis on adaptability and continuity that is particularly obvious in the integration of existing villages into the plan. However, we should observe that somehow the Swedish architect lacks the surveyor's skill in dealing with topographical details and plot structure, and one experiences some sense of artificiality in the layout of projected allotments. For his part Sundbärg seems far more concerned with the importance of architectural effects -perspectives with possible axial closure, for example – in the newly built districts.

Finally, the plan displays considerable variety—e.g. a wealth of possible picturesque effects – but compared to other projects discussed here, particularly the Danish ones, the soundness of its approach to conservation seems questionable (see *infra* for further details).

"For Byen og Borgerne"

Attempting as it does to balance the practical needs of accommodating social groups with more abstract needs such as satisfying "spiritual" and aesthetic requirements, Gellersted's entry takes a definite stand.[82] Accordingly, the city is presented as a matrix for the education and cultural development of its inhabitants. Yet the practical consequences of this stand are not really made explicit, beyond a general search to provide a satisfying framework for social and economic development. Zoning organisation is given a top priority in articulating the peripheries. High-density zones are mainly concentrated in the Valby, Sunby and Utterslev area, together with Brygerrvangen (already quite urbanised at the time), these areas looking like huge "free-floating" urban fragments. The linkage of Utterslev with Bryggervangen is thoroughly studied. An electric urban-railway ring is provided, with an underground connection towards the city centre. Layout details, especially for theses areas, are designed with great care, producing an urbanised extension with focus on simplicity of form. No flights of geometrical fancy are attempted and while Gellersted, Hallman and Sundbärg might rightly be described as sharing the same fundamentals in design, the results are no-

80 Stadsarkivet, Stadsingeniørens Direktorat, Byplankontoret – BP sager 1918-1984, Sag 977: memoir *Stor-Kjøbenhavn.*

81 *Idem.*

82 Stadsarkivet, Ejendomsdirektorat – Hovedjournalsager – Sag EJ 1150 /1925: memoir *For Byen og Borgerne.*

tably different. This is no doubt due to design practices influenced by differing professional backgrounds.

Gellersted's attitude seems quite restrained concerning architectural effect, with less emphasis on ornamental public squares. The few plazas designed are carefully organised, e.g. a square in the vicinity of Lersoe area exemplifying the designer's wish to adept the planned suburbs to the existing urban environment. Gentle curves are preferred to straight roads and squares present a closed aspect with civic buildings designed in a sober "monumental" or "picturesque" manner.[83]

In relation to the city core, no special protective device is considered. On the contrary, Gellersted's plan is one of the few plans to highlight an inner-city network organisation to which central connecting functions are ascribed. Moreover a ring road is provided on Christianshavn's bastions, the latter being conserved.

A few years later, in the absence of German competitors, Gellersted was to be the lone follower of the "Sittian"-influenced current of planning to enter the Canberra competition. While rejecting the English or Scottish model of old cities, as well as the American "wilderness of bricks and mortars", \ he significantly made a point in distinguishing his project from the so-called German style, saying that "Still less must it pay tribute to the German tendency towards building cities after medieval patterns."[84]

In fact Gellersted's entry adopted a sober nineteenth-century style of continental European city with its Ringstrasse, its monumental city district and its functional distribution. In the austral wilderness, the plan looks like an awkward if skilled plagiary of a densely urbanised model far removed from most of the "colonial" types of plans. This awkwardness can be partly explained by the conspicuous absence of the expected basis of this model, that is, a stock of inherited ordinary housing.

While sharing much of the Civic Art approach, Gellersted's design during this 1909-1912 period can already be seen as seeking to sever the links of strict allegiance to this current.

"Richesse oblige"

Hallman's project could be qualified as minimalist, both as regards the memoir and the drawing plan.[85] Feeders are shown stopping awkwardly short of the edge of the city centre, suggesting possible crossings as in Gellersted's plan. A weak deflecting thoroughfare is shown on the west flank of the city. Large portions of the existing primary and secondary network in the periphery are left untouched, but existing radial arteries are utilised in the periphery to vertebrate growth lines, suggesting long and unarticulated corridor streets. A few nuclei of urbanisation are clearly shown on communal land. The layout displays a somewhat sinuous pattern at times, which does not seem to flow as naturally Strinz's drawing does. The influence of F. L. Olmsted's landscaping forms on Hallman was noted already in the context of mining communities built in Sweden at the turn of the century;[86] however, it follows land divisions and road networks quite closely. The Sittian principle of multiplying squares in cluster patterns is applied quite systematically.

"Gefion"

Engineers Elliot and Påhlman presented an less developed entry, which essentially focuses along the same lines. The street network is fairly adaptive, lending the design a great deal of plasticity. Accordingly, architectonic effects are more subdued. A special attention is paid to the layout of an industrial port in the southern area of Kalvebod.

83 Idem, p. 23. It is specified in Gellersted's memorandum that no perspective drawings are provided with the plans. It is argued that the only use of such drawings is to seduce the jury. It should be noted that Gellersted's Canberra entry (in collaboration with Ivan Lindgren and Hugo du Rietz) was presented with lavish perspective drawings.

84 Quoted from John W. Reps, *Canberra 1912 – Plans and Planners of the Australian Capital Competition*, Melbourne, 1997.

85 Stadsarkivet, Ejendomsdirektorat – Hovedjournalsager – Sag EJ 1150 /1925: memoir *Richesse Oblige.*

86 Mats Ahnlund and Lasse Brunnström, "The Company Town in Scandinavia", in John S. Garner (ed.), *The Company Town, Architecture and Society in the Early Industrial Age,* New York & Oxford, 1992, p. 75-108, p. 92-93.

2.8 Overview of other Proposals

Of the nine remaining projects, two do not explicitly address the relation between the core city and the extension zone.[87] These two entries, with the addition of V. Ahlman's contribution, provide us with little details as to the few developed zones, but do give an overview of the programme of implementation. In the main, attention is devoted to traffic lines and districts linkage. The displayed limits of the Great Copenhagen are merely administrative.

The entry of Clausen provides more details. In the latter, the entire plan is filled out with detailed drawings of districts. This highly skilled and "architect-minded" type of project can be associated without hesitation with the Civic Art current, demonstrating leanings toward a Baroque type of design. Clausen's plan a high-density belt between Brønshøj and Utterslev. This zone is entirely vertebrate through a chain of Baroque plazas of all types (horseshoe, squared, round, etc.) with the central scheme radiating from Utterslev. On top of that a serpentine boulevard is well articulated to what could be described as a system of public squares. Parks are small but gardens quite numerous. The variety of patterns could almost be seen as a design extravaganza. But the plan is demonstrate a sound conception and skilled architectural practice. The shape of squares in particular is carefully designed, organising intricate clusters of blocks of housing. No indication is given concerning the city core. This plan demonstrates that the morphological approach recommended by Sitte had a strong echo in Denmark. This especially should be noted, as Clausen was to become by 1910 a member of the committee of the Akademisk Architektforeningen. As in Plesner and Mathiesen's entry, Clausen's plan is an architect's interpretation of Civic Art principles and "adaptability" is not a systematic concern. Built forms of some of the villages (Vigerslev, Husum) seem to be partly conserved and integrated into the general street network. The city limits are left open for further development. The graphic quality is good, obviously aimed at conveying the idea of a coherent physical urban unit. In contrast Clausen's written document remains only descriptive.

Finally, V. Ahlman's plans concentrates on a few areas of urbanisation, in relation to communal ownership in Bryggervangen, Valby and to a lesser extent Sundby. No layout details are given. Yet the City Archives have preserved plans of carefully designed blocks of housing of sober Baroque inspiration, with street frontages in serrated lines.

"Grönne Baand" deserves special notice, as this project seems to be the first full-scale extension plan authored by Hans Bernoulli. Unfortunately, we are left only with a copy of the overall plan.[88]

In his proposal, Bernoulli propounds his aim: a "quiet and harmonious" implementation of the project.[89] Bernoulli clearly refrains from suggesting any violation of the city core. In addition, the importance of ancient country roads in ensuring spatial and temporal continuity is underlined, and Bernoulli emphasises the advisability of maintaining the surrounding villages. Although his plans for the secondary extension network displays some rigidity, Bernoulli demonstrates a close affinity with the design principles of many of his Danish counterparts.

The six remaining projects are quite explicit concerning their treatment of the city core. Only two of them advise the dismantling of the fortifications. The "Julemærket" project of engineers Frölich and Klixbüll features a new district in Amager to be built in close proximity to Christianshavn. The plan of the Spanish architect Ferran Romeu, "Axel Hus" unfolds in each new district its Beaux-Art 'Grand Manner' style. Such a layout, with emphasis on axiality and symmetry of volumes and perspective vistas, is likewise expounded in a trivium road pattern toward the south of Amager Island. To the North this design comes into close contact with Christianshavn, de facto erasing the crescent-shaped form of the southern part of the city. By a matter of fact, Romeu opened his written document with:

87 For each project, which are referred to in this paragraph, see the corresponding notice in Chapter 2 with the archive references.

88 It has not been possible to trace them in Bertnoulli's collection in Zurich despite the efforts of the staff at the GTA Archives.

89 Stadsarkivet, Ejendomsdirektorat – Hovedjournalsager – Sag EJ 1150 /1925: memoir *Grönne Baand.*

”Pour l’extension logique de la ville” by advising “la démolition des murailles de Christianshavn, pour agrandir le port et le poser en contact avec Syndbyerne et convertir le district en quartier commercial.”[90]

As we have already mentioned, nothing could have been more alien to the dominant spirit of nostalgia that followed the demolishing of the City’s fortification. On the other hand, Romeu’s plan clearly delineates the existing villages to keep those outside the zoning’s proposal. But one cannot conclude on the assessment Romeu might have made whether to conserve the villages or not. There are no detailed site plans in the Town Hall Archives, and the memoir does not refer to that matter. Romeu was the only competitor to receive negative comments in the press. He certainly had not been acknowledged in Denmark as one of the period’s leading architects in Barcelona.

Among the remaining projects, the entries entitled “Storstad” and “Mindre parker men parkalléer” display a strong geometrical character. The “Storstad” booklet insists on a preference for tangential circulation for squares, short curved streets and short straight streets ending up on monuments and closed squares. The two authors propose the construction of an “English type of district”.[91] Engineer Rolf Erslev’s project is almost a caricature of what was often presented by architects as an engineer’s approach to design practice (for further details See Chapter 5, 7F) The main focus of Erslev’s project lies with the study of an underground mass transportation network. However, Erslev’s mention of the “beautiful fortifications of Christianshavn” and his advice to leave the surrounding areas free of any constructions is noteworthy.[92] Storstad concentrates on zoning repartition and traffic lines. The district is characterised by but a few squares, an unimaginative layout and rough connecting devices as well as an intersecting road network with little plasticity. Radiating thoroughfares unfold onto Amager.

Two last entries must be considered as quite developed. “Hafnia”, authored by Norwegian engineer E. Bjerknes recalls the Swedish project approaches already described, though it provides little detail on inner districts lay out.[93] The written document sets forth the aim of the author to adapt his plan as much as possible to the existing conditions of the road network and to develop existing potentialities. A ring of open spaces is supposedly linked by a system of alleys distinct from the traffic road. However, this scheme is much less elaborate compared to other projects. The core city as shown is fully integrated into the global traffic network; the fortification ring is also conserved.

”Bella” by the hand of architect Hygom and engineers Manicus-Hansen and Einsersen is a ‘comprehensive’ entry displaying what might be deemed a ‘middle range’ kind of grid that could be compared to Bernoulli’s entry. A north-south axis running through Christianshavn to Nytorv Square is suggested. This entry takes into account some of the features of the pre-existing layout and displays a large amount of detail. Carl Brummer singled out “The beautiful and picturesque roads set in terraces”.[94] This project, which might be interpreted within the context of the development of Den Fri Architektforening, received positive comments from the press. The written document confirms the wish of the authors to start the project by taking into account the contour lines. In particular, the idea is to conserve the character of the hilly top of “Bellahøj” and possibly to accentuate some aspects by implanting high buildings on high ground. The authors of the project also recommend the conservation of the “rustic” character of the old “entrance” to the city surroundings, namely Lyngbyvej.[95]

90 ”The logical extension of the city (…) the demolishing of the walls of Christiansand (sic) to enlarge the port, to afford some contact with Sundbyerne and to convert it into a commercial district” (our translation) Romeu’s memoir: Stadsarkivet, Ejendomsdirektorat- Hovedjournalsager, Sag EJ 1150/ 1925, kas. 3.

91 Memoir *Storstad: Stadsarkivet*, Idem.

92 Memoir *Mindre Parker Men Parkalleer*: Stadsarkivet, Ibidem.

93 Memoir *Hafnia*: Stadsarkivet, Ibid.

94 Carl Brummer “Bebyggelsesplan for kommunens ydre distrikter”, *Berlingske*, 21 January 1908.

95 Memoir *Bella*, p.2, Stadsarkivet, Stadsingeniørens Direktorat, Byplankontoret – BP sager 1918-1984, Sag 977.

5 CITY FORMS IN DETAIL

This chapter is devoted to the analysis of plans details according to a number of thematic. The figures that are arranged into seven plates provide the material for the following discussion. We consider plans as relatively autonomous discursive practices whose techniques can be scrutinised in relation to the development of a professional field, e.g. town planning, independently of effective implementation on the ground.[1] Moreover, the plans submitted to the Copenhagen competition were not requested with the intent of implementation, but to provide the city administration with orientations and ideas. Therefore, plans can offer insight into alternative design strategies of their time. They reflect specific configurations that might help elucidate the dynamic of professions and of the disciplinary field. In this sense, tools developed in the field of urban morphology (that is study of transformations as stratified over time in the built form) are of lesser use when considering projects presenting a synchronic image of the city. In this respect, plans have more to say about the imagination and ethos of planners, about professional rivalries and strategies, about the history of techniques of design and graphic style. They say less – at least directly – about the physical process the city is undergoing through.

The following paragraphs provide salient commentary on part of the existing graphic documents with respect to the nineteen entries. Some of the subject matter, which the analysis of the entries has already approached in Chapter 4, is considered here in depth. We have selected a series of plans' details that are arranged in eight thematic comparative sets. The details are taken from the general plans of a number of entries, which are kept at the Town Hall's Archives in Copenhagen, and the references are the same as the ones given in Chapter 2. Each graphic set is organised with reference to one thematic that is summarised in the set's title. Two plates are devoted to the design style of K. Strinz and of A. Raavad respectively. Five plates show a selection of elements from distinct general plans to illustrate planners' strategies in relation to a particular issue. At the end of this chapter, Box 4 sums up characteristics, which are commented here, as they can be analysed in the nineteen entries according to five main criteria.

1 Karl Strinz's Design – Plate 1: 1A & 1B

Squares play a central role in articulating space in Civic Art type of design practice. Asymmetry as a formal characteristic is usually developed according to what is thought being the natural development of old roadways. Framing new built spaces intends to show the greatest consideration for the existing conditions of the site, existing roads and lanes, and property boundaries, so as to make the best of topographical elements. Accordingly, 'free flowing' baroque patterns are greatly valued. The assessment of the square as a founding element of public space leads to paying particular attention to the creation of an attractive open space whose main function is certainly not to be a circulatory device for vehicles. Camillo Sitte succeeded in applying his principles to extension plans, which

1 Our analysis is informed by various approaches, including historical geography, urban morphology as linking architectural analysis, construction history and urban historical geography, and spatial analysis; see Harold Carter, *The Study of Urban Geography*, London, 1995, Anne Vernez Moudon, "The origins and development of the International Seminar on Urban Form", *Urban Morphology 1*, 1997, p. 3-10, Philippe Panerai, Jean Charles Depaule, Marcelle Demorgon, *Analyse Urbaine*, Marseille, 1999.

Karl Strinz's Design

Plate 1

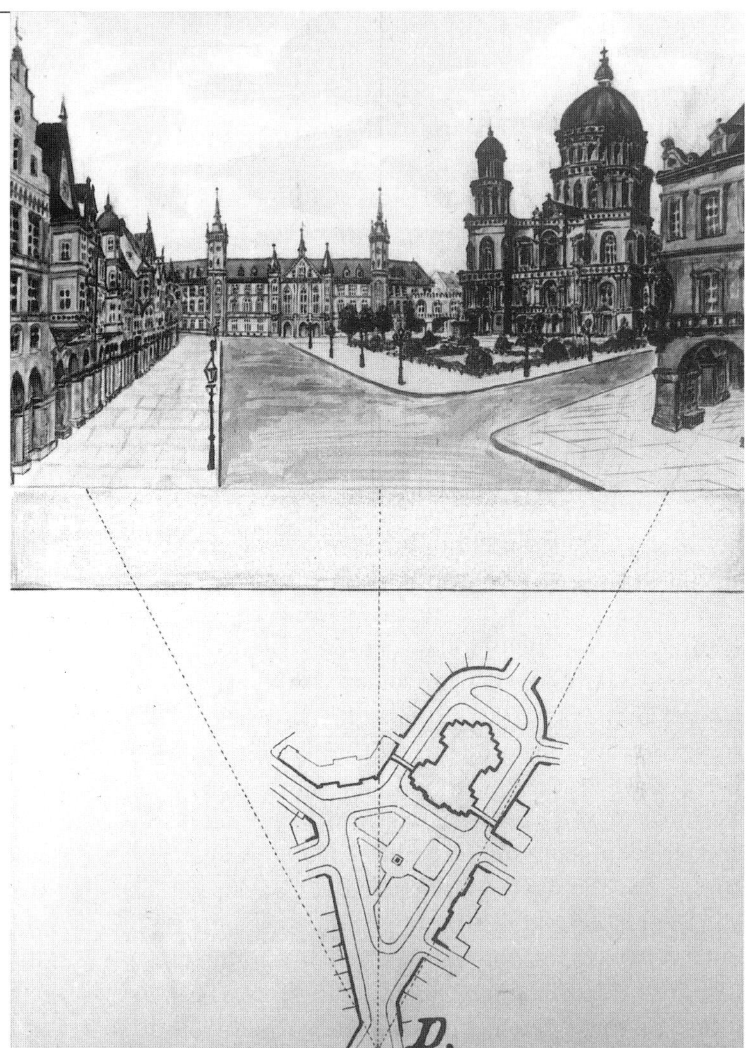

1a

1b

display a great variety of patterns trying to embody inherited parcelling and roads system. In his 1893 Munich plan, Karl Henrici systematically explored the three-dimensional options of the formula to generate myriads of irregular square patterns. Strinz's project pursues this line of thought with 30 different squares layouts that often are the outgrowth of available roads junctions, and the turbine plaza's principle is adjusted to topographical peculiarities and pre-existing roads network. Plate 1 shows the application of a set of rules laid down by the Austro-German school of design: tangential circulation, closure device, non-orthogonal implantation of buildings and decorative elements adorning plazas (fountains, statues, etc.). This complex layout is over emphasised by the surrounding buildings with ornamentation of various historical architectural styles – such as oriel windows, pinnacles, turrets, gables with a stepped outline, and arcades, which juxtaposes neo-Gothic, neo-Renaissance or neo-Baroque references. Accordingly, a 'Sittian device', namely arched porticos, marks the main view on the square (1 A) to convey a sense of completeness. If the perspective drawings can be seen as of dubious quality and with poor reference to Danish architecture, it still communicate the idea of 'rooted complexity' as stressed by the Austro-German school of design. Urban design skill of the Bonn surveyor, however, should not be assessed at the yardstick of his architectural drawings. The ability for gauging relationships between plots and roads network, and as a consequence a suitable treatment of building masses, has to be balanced against a poor command of drawing techniques and of the art of the architect.

2 Alfred Raavad's Design – Plate 2: 2A-2D

Raavad's design strategy for extension planning is three-fold: maintaining the existing villages while enhancing their centres, creating patterns for site plans, and developing "civic centres". Figure 2A shows an example of a housing cluster that Raavad labelled 'Meandering Gader'. The spatial configuration could be compared to an adaptation of the 'turbine plaza' typology, but as an orthogonal version of it. The main purpose of the somehow labyrinthine pattern is to create a quarter with public spaces protected from transit traffic. The central square is to be used as playgrounds, public garden, or any other collective use. Raavad envisioned organising this type of clusters as a parallelogram or a rhombus to be adaptive to the primary roads network at the scale of the master plan. This pattern could be replicated and integrated in-between existing thoroughfares, plots then being filled up with different types of buildings to lend each cluster its own volume and character. Raavad made use of this concept in his entry for the Canberra competition, though he applied it by following a straightforward orthogonal layout.

Figure 2B shows a civic centre model with features conceived primarily as symbols of Danes culture. On the large square a circle of granite stones and trees refer to the Nordic Ting (assembly) to illustrate the meaning of a tight community. The domed shape building the "people's palace", also suggests a harmony between nature and civic assembly while a circular ring of arcades affords a transition between inside and outside. Raavad believed that squares and public buildings could be the proper locations to exercise public control and generate a stronger urban feeling. Moreover, he recommended a decentralised administration at the level of the great municipality.

Figure 2C gives an example of leisure facilities with a watchtower proposed to enhance some of the "natural places" to be preserved in the new districts. As model installation, this pavilion is intended to increase public awareness about the surrounding landscape of moors and woods.

Figure 2D provides an illustration of street blocks. This grouping of buildings, termed "sluttet bebyggelse", is animated by a back line creating a contrasted effect, which is reinforced by gable-ended overhangs and towers enhanced by multi-coloured brick works. It is interesting here to notice that Raavad favoured low density housing in the annexed districts, which he perceived as part of a general trend toward democratic rights with access to individual housing units for the working classes. At the same time, he thought that this system should be departed from, to structure the city as such, of which density was a chief criterion. Raavad often suggested to consider the advantages

Alfred Raavad's Design

Plate 2

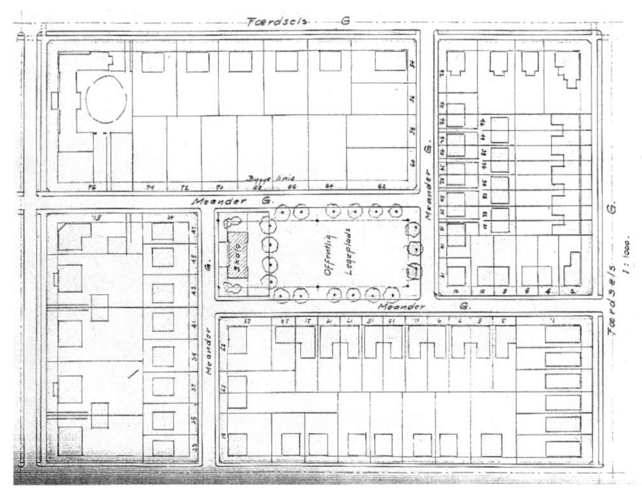

2a

2b

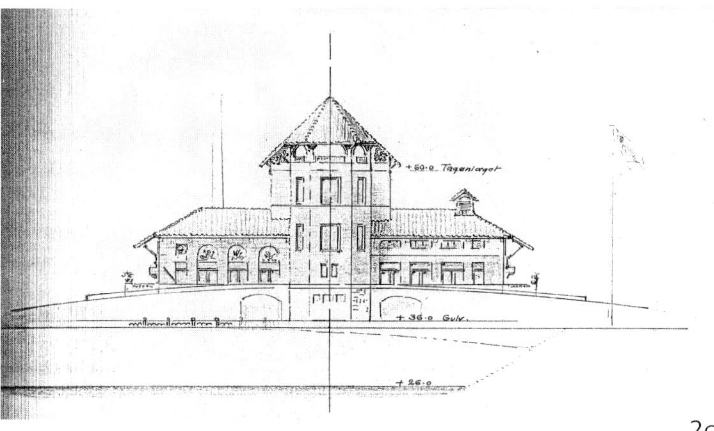

2c

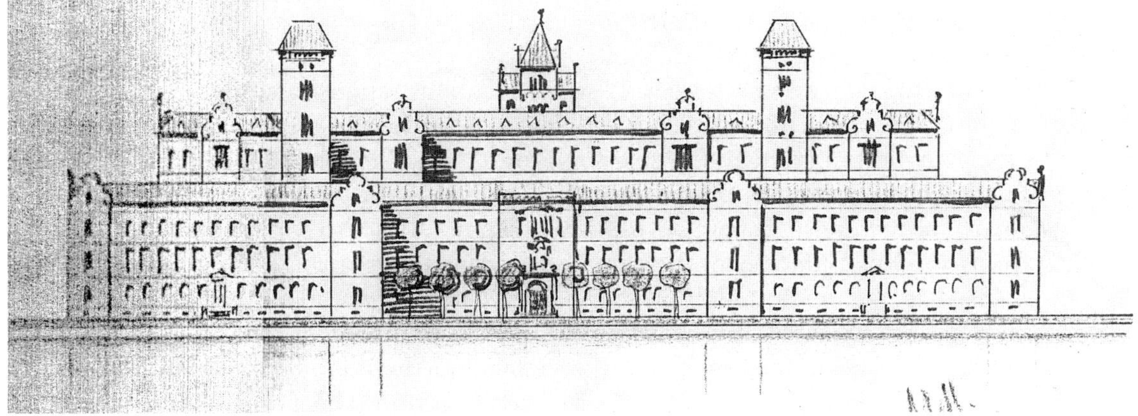

2d

those American high-rise buildings could have to develop a European city. Architectonic effects and monumentality thus should be associated with the growth of the city, and architects should be given enough room for free expression, he felt. This figure provides an example of one possible treatment of traditional street blocks, termed "Sluttet Bebyggelse" (closed block of constructions), with the back line creating a contrast effect, which is reinforced by gable-ended overhangs and towers enhanced by multi-coloured brick works.

In contrast to Strinz's design this can be qualified as 'transitional architecture', style's reference becoming minimal and quite indistinct.

3 Incorporating Villages – Plate 3: 3A – 3H

In the illustrations 3A, 3C, 3E and 3G are shown alternative options for integrating the village of Husum in the northwest of Copenhagen's extension as designed by Strinz, Bjerre, Raavad and Hallman. Meanwhile, illustrations 3B, 3D, 3F and 3H display the strategies propounded by the same competitors for the village of Vigerslev, south to Husum, bordering the western boundary of Copenhagen's extension.

It can be summarily assumed that the four town planners followed a common approach toward the conservation of the existing villages, though the schemes greatly differ from each other. One could characterise Strinz' approach as 'conservationist' in relation to Civic Art design. Oblong and crescent-like types of squares emerge in Husum and Vigerslev. Those central arrangements are planed as nuclei of urbanisation adapting to the radiating pattern of land plots in Husum, and to strip shaped forms in Vigerslev. We should notice that the conservation of existing buildings seems to be the exception rather than the rule – an example of building conservation is found south of the Husum Square. The method, here applied, supposedly springs from a thorough concern for the 'genius loci'. If the original place is formally unsalvageable as a whole, the new building or places subsumes some of the former qualities of the place, then transmitted to future generations.

In Bjerre's design (3C & 3D) the villages are merely traces as the focus of connecting lanes and roads. Despite strong emphasis on zoning, options for a likely development of these locations are not excluded, though the zoning partition splits village areas. Total obliteration, however, is avoided, but conservation is kept to a minimum. This exemplifies what one may call a 'middle range' approach.

Raavad's scheme (3E & 3F), on the other hand, should fall in the 'preservationist' category. The edges of existing villages are carefully delineated by pencil marks, and deflecting devices protect the connecting points. Possible integration of the "meandering gader" system (2A) is also displayed. Such a strategy is unique among the nineteen entries.

Hallman's plans (3G & 3H) show a radically different choice for the villages selected here. It is apparent that the corridor street of the main West-East thoroughfare closely borders Husum while splitting its south area in two parts. The likely connections are impractical, if not useless, and the village is left for rapid transformation. The treatment of Vigerslev is dubious; it seems to be kept untouched while a nucleus of urbanization is developed next to it. There is no indication in Hallman's plan toward the conservation of the villages. This suggest us that the 'Sittian school' of urban design was one option among others, at least in 1908, for Swedish planners who had placed the 'new German design' at the forefront of town planning.

4 The City's Boundaries and the Fortifications – Plate 4: 4A – 4E

The five illustrations show the treatment of Christianshavn's fortification on Amager Island by Strinz (4A), Bjerre (4B), Plesner (4C), Fischer (4D) and Raavad (4D).

Figure 4A shows a continuous green belt with a tree-lined ring boulevard. The bastions and moats are removed to be replaced by parkland. At the same time, the form of the fortifications is kept to maintain the break and the boundary's definition of the old defence structure. This project clearly refers to the op-

Incorporating Villages Alternative Design Strategies

Plate 3

3a

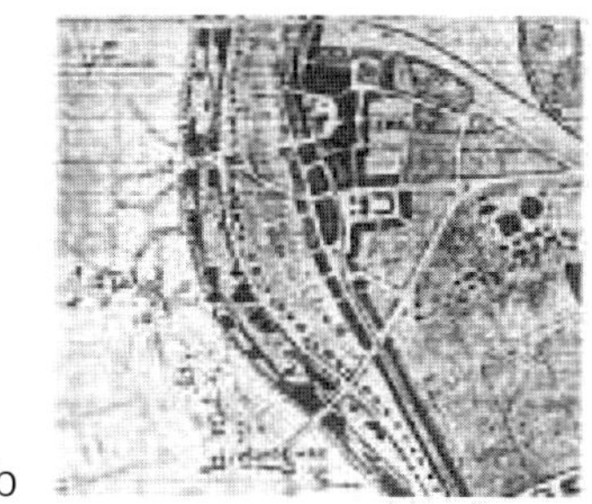

3b

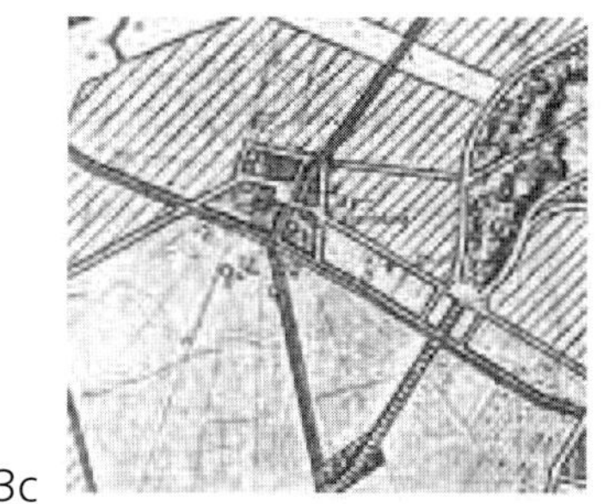

3c

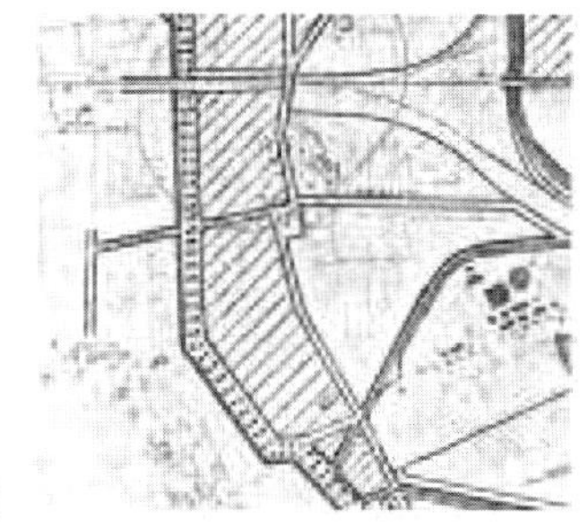

3d

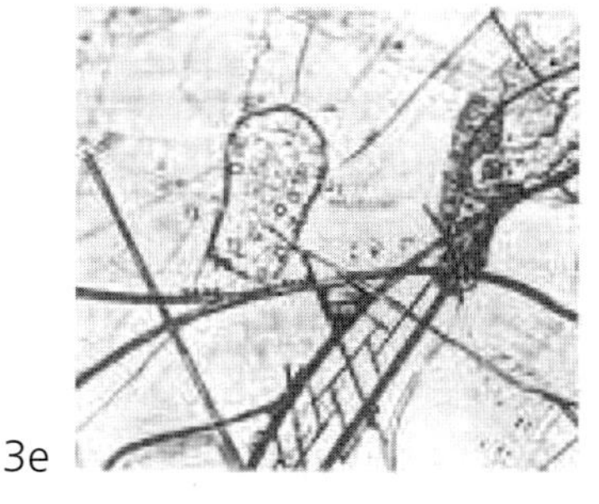

3e

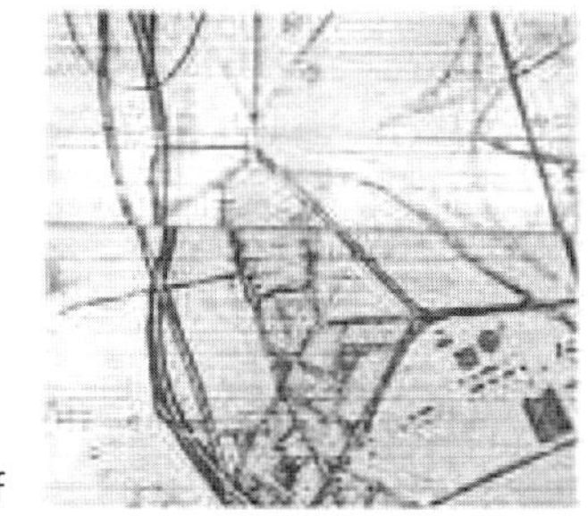

3f

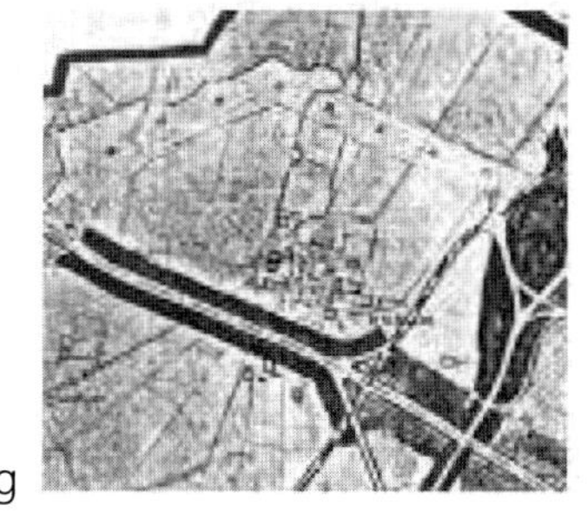

3g

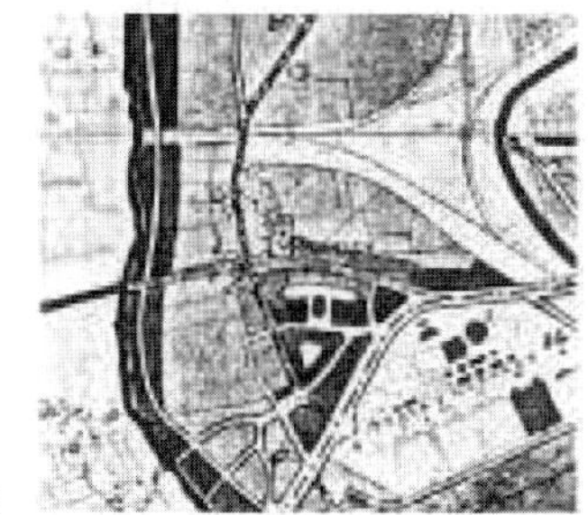

3h

tion, which had been earlier adopted for the City's western fortifications, thus competing what one may call the 'inner ring'. There is, however, one major difference with the west part: the former earthwork line is kept as a continuous belt. We notice here, as already mentioned, that the three intra-core connections include a suspension bridge crossing the central see way close to the Kastellet, which is added to the two existing bridges, Langebro and Knippelsbro.

In Figure 4B, the fortifications are with minor alterations conserved as a whole. A quadrant shaped layout of roads junction opens up Christianshavn on Amager Island, deflecting direct traffic pressure, and a small bridge is fitted in-between two bastions. A tree-lined boulevard and a park facing the fortifications aim to enhance the landscape. Bridge linkage is also proposed near the Kastellet. Importance is given to the tree-lined, continuous ring boulevard while Inner city junctions are not insisted upon.

Figure 4C suggests that the fortification area is to be left intact. No ring boulevard is planned, and a park with sports facilities similar to the project of Raavad is facing the city walls. There is also a new bridge linkage as in the previous projects and the prolongation of the two existing bridges circulation on to Amager is underlined.

Figure 4D displays a careful treatment of the bastions that are conserved. However, a new connection across the inner seaway runs as a central axis through Christianshavn and its walls. It links to a bridge, which should extend Nyhavn embankment in the city centre. This main axis recalls previous plans of Fischer that intended to develop the district of Christianshavn. Furthermore, the layout plans a double-lanes entrance through the fortifications, which is to be adorned with monumental aspects. A tunnel linkage is also added near the Kastellet. We see Fischer's proposal as twofold. On one hand, the purpose is to deflect the heavy traffic from the core city in balance with the similar option planned for the western part of the city. On the other, the choice is to strengthen intra-core linkage between the city and Christianshavn, which was perceived as a distinct part of the city as late as at the end of the nineteenth century, to allow for development schemes in the depressed district. With regard to the development toward Sundbyerne, the options of Fischer's project were to accommodate for an industrial area with worker housing and port facilities.

Figure 4E displays the direct encounter of what we have termed the first and third dimensions of planning. A highly imaginative blending of transformation and preservation characterises Raavad's design. The projected 'Øresund canal' would flow alongside Christianshavn's fortifications. It would bisect Amager Island while providing further south of Christianshavn a large area for an industrial district with a park as a buffer next to the fortifications. At the northern end, the bastions are also preserved with the sea environment, which form the background scene for a park with leisure facilities opening up to a beach. Yet, the arrangements along the new canal embankments are not specified in detail. The mode of linking Christianshavn to the centre is also left unclear, but this district is strongly connected to Amager with a number of underground links.

5 The City's Boundaries and Connections toward the Lakes – Plate 5: 5A – 5E

Strategies concerning the limits of the 'old city' toward the lakes often remained unclear in the entries, as the huge 'buffer zone' between the former line of fortifications and the previous limits of the municipal area, including Frederiksberg, were not formally part of the Competition's programme. The plans, however, indicate a variety of approach in relation to the future of the 'old city', which is not defined by a clear physical line. Strinz's proposal opens to the possibility of crossing through the city centre with three thoroughfares as shown in Figure 5A. Bjerre's plan, on the contrary, acknowledges historical boundaries. It does so by underscoring a tree-lined ring boulevard that secures the north-south traffic (Figure 5B). Plesner & Mathiesen's plan is rather silent about the matter (Figures 5C & 4C) and the same goes for Raavad's project, which does not recommend any West-East thoroughfares crossing the inner city (Figure 5E). As we already pointed out, Fischer's proposal tackles the question by widening an existing road to deflect part of the traffic pressure beyond the northern lake to-

The City's Boundaries and the Fortifications

Plate 4

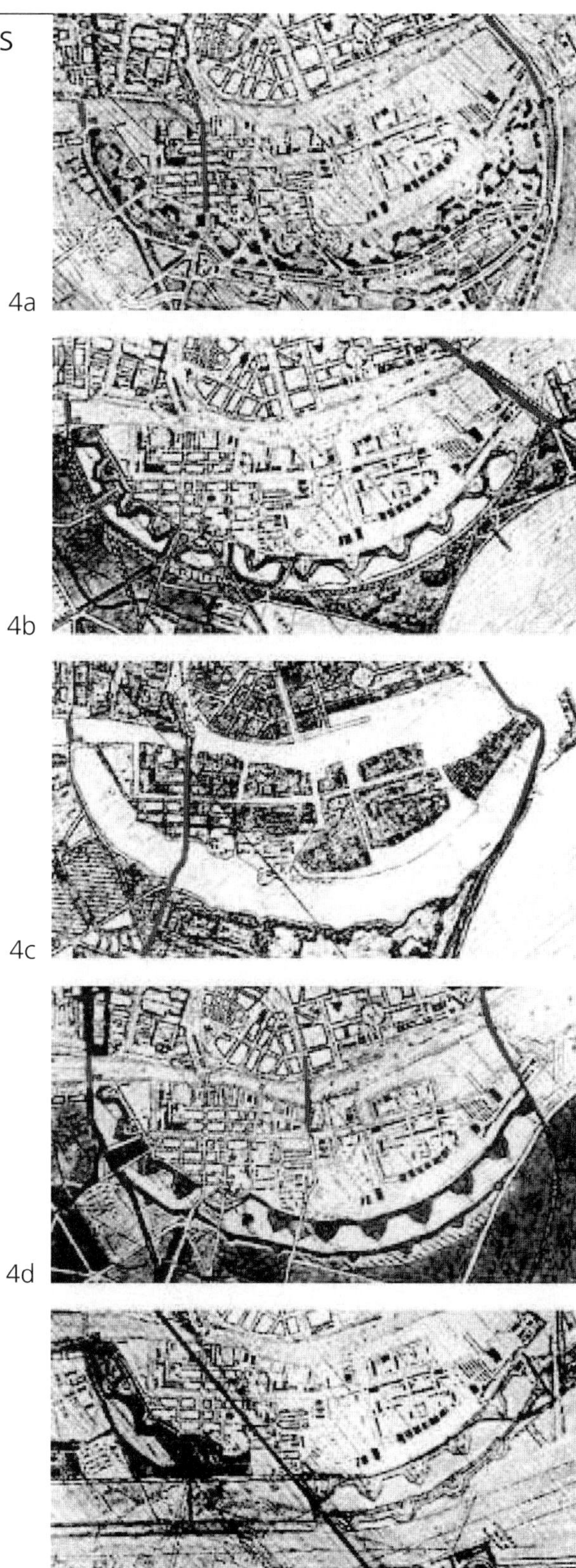

4a

4b

4c

4d

4e

The Old City's Boundaries and Connections toward the Lakes

Plate 5

5a

5b

5c

5d

5e

ward the Jarmer Tower junction. The scheme is clearly intended to avoid traffic junctions in the inner city. We notice here that the ring boulevard proposed by Bjerre can also be considered as a manner to lead the traffic away from the centre. This aspect of Fischer's layout drew much attention at the time of the Competition. Later, planners such as Olaf Forchhammer and Sten E. Rasmussen quoted Fischers' idea as a skilful and elegant solution (See Figure 5D).

6 The Great City's Macroform: the Treatment of Limits – Plate 6: 6A – 6F

By the time the competition was held, a law was passed that concerned the decommissioning of the system of fortification built during the years 1888-1892 as a defensive line to protect Copenhagen. This decision came as a result of a long political battle concerning the abandonment of the Capital's nine kilometres radius last ring of fortifications. This ring was made off a continuous one hundred meter large line of defence on the Vestvolden, the rest of it being constituted toward the North or on Amager (facing the sea) of a discontinuous line of forts and batteries. Most of this 'ring' was situated much beyond the limits of the annexed communes, only a small part being implanted north of Husum (appearing as a shadow on Raavad's plan, see 3 E). But for one, "Copenhagen Vaaben", none of the entries took into account this then obsolete system of defence as an actual constraint. However following the much heated debates the perspective of the decommissioning, scheduled for 1922 (according to the 1909 law) was there and the idea of the outdated conception of land defence could indulge for some competitors a renewed interest for a kind of new boundaries for the 'Great city'.

The idea of the city has, throughout history, been closely associated with the idea of limits. During the course of the nineteenth century whatever kind of city's limits – there were not only and always a means of defence – were progressively removed owing to the interplay of numerous factors. At the turn of the twentieth century, a shift in favour of low-density housing in conjunction with the outgrowth of towns, which was perceived as natural and desirable made the line between what was "in" and what was "out" of town a rather dubious issue. Many proponents of Civic Art underlined this 'obliteration of the line'. The representation of limits became extremely problematic for town planners. As professionals and 'city experts' they were continuously confronted with the question of how the new urban form was to take shape. In the meantime, some were not satisfied with being seen as defending outdated models of closed cities while the term 'conurbation' had already been coined. Different kinds of compromises as well as spatial innovations resulted from this dilemma, ranging from the infinitely expanding and replicable dense city of Otto Wagner (suggested by Raavad in the case of Canberra) to the symbolic, landscaped 'medievalist' inspired picturesque low walls, among other devices, as explored by Raymond Unwin to define "boundaries and approaches" of "towns, suburbs and new areas generally"[2].

The case of the 1909 Copenhagen competition illustrates the wide spectrum of alternatives as envisioned by planners attempting to express the relationship between the idea of city limits and a relatively symbolic continuity of the idea of city. Figures 6A & 6B display details of Bjerre's plan (north and west) with sections of the tree-lined ring boulevard imagined by the author as constituting the new spatial boundary. This boulevard relies on a succession of parks and lakes for its effect. The influence of the American 'park system' can also be noticed, even if the formal 'contrasted continuity' of the circuit is lacking. Figures 6C and 6D show the same locations as treated by Strinz. Here the choice is almost reversed, the continuity of the park belt being expressed through a combination of green and blue spaces. No close relation to the circumnavigator traffic line is suggested. The attempt is to inspire, at least graphically, the sense of a natural barrier quite apart from the main thoroughfares running parallel to it. The scheme is most likely inspired by the successive elaborations of the original plan of Eugen Fassbender for the Vienna com-

2 Raymond Unwin, *Town planning in Practice – an Introduction to the Art of designing cities and Suburbs,* London, 1911, p. 154.

The Great City's Macroform: the Treatment of Limits

Plate 6

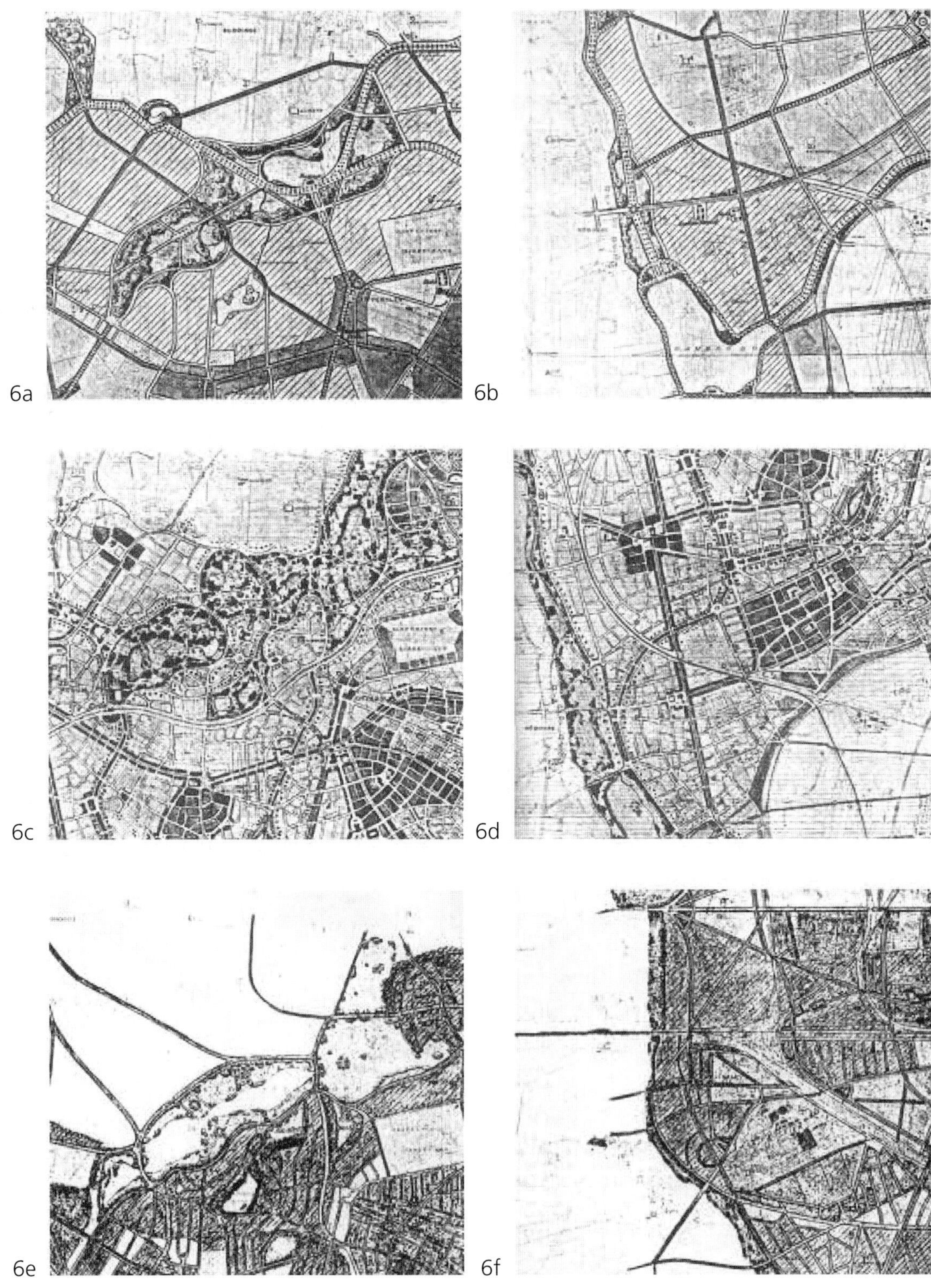

6a 6b 6c 6d 6e 6f

petition in 1894 (second prize). The concept of a green belt, designed as a sixth outer concentric zone, 750 metre large, was further developed by Fassbender in 1898 with the project '*Volksring*' presenting the detailed layout of a civic leisure belt[3]. Henreich Goldemunds, an Austrian engineer, presented the project 'Wald –und Weisengürtels' at the Paris exhibition in 1900, which stressed the natural and hygienic character of the scheme. The municipality of Vienna eventually adopted this scheme in 1905, and we believe that it is a reference in Strinz's project. This proposal was much appreciated in Copenhagen. However, some critics judged the 'barrier' too thin to create a significant delimiting effect. The idea of polarising residential housing toward the outskirt of the new municipal area, which characterises Bjerre's scheme, was commented as a desirable and realistic option. Figures 6E & 6F show how Plesner and Mathiesen explored a somewhat similar choice. Here, too, the aim is to attract residential housing. The belt, however, is far from continuous.

7 The New Districts' Layouts – Plate 7: 7A – 7 I

This set groups several examples of design style in which an urban network had to be projected onto virtually open land. The patches of plan, which are here selected, are all different, as the entries often identified different locations to focus urbanisation. The patches elicited a wide variety of design mechanisms, even though a few of these might be superficially termed 'Sittian'. Figure 7A displays a sample of Strinz's design. Here the surveyor had to create something from virtually 'nothing'. Nevertheless, a system of short and slightly bended streets is incorporated to the larger network. Figure 7B shows Bjerre's attempts to create a measure of urban polarity through focal point and symmetrical ordering of a forked device. Meanwhile, Figure 7C displays a full-fledged deployment of Raavad's "meandering gader" system. Figure 7D details a patch of Hans Bernoulli's urban design. While sharing a similar approach the layout might prove relatively stereotyped in comparison to Strinz's design (7A). Yet, the guidelines of Civic Art approach, including the design of short streets, are closely considered, though one can notice a degree of rigidity and artificiality in searching for 'irregularity' and 'effect'. Figure 7E provides an example of Gellersted design. The bell-shaped form, following natural declivity, and the main roads and lanes radiating out south of Utterslev create a new, reasonably diverse urban unit. Figure 7F illustrates Erslev design concerning the northern extension adjacent to the area of Utterslev. Here, the design relies almost exclusively on a variety of geometrical patterns and some variation is achieved via the juxtaposition of distinct geometrical forms. This kind of uttermost formal layout has been sometimes dismissively and polemically labelled as 'German design'. Camillo Sitte characterised this type of design as 'engineer's romanticism', which would have been an attempt from the civil engineers to answer to the mounting critics in the 1880s on the supposedly unimaginative orthogonal style of their design. It is interesting here to notice that this kind of 'dried up romanticism' had often prevailed in the residential suburbs of colonial cities.

Figure 7G shows Plesner and Mathiesen's plan concerning the area of Utterslev whose treatment should be compared with Figure 7E owing to a similar bell-shaped form and inferior treatment of streets distribution. The same area is the focus of Figures 7H and 7I as treated by Sundbärg and Hallman respectively. Despite strong similarities in their design with some degree of artificial complexity, the scales of streets and squares are quite different. Moreover Hallman's technique generates a more informal interplay of figures.

3 For a full report on Fassbender's scheme, see Kurt Mollik, Hermann Reining, Rudolf Wurzer, *Planung und Verwirklichung der Wiener Ringstrassezone*, Wiesbaden, 1980, p. 361-363 & p. 375-379.

New Districts: Alternative Layouts

Plate 7

7a

7b

7c

7d

7e

7f

7g

7h

7i

8 Raavad: "Midtvejen af park og boulevard beltet"

Raavad's entry belongs to a minority of projects presenting Great Copenhagen as a spatially limited entity. The proposal of "middle park alley" is explicitly intended to stress that a succession of rings surrounding an expanding city is a historical process which characterises Copenhagen. Raavad's project aims at integrating existing but fragmented natural entities, such as lakes, marshes and woodland, around an eight km-long "Corso" or Mall. The design provides for some public amenities and recreational areas to be connected onto this belt. This scheme reflects to a superior scale the principle of public place of amusements, which the Tivoli garden had established in the mid- nineteenth century. This systemic interpretation of a Greater City belt is to be compared with the narrative dimension of an undulating ring as proposed in the project Urania, and with the more formal tree-lined connecting boulevard displayed in the project Tre Træer. (See, Plate 6A-6F).

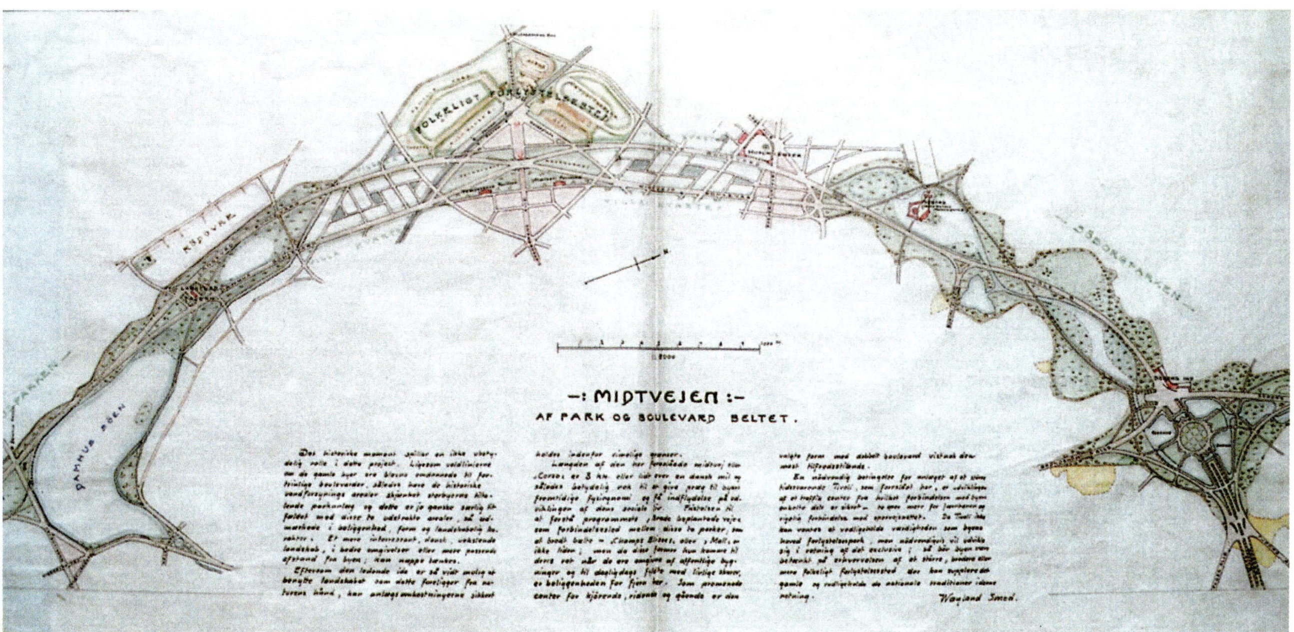

Alfred Raavad, *Midtvejen af park og boulevard beltet,* see references p. 52. Photo by the author.

The nineteen Entries according to five Criteria

Entries	A	B	C	D	E
1. Gefion	△	△			
2. Urania (1st pr.)	△	△	△	△	△
3. "+"	△				△
4. Tre Træer (2nd pr.)	△	△	△		
5. Anno 1977 (4th pr.)	△	△			△
6. Hafnia	△	△	△		
7. Julemærket for 1908					
8. Wayland Smed (selected)	△	△	△		△
9. Grønne Baand	△	△			△
10. Storstad	△				
11. For Byen og Borgerne	△			△	△
12. Mindre Parker men Parkalléer	△				
13. Bellla	△	△			△
14. Millionbyen	△	△	△	△	△
15. Københavns Vaaben 1296 (3rd pr.)	△		△		△
16. Et kløverblad	△	△		△	△
17. Stor-København	△	△			△
18. Richesse oblige	△		△		△
19. Axelhus		△			△

Box 4 A- Conservation or preservation of Christianshavn's fortifications. B- Conservation or preservation of incorporated villages. C- Design of limits for Great Copenhagen. D- Road system's layout adjusted to the existing one. E- Layout oriented toward dense built areas.

Entry n° *2, Urania.* General plan, see references p. 45-46. Photo by the author.

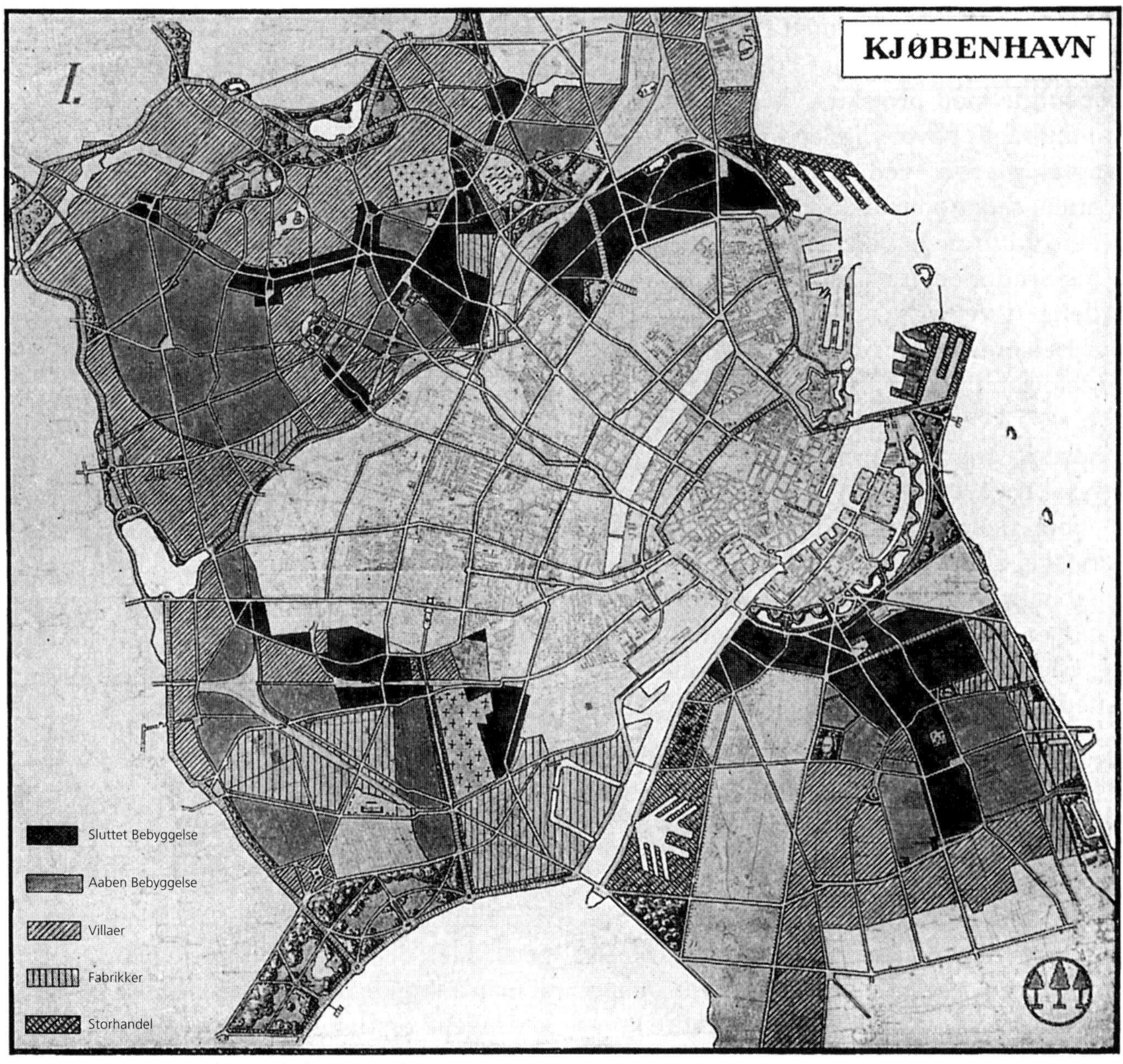

Entry n° 4, *Tre Træer.* General plan, see references p. 48. Source: O. Forchhamer (red.), *København – De indlemmede Distrikter byplanmæssig Udvikling 1901-1941*, Copnhagen, 1942, p. 25.

Entry n° 4, *Tre Træer.* General plan, detail with focus on the Old City' boundaries, see references p. 48. Photo by the author.

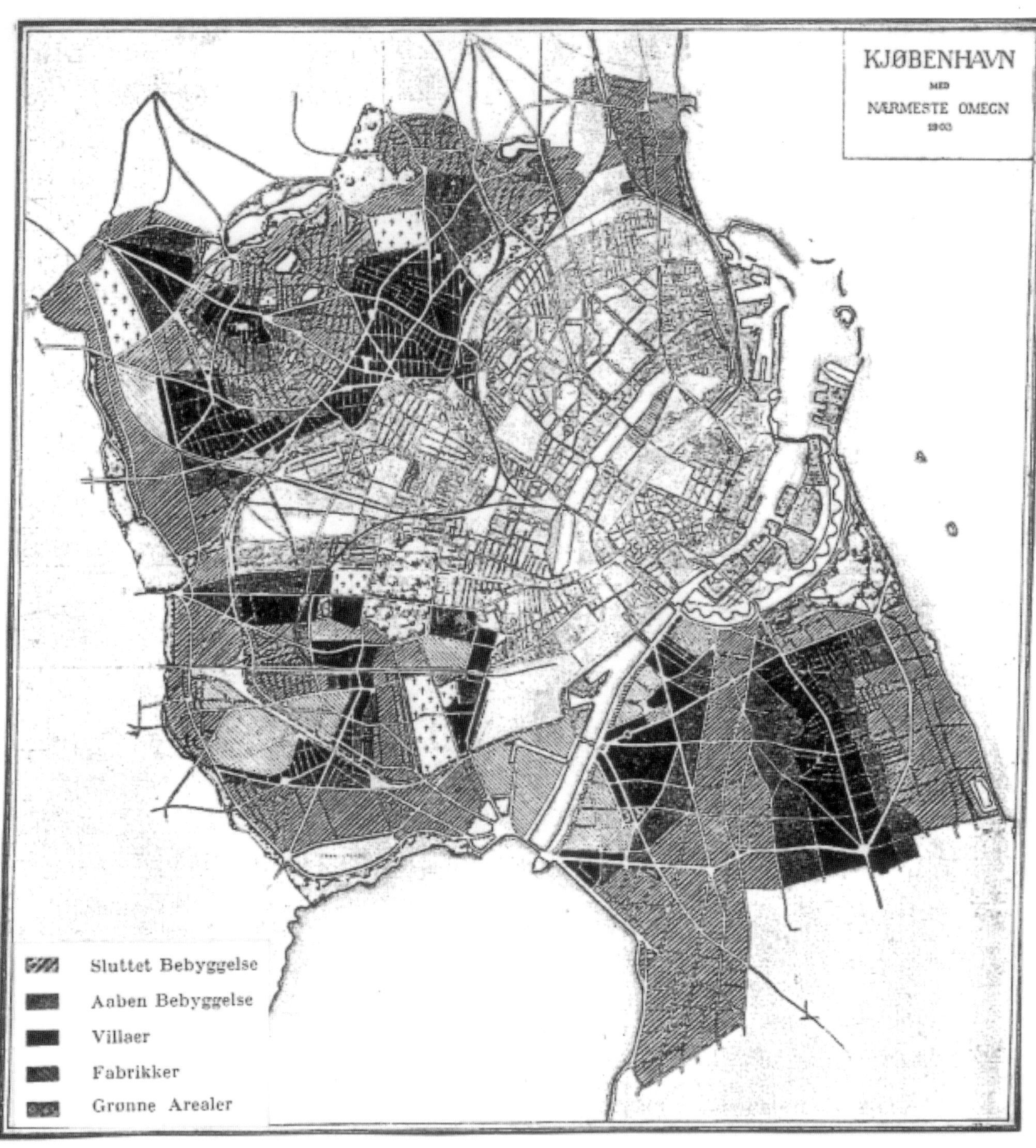

Entry n° 15, *Københavns Vaaben 1296.* General plan, see references p. 60. Source: O. Forchhammer (red.), *op. cit.* p. 26.

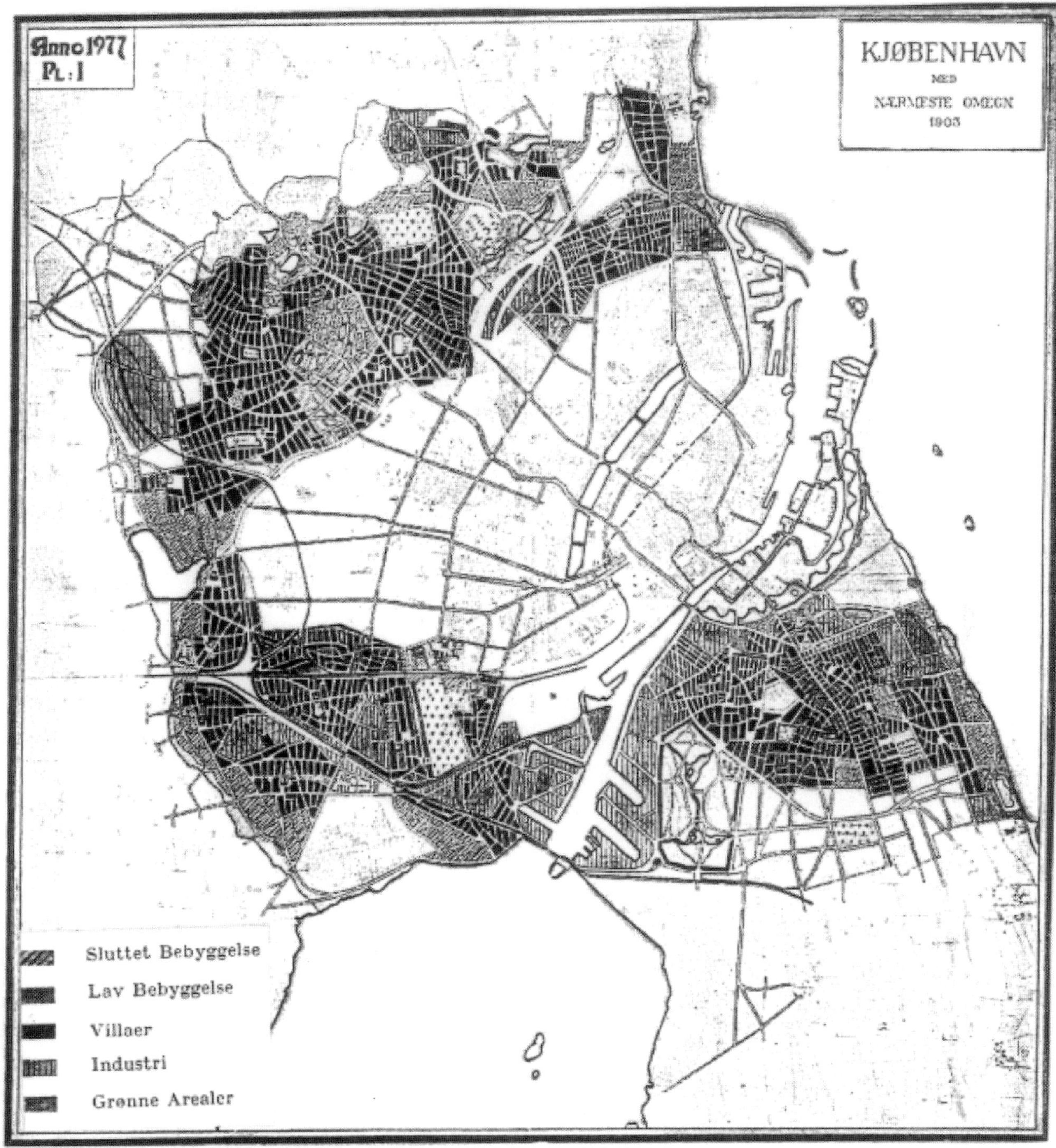

Entry n° 5, *Anno 1977.* General plan, see references p. 49. Source: O. Forchhammer (red.) *op. cit.*, p 27.

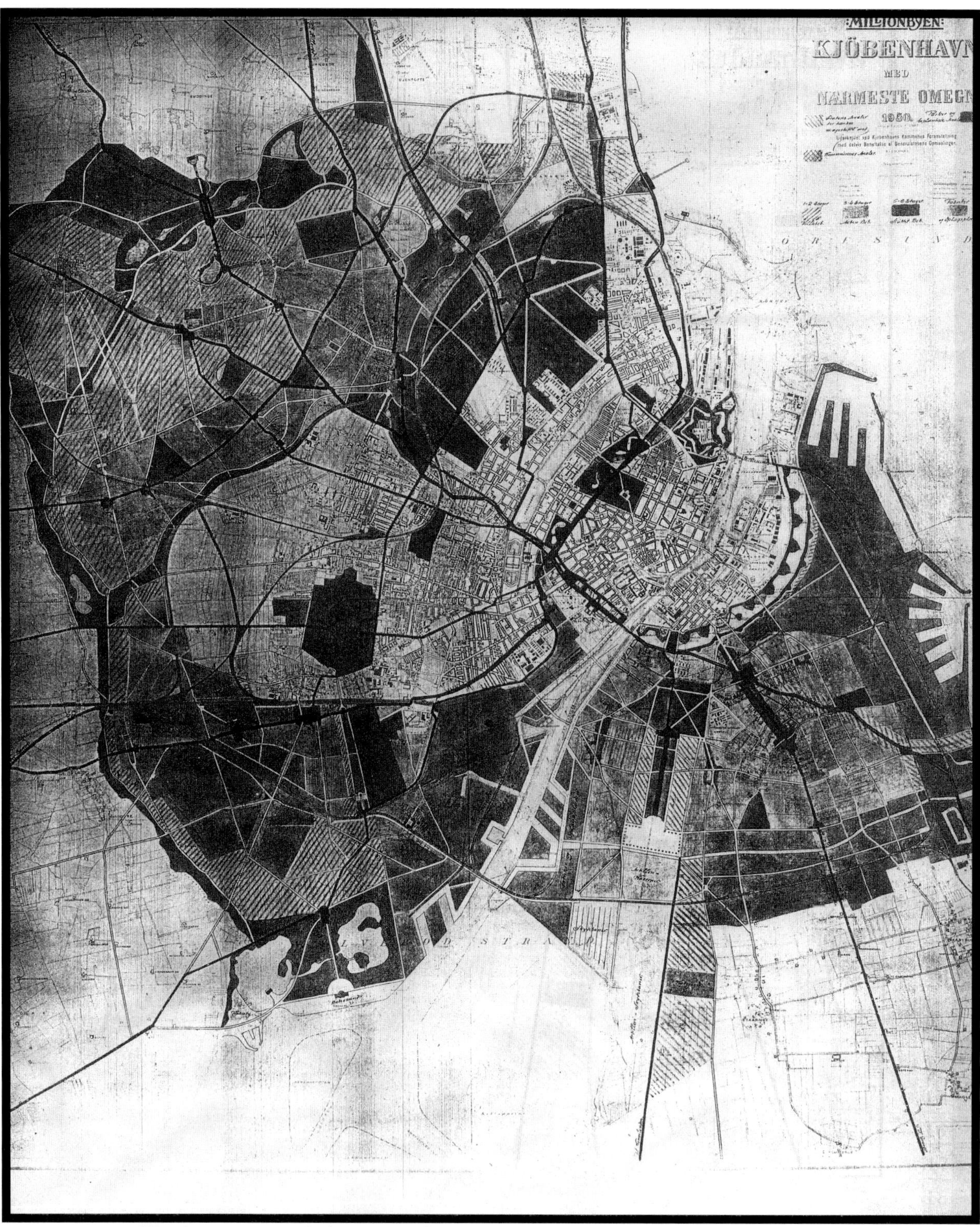

Entry n° 14, *Millionbyen.* General plan, see references p 58. Photo by the author.

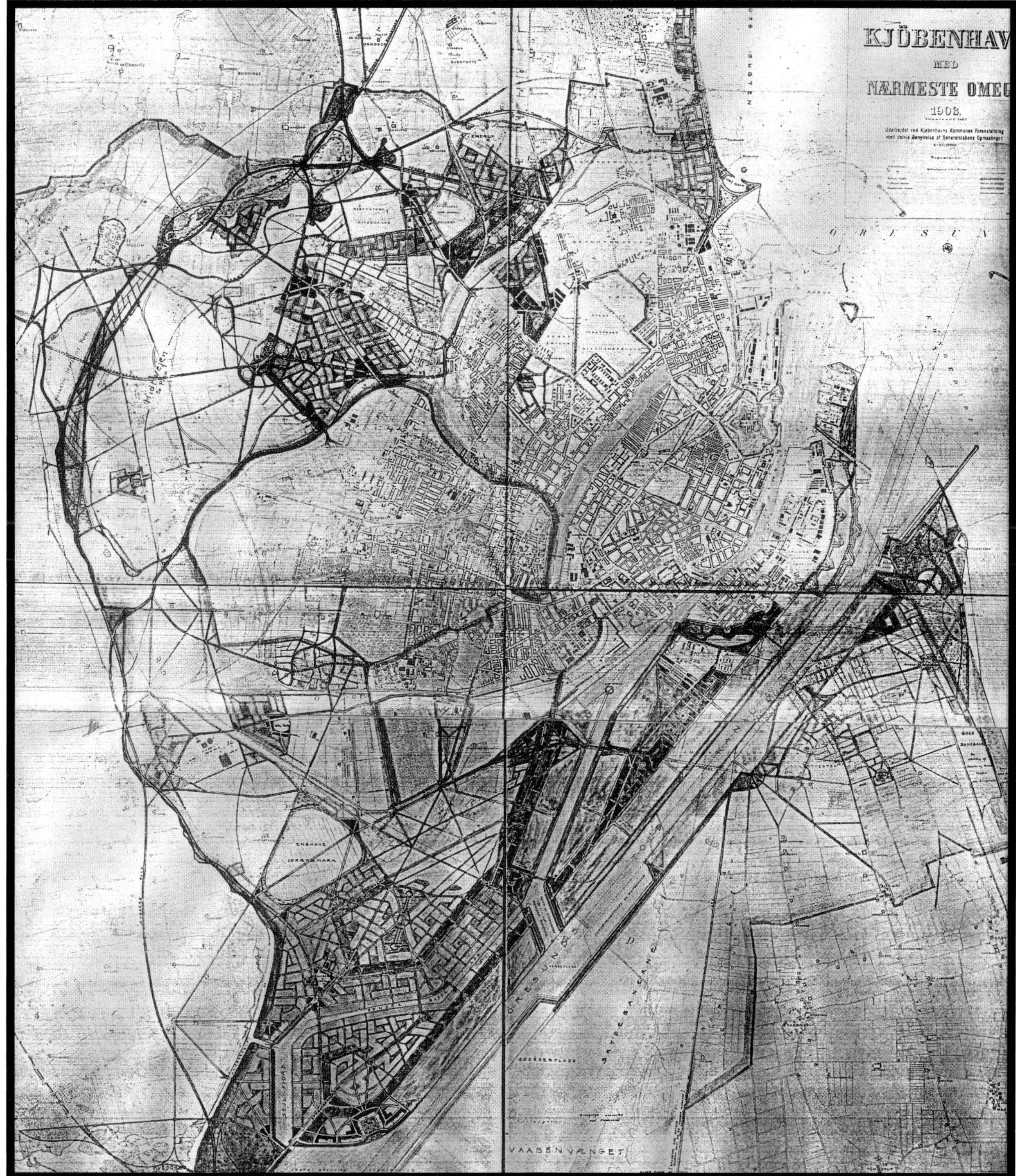

Entry n° 8, *Wayland Smed*. General plan, see references p. 52. Photo by the author.

PART III

TOWARD THE HISTORIC CITY

The third part of this book focuses on the evolving perceptions of the city centre at the time of the competition both in relation to extension planning and to the concept of *Bevaring* (conservation) that was developing.

In a different historical setting, the French colonial empire, the desire to ensure the global conservation of the "historic city" found expression by the 1920s. The 'historic city' in this case corresponded to what was often described on surveyors' maps as the 'indigenous city'. The concept of *'ordre de ville'* was coined by the colonial authorities to suggest that tradition and modernity could coexist in so far tradition and modernity were enclosed within almost autonomous spatial cells. The institutional and legal framework established to this effect, and what we may call colonial conservation, epitomised and realised the dream of disconnecting fragments of time-space entities.[1]

In Europe, such time-space fragments could only seldom be integrally preserved. This was only possible when relics of the built environment could still convey an impression of enclosed wholeness. The city of Carcassonne for instance, failing appropriate conservation legislation, was reclassified as a military area in 1820 to avoid further destruction (this was well before Viollet-le-Duc was commissioned for the restoration of the entire fortification).[2] The municipalities of other cities, such as Aigues-Mortes or, on a much larger size, Avignon, proved to have a sort of interest in their surviving town walls and monuments. However, the concern for the ordinary built environment enclosed within the town walls remained generally limited. A case in point was the city of Venice on the map of the Grand Tour: It was only thanks to the protection of its lagoon that it escaped the encroachments to which most other towns fell victim. By the end of the nineteenth century, Rothenburg ob der Tauber, a fortified city with a substantial urban fabric, was widely praised for action in favour of conservation both in the Nordic countries and in England even becoming a direct source of inspiration for Raymond Unwin's design of Hampstead garden suburb. Finally, 're-building' strategies were sometime elaborated, as was the case in Barcelona. There, the much differed and only partly implemented redevelopment scheme for the city centre came to collide by 1907 with the new values attached to the revival of the 'national' heritage in Catalonia. The resistance offered to the threat of sweeping clearance came in the form of the 'Barri Gotìc', or the project to realise a homogeneous 'Gothic' enclave regrouping and recomposing around a nucleus of original edifices a number of ancient buildings collected in the course of sweeping clearances.[3]

1 On this aspect of conservation introduce by the French 1912 Protectorate over Morocco see, Hélène Vacher, *Projection coloniale et ville rationalisée – le rôle de l'espace colonial dans la constitution de l'urbanisme en France, 1900-1931*, Aalborg, 2001, p. 139-145.

2 See Jukka Jokilehto, *A History of Architectural Conservation*, Oxford, 1999, p. 147-149. The same mechanism of "military protection" of the city walls was used in Morocco before a comprehensive strategy of conservation was worked out.

3 On this project, cf. Joan Ganau, "Town planning and conservationist policies in the historic city centre of Barcelona (1860-1930), in *Planning History*, Vol. 19 n°2/3, 1997, p. 23-31.

Except a few significant examples however, the trend to transform a densely built centre generally did prevail and cities started to suffer from 'perpetual public works',[4] while the 'historic city' mostly survived in the shape of a ghost from the past.

The relation between planning and conservation seems to be an asymmetrical one. It has long been assumed that the legitimacy of planning lays in its capacity to solve problems efficiently, in response to social and technical needs using, that is, a mainly quantitative approach. On the other hand, conservation concerns, rather the preserve of connoisseurs, were not believed to satisfy basic social needs. However, such simplistic views do not give an accurate account of the complex interplay between social forces and urban forms.

What we are looking for is that set of circumstances that could be roughly identified here with the 'second industrialisation'. This caused the reorganisation or redistribution of urban space to be perceived as a historical phenomenon, also giving rise to specific planning approaches. In Copenhagen, the inner city was never the subject of a global remodelling project, even though numerous efforts were undertaken to discuss and elaborate a new profile for the city centre, as numerous public and private building activities were putting pressure on the existing built environment, maintaining a lively debate between the supporters of conservation and the advocates of change.

We want to follow up some of the issues in this debate, in which the notion of civic improvements was often drawn upon. We want to analyse the progress, shortcomings and ambiguities of the conservation movement in this context, and document the complexity of the positions involved.

Debates on conservation issues were not bi-polarised but multi-polarised, and tensions between conflicting strategies created new fields for professional intervention. Chapter 6 discusses the process of designation, the unfolding of the diversity of motives behind conservation and finally the emerging notion of an 'old city', while Chapter 7 discusses some of the major contributions from 'conservationists' and gives a closer look at some societies' concern with beautification, the study and the protection of the historic fabric.

The first decade of the twentieth century, as witnessed by the composition of some of the associations we are looking at, saw the steady extension of the social base for urban conservation. The growth of the support for conservation, among middle-class professionals at least, and its increasing, if limited, endorsement by the general public, was reflected in both the liberal and the conservative press. Accordingly, the heightened awareness about the historical, methodological and technical issues related to conservation is all clearly perceptible.

This interest for urban conservation encompassed a vast array of motives, which emphasized the sense of uniqueness emanating from forms of the past, or rather the visual quality and complexity of historical ensembles, and the narrative support for transmitting cultural values. Urban conservation could be understood as a counterforce, through the perpetuation of historic markers, against an emerging townscape that was becoming increasingly, despoiled, dull, and standardised, a landscape epitomised by the 'repulsive' outer districts, which had been built in the second half of the nineteenth century between the former ring of fortifications and the extension zone.

Through the interference of spheres involving the different aspects of the demolition-cum-construction process, we shall look for organisations and personalities working towards the formation of the cultural image of the '*gamle København*'. It was also during that period that the debate was initiated about the requirements and the extent of the conservation strategies to be implemented.

Although far from exhaustive, the material we have selected for investigation nonetheless reflects a wide spectrum of opinions and highlights the plurality of meanings given to the notion of 'old city'. In effect, the 'old city' became a touchstone as concerns spatial designation. In Copenhagen, the notion of 'old city' happened to correspond to the city centre and therefore coincided with the idea of centrality attached to the 'Great city'. The 'old city' could be seen as a collection of inherited fragmented relics; or as a historic, cultural and aesthetic whole where had taken place a process of selection of urban forms; or simply as a topographical label indicating a densely-built centre

4 We borrow from Peter Hall referring to Paris, in *Cities in civilizations, Culture, Innovation, and Urban Order*, London, 1999.

the 'old city' being in this case more or less confused with the idea a 'city district', a business centre emerging as a complementary functional unit to the low-density housing schemes planned in the extension zone.

The geography of the 'old' Copenhagen was thus intricate and manifold. There was a strong underlying strain between the wish to protect picturesque fragments in their social and cultural wholeness, and the great many of modernising projects, which nonetheless had to be wrapped in a 'historical garb'.

Elaborated by some of the most talented master-builders and architects of the period, the "arts and crafts" type of architecture strived to integrate tradition and innovation in a balanced fashion. It shunned all forms of eclecticism (understood here as an opportunistic stylistic combination and not as a stimulus for innovation) and tried to go beyond the limits inherent in historicist constructs. Such attempts can be interpreted as the desire for redemption from the merely utilitarian architecture of the liberal years of the nineteenth century. Yet it was also a quite successful figure of aesthetic and cultural compromise with the historicity encapsulated in the inherited urban form.

Several contributions and debates to be found in the press show that arguments in favour of conservation and even a framework for intervention were already well developed, with diagnoses and strategies formulating a complete range of policies from micro- to macro-structures. In fact, conservation strategies applied throughout Europe from the second half of 1970s, such as selective de-densification, the opening of inner-block walkways, the attention paid to the surroundings of monuments, the respect of the hierarchy between buildings, etc., were already being put forward at the time. The rebirth of the Society for the Beautification of the Capital City and the development of 'sister' organisations of more specialised scope are closely linked to the new drive for urban conservation. It could be argued here that most of the former Society's interventions were anecdotal in terms of town planning, and that a conservation finally had, at last, little impact in practical terms. However, such a line of argument would overlook other important factors. In the period considered here, the conservation of major urban sites such as the 'Kastellet', the remaining southern fortifications and even the canals could not be taken for granted.

The 1909 Competition turned out to be a strong spur in the creation of what we might call a *heritage conjunction*, bringing together macro-urban planning strategies that incorporated a conservationist dimension with a movement dedicated to the maintenance of a relative continuity for the inner city. Part III will therefore make more explicit the elements that allowed this conjunction to form. In this respect, it is no coincidence that, but for one exception, all of the Danish architects participating in the 1908 Competition were affiliated to the Society for the Preservation of Old Buildings. Equally to be noted is that most of them were also members of the Society for the Beautification of the Capital City.[5]

5 This society had appointed landscaper-gardener and gold medal winner in the 1902 Düsseldorf exhibition Edvard Glæsel to sit on the 1908 jury. The role of Nyrop should obviously also be mentioned here. For more details see Part I.

6 CONSERVING THE CITY, PERCEPTIONS AND STRATEGIES

1 The Debate about Conservation in Europe, 1890-1914

The genealogy of a discourse on the city and a serious concern for city form has also been traced back to the Italian Renaissance. It has been stressed that the notion of 'old city' as a distinct spatial and temporal entity appeared much later.[1] It is generally assumed that the notion of the historic monument has followed a triple extension process: "typological, chronological and geographical".[2] Thus, the interest for conservation was first aiming at the protection of de-contextualised artefacts and the inventory of selected edifices was progressively extended to surrounding remains or testimonies, partly under the influence of archaeological methods. Ultimately, sites and landscapes were to be integrated. The French example highlights the strength of institutional processes. The Revolution and the following escheat of goods of the old regime quite rapidly led to a "de-consecrated and analytical"[3] version of conservation giving birth to a systematic model of compiling historic buildings.[4]

However, the study of this thematic in various European contexts show highly differentiated practices and formulations regarding the notion of urban heritage. In Sweden, early cultural historiography influenced by the thinking and the works of German scholars has early on associated the notion of "old city" to values of nationality and fellowship toward the past.[5] Therefore, the formation of an urban heritage has been established by ensuing scholarly and scientific approaches, investigating their 'documents' by also looking at the 'surroundings' of historical edifices. This was also much helped by the network of local or national associations mobilised to save monuments and sites. Monuments were perceived more as links to a common past than as a collection of artistic artefacts. This approach firmly anchored the monument within this site as either artificial or natural. Importance was given on sensitive perception of built and/or natural environment, often qualified as picturesque. This environment was understood as a cradle of cultural meanings, which should be transmitted to insure the self-perpetuation of the community. In the two first decades of the twentieth century, this type of approach tended to be integrated to planning policy, as a "counter-force" to the disruptive effects unlashed by industrialisation which was supposed to help controlling the scale of urban redevelopment.

The idea of an intrinsic historical and artistic value attached to the ordinary built environment was explicitly formulated several times by John Ruskin (1819-1900) in particular in his work the "Lamp of Memory":

"To this day, the interest of their fairest cities [Italy and France] depends, not on the isolated richness of palaces, but on the cherished and exquisite decoration of even the smallest tenements of their proud periods".[6]

1 Françoise Choay underlined that there is a gap of several centuries between the "invention" of the monument as an historic artefact and the notion of city as a monument in *L'Allégorie du patrimoine*, Paris, 1992, p. 135-141.

2 Idem, p 12.

3 See, Dominique Poulot, "Introduction générale", in Daniel J. Grange, D. Poulot (dir.), *L'esprit des lieux, le patrimoine et la cité*, Grenoble, 1997, p. 20.

4 On the main characteristics of this 'universal' model, cf. Dominique Poulot, "Le patrimoine universel : un model culturel français", *Revue d'Histoire Moderne et Contemporaine*, January –March 1992, See also John Delafons, *A Policy History of the Built Heritage 1882-1996*, London, 1997, p.12.

5 Ola Wetterberg, *Monument och miljö. Perspektiv på det tigiga 1900-talets byggnadsvård i Sverige*. Gothenburg, 1992.

6 John Ruskin, *The Seven Lamps of Architecture*, New York, 1989, p. 182.

This approach was the logical consequence of the belief that the "domestic architecture" was "the beginning of all others".[7]

In general, "old cities" have been acknowledged as self-contained units, which were defined by their form and type of spatial limits, when new districts were to be laid out on different patterns. The feeling of time gap then developed with the discontinuity of physical development. That was particularly so with the "embellishment" planning era of the eighteenth century. Voltaire's remarks on old pattern of street forms in Paris are a case example of subjectivist statements suggesting the idea of a 'dual city'.[8] It should however, be noted that contemporary judgement about the gap between 'enlightened' planning and traditional patterns was not one-sided and not necessarily disqualifying for the later.[9] Besides changes in parcelling and streets patterns, the changing characters of city limits has probably been a dynamic element behind the identification process of 'modern' and 'old' urban space.

The weakness of our quantitative and qualitative knowledge concerning the debates about urban limits has recently been underlined.[10] The process on the abolishment of fortifications and the 'freeing the city' in continental Europe indicate long tortuous and contradictory approaches involving institutional, professional as well as cultural aspects. It does not seem that these approaches should be reduced to bipolarity between conservative and conservationist patricians versus liberal minded ascending classes. Each city has its own process of formation of urban spatial entities depending of the positions and choices of the landed proprietors, the policy of industrial elites, the geographical location of the city, its size and rank, etc. However, in most cases the treatment of limits has contributed to raise awareness about the relative cohesiveness of the built environment of specific areas and to stimulate debates and planning strategies about their role in the future.[11] Obviously, the oldness of the built environment is a much relative notion and the handling of physical limits is essentially an indicator for evolving functions and change of societal and cultural values.

By the end of the nineteenth century, the generalisation of extension planning in Europe, and the fast changing characters of big cities, had brought back some of the questions of planning toward the centre under the heading: "what to do with old centres"? Replies were essentially the product of two factors: the orientations of school of planning, and the specific path of development followed by each city. In most metropolitan cities both developments were closely interwoven. Below, we shall succinctly present the few major orientations that participated in structuring the field of urban conservation in Europe.

1.1 Vanishing Cities

For extensively redeveloped World cities such as London or Paris the question has been, one could argue, resolved relatively early in the sense that what could have been the 'old city' and the 'metropolis' were mutually entangled. For instance: "Almost all the vestiges of mediaeval and Tudor buildings in the City of

7 Idem, p. 181.

8 Old Paris was characterized by Voltaire as "très incommode et irrégulier" (very inconvenient and irregular), in "Des embellissements de Paris", *Oeuvres*, Vol. 30, Paris, 1792, p. 1-12, p. 3.

9 For instance, E. G. von Willebrand (in the end of the eighteenth century) is quoted by George R. Collins and Christiane Crasemann Collins, *Camillo Sitte and the Birth of Modern City Planning*, London, 1965, p. 121.

10 The lack of knowledge we have about the demolishing campaigns, and especially about the debates leading to it and the formulation of alternatives projects, was pointed out by Marcel Roncayolo, *Lectures des villes, Formes et temps*, Marseilles, 2002, p. 38.

11 In the case of Geneva, Brulhart gave a detailed account of the struggle G. H. Dufour, a military engineer, led to maintain the fortification system of the town, eventually producing skilled designs of landscaped treatment. In 1849, this attempt was ultimately to be defeated after thirty years of projects and counter projects. See Armand Brulhart, *Guillaume Henri Dufour, Génie civil et urbanisme à Genève au XIXe siècle*, Lausanne, 1987. For a critical assessment of Paris fortifications built in 1844, see Jean Louis Cohen et André Lortie, *Des fortifs au périf, Paris, les seuils de la ville*, Paris, 1991. For an account of the alternative projects concerning the northern Copenhagen fortifications areas, see Axel Holm and Kjeld Johansen, *Københavnske Bysamfund og Kommunens økonomi, 1840-1940*, Copenhagen, 1941, p.16-23.

London, and in many provincial cities, were swept away".[12] Consequently, early conservationists turned their efforts mainly toward suburbia or secondary towns. In Paris, Haussmann's rebuilding plans were concentrated on thoroughfare networks and parts of the urban fabric were destructed as a result of clearance schemes.[13] However, entire areas were left almost intact. Therefore, conservation was a case-by-case question dissociated from the idea of a neatly delineated city centre.

Set up in 1898, the *Commission du Vieux Paris* worked by following a methodical framework based on topographical surveys and archives. One of the first tasks of the commission was accordingly, to resume the photographic coverage of the capital, which had started under Haussmann. Inventory and archaeological excavations were the main activities. Conservation was recommended "as far as possible" and the third sub-commission (of the commission) was to consider "picturesque and artistic aspects".[14] During the years 1898- 1908 the commission was interested in the conservation movement in Europe, and especially in the "mouvement d'Art Public" (See, Chapter 4). In 1898 the Commission carried an extensive report. Numbers of municipalities were being questioned on conservation procedures. Norway was singled out for its 1851 special provision protecting archaeological remains in case of public work operations. France was, however, left with the privilege of having set up the first municipal commission.[15] Vandalism was time and time again denounced, and by the end of the first decade of the twentieth century it was suggested that all demolition projects should be submitted before obtaining authorisation.[16] Member of the Commission from 1907 onward, archivist and historian Marcel Poëte (1866-1950), soon played a central role.[17] Closely associated with the early town planning movement in France, he and architect Louis Bonnier (1856-1946) co-authored the first full- fledged work on Paris extension.[18]

Poëte's experience in urban conservation was nourishing his understanding of urbanism. His work was concentrated toward laying the theoretical foundation for urbanism, through the exploration of the mechanisms of city growth perceived as a form of 'organic' adaptation. Despite his first-hand practical experience in historic topography, no general strategy or comprehensive proposals about urban conservation emerged from an interplay of activities involving researches, conservation concerns as well as the teaching of urbanism in the aftermath of the World War I.

1.2 The Place and its Social Dimension

An early comprehensive approach to city conservation can be found in the work of Patrick Geddes (1854-1932) living aside the general reflections developed in the second half of the nineteenth century by John Ruskin and William Morris among others. Geddes's contribution to the early town planning movement has been abundantly documented and researched.[19] For our purpose it is sufficient to re-state some of the basic principles formulated in his 1904 report to the Carnegie Dunfermline Trust. This report is singled out as it states its basic method of a full-fledged conservation, – with large sections discussing "treatment of ancient buildings", "threatened conservation" and the like. Geddes took an unusual strong statement by writing:

12 A. Delafons, *Policy... op. cit.*, p. 43. The Society for the Protection of Historic Buildings was created in 1877.

13 Emile Fournier, *Paris démoli*, Paris, 1855. For an account of the Haussmannian approach, see François Loyer, *Paris XIXe siècle, l'immeuble et la rue*, Paris, 1994.

14 Commission du Vieux Paris, *Procès Verbaux*, Paris, 1899, p. 1.

15 Idem, "séance du 5 mai" 1898, p. 10.

16 Ibidem, 1908, p. 106.

17 On Marcel Poëte, see Donatella Calabi, *Marcel Poëte et le Paris des années vingt, aux origines de "l'histoire des villes"*, Paris, 1997.

18 Marcel Poëte & Louis Bonnier, *Commission d'Extension de Paris, Aperçu historique et considérations techniques préliminaires*, Paris, 1913.

19 See, Helene E. Meller, *Patrick Geddes: Social Evolutionist and City Planner*, London, 1990. Lilian Anderson looked at Patrick Geddes and Camillo Sitte from the point of view of their struggle against "bureaucratic rationality" in planning. However, the question of urban conservation is marginal to that study; see Lilian Anderson, *Mellan byråkrati och laissez faire, En studie av Camillo Sittes och Patrick Geddes stadsplanerings-strategier*, Gothenburg, 1989.

"Not only have old quarters been everywhere demolished in the name of progress and hygiene, but even the permanent buildings which it was intended to disclose have been largely destroyed by their restorers".[20]

Considering old buildings Geddes advocated "a fair trial before condemnation". He urged, "not to rush on the altar of hygiene" and fought well entrenched cliché:

"Decaying matter and smells, the germs which produce these, are not in the stone of the building, but in the dirt superficial to these".[21]

At a macro-urban scale Geddes criticised the spatial consequences of Haussmannian streets widening schemes: they generate impracticable plots of lands. In general he denounced "superficial spaciousness" of the wide boulevard opened at the cost of "ample courts" and "old gardens".[22]

His alternative strategy is:

"To improve the old and build new quarters beyond, so slackening the pressure of population upon habitation, not increasing it".[23]

Geddes' approach to conservation is essentially based on his sociological view, which is underpinned by an evolutionist and "vitalist" philosophy, and history is used as an analytical tool to grasp the spatial and temporal complexity of present. The idea of continuity is linked to the acknowledgement of this very complexity. As a result, Geddes also provided architectonic analyses. In his 1904 report, he inserts 'transitional' styled architecture with a strong historicist leaning in the existing fabric. In the following decades, Geddes developed his "civic" and "diagnosis" survey. Time and time again, Geddes pointed out that "the policy of sweeping clearance [was] "the most disastrous and pernicious blunders in the chequered history of sanitation".[24] This approach of 'conservative surgery' was to be the ultimate outcome of this belief, and can be rightly interpreted as a systematic method for urban conservation developed right in the heyday of extension planning. Geddes' first incitement in getting involved with urban planning had been initially stimulated by his dissatisfaction with the socially depressed social fabric of Edinburgh. For him conservation was a logical extension of social upgrading of depressed districts based on a steady and carefully studied programme of transformation.

Although, much original and part of a willingly systematic method of planning, Geddes' approach to urban conservation should draw our attention to a greater plurality of view than generally assumed on hygiene and old urban fabric at the turn of the twentieth century. The same year, a member of the Czech delegation gave to the First International Congress of Hygiene and Housing a full report about the old city of Prague. His position might have been isolated within the Congress. Anyhow, the paper presented by this physician concluded that no statistical evidences could be given in disfavour of health standards in the old city.[25]

1.3 The Old City as a Cultural Cradle

Camillo Sitte's sudden pledge for a new way of comprehending the city fabric was the direct result of his contempt for the way Vienna had been redeveloped after the ring competition of 1857. His work, *Der Städtebau nach seinen Künstlerischen Grundsätzen*, however, was drawing its strength from a larger background.[26] Ambition here was to set up a theory about

20 Patrick Geddes, *City Development, A report to the Carnegie Dunfermline Trust*, Shannon, 1973. p. 11.

21 Idem.

22 Ibidem.

23 Ibid, p.12.

24 Jacqueline Tyrwhitt (Ed.), *Patrick Geddes in India*, London, 1947, p. 45 (the texts are related to the survey carried in India by Geddes during the First World War).

25 The title is particularly indicative: Dr. Ladislas Prochazca, "Sur la prétendue opposition des exigences de l'hygiène moderne avec la sauvegarde du caractère historique des villes", *Premier Congrès International d'Assainissement et de Salubrité de l'Habitation*, Paris, 1905, p. 108-112.

26 Camillo Sitte, *Der Städtebau nach seinen künstlerischen Grundsätzen*, Vienna, 1922. Among the numerous studies undertaken on Sitte's writings, we refer here to Françoise Choay, *La règle et le modèle*, Paris, 1980, p.312-315; Daniel Wieczorek, *Camillo Sitte et les débuts de l'urbanisme moderne*,

the processing of urban forms. In this pursuit, old cities were used as both inspiration and resources. The pledge for conservation was implicit, and considered as self-evident. Before all, Sitte was, after discovering history natural laws, explaining the secret of coherent diversity, which made for the attractiveness of the old city. Consequently he also looked for suitable rules, patterns and knowledge in order to produce some form of urban continuity. He strove to present figures of unavoidable compromise with the modern city. Therefore, the place assigned to city-conservation was part of the general strategy of continuity and compromise.

Sitte has been studied and much commented for his writings, less for his own planning achievements.[27] Sitte's plans display an erudition and skill in design that dismissed any assimilation with some medievalist schemes later attributed to the 'German school' by the Modern Movement historiography.[28] In fact, each pre-industrial period was mobilised, combined and one may say, transcended. If Sitte was puzzled by the widespread success of his *Städtebau*, the impact of his later exposed theories on city building was paradoxically downsized in his own city during the period of the Great Vienna competition of 1892-94. His uncompromising position on city conservation contributed to his likely marginal position. Conceived in the 1850s, one of the particularities of the Ringstrasse system was to have provided for a buffer maintaining the 'Altstadt' as an almost intact unit. This has been remarked by Gustavo Giovannoni as "the most monumental urban achievement in modern time" making the Altstadt a virtually detached district.[29] In this light, Sitte's infuriated reaction to the redevelopment scheme proposed in the aftermath of the 1892 competition was to be expected. Among other observations, Sitte made it clear that baroque buildings should be left untouched, and that the adjustment of old squares to modern urban traffic would bring death to the Altstadt.[30] For him, the Altstadt should still radiate as the cradle of urban forms, potentially open to regeneration.

Extension or layout plans allow us to verify the orientations taken by Camillo Sitte in the aftermath of the publishing of his Treaty in this regard. Among an important number of middle-sized projects, Olmutz in 1893 is a significant step. The city remains a fairly demarcated unit with its six pierced town walls, faced by a long ring of building blocks itself surrounded by a park ring displaying an intricate lacework of alleys. While the post earth-quake plan of Ljubljana in 1895 insists on minimal alteration of the existing urban form, the 1903 plan of Marienberg displays an elaborate lay out system of small squares, ramified street network, tangential circulation, differential levelling, hooked street ends, and inner housing blocks public space, all devices intended to soften transitional spaces between old and new urban units. Siegfried Sitte's entry for Gothenburg in 1901 is already quite close to the carefully designed Marienberg scheme.[31]

Although miles a part and respectively grounded in art history and applied arts and in sociology and

Brussels, 1981; George R. Collins and Christiane Crasemann Collins, *Camillo Sitte and the Birth of Modern City Planning*, London, 1965; Carl E. Schorske, *Fin-de-siècle Vienna, Politics and Culture*, Cambridge, 1981.

27 Shortly after writing his book, Sitte had been involved in many projects in relation to the following cities: Privoz, Ljubljana, Marienthal, Tepliz, Eichwald, Reichenberg. For a more complete list, see G. R. Collins, Camillo… op. cit., p. 113-114. On Sitte's epigones, cf. Guido Zucconi (ed), Camillo *Sitte e i suoi interpreti*, Milano, 1992; also the analysis of Breda Mihelic, "Ljubljana, 1895-1937- De la ville régionale à la capitale slovène", in Eve Blau, Monica Platzer (dir.), *L'idée de la grande ville, l'architecture moderne d'Europe centrale, 1890-1937*, Munich, 2000, p. 196-204.

28 By referring to this current we allude first to Siegfried Giedon (Le Corbusier can hardly be quoted in this regard). See especially Siegfried Giedon, *Space, Time, Architecture*, Cambridge, 1959.

29 "Ma il Ring Viennese, forse la più monumentale concezione edilizia dei tempi moderna, è qualcosa di più: è une vasto spazio che distacca I quartieri esterni dall'interno ed impedisce che lo imprigionino e lo soffochino; è la linea massima del movimento e degli affari che circola intorno alla vecchia città senza penetrarvi", in Gustavo Giovannoni, "Vecchie città ed Edilizia Nuova", *Nuova Antologia*, Fascicolo 995, 1913, p. 449-472, p. 462.

30 See R. G. Collins, Camillo… op. cit., p. 44.

31 On Camillo Sitte and Siegfried Sitte's plans, see Rudolf Wurzer, "Franz, Camillo und Siegfried Sitte, Ein langer Weg von der Architektur zur Stadtplanung", *Berichte zur Raumforschung und Raumplanung*, (33), 1989, p. 9-34.

social practice, Sitte's and Geddes' vision of the 'old city' did converge to some extent.[32]

1.4 Municipalism and Conservation

As Burgomaster of Brussels between 1881 and 1899, Charles Buls (1837-1914) steadily developed a pragmatic approach of city building and of conservation initiated with the restoration work of some of the "Grand' Place" buildings since 1883 onward.[33] As other parts of the old city, the "Grand' Place" had been damaged by the French bombing in 1695. Having been partially rebuilt and 'restored', the place was by the end of the nineteenth century in a much dilapidated shape. Buls' project of the restoration of a significant cluster of civilian buildings did much to establish his fame as a staunch conservationist in Europe. For once it was proved that not only it was possible to carry out restoration work by convincing the owners and to instil the idea of maintenance, but also to correct previous mishandling by carrying partial reconstruction of degraded or destructed parts. He was perfectly informed of the growing body of scholarly literature and work on conservation. However, his vision of urban conservation was part of a much larger interest for social reform and education. Monuments and ordinary buildings had to be transmitted to new generations in order to promote civic pride and awareness about national traditions and crafts. Therefore restitution could be admitted when necessary to convey a feeling of cohesiveness. A compromise could be done in time to balance 'scientific' conservation with artistic and aesthetic considerations. Built remains in their different shapes were marks and roots that protected a society engaged in a path of transformation. Remains should not be distorted, however, they still should be understandable for non-specialised citizens in order to stimulate civic mind. To achieve that end, Buls proceeded mainly through incitement measures and negotiations. However, compulsory purchase was to be later and used as "a last resort" step, a dissuasive weapon against indiscriminate destruction.

Buls' approach, based on fieldwork practice in Brussels, was summarised in his 1893 pamphlet on 'cities aesthetics'.[34] Freed from his tenure as a Burgomaster after 1899, Buls was widely recognised as a specialist in urban conservation and managed to exert some influence on the professional milieu, especially in Rome.[35] With the Art Public movement developing in Brussels, and the strong influence in the Belgian capital of German planners as Joseph Stübben, Buls realised, that his quest was not an isolated one in Europe.[36] By the turn of the century, he eventually discovered that through his pragmatic approach he had come next to some of Sitte's findings in studying urban form. Buls' action continued on focusing on a practical way to promote urban conservation. For him 'modernity' should be beaten on its own ground by proving through case-by-case studies that better financial, cultural and aesthetic solutions could be found.

32 The parallel between Geddes and Sitte has been underlined by many authors, quoting Geddes' project of "outlook tower" and Sitte's project of "Holländer Turm", as receptacles of culture creativity. Collins stated "it is hard to imagine two city planners of the same generation who were more widely separated in interests than Sitte and Geddes", cf. R. G. Collins, Camillo… op. cit., p. 15. According to Lilian Anderson both men were, beyond their differences, opposed to a bureaucratic form of rationality and in favour of public participation in town planning, even if in an undeveloped form. We should note that Geddes was deeply impressed by his 1909 tour in Germany and referred to Sitte as "that admirable architect of Vienna, who has done for the appreciation of the medieval city as a whole what the romantic revival did for its cathedral or town house", cf. Patrick Geddes, *Cities in Evolution: an Introduction to the Town Planning Movement and to the Study of Civics,* London, 1915, p. 200-202.

33 Mina Martens, "Buls", *Biographie Nationale*, published by Académie Royale des Sciences, des Lettres et des Beaux Arts de Belgique, supplément T. II, Fascicule I, Brussels, 1858, p. 231-236. For a comprehensive analysis of Buls's contribution, see Marcel Smets, *Charles Buls, Les principes de l'art urbain,* Liège, 1995.

34 See Charles Buls, *L'esthétique des villes*, Brussels, 1893.

35 M. Smets, *Charles Buls…* op. cit., p. 153-156.

36 Buls came first to learn the achievements of the 'Austrian-German school' through Joseph Stübben who was acquainted to Leopold II. However, it seems that Buls discovered Sitte through the imaginative translation of Camille Martin. See *Idem*, p. 148-151.

1.5. Conservation as Professional Expertise

In Rome, the very complexity of the archaeological 'palimpsest' of different layers of the eternal city within its walls, and the centuries old tradition of antiquarians pilgrimage had favoured, after much debate and arguments between archaeological purist and amateurs of the picturesque, a conciliatory treatment of preservation and landscaping of the ruins.[37] It is no surprise that the enormous body of writing produced during more than half a century by the engineer, architect and art historian Gustavo Giovannoni (1873-1947) has been strongly articulated in the thought and practice of the development of Rome.

His two essays published before the First World War looked for general principles aiming at integrating urban conservation within town planning theory. Giovannoni's first essay, "Vecchie città ed Edilizia nuova", is primarily an informed and academic account of the progress of old city conservation in Europe, and secondly an analysis of the ongoing development after the general plan of Edmondo Sanjust di Teulada had been established in 1906-1909.[38] Through the study of a specific district of Rome, the second piece expounds in detail a systematic method of intervention on the old urban fabric through what Giovannoni calls "il diradamento", or, the thinning out of the existing built environment.[39] Modernity could finally encapsulate innovation and conservation in a coherent and complex unit as long as the specificity of each spatial sub-unit is acknowledged and duly treated. This infers various kinds of strategies to treat the macro-form as well as the clusters of dwellings. The general principle is to release the old centre from the transit traffic pressure through various strategies.

Giovannoni quotes the ring system, as non-feasible if the core city is too spacious. Then, the "dual system" is a product of a shifting of the centre. Berlin is quoted as an "imposing example" and Strasbourg as a completed one.[40] However, Rome shows precisely the limit of those models, since an appropriate layout should consider particularities of the topography and of the socio-economic tendencies of development. Conservation should thus relate to the discrete situation of each spatial entity. It is tempting to compare Giovannoni's method of "diradamento" to Geddes' "conservative surgery". The operative techniques look quite similar, with the purpose of lowering housing density, 'cleaning up' in-built accretion and finally by giving some sense of historical and cultural grounding. But at least two important differences must be insisted upon.

Firstly Giovannoni not unlike Egil Fischer emphasised on the necessity to connect the different scales of conservation procedures. Secondly his approach is fitted in a techno-artistic professional practice, while Geddes' method is primarily rooted in a process of civic mobilisation. Giovannoni analysed old cities and old districts as recently destabilised units. Professional techniques that fuse the knowledge of the architect, the erudition of art historian and the new possibilities of civil and urban engineering should allow to reverse this urban process and to re-stabilise a socio-spatial unit inserted in the larger framework of modern urban development.[41]

1.6. About Conservation in a Colonial Set Up

Vilhelm Lorenzen accurately observed the relatively rapid development of a conservation framework in colonial or semi colonial countries. By the time Giovannoni was laying the bases of a systematic urban conservation, another concept of urban conservation was formulated within the context of the newly imposed French Protectorate on Morocco. From November 1912 onward city walls and fortifications complexes were listed and the surrounding zones declared

37 On the influence archaeological findings had on the elaboration of the regulation plan of Roma, see Guido Zucconi, "Le destin de la Rome antique au début du siècle", in Yvon Lamy (dir.), *L'Alchimie du patrimoine, discours et politiques*, Talence, 1996, p. 287-303.

38 Gustavo Giovannoni, "Vecchie città… op. cit., p. 449-472.

39 Gustavo Giovannoni, "Il "diradamento" edilizio dei vecchi centri- il quartiere della rinascenza in Roma", *Nuova Antologia*, Fascicolo 997, 1913, p. 53-76.

40 G. Giovannoni, Vecchie … op.cit, p. 462.

41 G. Zucconi has established a powerful relation between Giovannoni's urban conservation approach and his attempt to create the profile of a new professional actor, "gli architetti integrali", assuming a key role in town-planning; cf. Guido Zucconi, *La Città Contesa, Dagli ingegneri sanitari agli urbanisti (1885-1942)*, Milan, 1989, p.123-128.

as "non aedificandi".[42] In most cities of Morocco, particularly imperial cities, a clear-cut separation was therefore installed between the old "medina" and newly built "European" centres. From that moment, General Hubert G. Lyautey justified this policy in the name of safeguarding the very independence of indigenous cities' cultural tradition.[43] To preserve this picturesque, modern installations should be kept at bay. Lyautey later coined the notion of different "ordre de ville" living side by side.[44] Three consequences followed: Conservation was part of state duty and presented as a factor of renewal for the Moroccan civilisation; the endeavour for 'genuineness' should govern; build heritage had to go through a systematic objectifying process. Finally, multi-polarities characterise urban development.

By and large, this urban policy must be understood as a 'policy and theory of expediency' in the context of a pre-war Protectorate, just tolerated by rival European powers. More narrowly understood, this policy was also a convenient device to minimise investments in the infrastructure of the 'medinas'.[45] However, besides the obvious opportunism of this conservation theory and practice, an entire process of 'planning for conservation' was effectively engaged with a rapid built up of procedures, restoration techniques and general conservation paraphernalia. This was also to have a long-term cultural effect on planners and conservationist lobbies in France. Between the two world wars the safeguard of the Moroccan cities was widely acknowledged in the press of architects and municipal professionals as evidence of how the old built environment could withstand the onslaught of modernity and coexist in parallel to other urban forms.

42 *National Archives, Paris, Fonds Lyautey, 475 AP/169*, Firman du 1 novembre 1912.

43 On the discourse and practice of the authorities of the French Protectorate on conservation, see, H. Vacher, *Projection... op. cit.*, p. 139-145.

44 Lyautey summed up his conceptions on conservation in "Comment on sauve l'art d'un pays", (Conférence donnée à l'Université des Annales le 10 décembre 1926), *Paroles d'Actions: Madagascar, Sud Oranais, Oran, Maroc (1900-1926)*, Paris, 1927, p. 444-457.

45 See Janet Abu-Lughod, *Rabat, Urban Apartheid in Morocco*, Princeton, 1980.

1.7 From Conservation to Safeguarding Strategies

A few conclusions can be drawn from the above overview on urban conservation. We have hinted earlier on the fact that relatively little is known of the historical relation between the planning discipline and the transformation of inherited built entities. Even less is known about the way this problem was tackled within competition entries during the 1880-1914 period.

The concept of conservation of the inherited built environment was clearly established in Europe before the First World War, and there also were experiments in some colonies, and strategies to actively enforce conservation were tried out. Urban conservation can thus by no means be seen as a product of 'post-modernity' and of the weakening expansion of the 1970s. In fact, it could be argued that most of the complex technical, societal and cultural issues linked to conservation were thoroughly developed during the above-described formative period.[46]

More precisely, its seems that two phases can been distinguished. The last two decades of the nineteenth century were maturation phases. Conservationist lobbies and antiquarians were slowly gathering strength to block off some aspects of the destructive process. The growing corpus on restoration practice and the heated debate on the very purpose of conservation were also fuelling general awareness about the threatened destruction of the inherited urban fabric. This process eventually culminated in most countries with the establishment of specialised extra-municipal commissions in charge of the survey and minimal protection of fragments of the 'old city'. By the first decade of the twentieth century, this *first line of defence*—namely the attempt to prevent the destruction of individual buildings—was reinforced by a general shift of paradigm in the design of layout plans with the advent of Civic Art.

46 Relations between economic slow down and interest for conservation have been noted in reference to the late nineteenth century. However, simple causal links are difficult to establish. Cf. Peter J. Larkham, *Conservation and the city*, London and New York, 1996, p. 58-59.

However, at least for capital cities, the developing 'conservation paradigm' was largely offset by the 'city-building' paradigm whereby the centre of the enlarged city was intended to harbour an intensified locus of exchange for business and services activities. This irradiating centre was conceived as a pulse both as a point of departure for extending the thoroughfares and the built environment and as a point of attraction for catching energies from proximate and distant environments.[47] This intensification of centrality was associated with a more or less rapid renewal of obsolete built environments, as well as an acceleration of the building cycle, and involved a social and political compromise that saw the reallocation of popular housing within the suburban areas. However, this seemingly 'unavoidable' trend that drove the transformation of great cities in the 1880-1900s was far from manifesting itself in a uniform manner.

We have already mentioned Sitte's strong opposition to Karl Mayderer's 1895 *Generalregulierungsplan* for the Vienna *Altstadt*, and Giovannoni's enthusiasm for the Ringstrasse as an efficient de-connecting device. In this case, studies have effectively shown the considerable smoothing impact of the Ring on the city-building process in the *Altstadt*, and the quick silting up of Mayderer's project, in spite of its limited and cautious character and its pledge to maintain the "historisches Stadtbild".[48] With a very different type of urban form, the case of Berlin tends to show the slow progression of street-opening and widening schemes undertaken in the *Altstadt* in the second half of the nineteenth century, and the dubious profitability in the end of corresponding urban-clearance projects for the municipality on the eve of the 1910 international competition for the Greater Berlin.[49] Based on the awarded competitions entries, it has been suggested that planners of different backgrounds and supporters as well as opponents of the *Grosstadt* shared some common presuppositions at least for the capital of the Wihelmian Reich, namely the city-building process to be applied to the *Innenstadt*. The image of Berlin evidenced in the entries naturally reflected the importance given to the aspect of monumental grandeur that was deemed suitable for a *Weltstadt*.[50]

Despite their 'Sittian filiation', however, neither Jansen (first prize) nor Brix and Genzmer (first prize) devised specific approaches towards the centre, notwithstanding the notable will of the initiators of the Charlottenburg Seminar to mark off Berlin's former limits. Basically all awarded projects shared the city-building paradigm, with a strong accent on a network intensifying circulatory moves and making the city centre spectacular, with the possible enhancing 'theatre' of private constructions prolonging the architectonics of public monuments.[51] The differences therefore are more about accents and monumental radicalism than about general orientations. Entries oscillated between, on the one hand, a minimalist form of intervention on the *Altstadt* and the will to retain some mixed activities in the city centre, as suggested by the Havestadt & Contag entry (fourth prize), and on the other hand, widespread monumental interventionism. The Eberstadt, Mörhing & Petersen project (third prize) actually involved an activation of the city-building process. Finally, one should insist upon the fact that the Berlin competition, besides its symbolic dimension for the Reich, was a private venture sponsored by the professional Berliner milieu and conceived essentially as a catalyst for architectural endeavours.

As documented above, it remains that for a growing number of professionals 'extension plans planning' was

47 See, J. Rodriguez-Lorez "Stadt-Umbau und Elendsviertel, Zur Grundrentenbildung in der Innerstadt", in Gerhard Fehl, Juan Rodriguez–Lorez (ed.), *Die planmäßige Erneuerung europäischer Großstädte zwischen Wiener Kongress und Weimarer Republik*, Basel, 1995, p. 319-334.

48 Renate Banik-Schweitzer, "Zugleich ist auch bei der Stadterweiterung die Regulierung der innern Stadt im Auge zu behalten. Wiener Altstadt und Ringstraße im Tertiärisierungsprozeß des 19. Jahrhunderts", in Gerhard Fehl, Juan Rodriguez–Lorez (ed.), *Die planmäßige... op. cit., p. 127-147.*

49 Dieter Radicke, "Stadterneuerung in Berlin 1871 bis 1914. Kaiser-Wihelm-Straße und Scheunenvierteln", in *Idem*, p. 239-248.

50 For an in depth discussion of the awarded entries cf. Erich Konter, "Verheißungen einer Weltstadtcity. Vorschläge zum Umbau "Alt-Berlins" in den Preisgehkrönteen Entwürfen des Wettbewerbs Groß-Berlin von 1910", in *Ibidem*, p. 249-272.

51 On these aspects see, Wolfgang Sonne, "Ideen für die Großstadt: Der Wettbewerb Groß-Berlin 1910" in Thorsten Scheer, Josef Paul Kleihues, Paul Kahlfeldt, *Stadt der Architektur. Architektur der Stadt, Berlin 1900-2000*, Berlin, 2000, p. 67-77.

also viewed in relation to what was happening to the 'old centre', or what Cornelius Gurlitt (1850-1938) had called the "absorption of the heart of the old centre".[52] If the new developing techniques of the town plan were to be 'rational', they had to include old as well as new built environments, and urban growth should cease to be synonymous with systematic renewal and with the programmed death of old districts. On the contrary, they should seek a renewed equilibrium between different types of built environment.

The strategies elaborated within the Civic Art movement to erect this *second line of defence* were varied. Cornelius Gürlitt for instance advised caution and moderation to conservationists, considering that "the old stuff offends the bourgeois mind". Similar realism was also recommended to the amateurs of the picturesque, advised to consider, before falling into proselytism, the practical side of "living in and maintaining a house crippled with mortgages and several centuries old".[53] We can briefly sum up his proposals, as they largely reflect positions that can be found within the Civic Art movement and Art Public congresses:

* Combat the encroachment of advertising, its possible taxation.
* Ease traffic by prohibiting overtaking in town as well as high speeds in general. Avoid the introduction of tramways, considered as Trojan horses for street-widening schemes.
* Fragment traffic pressure toward the centre and design ring-road systems comprising suburban inter-connections.
* Facilitate "neighbourhood" traffic, posing no risk to the Old City and also safeguarding local activities.

The effect of the city-building process is fully acknowledged with all its social consequences, though no global strategy is devised. However, Gürlitt did note that, "whatever our political and social ideas", such a process must be duly considered—the maintaining of popular elements and of small activities within the city core being of prime importance.[54]

The basic statement is to acknowledge that the centre cannot be sustained as a functional entity for the Greater City and must thus be thought of as a specific unit. As we have shown in the paragraphs above, such a set of ideas that could be converted into operational planning was the result of an interplay between the development of the planning discipline and the prevailing trend of urbanisation happening in cities and putting municipal services as well as town councils under pressure for responses.

We should note that most of these safeguarding strategies were not fully elaborated in the core countries of Europe. They were in fact much more developed and sophisticated in the peripheries, were pre-industrial relations and cultural traditions, though also quickly eroding, remained relatively strong. There, the plethora of effects accompanying modernity could be given a 'second thought'.

We will now examine the development of conservation ideals and practice in reference to Copenhagen's city centre at the time of the competition.

2 Copenhagen and its Spheres of Transformation

We do not intend to give here an account of the transformation of the 'inner city'.[55] We restrict ourselves to only a few aspects of the demolishing and building process in relation to the development of conservationist concerns that will be explored from different angles in the following paragraphs.

From 1915 onward, the journal *Før og nu- Historisk topografisk Tidsskrift*, founded and edited by the philanthropic glove manufacturer Francis Zachariae

52 M. C. Gürlitt, *Conservation du Coeur d'anciennes villes, Traduction d'une conférence de M. Gürlitt à Salzbourg, suivie de La conservation du Coeur de la ville de Bruxelles de C. Buls*, Brussels, 1912.

53 Idem, p. 7.

54 Ibidem, p. 16.

55 For an extensive survey of the city's transformation according to each district, see B. Bramsen (red.), *København før og nu – og aldrig*, Copenhagen, 1987-1990. See also the process of transformation as analysed by O. Forchhammer, *København... op.cit.*

(1852-1936), provided its readers with an impressive record of a city under change. It printed side-by-side pictures of urban locations of "yesterday" and of "today", reflecting a rising awareness of the mounting tide of modern constructions.[56]

The term 'old city', as generally used in this book, refers to the former 'walled city' of the mid-nineteenth century. However, it should be underlined that what the contemporaries generally meant with the 'gamle by' was a smaller urban space in which Christianshavn, founded by Christian IV and integrated to Copenhagen's municipality in 1674, was not included. Neither Slotsholmen was thought being part of it. The 'gamle bydel' encompassed on nine quarters south of the main axis Gothersgade and the seventeenth-century extension of 'Ny København'. The "gamle bydel" had suffered from several fires in the eighteenth and early nineteenth centuries, and we shall see that this factor was to be used in the debate about conservation. While the notion of 'old city' meaning all the pre-industrial urban units had not yet consolidated (certainly not from an administrative point of view), the idea was nevertheless quite alive, as illustrated by Larsen and Schiødte's 1894 book *Gamle Kjøbenhavnske, Huse and Gaard*, covering all the area, which had been fortified by Christian IV, as well as remaining patches of bucolic surroundings.

Studies have analysed the city-building process that took place in the inner city in the second part of the nineteenth century and the shift from a residential city to an industrialising Great City, marked by a general tendency toward functional specialisation.[57] The impact of such a process on the physical fabric of the inner city could already be felt by the mid-1870s, with the London model of the 'city district' gaining strong ground within Copenhagen's administration.[58]

56 The issue from 15 November 1915 was mostly dedicated to the destruction happening within the city.

57 See, Ole Hyltoft, *Københavns industrialisering 1840-1914*, Aarhus, 1984. On the city –building process as such see, Casper Jørgensen, *Aspekter af citydannelsen i København: En analyse af samspillet mellem funktionsskift og kommercielle bygninger i det indre København ca. 1870-1911*, unpublished Master Thesis, University of Copenhagen, 1986.

58 *Idem.* We should note that a number of British civil engineers and consultant firms in Denmark were very active in Denmark during this period.

As a whole, the 'old city' saw its population steadily diminish since 1860, with a sharp decline during the 1880s, though Christianshavn was an exception to this process. Between 1880 and 1901, the inner city proper lost 22,786 inhabitants, and 22,835 between 1901 and 1911.[59] The former walled city, despite urbanisation schemes such as Gammelholm, had lost one third of its inhabitants in three decades. Finally the "Gamle bydel" as such had fallen from 67,087 in 1860 to 27,887 in 1911, with an especially sharp decline in the 1880s, in the quarters of Købmager and Rosenborg.[60]

Different forces were at work, reshaping the urban form and generating what we might call a 'sphere of transformations'. As a result, one would expect there to be an obvious relation between the transformation of the built environment, the creation of new perceptions of urbanity and the development of conservationism. However, the interplay of these dimensions is far from clearly established. We have attempted to figure out the general movement imposed upon the built environment on the map of the city, which was edited in 1906. (See, the map *Spheres of transformations*). The destruction of part of the urban fabric awoke curiosity, the interest of connoisseurs, and possibly anger. It also left many quite unconcerned.[61] The different 'spheres of transformations' therefore evoke a fairly open spectrum of attitudes, ranging from definite approval to the vociferous denunciation of a 'culture of destruction', with its heroes and villains. Each sphere of change had its own symbolic resonance, its specifically motivated public, its own intricate debate and also its well-entrenched vested interests. The result of this interplay is partly what determines further transformations or possible counter-moves, from partial freeze to possible conservation attempts.

In 1900 Copenhagen, a first sphere could be associated with projects dealing with the creation of new public and official buildings. The notion of "re-foun-

59 This calculation concerns the former walled city (Byen indenfor den gamle Voldlinie) only, See A. Holm, K. Johansen, *København... op. cit.*, p. 45.

60 These details are based on the numerous tables provided by C. Jørgensen, *Aspekter... op. cit.*

61 For a proposal of methodical exploration of group motivations, see J. P. Larkham, *Conservation ... op. cit.*, p. 109-252.

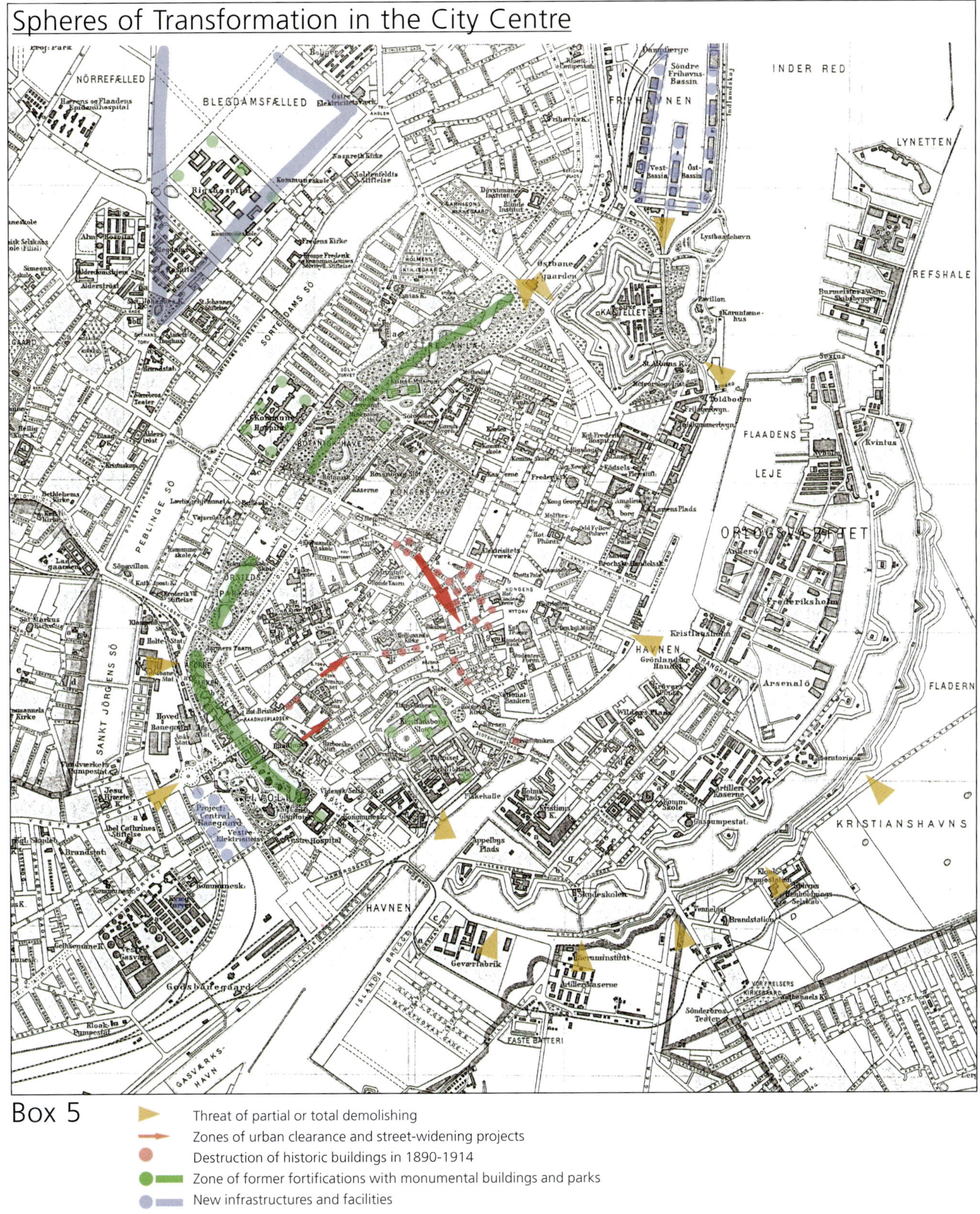
Spheres of Transformation in the City Centre
NÖRREFÆLLED
BLEGDAMSFÆLLED
FRIHAVNEN
INDER RED
LYNETTEN
REFSHALE
SORTEDAMS SÖ
PEBLINGE SÖ
SANKT JÖRGENS SÖ
ØSTRE ANLÆG
BOTANISK HAVE
KONGENS HAVE
KASTELLET
FLAADENS LEJE
ORLOGSVÆRFTET
Frederiksholm
HAVNEN
Arsenalö
FLADERN
KRISTIANSHAVNS
TIVOLI
Vestre Hospital
Appelbys Plads
Geværfabrik
Artillerikaserne
FASTE BATTERI
GASVÆRKS-HAVN
ISLANDS BRYGGE
Godsbanegaard
Box 5
Threat of partial or total demolishing
Zones of urban clearance and street-widening projects
Destruction of historic buildings in 1890-1914
Zone of former fortifications with monumental buildings and parks
New infrastructures and facilities

dation" could even be suggested to qualify the symbolic shift associated with the erection of the new town hall.[62] This sphere is not to be analysed simply in a context of demolition and construction, but also in relation to a relative 'urban vacuum', namely the poor state of important parts of the city fabric. Some of the buildings damaged after the bombing of the city by the English Navy in 1807 had remained in poor shape throughout the nineteenth century. The situation was even worse in the very core of the city: since the great fire of Christiansborg palace in 1884, Slotsholmen had more or less gone to rack and ruin.[63] What remained of the Royal Palace was basically a huge carcass, at a time when the New Town Hall was rising to prominence as a symbol and tool of municipal power. The evolution of the city's image was not only related to the reconstruction of Christiansborg, a project for which there was an invitation to bid in 1904, it was also conditioned by the slow reorganisation of Slotsholmen with the construction of the Royal Library.[64]

In the first half of the century, the demolition of old structures, the opening of new streets, the filling up of canals and of old harbour and docks had been going on bringing much change to Slotsholmen's atmosphere. The district's new profile remained uncertain till Thorvald Jørgensen's (1867-1946) project won in 1906. Martin Nyrop's 'Italo-Nordic' Town Hall inaugurated in 1905, which was to become the jewel of the National-Romantic movement, located on the site of the dismantled western fortification line and whose construction started in 1894, was conceived as a symbolic link between the 'old' and the 'new' capital city. This was also the case of the third railway station, designed by H. Wenck and built in 1908-1911: a 'national styled' building made of elegant carpentry and sober brick masonry.[65]

Jørgensen's unimaginative massive neo-baroque structure, which was erected between 1907 and 1928, already seemed to move the city away from the National Romantic period.[66] It re-anchored the very heart of the city in its early 1800s. The re-foundation appears as a 'de-doubling' of the once prevailing image, the symbols of the Burghers' city standing next to the former place of residence of the Absolutist Era.[67] At the same time, 'urban vacuity' and the prospect of restructuring the heart of the city had created a desire to excavate and to look for historical roots. Taking advantage of the numerous projects launched on Slotsholmen during these years, the National Museum's Archaeological Office searched for the remains of King Absalon's fortress, the city's founding father, and multiplied excavations that might throw some light on the city's early development. (See Chapter 7) Engineers and architects alike were mobilised in this survey work.

A second sphere can be distinguished as the by-product of street-widening and urban clearance schemes launched in many districts at the same period. Important privately founded schemes had already been carried out in the 1870s along Østergade, extended in 1907 to connect up with the newly opened Christian-IXs Gade. The press took a spearheading role in a cam-

62 The concept of 're-foundation' was put forward by André Corboz, *Le territoire comme palimpseste et autres essais,* Paris, 2001, p. 133-172. It implies that some minor alterations, transformations and creations in the prevailing structure of the city (for instance the erection of a public building) may provoke a new repartition of symbolic spaces. Two conditions must be fulfilled for a 're-foundation': the emergence of a political counter-power and some minor change in the physical layout. It could be argued that both conditions had been fulfilled in the case of Copenhagen. Obviously, this aspect should require a much more detailed study. Our only purpose is to point out the shift of 'focus', emerging with the erection of the town hall. Accordingly one should also note that the vote of the financial package relating to the rebuilding of Christiansborg Palace had been long postponed.

63 Christiansborg Palace, built by Nicolaj Eigtved (1701-1754), burnt down in 1794. Christian F. Hansen designed the new palace built in 1805-1828, which also burnt to ashes in 1884. An architectural competition was held in 1888 to select the design for a third Christiansborg Palace (seven prizes were given). However, the whole project had been de facto frozen till the end of the century.

64 The building of the New Royal Library was carried out by architect Hans J. Holm (1835-1916) during the years 1900-1906.

65 H. Wenck, "Centralbanegaarden nu og siden", *Illustreret Tidende*, N. 17, 1910, p. 215-216.

66 Three first prizes were respectively given to Andreas Clemmensen, Thorvald Jorgensen (1867-1946), and Martin Nyrop.

67 A. Corboz distinguished two configurations of 're-foundation' according to whether the raising authority wipes out or is composing with the former power: *Le territoire... op. cit.*, p. 157-158.

paign against "ill-fitted" streets and clusters of buildings. These projects were de facto reviving plans for a commercial district that had been formulated in the first half of the nineteenth century.[68] But mixed feelings were also expressed and the destruction of old plot structures was questioned, while widespread archaeological and historical surveys were actively encouraged.[69]

Studies have identified an especially important period of building activity in the years 1895 to 1911.[70] By the turn of the century, numerous projects still in progress had already made their mark on the urban fabric. Such was in particular the business-district scheme described as "opening a large route toward the future" around the enlarged Kristenbernikovstræde and Antonigade during the years 1896-1900, which was supported by the municipality.[71] So were also smaller schemes such as: the Nygade street-widening of 1898-1900, branching out into Gammel Torv; the Farvegade-Gåsegade street-widening in the vicinity of the new Town Hall in 1905-1907; and the important clearance operations in the area of Brøndstræde, Vognmagergade, and Møntergade after 1906. Widespread street-widening-cum-opening schemes were undertaken between 1905 and 1912 in the neighbouring of the new street Christian-IX mentioned above. It is worth mentioning here that it was precisely one of these major street-widening schemes that was sent, along with other projects, to represent Denmark at the 1910 Berlin Exhibition. This plan was criticised by Theodor Goecke, the editor of *Der Städtebau,* who underlined both the lack of fundamental purpose and heavy handling of the project. It was compared negatively to a skilfully designed scheme in old Vienna that preserved the complex pattern of streets. In brief, from Goecke's point of view, this project exemplified an outdated nineteenth-century model of street opening[72]. This cold reception is even more ironical when one recalls that W. Hegemann had strongly hoped to obtain the competition entries instead of this patchwork of projects for his Berlin Exhibition.

What we have called the second sphere of transformation was associated with a sharp reduction in the number of residents in major commercial streets (Østergade lost two thirds of its population during the 1880s).[73] Even major squares were affected by transformations. Kongens Nytorv and to a certain extent Gammeltorv were under intense speculative pressure.[74] The development of international-class hotels and the construction of department stores were denounced by a vocal minority for their trite and oversize design. Some authors have drawn attention to the evolving urban semantics, with the emergence circa 1880 of terms like 'forretningsbygning', 'city' appearing in the 1870s and becoming commonly used with the concept of 'city-gade' by 1890. Also influenced by the British model were the warehouses, built during the same years for the storage of commercial goods.[75] While a significant number of urban redevelopment schemes were privately founded, the municipal council backed the drive to create a "city district", providing stores, offices and high-standard housing. By 1908 a new by-law had opened up the possibility of state loans for launching urban clearance and social upgrading

68 The role of Det Kjøbenhavnske Byggeselskab founded in 1872 and backed by the magnate Tietgen has been instrumental in bringing this scheme to fruition. See Vibeke Petersen and Inga Christensen, "Stuktidens vindskibelighed. Sanering for de fattige, boliger for de fine", *Historiske Meddelelser om København,* 1982, p. 136-171.

69 See especially "Nyt og Gammelt", *Architekten,* N. 14, 5 January 1907, p.136-139. For detailed report on these schemes, cf. *København Før og Nu aldrig,* 1980, Vol. IV, and Vilhelm Malling, *Rundt i byen, Lidt stof til eftertanke,* Copenhagen, 1959, p. 41-45.

70 See C. Jørgensen, *Aspekter... op. cit.,* esp. p. 64-79.

71 See Borgerrepræsentationens Forhandlinger 2 November 1902, Copenhagen, 1903, p. 1075.

72 See Theodor Goecke, "Allgemeine Städtebau-Ausstellung, Berlin 1910, *Der Städtebau,* 7/8 Heft, 1910, p. 73-92, p. 79. In fact, the design was of a thoroughfare running parallel to Gothersgade before bending southward, linking Nørrevoldgade to Holmens Kanal The street widening project was to develop along the axis of the following streets: Tornebuskgade, Aabenraa, Vognmagergade, Gammelmønt, Kristenbernikovstræde, and Holmensgade. The final part of this entire scheme was realised much later.

73 For details, see Michael Koefoed & H. Weitemeyer, *Trap Beskrivelse af Denmark,* Vol. I, 1906 p. 446. Between 1880 and 1901, the number of inhabitants in Adelgade passed from 5.015 to 3.920, Borgergade from 4.678 to 3.818, Kjøbmagergade from 1.286 to 759, and Østergade from 956 to 342.

74 For instance, the building of Grundejerer Banken implanted in 1910 on Nytorv, and the building designed by Aage Mathiesen at the angle of Gammel Torv and Frederiksberggade.

75 C. Jørgensen, *Aspekter... op. cit.,* see chapter 4.

projects.[76] In those years, *Politiken* reported on a rough partition whereby the 'city district' was progressively gentrified. The daily noticed the sharp increase of right-wing votes within the newly built perimeter, while a social-democratic periphery was building up.[77] At the beginning of the century, the journal *Architekten*, ran a special section commenting on the 'old and new' in the transformation of streets and squares. The widening of streets was generally accepted, but with some reluctance according to context. Occasional mention was made of the picturesque of some old clusters, while the drive towards modernisation was generally praised.[78] Such schemes even came to threaten Christian IV's famous massive structure known as the "Round Tower". As the tower stood in the way of an important street-widening project, leading architects competed to find a happier compromise, Anton Rosen (1859-1928) even suggesting shifting the tower.[79] For once however, the irresistible force of modernity stopped short of the immovable past.

A third sphere of transformation could be more closely linked to the destructive pressure exerted on historic buildings of recognised architectural quality. The demolition of remarkable buildings such as the Nybørsen, known as the Six Sisters (see infra and Plate 12), or the Løveapotek designed by Caspar F. Harsdoff (1735-1799) and demolished by 1908, reminded the citizens of the sudden fragility of buildings that were part of the city's traditional iconography. Yet, ordinary timber-framed houses were going by the dozen, arousing little protest. However, surveys and photographic campaigns were increasingly encouraged, indicating a growing uneasiness with destruction. The role of the association Østifternes historisk topografiske Selskab was decisive in the undertaking of a systematic inventory of the old buildings and its publication issued detailed survey and history of townbuildings that were to be demolished. (See Chapter 7) In 1899, this society gave a detailed account of the timber-framed building 'Admiralsgaard', and its periodical *Fra Arkiv og Museum* issued an impressive list of valuable buildings that had vanished in 1906.[80] As late as 1913, and notwithstanding strong protests and widespread indignation within the Municipal Council, one of the city's finest Renaissance buildings, 'Efterslægtens bygaard', was torn down. In contrast, the restoration of the eighteenth century Kanneworffske house on Kongens Nytorv, with a shop on the ground floor, was an indication of a newly developing tendency.[81] With regard to new constructions, architects were usually advised by the Academy to use caution. Blatant eclecticism was condemned when new constructions were planted next to buildings of historic value, and by 1905 the Academy was campaigning to develop a legal framework bringing statutory protection to secular buildings of historic interest.

A fourth sphere of change can be associated to the attempts at beautifying squares or important locations, but also at historicist 'reconstruction' operations on unfinished monuments. Towers, spires and domes floating over a sea of gabled frontages and steep roofs punctuated the skyline of the city. As in the rest of Europe, especially Germany, art historians and architects frequently discussed the advisability of 'completing' church with their spires. Painters and artists gen-

76 Law N° 160, of May 27, 1908. The laws of March 29, 1887, and February 26, 1898 on worker housing made room for expropriation, but were little used. See, Indenrigsministeriets Saneringsudvalg *Betænkning*, Copenhagen, 1938.

77 Gustav Philipsen, "Valget og Kjøbenhavn", *Politiken*, 29 May 1909.

78 "Københavns Foryngelse", *Illustreret Tidende,* 29 November 1908, p. 105-106. With photos of inner courtyards and drawings in the "picturesque style" by Emil Krause (1871-1945) together with the photos of an impressive corner building implanted, in "Det Nye København" *Illustret Tidende,* 14 March 1909, p. 291-294.

79 "Rundetaarns flytning", *Architekten,* N 3, 1 November 1898, p. 17-19.

80 On this building see, Aage Mathiesen & Chr. Axel Jensen, "Bremerholms Admiralsgaard udenfor gamle Østerport (1). Oplysninger om Admiralsgaard udenfor gamle Østerport", *Fra Arkiv og Museum*, Vol. 1, 1899-1902, p. 191-207, and Chr. Axel Jensen, "Admiralsgaardens Stilling i dansk Bindingsværks Historie", *Fra Arkiv og Museum,* Vol. 1, 1899-1902, p. 207-218. For an overview of demolished buildings see particularly "København", *Fra Arkiv og Museum*, Vol. 3, 1905-1908, p 227 –228 & 438-439.

81 On this project, see "Det Kanneworffske hus", *Architekten*, N 35, 27 May 1905, p. 349-352. For a systematic inventory of the preserved buildings see, *Historiske Huse i det gamle København – Fortegnelser over bevaringsværdige ældre bygninger i Bispestad og Ny København*, Copenhagen, 1972.

erally were also expressing their concern over the city's townscape, placing aesthetic value as they did on the vulnerability of the soft Danish landscape. Critics focused particularly on the new spire proposed by brewer and patron of the arts Carl Jacobsen, a project contested by a sizeable group of staunch preservationists. The Copenhagen spire-mania, inspired by an ideal of "beautification", came under heavy criticism for two sets of reasons. First, it became anathema according to the new approach to restoration, which favoured preservation along Ruskinian principles; second, the possible snowballing effect on the surrounding urban fabric was much feared by some of the observers.[82] Such reconstruction schemes contributed to accentuating the divide between 'preservationists' and 'conservationists'.

This outline of several closely interrelated aspects of the transformations affecting the inner urban form is by no way exhaustive. In particular, V. Lorenzen pointed out a fifth sphere of micro-scale changes as having a powerful impact (see Chapter 7). According to him, the cumulative effects of such changes had a decisive role in hastening the obsolescence of the urban fabric.[83] This overview, however, suggests that the strategies and motives with which professionals and amateurs alike worked on the inherited urban fabric were many. Historicity was codified in several distinct, though not necessarily conflicting manners. The notion of 'historic city' nevertheless took shape, not only from the multi-dimensional process of transformation occurring in the inner city, but also from the 'grey area' of peripheral districts springing up after the dismantling of the fortifications. This buffer zone separating the city from its still open land surroundings had evolved as a non-planned, non-rural yet non-urban area, which was widely denounced by the end of the nineteenth century for its 'disorder' and 'ugliness'. It was possible to rhetorically use its ghastly aspect to promote planning ideals with low-density housing and open spaces, but also to suggest the need for the preservation of the inherited urban core. This illustrates how the process of inner transformation and of peripheral extension were intricately linked in the slowly emerging image of the Great City. Thus, with archaeological excavations and extension-planning schemes constituting the two extremes, this period saw both the past and the future of the city simultaneously put under scrutiny.

We shall now explore in more detail the development in 1900 Copenhagen of a body of thinking on urban conservation, by considering the role of the general and the specialised press that contributed to shaping the city's new profile.

2.1 Representations of City's Territories

In order to apprehend the rising awareness about heritage between 1900 and 1914, we have paid particular attention to statements that qualified or disqualified the city's heritage. We have selected three daily newspapers: *Politiken, Social-Demokraten, Berlingske Politiske og Advertissementstidende,* and the weekly *Illustreret Tidende*. The years 1907-1909 have been systematically consulted.[84] In parallel, we have carried out, over a much larger period (1898-1914), an extensive probe of *Architekten*, the journal of the Society of the Architects of the Academy and *Arkitekten-Tidsskrift for Bygningsvaesen*, the journal of the builders and the building industry. Finally, we have occasionally drawn on other publications of associations geared toward conservation issues.

The values put forward to justify or to condemn demolition as well as building implantation are frequently non-explicit, often contradictory and transitory.[85] They represent, however, an important aspect

82 A project designed by architect Andreas Clemmensen, including a 'cloister' like new square, was much discussed by the time of the competition, see "Arkitekt Clemmensens forslag til ordning af Nicolai Plads", *Illustret Tidende*, 16 February 1908, p. 321-322.

83 J. P. Larkham noticed a similar process nowadays: "the cumulative impact of such individually relatively minor changes on the conserved townscape..." in *Conservation...* op. cit., p. 200.

84 *Politiken* was founded in 1884 and became the mouthpiece of Det Radikale Venstre in 1905, (24,500 copies in 1906); *Social-Demokraten* had been published under this title since 1874 (50,000 copies in 1906); *Berlingske* was founded in 1833 (15,000 copies in 1906). For more details see, J. D. Søllinge & N. Thomsen, *De Danske Aviser, 1634-1898*, Vol. 2: 1848-1917, Odense, 1989.

85 We use the term 'value' according to the meaning given by Alois Riegel .

of the discourse held on the town. Being positively qualifying or disparaging, these statements are established according to a complex web of 'urban intrigues' that accompanied transformations.[86] We attempt to show that these intrigues were numerous in Copenhagen at the beginning of the twentieth century: for instance in relation to the colouring of the facades, the restoration of church spires operations concerning street widening schemes or the treatment of the remains of the fortifications. All these intrigues underlie an ongoing process of designation for the setting up of the different areas of the town. This process of designation is studied by following three main tracks.

First, we shall look at the old town 'by default', namely a town described negatively in relation to its insalubrious areas. We have noticed the discourse of the first generation of town planners drew upon the philosophy of evolution and organicism, which is also potent in the discussion about the fate of 'old buildings'. The link between organic metaphors and aversion for the process of ageing with regard to artefacts has been outlined:

> "Organic terminology strengthen such biases, and indeed is often used to put the new and fresh in the best possible light, the old and stale in the worst".[87]

Second, we shall see the city, favouring the discovery of fragmented pieces of the 'picturesque' city. And lastly, we shall look at the city perceived as an urban monument demanding care and enhancement.

2.2 Modernity, Practicalities and Hygiene

In 1900-1901, *Arkitekten – Tidsskrift for Bygningsvæsen*, the journal of the building industry, contested the overriding fashion throughout the press to promote all that is related to the past or smacks of antiquity. In a leading article entitled "Devotion for our ancient buildings", two lines of arguments take an opposite view to the stand of admirers of old buildings. The first set of arguments refers to the almost complete destruction of medieval Copenhagen, two fifths of which were totally destroyed during the great fire of 1728 and the 1795 and 1807 disasters that completed the destruction of buildings that held architectural value. The buildings that replaced them are said to have been built in haste, often with poor means. In most cases, it is believed that they hold little or no architectural interest. Considering that the town was finally 'rebuilt' in the 1830's, it is stressed that these constructions offer only a feeble "antique value" and are not worth a "sentiment of devotion". All those whose "duty" was to protect ancient architecture and resist demolition had therefore no real issue to raise.[88]

Secondly, it is alleged that health and convenience reasons lead to the demolition of "squalid slums almost in ruin" and their replacement with decent housing, even if, from time to time, for convenience, this could have occasioned "the loss of a characteristic gable, a door, or some interesting wrought iron work as evidence of past know-how".[89] The topic of hygiene, which reflects the importance attached to the utilisation of buildings in that they should guarantee the health of the occupants, is systematically brought into play to validate the demolition of decrepit urban fabric. Several articles in *Social-Demokraten* were devoted to the rehabilitation of the quarter of the "Vognmagergade" in April and June 1909. The operation is compared to the earthquake in Messina. It is in the name of hygiene that "dirty shacks and unhealthy alleys" are at last demolished and replaced by healthy housing and enlarged roads letting in air and light. (See, Plate 9) In opposition to picturesque beauty that might be evoked by the "artistic minded", there is another form of beauty that springs form the dissolution of the remnants of the 'Holberg era', which compromised the life of its inhabitants.[90] Remarks can be

86 By concretely or abstractly appropriating spaces (for instance through representations), urban professionals, leading citizens, and associations contribute to the ongoing process of space territorialization. See Claude Raffestin, *Pour une géographie du pouvoir*, Paris, 1980, p. 129.

87 See, David Lowenthal, *The past is a foreign country*, Cambridge, 1985, p. 128

88 For a circumstanced account of the great fires' destruction of the old city, see O. Forchhammer, *København... op. cit.*, p. 171-194.

89 "Pieteten mod vore gamle bygninger", *Arkitekten – Tidsskrift for Bygningsvaesen*, N. 351, 14 June 1901.

90 "Nedbrydningen i Vognmagergade-Kvartet", *Social-Demokraten*, 6 June 1909.

even more aggressive. Some papers contemplate with unmitigated joy the erasing of "hæsligt" (hideous) and "svinsk" (filthy) clusters and give laudatory comments about the implementation of the new Christian IX complex of buildings.[91]

In the context of the March 1905 election campaign, *Social-Demokraten* published a series of articles entitled "Copenhagen, the people's town" (see Plate 11/B). The 'right wing' is accused of having nothing better to put forward than an old 'social-democrat' project to 'demolish insalubrious areas'.[92] The "anti-socialists" are qualified as being "anti-hygiene" and the first article concludes:" disinfect our town in March and keep the air clean!"[93] The series goes on pointing out that the municipality over a period of ten years, brought to all inhabitants: "one of the healthiest towns in the world".[94] The work done to improve urban health conditions are recalled: drinking water in buildings; collecting and purifying sewage waste before it is discharged into the sea; the building of hospitals, schools and housing according to sanitary prescriptions and last but not least, the carrying out of demolition of "slum areas". The articles widely use organic metaphors to describe these urban transformations and give them a moral significance. Accordingly, the new town hall is described as the "heart of the city" from where "life's pulse is regulated".[95] It is also the "house where the work is done to bring air and light" and regulate the "harmonious and natural growth of the city". The old town stands out the background, a discredit, so to speak: it is a place of primitive living conditions, which "unfortunately continue to exist even until now", though they belong to the past that ought to be eradicated.[96] This past, and how it is dealt with, is obviously an important issue.

Is urban renovation not closely linked to an educational mission towards the inhabitants and bent on wiping out all signs of ignorance and subjugation? And so, the image of the body, which becomes a common noun representing urban development, seems to imply an ideal that would be a new harmonisation between the political spheres, the space of the city and its citizens, and the newly developing town, seen as a social/physical territory.

Though hygiene was mostly a topic of the trade journal of the engineers, the periodical Architekten also touched it upon. The health question is articulated to both the ideas of cleanliness and beauty, as V. Koch contended in 1901 when demanding that the upkeep of the outside of the buildings and their surroundings be subject to regulation.[97] It also concern architects on the look out for orders for modern buildings. They were compelled to master new techniques of construction owing to the growing use of electricity, gas, sanitary equipment and the like. In an article entitled "New and old", the Academy's official publication takes note of the renovation project and the regulation of the Vognmagergade area, "which has been abundantly discussed in the daily press".[98] The eradication of the "black continent" is justified in the name of hygiene and morality. Nevertheless what is happening to the "artistic values" and the importance of "antiques" must be still regarded "with piety".

It is admitted that, some cultural evidence from the past could occasionally be sacrificed- a sheer necessity to put up new buildings in keeping with the modernisation of the capital city. It was, however, recommended to young architects in the Foreningen of 3rd December 1892 (see Chapter 7) that they record by drawing or photographing, all buildings and architectural details of interest, while paying close attention to the picturesque, lively, narrow and winding streets of the old town. In *Politiken*, we notice a common perception feeling of inexorable movement, albeit tainted with regrets, in the description of the demolition of buildings on Stænstræde.[99] In this case it is, above all, the noise and the length of the fencing, enclosing the site works, which the paper comments on. Moreover, feelings about similarly spectacular as-

91 See unspecified article dated from 28 September 1910 about "Nyt Gadeprojekt i København", Landsarkivet Sjælland, FHF /gen. Sager, pk. nr. 11.

92 "København som folkets by", *Social-Demokraten*, 2 March 1905.

93 "Idem, 9 March 1905.

94 "Ibidem, 24 March 1905.

95 "Ibid., 9 March 1905.

96 "Nedbrydningen i Vognmagergade-Kvartet", *Social-Demokraten*, 6 June 1909.

97 "Er Kjøbenhavn renlig?", *Architekten*, 13 December 1901, p. 89-91.

98 "Nyt og Gammel", *Architekten*, 5 January 1907, p. 136-139.

99 "Gamle Huse eller Nye", *Politiken*, 10 June 1907.

pects of city modernity, such as the new webs of phone wires, are equally mixed. Why not to hide the wires in the ground, asks *Politiken*?[100] Complaints about advertisements spoiling the street scenery are a recurring thematic in the same vein. However, doubts about rising utilitarianism and commercialisation of the public space rarely exceed a vague nostalgia. Dilapidated areas should pass away and alternative options of the Geddesian type are seldom, if ever, considered.

A point of view firmly in favour of the "rejuvenation of Copenhagen" is to be found in the weekly *Illustreret Tidende*, which only touches rapidly on the disappearance of "old time souvenirs": the numerous and interesting picturesque buildings with their covered alleys. The article deals with the shortcomings of the new street layout proposed by the town authorities, as opposed to other projects that are equally modernising.[101] Several photographs show buildings destined to be demolished. A year later, always on the same subject, and in the same vicinity, pictures of the new buildings are shown in order to underline the re-appropriation of the new over the old, "poor and unhealthy", and the opening up of a new road system, "these arteries that are the ideal condition for circulating the blood of the town". The "old town" has metamorphosed and given a new dignity.[102]

2.3 The Picturesque City

The emergence of the 'old town' as a valuable historic centre should also been associated with a picturesque approach to the inner Copenhagen, and based on an abundant production of drawings and urban paintings, the study of which could not be included in this book. In parallel with statements on 'modernity' that concern the technical and sanitary progress, there is a series of fragmented picturesque (malerisk) visions that would have to be inventoried in order to apprehend the main themes that underline how the sites were actually perceived as representative of a "surviving" past.

There are two urban representations that can be easily identified, one being concerned with that which is measurable or quantifiable and statistics offering a clear cut view, and a second less distinct picture that may become apparent through direct observation, and wide aesthetic and cultural knowledge.

Far from being reduced to the juxtaposition of several romantic stereotypes, writings by scholars a current encompassing professionals and amateurs alike, attempts to make tangible the atmosphere (stemning) of the 'old Copenhagen' areas. This picturesque approach, whilst focusing on particular buildings for their originality, their beauty or their appearance, also takes into account wider aspects of the urban scene. The architectural quality of the buildings and evidence of high culture architecture are, in this case, of secondary importance.

To identify and recognise the atmosphere of the place, it is accounted for ordinary activities of the people especially where country land merges with town land as well as for features, such as the forms of streets, trees enhancing a facade, the variety of colours, which occurs from the composition of different elements as water and vegetation with the buildings. The appreciation of the patina as marks of age is not expressed as a taste or a cult for bygone past with a bias against the present. It rather reflects respect for testimony of the past whose marks are valued as components of an integrative process, which moulds the passing of time on the city's form.

The picturesque and the atmosphere are also underlined in the silhouette of the town unveiled on different occasions and from different angles. This succession of perspectives creates a unity and shows the town as a whole in time and in space. This approach is present, more or less clearly, throughout the political and specialised press, albeit compared to the former most often in a minor way.[103] Two characteristics mark this way of perceiving the 'old town' throughout the

100 "Fra det Kjøbenhavn, der forsvinder", *Politiken*, 16 January 1908.

101 "Københavns Foryngelse", *Illustreret Tidende*, 29 November 1908, p. 105-106

102 "Det nye København, Christian-IX-gade kvarteret og byens centrums udvikling", *Illustreret Tidende*, 14 March 1909, p. 291-294.

103 For a full fledged presentation of this picturesque approach, cf. A. Larsen and E. Schiødte, *Gamle Kjobenhavnske Huse og Gaarde*, 4 Hæfter, Copenhagen, 1894-97.

slowly unfolding discourse on historical urban space. On the one hand, the 'picturesque' points out that the main qualities of ancient buildings lie in the way original and always unique details and variations are displayed, which arise interest and revive imagination. It is a digressive and poetical approach to the city. Thus, the scenery of the bastioned fortifications of Christianshavn offers an idyllic decor, which was preserved by numerous projects in the 1909 Competition.[104] On the other hand, the loud and frequent denunciation of modernity becomes almost stereotyped. The modern city is essentially a grid of long straight roads and dull rows of houses. (See Plate 10 A)

Numerous articles about the disappearance of buildings are written in the form of epigraphs. While reporting demolitions, *Politiken* regrets the passing of this or that building or shop. No revolt here, but a resigned and melancholic ode to memory[105]. Sometimes, however, critics are more harshly formulated. This is particularly so in relation to public squares heavily charged with Copenhageners' collective memory. For instance, *Illustreret Tidende* published an 1898 view of Amagertorv. An eclectic corner building vaguely reminiscent of the Nordic Renaissance overshadows the built environment of the square. Next to this picture, the periodical provides an older perspective of the square, extracted from the *Den Danske Vitruv* by Lauritz de Thurah, and comments:

"Amagertorv, der bærer sin egen Tids periodes ejendommelige Træk, blive ombyggede uden Plan og uden Tanke for den kunstneriske virkning. Da brydes alle oprindeligt beregnede Forhold, og Harmonien, Stemningen, Virkningen er borte med det samme".[106]

In 1899, the magazine *Arkitekten -Tidsskrift for Bygningsvaesen* published a letter from a reader, who suggested a means of retaining the memory of ancient buildings. Why not follow this "loyal attitude" of the owner of one town building, who replaced it by a new one, and displayed on his frontage the picture of the demolished construction in the form of the sculptured medallion.[107] This example follows the picturesque codes and represents the building integrated in its past "natural" environment. This sort of proposal seems to have had a certain appeal to Copenhageners. Another similar initiative was actively encouraged by the review *Arkiv og Museum* during the same years.[108]

2.4 The City as a Monument

The 'old town' also emerged into light as wide critics mounted in contention about the disappearance of particular ancient buildings. Here, the old town gains in wholeness, and the city takes on the appearance of a monument possessing historical, artistic and cultural qualities. In connection with the picturesque elements, the press frequently established a symbolic link between its own existence and the city's image. Some papers published medallions of Copenhagen's profile with its domes and spires. Others periodically choose to show a highly symbolic roof ridge, such as Nyrop's town hall. (See Plate 8)

The fear of losing the characteristic architectonic qualities of the town and the peculiarity of its built environment was frequently expressed in the last decade of the nineteenth century. One 'intrigue' especially reflects the acute tensions between preservation concerns and the strategy of historicist architecture. It crystallised around an impressive cluster of late Renaissance buildings known as the "Six-Sisters" situated next to Børsen (the Old Stock Exchange) and a jewel of Christian IV-period. (See Plate 12) We already mentioned that representatives of the entrepreneurs' milieu of the building nascent industry mocked the "newly fashionable and immoderate taste" of architects for historic buildings.[109] The fact that a 'historicist' design was purposely chosen for the Danish pa-

104 On the fortification areas, see, *Idem, Hæfte 1.*, p. 9.

105 *Politiken,* 10 June 1907.

106 "(The square) Amagertorv has been refurbished without plan nor artistic thoughts. Pre existing relationships have been destroyed and consequently former harmony, atmosphere, and effect have disappeared", (our translation) *Illustreret Tidende,* N. 49, 4 September 1898, p. 794-795.

107 *Arkitekten -Tidsskrift for Bygningvaesen,* N. 271, 1 December 1899.

108 *Fra Arkiv og Museum,* 1903-1905, p. 188.

109 "Pieteten mod vore gamle bygninger", *Arkitekten- Tidsskrift for bygningvaesen,* 14 June 1901.

vilion at the 1900 World Exhibition in Paris had been sharply criticised in Denmark at this very moment; commentators pointed out that its paraphrase of timber framing architecture was ridiculous in an age of "fairy-electricity".[110] For once, *Arkitekten Tidsskrift for Bygningsvaesen* had backed a project designed by a civil engineer aiming at restoring the integrity of the "Six Sisters". First published in the *Illustreret Tidende,* the project of engineer Otto Jünger presented an impressive elevation of the cluster of buildings before and after restoration. (See Plate 12 A & B). The engineer quoted the example of Rothenburg-ober-Tauber as a successful conservation endeavour and called upon the likely pitiless judgement of posterity. For him the atmosphere of the old port should be defended against "aesthetic vandalism".[111] One main argument was the necessity to maintain the high quality of authentic Seventeenth century architecture within the surrounding of the Old Stock Exchange.[112] *Politiken* published a petition and articles arguing in defence of the building block.[113] But, Privatbanken, who had purchased it, turned a deaf ear to protests. Despite repeated attempts of rescue, the 'Six' remained scheduled for the wrecking ball and by the turn of the century, the late Nordic Renaissance buildings was no more; some remains were collected by the National Museum. *Arkiv og Museum* published a substantial report on the buildings with quite a touch of regret and disapproval.[114] (See Plate 12 D & E) Here too, one can observe the fluidity of postures as, *Arkitekten-Tidsskrift for Bygningsvaesen* eventually hailed the "tasteful" project authored by architect Axel Berg (1856-1929), claiming that it was in tune with the Old Stock Exchange.[115] At last, historicist architecture had prevailed over a well-defined preservation proposal concerning a remarkable building block set in the core city, a few yards away from Christiansborg Palace. (See Plate 12 G).

During this period, *Architekten* recommended that all buildings, built prior to 1870 and earmarked for demolition should be surveyed and systematically indexed for the national museum's collections. In the meantime, a great many of comments published in the columns of the review strongly advised the architects' corporation to take into account the surroundings in which new buildings are to be integrated.[116] One observes a significant relation interplay between scientific and scholarly approach and a more emotional awareness, sentimentalised discourse of chronicles concerned with the recognition and the handing down of traditional and popular arts and crafts which were both involved, perceived as national heritage, and which were endangered by the transformations of the urban fabric.

Numerous initiatives on the borderline of both sensibilities exemplify a growing interest for conservation.[117] However, the protection of the 'old town', was not included in the contradictory professional debates and discussions in which conflicting interests between the various building corporations concerning 'historical buildings' were frequently brought up. For instance, an article in *Architekten* presents the modification of a porch in order to widen a shop window. This is seen as an "interesting example of adaptation". Yet, in a following issue, the demolition of this very baroque porch is stigmatised as "an act of violence and brutality", and it is underlined fact that neither Foreningen til Hovedstadens Forskønnelse nor the Academy raised the issue.[118] A few years later, the *Forskønnelsen* magazine reproduced the picture of both the old and new porches to illustrate common "vandalism".[119]. Moreo-

110 See, Michael Ottosen, *Dansk bygningsrestaurering historie,* Aarhus Arkitektskolens Skriftserie, 1984, p. 24.

111 "Nybørs i København ", *Arkitekten -Tidsskrift for bygningvaesen,* N. 230, 17 February 1899, p. 152-153. The article supports the restoration project and suggests that the stock exchange traders could fund the project, because they would directly benefit of it.

112 The project was presented by Otto Jünger: "Nybørs", *Illusteret Tidende,* 21 August 1898, p. 768-770.

113 See *Politiken,* 27, 29 January 1899; and 8 February 1900.

114 Axel Jensen, M. Mackeprang, "Nybørs kaldet "de seks søstre", *Fra Arkiv og Museum,* 1899-1902, p. 136-159.

115 "Den ny Privatbankbygning", *Arkitekten-Tidsskrift for bygningvaesen,* N. 324, 7 December 1900.

116 *Architekten,* 1 August 1899, p. 204-206.

117 For instance, a collection of 300 pictures concerning destroyed buildings was assembled by the Town Hall's librarian. The journal issued an appeal to its readership to develop the collection: "Det Gamle København", *Arkitekten-Tidsskrift for Bygningsvæsen,* N. 249, 30 June 1899.

118 See *Architekten,* N. 4, 24 October 1906, p. 36-37 and *Architekten,* N°5, 3 November 1906, p. 47-48.

119 This was part of a survey of the doors and porches of the city, see "Porte og Døre", *Forskønnelsen,* 1914, p. 65-82.

ver, the debate on the theory of restoration, which gained momentum in 1908, brought forth some confusion among circles favouring conservation generally. Numerous articles criticise the dominant conception in the second half of the nineteenth century concerning the restoration of buildings, churches in particular, which aimed at restoring in the original style.[120]

When the operation involves historicist reconstruction rather than restoration, the confusion is at its utmost. On reading the daily and weekly press it is apparent that the figure of the town, was a chief issue during the heated debate that surrounded the spire of the Church of Saint Nicholas, a remnant of the building that had burnt down in 1795. Butcher's stalls surrounded it, the main meat-market of the city.[121] Those in favour of the restoration, which should commemorate the Reformation, referred to the silhouette of the town with its towers and steeples. Usually others, radically opposed to "modern antiques", preferred to keep the "sacred" ruins as they stood.

They also feared the 'spill over' effect, which the project would likely generate, that is the rehabilitation of the whole square and its vicinity that the work would epitomise. Carl Jacobsen inspired the project for the restoration of the steeple. He offered the Municipal Council to sponsor the scheme, while the Carlsberg foundation opened in 1902. A controversy soon arose and arguments were exchanged throughout architectural and historical publications. Numerous projects were formulated. For instance, the design of the architect Christian Hansen (1854-1930) modelled after a Berlin project was presented in *Architekten:* The composition includes an arcaded plaza and a 'cloister' to give some 'framing' to the steeple. The 'cloister' was to be linked through a long arcaded pathway to the Østergade and to serve as a large "commercial palace". The feared snow balling effect was, then, materialised.[122] We already mentioned the project by the architect Andreas Clemmensen (1852-1928) who originally was reluctant to the spire project. Presented in winter 1908, the sketches suggest a historicist reconstruct of the immediate surroundings of the church.

Peter Johansen and the Foreningen til Hovedstadens Forskønnelse backed this scheme.[123] (See Chapter 7). Despite the wide publicity given to this project, enthusiasm was circumscribed. Architect H. Kampmann ironically commented about Clemmensen's sketches as made by a "Master of placard".[124]

The very idea of modifying the profile of the square with the symbol of the Reformation was dismissed as 'historical forgery'.[125] However, the Academy gave its absolution for the spire project on the grounds of formal architectonic quality, and a change in the Municipal Council opened the way for the implementation. The spire, conceived by architect H. C. Amberg, who had been in charge of the restoration of the cathedral in Ribe between 1883-1904, finally emerged in August 1909. It was saluted by *Architekten* as having a positive "Virkning i Omgivelserne" (effect on the surroundings).[126]

In the following years, the debate on the reconstruction of the 120 metres high spire of the Church of 'Our Lady', which had been designed by Christian Frederik Hansen (1745-1845), divided two firmly opposed parties. On one side, the architects Borch, Rosen, Brummer, Nyrøp and Jørgensen supported the project, on the other the painter Viggo Johansen, the director of the Museum Mackeprang, and the architect H. B. Storck among others were strongly opposed to it. The group of young architects who had left the Academy in protest against its conservative teaching (they founded Den Fri Architektektforening in 1909) came into the argument by joining the detractors of the scheme and helped to make the second initiative for the reconstruction of a spire a failure.[127]

120 For an analysis of the debate about restoration in *Architekten,* see Michael Ottosen, *Bygningsfredningsloven-historie og princip,* Aarhus, 1984.

121 See Hans Edvard Nørregaard-Nielsen, *Ny Carlsbergfondet 1902-2002,* Copenhagen, 2002, p. 239-241.

122 Cf. Chr. Hansen, "Nikolaj Plads", *Architekten,* N. 18, 1 February 1908, p. 256-258.

123 Cf. "Nikolaj-Spiret og Arkitekt Clemmensens Plan - Forskønnelsesforeningen vil holde stort Møde til Guunst for Spiret", *Politiken,* 19 January 1908.

124 Cf. "Nicolaj. En Holmgang mellem Brygger Jacobsen og Anders Hvass", *Politiken,* 30 January 1908.

125 Cf. Frederik Rasmussen, "Nikolaj Taarn", *Architekten,* N. 24, 16 March 1907, p. 236-237.

126 K. Varming, "Nikolaj Taarn", *Architekten,* 4 September 1909.

127 For a detailed account, see Nina Dahlmann Olsen, "Den Fri Architektforening, Foreingen som markerede et stilskifte i dansk arkitektur", *Architectura-10,* Copenhagen, 1988, p. 102-108.

Reflecting a rising awareness about the wholeness of the inherited built environment, the emergence of the 'city as a monument' is also the result of other initiatives, which we can only here give a glimpse of. From the beginning of the century, the revival of the Foreningen til Hovedstadens Forskønnelse was associated with a number of spectacular projects. For instance, the action for colouring clusters of old buildings was designed to bring to public attention the quality of a fabric, which was neglected and would disappear in due course. Whether such campaign was critical or not in arising public interest in conservation is difficult to assess. Moreover, artistic circles were doubtful about the aesthetic value of the buildings' coloration. Yet, it can be assumed that initiatives of various kinds and their related debates brought forth the 'old city' as an inherited monument. On this monument were engraved aesthetic quality and knowledge of home architecture and construction which was argued for as a guarantee that 'bad taste' could be repelled and 'hjemme Bygningskunst', or 'national architecture' or more literally 'homely building art' could be secured and developed.

Plate 8

8A
Politiken, 4 July 1914.

Nr. 21 København, den 20. Februar 1910 51. Aarg.

8B
Illustreret Tidende,
20 February 1910.

ARKITEKTEN

1900 1901

· TIDSSKRIFT · FOR · BYGNINGSVÆSEN ·

ORGAN · FOR · DEN · DANSKE BYGGEINDUSTRI · · · 5 · OKTOBER · 1900 NUMMER · 315 REDIGERET · AF · ARKITEKT · · · ALFRED · MØLLER

8C
Arkitekten – tidsskrift for Bygningsvæsen,
5 October 1900.

ORGAN . FOR . DEN . DANSKE · BYGGEINDUSTRI — 29 . SEPTEMBER . 1899. — NUMMER · 262. REDIGERET . AF . ARKITEKT ALFRED · MØLLER

8D
Arkitekten – tidsskrift for Bygningsvæsen,
29 September 1899.

Plate 9

9 A "Licitationer", *Social–Demokraten*, 27 April 1909.

9 B "Nedbrydningen i Vognmagergade- Kvartet", *Social–Demokraten*, 6 June 1909.

9 C "Nedbrydningsarbejdet i Strandstræde", *Politiken,* 10 June 1907.

Parti fra Vognmagergade.

NAAR STORBYEN UDVIKLER SIG

HVOR GAMMELT OG NYT MØDES

9 D "Naar Storbyen udvikler sig hvor gammelt og nyt mødes", in Otto Asmussen, *Kjøbenhavn, som den er og som den burde være,* Copenhagen, 1914, p. 129.

Plate 10

Den gamle Jagtvejs Omdannelse til Boulevard

10 A "Den Gamle Jagtvejs Omdannelse til Boulevard", *Politiken,* 31 May 1914.

Pladsen foran Nyhavns Kanal, som den i disse Dage ordnes.

Et „Landgangstæppe".

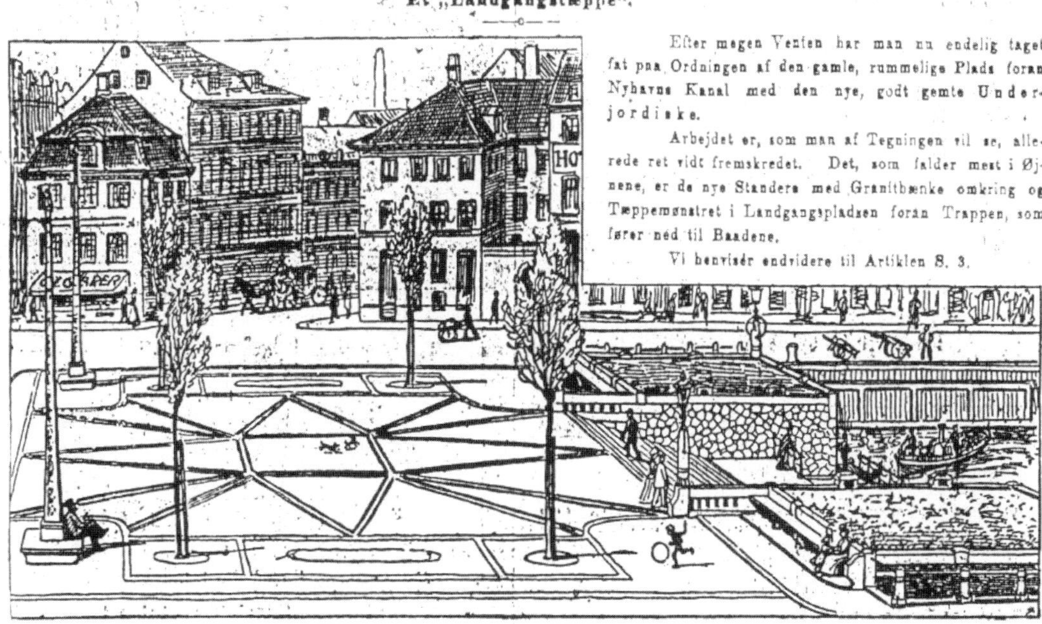

Efter megen Venten har man nu endelig taget fat paa Ordningen af den gamle, rummelige Plads foran Nyhavns Kanal med den nye, godt gemte Underjordiske.

Arbejdet er, som man af Tegningen vil se, allerede ret vidt fremskredet. Det, som falder mest i Øjnene, er de nye Standere med Granitbænke omkring og Tæppemønstret i Landgangspladsen foran Trappen, som fører ned til Baadene.

Vi henviser endvidere til Artiklen S. 3.

10 B "Pladsen foran Nyhavns Kanal, som den i disse Dage Ordnes", *Politiken*, 17 May 1907.

Plate 11

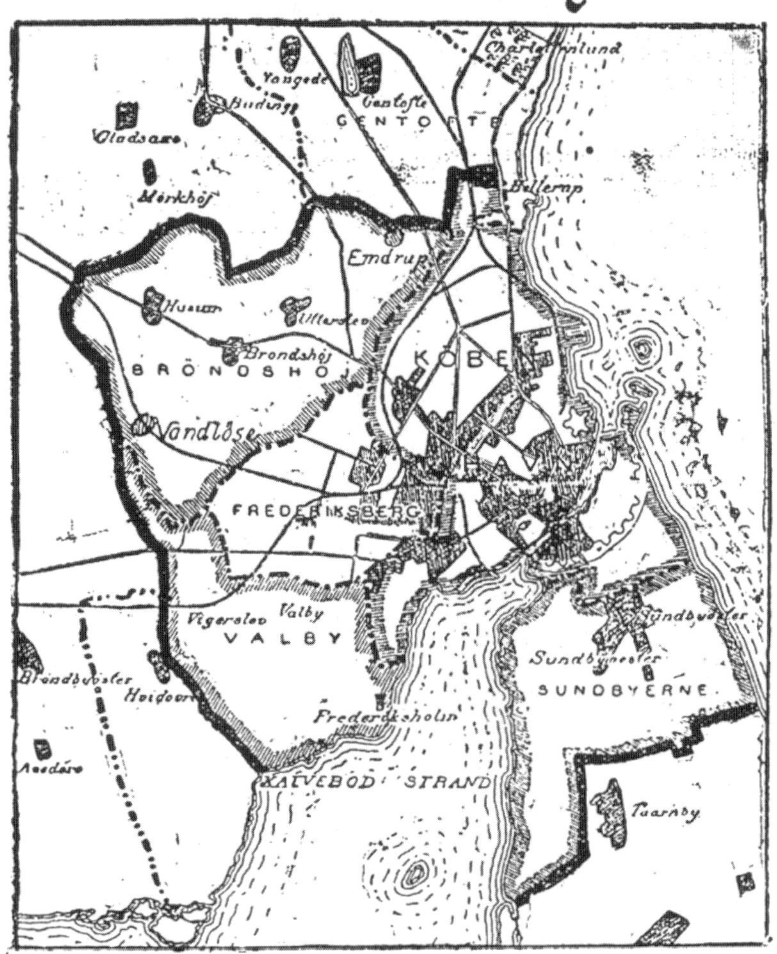

11 A "Stor-København",
Social–Demokraten, 20 April 1900

11 B "København som Folkets By",
Social–Demokraten, 16 March 1905.

Nybørs or "de seks søstre"

Plate 12

12 A "Nybørs tilbageførte ydre", *Illustreret Tidende*, 21 August 1898, p. 769.

12 B "Nybørs nuværende ydre", *idem,* p. 769.

12 C "Nybørs set fra Børsbroen", *Fra Arkiv og Museum*, 1903-1905, p. 137.

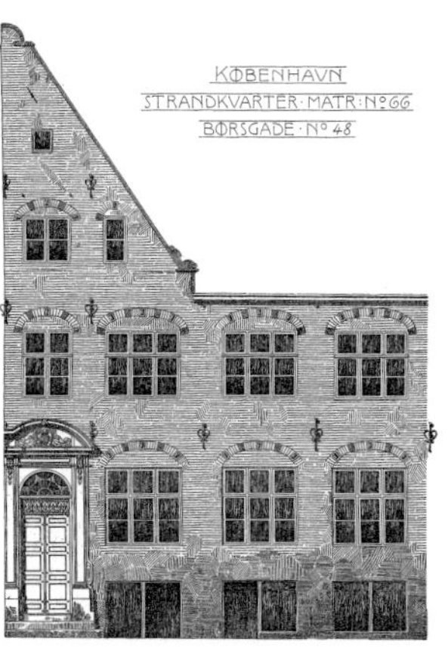

12 D "København, Strandkvarter Matr. N. 66, Børsgade N. 48", *idem* p.146

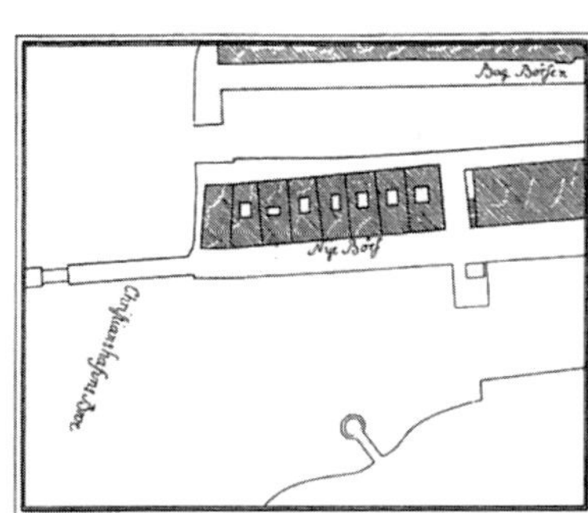

12 E "Grundplan af Nybørs, efter Geddes Kvarterkort 1757, *idem,* p.144

12 F "Martin Borchs projekt til Privatbanken i Børsgade 1900", in Knud Millech & Kay Fisker, *Danske Arkitekturstrømninger 1850-1950*, Copenhagen, 1951, p. 225.

12 G "Axel Bergs projekt til Privatbanken i Børsgade 1900", *idem*.

The Picturesque Copenhagen

Plate 13

13 A "Gaardparti fra "Tre kroner" i Tornebuskegade", in Erik Schiødte, Alfred Larsen, *Gamle Kjøbenhavnske Huse og Gaarde, Hæfte III, Kjøbenhavn nordøstlige del,* Copenhagen, 1896, p. 77.

Fra de gamle Beværtningshaver i Pilealléen, der forsvinder.

13 B "Fra de gamle Beværtningshaver i Pilealléen, der forsvinder", *Politiken*, 25 May 1914.

7

'OLD COPENHAGEN', FROM SURVEY TO ACTION

1 Conservationists and the 'Old Copenhagen'

University professors, cultural historians, art critics, curators, artists and architects were joining forces to elaborate a scientific corpus on the city history and on the history of particular buildings. A number of amateurs who were passionately concerned with the national heritage and worrying about the rapidly changing urban and rural landscapes also contributed in a significant way to this corpus. A great many books devoted to the 'Old Copenhagen' were published at the turn of the century, and the work *København i gamle dage og Livet i Kobenhavn* by Bering Liisberg that came out in 1901 provides one example among many.[1] It was also in 1901 that a collection was established and housed in the premises of the Town Hall as a museum of the city's history.[2] These endeavours were forwarded with an accumulation of architectural drawings, photographs and surveys, which had been undertaken under various initiatives, sustaining the project in compiling a systematic inventory of the urban fabric, history and culture.[3] Diverse circles of people from different backgrounds converged on the issue of the process of transformations affecting ancient buildings, landscapes, built fabric and townscapes. The spectrum of concerns was broad, ranging from interest in architecture and history to folk culture and crafts techniques. This process of physical transformations was often perceived as new in its scale and pace, endangering the identity of the society with the risk of a swift debasement of its historical and cultural roots.

There nevertheless was a wide gap between the development of an organised body of thought on the inherited urban fabric and a variety of informal, impressionistic views, whether informed or not, of the undergoing changes of the city. Preservation or specific conservation issues, and concerns about 'art in the city' were not necessarily leading —as it has been abundantly shown throughout the twentieth century— to a social, aesthetic and philosophical ideal addressing the change of the townscape as a whole, and for that matter even less to a strategy promoting conservation for the city or for part of the city. To gain wide social acceptance, planning ideas had to come as part of an easily identifiable ideal type such as the 'garden city'.[4] A number of conditions were required to favour the emergence of a parallel ideal-type that could be called 'the conserved city'. The speed and widespread character of change within the built environment should be widely acknowledged. Prerequisites should also be secured for a contradictory debate to last for a reasonable period of time. For instance, studies have shown that contradictory debates hardly occurred in post-World War II Germany, as concerns the rebuilding of the urban fabric, with the imperative criteria of 'urgency' and 'efficiency' being called upon to obstruct possible alternative reconstruction schemes.[5] In Poland, brutal subjection led, notwith-

1 Henrik Carl Bering Liisberg (1854-1929) studied history at the University of Copenhagen. Since 1883 he worked at the Royal Danish Collection housed in the Rosenborg Palace in Copenhagen and eventually became the administrator and inspector of the museum. He wrote a number of books on Danish history, including *København i gamle dage og Livet i Kobenhavn*, published in Copenhagen in 1901.

2 In 1917, this museum was renamed Københavns Bymuseum and opened to public in 1925 in the Town hall attic.

3 We should note that Hugo Matthiessen (1881-1957) took the initiative of a vast photographic survey at a later stage, in the years 1913-1922 . This work encompassed the built environment of 75 'Købstæder'.

4 Peter J. Larkham, *Conservation…op.cit*, p. 84.

5 See Paul Jürgen, "Der Wiederaufbau der historischen Städte in Deutschland nach dem Zweiten Weltkrieg" in Cord

standing at least equal financial constraint, to the total reconstruction of substantial part of the urban fabric. With reconstruction in post-war France, functionalists' attempts at implementing innovative schemes were for the most part ultimately thwarted, following much heated controversy.[6] It is, thus, not enough to identify the causes of the global trend toward obsolescence and dilapidation of the urban fabric; it is also a matter of elaborating comprehensive alternative strategies that can be given practical expression by groups of actors sufficiently anchored within social forces.

We have shown the existence of a fair degree of awareness in the general public of the 'ageing' process that the urban fabric was going through; we have also seen that, quite decisively, some town-planners were indeed considering specific schemes to apply to the core city to avoid too disruptive encroachments. We shall now look at the approach of contemporaries to the particular context of Copenhagen's 'old city'. To this purpose we have selected a few contributions to the problematic of conservation, which were chosen because of their common ambition to consider the 'old Copenhagen' as a whole and assess the ongoing process of transformation. We shall see, however, that these documents widely differ in content and perspective; some are devoted to record 'Old Copenhagen', while others are formulating alternatives to the ongoing process. These contributions have been selected because they are also related to the inter-professional debate. We have chosen four texts along the above criteria over the period extending from 1894 to 1914. They are respectively from Erik Schiødte, Peter Johansen, Nicolaus Lützhøft and Vilhelm Lorenzen. E. Schiødte was an architect, P. Johansen an academic and a painter, N. Lützhøft an art critic and V. Lorenzen a historian of cities and architecture. Johansen and Lützhøft were involved in the association Foreningen til Hovedstadens Forskønnelsen, and Lorenzen was a mouthpiece of the Conservation Movement for more than half a century as a pillar of Foreningen til Gamle Bygningers Bevaring. We shall summarise their approaches and assess their contributions to the debate on the 'old city', before to discuss the spread of conservationism through different civic societies in the second part of this chapter.

Meckseper and Harald Siebenmorgen (ed.), *Die Alte Stadt: Denkmal oder Lebensraum? Die Sicht der mittelalterlichen Stadtarchitektur im 19. und 20. Jahrhundert*, Göttingen, 1985, p.114-156. For a brief commentary on war destruction and civilian redevelopment see, Anthony M.Tung, *Preserving the World's Great Cities, The Destruction and Renewal of the Historic Metropolis*, New York, 2001, p.17.

6 See for instance the strong rejection of Le Corbusier's plan for the reconstruction of Saint Dié in the Vosges: Anatole Kopp, Frédérique Boucher, Danielle Pauly, *L'architecture de la Reconstruction en France, 1945-1953*, Paris, 1982, p. 151-155.

1.1 The Realm of Saturn

Erik Schiødte (1849-1909) studied architecture at the Royal Academy (1869-1875) and was strongly influenced by Hans Jørgen Holm (1835-1916), then professor at the school of Architecture, as he developed special interest in 'traditional' architecture. Schiødte was involved from 1876 onwards in the survey of ancient buildings, occasionally, in restoration works, and became associated with programmes of the National Museum. He joined the Østifternes historisk-topografiske Selskab on the year of its foundation.(See infra) He had been a founding member of Akademisk Architektforening (the Society of Architects of the Academy) in 1879, and in 1893, together with V. J. Murk-Hansen and V. Koch, he was editing the architectural drawings portfolio *Ælder Nordisk Architecture* (Old Nordic Architecture) commissioned by the Church Ministry. In the meantime he developed a fairly extended and creative practice as an architect. His sober neo-Nordic wooden fishery pavilion built for the 1888 Nordic Exhibition showed an affinity with vernacular craft and building as well as sensibility and inventiveness free from any leaning for pastiche.[7] In the 1890's, he was commissioned by the Frihavn Company to design a number of buildings, including the head office (1893)and the custom office (1894). His joint project with Rogert Møller for a large building complex in Christianshavn with staircases towers creating a 'comb like' pattern reminds of the large-scale housing estates in Vienna, which were designed in a

7 For a short biography and the reproduction of a few projects, see *Architekten*, 8 December 1909, p.121-125; and *Dansk biograpisk Lexikon*, Vol. 21, 1941, p. 149-150.

'palace' style for low-income people.[8] Schiødte, whose education included philosophy and literature, wrote also extensively in different papers about art and architecture. In 1894, under the sponsorship of the Society *Fremtiden*, he published in collaboration with the draftsman and painter Alfred Larsen (1860-1946) the first volume of the series *Gamle Kjøbenhavnske Huse og Gaarde* (Old Houses and Mansions of Copenhagen). This could be seen as a 'manifesto' on a vanishing city —not only the 'old city' but also its surroundings— the subject of the fourth volume published in 1897. The authors keep off an academic history or an architectural account of Copenhagen. The purpose is to depict the ordinary yet characteristic built environment made of ancient buildings that are often in a derelict state :

"De maa tale for sig selv, som de staar den dag i dag, de Gamle Huse, og som de her aftegnede, med de Forandringer og Omformninger, som Tiden og Brugen har medført".[9]

The seemingly digressive text, which is composed with a great many fine drawings, is articulated with different levels of writing. The first level combines accuracy of details and liveliness of form, which are intended, through cultural history, to convey the *stemning* (atmosphere) of the place.[10] Thus, the emphasis is laid not so much on significant buildings from a historical and architectural point of view as on the streets, alleys and yards forming the network of a picturesque built environment characterised by its bold architectural quality.[11]. (See Plate 13/A) There is no much room in Larsen's drawings for Amelienborg or other major monuments, nor are the town's eighteenth-century palaces and mansions devoted much space (16 views) compared to vernacular clusters or timber-framed buildings (30 views).[12] The city's architectural character is perceived as neither spectacular nor ostentatious —Copenhagen does not need to compete with other European capitals on that level. The very quality of the city is said to reside in the close spatial and historical integration of many diversified and softer elements such as blue water, and green trees contrasted with boat pools, red gabled roofs and verdigris spires in a balanced equilibrium.[13] The drawings and the texts, taking the reader for an imagined visit on foot through the town, emphasise the atmosphere of quietness and the harmony of forms, with gently curving streets slowly revealing the variety of townscape views and facades.[14] Regret is clearly expressed about the apparent little awareness of this *stemning* by the people who live there while it is highly praised by visitors as unique.

A second level of writing, often using small sentences, such as "a little time ago", "still recently", suggests the voracious "teeth of time" at work. Here and there, remarks are made about recently pulled-down buildings, the encroachment of "new wings" on old mansions, dilapidated houses, etc. Nonetheless, the short, mild turn of phrases expresses the swiftness of change and the speed of decay.

A third element is put forward to explain this change, though not quite explicitly: the cardinal social process whereby the city's original population has been displaced and replaced. Even then, old houses had long ago drifted into the hands of the bourgeois classes, with the ensuing partition of space and rising density, tenants and workers having been displaced to cheap habitations erected in the backyards. The built environment had fallen prey to the "mercantile modern spirit" that was perceived as the very engine of these negative changes.[15]

A fourth and last level comments more incidentally and soberly on possible remedies: collections of drawings and surveys should be made to help craftsman and architects[16], laws should be enacted to protect buildings of artistic, architectural and historical

8 Rogert Møller (1844-1918) was the co-author of this housing project (more than two hundreds apartments) for the building society Aladdin in 1900-1901, see Millech, *Danske... op.cit.*, p. 251. The drawings are kept in Kunstakademiets Bibliotek, Samlingen af Arkitekturtegninger, with the reference ES 14 108.

9 "Buildings must speak for themselves, reflecting as they do the transformations and changes they have gone through over time." (our translation) see, Larsen and Schiødte, *Gamle... op.cit.*, Haefte (3), p. 76-79.

10 Idem, Haefte (4), p. 127.

11 Ibid., this is particularly stated in Haefte (3), p. 79.

12 We consider here only the three first volumes encompassing Christianshavn and the 'old city'.

13 Ibid, for instance Haefte (2), p. 40.

14 See Haefte (1), p. 47-48.

15 Ibid., p. 119 and 105.

16 Ibid., p. 29.

value[17]—with the implicit wish throughout that Copenhageners should become aware of the quality of their city.

However, the writer seems to be under no illusions about a possible reversal, nor about the squalid conditions of some part of the picturesque quarters.[18] In the end, life has to prevail over remembrances and monuments.[19] What is hoped for is a less "mercantile" and more aesthetically conscious twentieth century.[20] Moreover, the picturesque city is not an empty city, and the role of people in the streets, squares and markets is often recalled, even if the social aspects of Larsen's aesthetics remain minimal. 37 drawings are devoid of any human presence, 51 present casual street scenes—mostly relegated to a distant background and rather serving as scale indicators. In most of the remaining views there are to be found children, working women, casual passers-by and sometimes people chatting. There are no real attempts at making poverty esthetical, on the contrary rampant poverty is to be perceived distinctly as a no-romantic attribute of the city. In the end, Schiødte and Larsen's message remains ambivalent. The picturesque and its associated qualities are shown as fragile. It remains a privilege enjoyed by the happy few in the position of an observer, and especially by lone travellers catching the fleeting image of a vanishing city and a vanished time.

1.2 Architectonics and Harmonics

The second contribution is from the painter and art critic Nicolaus Lützhøft (1864-1928) who addressed the question of the "picturesque city" in his article *Det maleriske København* (The picturesque Copenhagen) published in the journal *Førskonnelsen* in 1911. Close to the school of painting in Fyn Island, and also a musician (he taught song at the Franz Liszt Academy in Gotha), Lützhøft combines both sensibilities in search of a definition of the "picturesque" townscape.[21] However, the author also directly addresses the process of change of the urban fabric and the formation of the "Stor Stad", giving a large number of examples.

Lützhøft's essay is quite remarkable for its attempt to discuss how the "picturesque" of the townscape can be characterised. The text draws its strength from a rather crude dualism. First of all, the modern spaces are disqualified as boring. The modern city is compared to a devouring Moloch, at that time an alternative image to the 'giant octopus', which is full of "ostentatious" architecture. Speculators promote low quality housing and short-sighted vandalism is prevalent. As with Schiødte, the 'picturesque' city exists in a somewhat parallel dimension, almost hidden to those for whom it is their daily environment, however perceived by the foreigners or the travellers who can compare and immediately distinguish what is place-specific. The "picturesque" of the city is understood as the result of manifold factors that have accumulated through accidental development and coalesced through generations. Natural factors or artificial creations (architectural qualities) are not of prime importance. The picturesque is essentially the product of a harmonious setting enhanced through long lasting "relations". As with musical chords, individual elements remain secondary, it is the relations between them that are essential. Thus, beauty does not flow from design but from the carefully integrated natural and man-made elements. This dimension is a kind of open secret, however, little place it is usually left in main streets. The 'picturesque' is always place-bound, and therefore unique. From this point of view it can be compared to an irreplaceable old tree. Thus, the "picturesque city" is highly fragile, and is put at risk if elements are unduly withdrawn. Lützhøft abundantly illustrates this aspect, drawing up with talent an inventory of a city undergoing radical change.

The author does not adopt an exclusively antiquarian attitude. His plea for softness of line, for locally bound character, and for a provincial atmosphere should not be interpreted as the conservative complaint of a disgruntled patrician. His criticism of city modernity revolves round the idea of 'absurdity'. The mechanisms underlying this absurdity are left implicit, though tangible examples are given. For instance, the following question is raised: why invest huge amounts in laying out artificial parks, when existing 'picturesque' open spaces such as the fortifications are aban-

17 Ibid., p. 100.
18 Ibid., for instance pp. 35, 36 in Christianshavn.
19 Ibid, p. 112.
20 Ibid., p. 67.
21 See *Dansk biografisk leksikon*, Vol. 9, p. 269.

doned or even due to be demolished? Such criticism also applies to the new practices of city dwellers. Why rush to houses in the country in spring and summer, when plenty of natural and beautiful spaces are available in Copenhagen itself, with the sea and landscape on its fringe? Accordingly, the spirit of modernity is associated with a tendency to spoil one place in order to generate a need for other places. The architectural heritage can be left to decay to the point of justifying reconstruction in consequence of this 'modern' attitude.

The concluding message of Lützhøft's article leaves open the problem of the specific value of modernity, restricting itself to the question of its mastery.[22] A few orientations are then suggested. Inner-city modernisation should be closely looked at. New building should be allowed to be erected only when seriously needed, and the impact on "city physiognomy" assessed. Even ordinary housing without obvious architectonic attraction should be considered, constituting as it does the first level in the scale of architectural quality. The maintenance and care of old buildings should be given a high priority. The author does not exclude the production of built environment. He actually praises the "singular" example of Fritz Koch's (1857-1905) Baroque-influenced building "Gotfred Tvede" from 1903. More generally, Lützhøft acknowledges the painstaking and long process of discovering what could be a "local character". He therefore encouraged the movement of young architects who gathered in *Den Fri Architektforening* to develop a *hjemlig* (homely) perspective on design and construction. Those suggestions also carry social implications. In a depressed district like Christianshavn for instance, the fortifications could make use of open spaces. As a rule, less importance should be attached to anecdotal embellishments such as fountains and statues, and more emphasis placed on improving existing valuable sites, where cosmetic treatment should be avoided in favour of straightforward maintenance.

22 "Fremskridtets Vej maa under Tiden kunne tvinges udenom, ikke al Tid over Ruinerne af vor Arv fra Fortiden" Nicolaus Lützhøft, "Det malerisk København", *Forskønnelsen*, n°5, 1911, p. 75-83, p. 83.

1.3 Design in Context

The third contribution, selected here, is from Peter Johansen (1858-1939), adjunct professor of art history at the Academy and founding member of Foreningen for National Kunst in 1900. Johansen was an exponent of Foreningen til Hovedstadens Forskønnelse. He was also described in the press as a staunch champion of heritage, in connection with the founding meeting of Foreningen til gamle Bygningers Bevaring" in 1907.[23] (See infra). Johansen's article is chiefly concerned with the relationship between urban expansion and inner city transformation. It also addresses the conjunction of spatial transformations and social change, and describes in some detail the ongoing process of city building within the city and in the suburbs. We will concentrate here on the first theme.

The threat to the city centre is seen as the result of an evolution having deeply affected the inhabitants' ties with their built environment. Not only has the patrician character of the inner city been weakened over the nineteenth century, but also above all the relation between tenants and owners, and their dwellings has been impaired. To Johansen, the old city is basically a collection of "hjemme" (homes), of intimate links forged across generations between the inhabitants and their dwellings. Those links have often been severed, further altering the interest that inhabitants had in the care of buildings and the surroundings. In others words, "hygge" (atmosphere of intimacy) is no more, and even old mansions have become little more than "rented wardrobes". The rapid growth of the city brought highly speculative pressure on the centre, making it difficult to organise the protection of its physical fabric. Johansen sums up the common trend as "stupid and brutal toward the old" and "uncouth with the new". He also laments the "passivity" of town dwellers toward what is happening to their city. Moreover, he stresses that the "practical needs", which are invoked to justify anything in both suburban extensions and town centre, are scarcely more than a mask allowing speculative interests to minimise other needs of equal importance.

Furthermore, this contribution is a clear advocacy

23 See "Gamle Huse", *Berlinske*, 24 May 1907, and Weilbach, *Dansk Kunstnerleksikon*, Vol. 4, 1995, p. 159.

for new methods as concerns town planning. It considers that the old nineteenth-century plea for "rational order" has ended in reductionism, and insists on provisions to regulate communal land and secure forecasting developments. It is suggested that the London's 90-year leases' method may be applicable at home. As concerns existing elements of the 'old city', such as the remaining fortifications, they should be not only preserved but also put to imaginative use. Greater consideration should be shown to the character of the place generally. It should be possible to check the thoughtless implementation of "practical needs" in urban layout, which revealed its effects in the lakes' area and in Nørrevoldgade, being neither a new urban centre nor a public walking site.

Johansen sees the building process in the town centre as one of "progressive reconstruction". He argues that some careful clearance may be carried out within high-density districts without, however, traffic being given undue priority against other needs. Careful attention should also be paid to the integration of new buildings such as department stores, when they are really needed. The long plots of land typical of Copenhagen's centre should also be treated imaginatively. Johansen deplores the "petty-bourgeois" importance attached to street frontages. There would be many ways of putting back plots to good use, with dwellings opening onto inner gardens or with banks and public buildings constructed without undue frontages. It is also suggested to open pedestrian passages through inner courtyards, possibly provided with small shops.

Johansen was obviously no proponent of the "Great City" concept, while not anti-urban either. He directly questions the ultimate benefit of ceaseless urban expansion, especially in the Danish context. Giving a large number of imaginative examples taken from his travels through Europe, particularly in Spain, he still believed in the practical possibility of adapting the "old", and generally strove for a more open concept of contextual rationality.

1.4 Negotiating Conservation

The final contribution is taken from the abundant production of Wilhelm Lorenzen (1877-1961). As Johansen, Lorenzen was a founding members of Foreningen til gamle Bygningers Bevaring, and both the articles we selected were published in 1914. While Johansen's article addresses the dynamic of city building in relation to "old" and "new" space, Lorenzen's contribution specifically focuses on conservation issues; it was published in the book *København, som den er og som den burde vaere*, edited by Foreningen til Hovestadens Forskønnelse, which can be considered as a manifesto to link modern town planning topics with concerns for Copenhagen's built heritage.[24]

Lorenzen looked for an affordable treatment of conservation, at a time when heritage was not yet acknowledged as a cultural value. He advocated a realistic compromise between contrary ideas and attitudes toward the inherited city by developing arguments that could be heard and agreed with by an urban elite tempted by quick speculative gains or by the modernisation of the city's fabric. On the one hand, he acknowledges the need for change. On the other hand, he tries to shame the anti-conservationist lobby. He admits that depressed districts need not be conserved, because the "physical and moral hygiene of a great city requires transformations". However, when historic streets and squares are concerned and disfigured by flashy, pretentious modern architecture that alters the atmosphere of a whole street, then, the author call for public action.[25]

Here, the "picturesque city" literally recedes into the background. Schiødte and Larsen's Copenhagen and Lorenzen's city do not partake of the same dimensions and architectural qualities. This is particularly striking when comparing the style and subjects of the drawings chosen by Larsen on the one hand and by Kr. Kongstad. The later, for instance, depicts very few timber-framed or simple vernacular buildings (see Plate 9/D). It is interesting here to notice that Bering Liisberg, who praised the quality of Kongstad's drawings, ostensibly acknowledged the effort made to accurately represent Copenhagen's heritage without failing prey to pictorial romanticism.[26] Kong-

24 Lorenzen, Wilhem, "Om bevaring af gammel bygningskunst", in Otto Asmussen, *Kjøbenhavn, som den er og som den burde vaere*, Copenhagen, 1914, p. 117-128.

25 Idem, p. 118.

26 See the commentary of the book by Bering Liisberg, "Kjøbenhavn som den er og som den burde vaere", *Forskønnelsen*,

stad's work may well reflect a widely defensible heritage while Larsen drawings are looking more as epitaphs.

Nevertheless, it should be underlined that the illustrations in both books are centred on civil architecture. Larsen offers a profusion of perspective drawings of clusters of buildings. Similarly, Kongstad's view of Copenhagen is not restricted to its monumental heritage. However, singled front elevations are often privileged, and illustrations focus on homogeneous squares, avenues and streets as to underline the arrangement of the main streets and its network to be part of the urban heritage.

According to Lorenzen, whatever contributes to the "physiognomy" of the city should be taken into account. Any additions to the townscape ought to be carefully analysed, and respect existing buildings. Thus, new construction should be restricted to a minimum in the town centre, while modern architecture is given enough of a free hand in the rapidly developing suburbs. A distinction should be made between public estates and private property: the former, largely made up of historic monuments, should, in theory, be automatically protected; the latter, comprising most of the built environment, should be tackled with by various measures. For instance, landowners ought to be held responsible for the maintenance of their buildings, while a degree of adaptation to modern needs should be acknowledged. Conservation thus means defining the degree of change that is advisable, with the risk of a divorce between scholarly attitudes and conservationist pragmatism.

Besides these general considerations, Lorenzen underlines the significance of micro-scale changes:

> "Og det er ved disse bestandige, altfor upaaagtede Smaarevolutioner i vor Bys Arkitektur, den store, stille Revolution en skønne Dag vil være fuldbyrdet, hvor Kjøbenhavn helt igennem er bleven en temmelig ligegyldig europæisk Storstad af det almindelige Gennemsnit, hvis vi ikke i tide passer paa og har vor Opmærksomhed henvendt paa denne Udvikling".[27]

1914, p. 83-84. Liisberg nevertheless regretted the reluctance of the draftsman to represent the defacing transformations occurred on some buildings. Concerning the 1914 collective book sponsored by the Forskønnelse, we should underline the fact that the jacket offering the view of the roofs and skylines of the city is almost the only 'picturesque' vernacular view.

The setting up of ground-level shops in architecturally sensitive buildings is a test case there. Lorenzen contemplates two alternative options, which could be acceptable to secure the conservation of the built fabric. One may call 'facadism' the first scheme, which consists in radically transforming the inside of a building without altering its external appearance, its frontage especially. On the other hand, careful adaptations can be approved, and architects should be encouraged with awards for creative design in keeping with the style of the building.

Lorenzen's contribution primarily aims at sensitise leading citizens and municipal officials alike to the city's historical, artistic and cultural value, and to the swift pace of transformations, which can led to its vanishing without much notice. It is architecture and not the *stemning* that is given a central role to focus on urban culture, though insistence on "architectural quality" could endanger the efforts to grasp the city in a single image, a risk Lorenzen is aware of. Yet, it seems that Lorenzen believes in the positive effect, which incentives may have for architects and landowners alike in relation to the goals of conservation. It is agreed that preservation entails some sacrifices, and social recognition of whatever effort in the 'right' direction should broaden awareness of the architectural legacy and secure an opinion in favour of conservation.

2 The Movement for Conservation

In the first part of this book, we showed that most of the Danish architects who competed in 1908 were members of one or several associations, or institu-

27 "Those small imperceptible alterations in our city architecture make for a silent revolution of the whole city that will be one day accomplished – Copenhagen will become a much ordinary middle sized European town if we don't tackle in time this course of affairs." Lorenzen, *Om bevaring… op.cit.*, p. 126-127.

tions, whose activities buttressed urban conservation generally. We shall now document some of these organisations, namely Foreningen til Hovedstadens Forskønnelse, the Østifternes Historisk-Topographisk Selskab and finally Foreningen til Gamle Bygningers Bevaring, and look for the cultural tradition in which they operated as concerns the handling of the built environment. This selection does not mean that other important actors did not contribute to this process; we already mentioned the contribution of the Akademisk Architektforening in defining guidelines for conservation, and the role of Den Fri Architektforening in restoration issues. There are indeed a great many actors, individuals or organisations, that would deserve systematic investigation to embrace the sphere of the movement for conservation at the beginning of the twentieth century in Copenhagen and in Denmark generally. Moreover, there are two dimensions of technical and social practices in close relation to the evolving cultural attitudes toward the built forms that the scope of this study does not allow us to consider in detail.

The first dimension relates to the role of architectural surveys in the "re-discovery" of the country's traditional architecture at the end of the nineteenth century. Published in 1884 under the aegis of the Church and Education Ministry, the series *Ældre Nordisk Architektur* (already mentioned in relation to Schiødte) made a wide range of drawings available in the following years. Edited under the supervision of V. Dahlerup, Hans J. Holm, O. V. Koch and H. Storck, the portfolios printed extensive surveys of churches, castles and residences in Denmark and Sweden. The scope of the surveys was progressively enlarged in the years 1908-1913, and came to encompass a significant number of rural and urban timber-framed buildings.[28]

Another important initiative may have had even greater impact, both in terms of professional dynamics and in terms of the range of types of buildings covered. In 1892, students at the Academy of Architecture had formed the association Opmaalinger-Foreningen af 3. December 1892, with the purpose of promoting surveys of ancient buildings as part of architect education and to awaken interest in traditional architecture among fellow students. Since 1898, it received subsidies from the Church and Education Ministry as well as the Academy. By 1903, with its 86 active members and 246 passive members gathering professors, architects and master craftsmen, it had acquired a real influence as a complement to the teaching of the School of Architecture.[29] Between 1894 and 1932, the society published lavish surveys of buildings of all kinds. The society was above all a students' association organising study tours, lectures, exhibitions and competitions, which could prove of some weight in the appointment of professors. In the first decade of the century, the society devoted much of its work to the survey of fast disappearing civil urban architecture. At the same time it forged strong ties between archaeological and architectural practices with its extensive survey and excavation campaigns in different regions of the Eastern Mediterranean. In fact, the Opmaalinger-Foreningen succeeded in nourishing two kinds of architecture: helping to preserve the tradition of the local "Danish architecture" favoured by the romantic stream, it also paved the way for the neo-classical revival that took shape around 1915.

The second field we ought to mention is partly linked to the former. The movement emphasising the return to stylistic sobriety and plainness of traditional Danish architecture was intimately linked to what we may call the movement for the historical survey of the built environment. At the turn of the century, P.V. Jensen Klint's (1853-1930) action, which motto was "to safeguard the old and to give rule and guidance to the new", was particularly significant in trying to anchor modern building techniques in Danish constructive culture.[30] V. Lorenzen echoed this appeal: he thought that a reform of the technical schools could be a decisive factor toward upgrading the average quality of construction.[31] Klint's efforts to promote

28 The Portfolios are edited under the responsibility of V. J. Mørk-Hansen, V. Koch and Erik Schiødte from 1893 onward, than later under H. Storck once more.

29 We draw here from Henrik Egede Glahn (red.), *Foreningen af 3. December 1892 – Festskrift i anledning af 100-aarsdagen*, Copenhagen, 1992.

30 See P.V. Jensen Klint, "At vaerne det gamle og saette skik paa det ny eller en reform af vore bygningsskoler", *Architekten*, 6 october 1906, p. 6-11.

31 V. Lorenzen, "At saette skik paa det ny", *Architekten*, 20 Oktober 1906, p. 30-31.

the Danish tradition of the master-builder as well as new standards in building education against the rampant eclecticism or "free historicism" of nineteenth-century architecture aroused interest, suspicion and anger alike.[32] The mediocrity of the expanding urban fabric was a recurrent topic in the professional debate of those years, both within and outside academic circles. Numerous attempts were undertaken to reverse what was described as the tide of "ugliness" that was threatening to engulf towns and landscapes.

Once Martin Nyrop took over F. Meldahl's professorship at the Academy's School of architecture in 1906, a committee was set up, including U. Plesner, for drawing samples of "good" and "bad"-quality buildings throughout the country. The project was to design some guidelines for ordinary construction to craftsmen or non-academic architects and took shape with the assistance of architect Poul Holsøe who devoted his efforts to set up the "Akademisk Architektforenings Tegnehjælp" (the Academy's council for design guidance) in 1907. This initiative is characteristic of the current for improving domestic architecture, and it can also been seen as one component of the endeavour to reform the training of builders at the technical schools, aiming at enhancing both artistic and cultural knowledge alongside technical knowledge.[33] In the meantime, the Academy of Arts resumed its project of opening a technical curriculum for construction in the summer of 1908.[34]

However, some architects were of the opinion that the strong focus given on the technical dimension of construction in the education of architects did not answer some key questions. In a lecture given to representatives of crafts and industry, an architect emphasised that his corporation should consider how to build cheap and fast to secure the path to modernity. This meant using new materials and imported ones, implementing the techniques of emerging industrial construction, and designing new types of building, such as dairies, slaughterhouses and the like. In the same breath, he drew the attention of his audience to the fact that some other countries, which were going through the same process of transformations affecting the built environment, had nevertheless enacted measures to protect their built heritage.[35]

Whatever the diagnoses of the professionals, the first decade of the twentieth century displayed a wealth of attempts and initiatives aiming at mastering the "first" and "second" industrialisation that in Denmark were making their marks on the country almost simultaneously. It appears that in the field of construction, conservation was increasingly understood as part of this mastering process. We shall now explore the role of some organisations in that perspective.

2.1 Foreningen til Hovedstadens Forskønnelse

Founded in 1885, Foreningen til Hovedstadens Forskønnelse (The Society for the Beautification of the Capital) (FHF), had long been dominated by notables, among whom the brewer Carl Jacobsen (1842-1914).[36] At first, peopled by many of the capital's wealthy and artistically-minded citizens, the society mostly concerned itself with upgrading Copenhagen's cultural prestige, according to its motto: '*skøn by skaber ry*' (Beauty brings fame to the City). It funded ornamental structures to adorn the public space, such as statues and fountains, and as such supported artistic production as in the time-honoured Danish tradition of 'urban art'. The society gave little evidence on the circumstances of its creation. It seems to have had as a forerunner a committee founded around 1842-1845, an initiative closely linked to the municipal authorities and apparently almost stillborn.[37] It seems diffi-

32 The articles P.V.Jensen Klint wrote about this topic were published as a book: *Bygmester Skolen*, Copenhagen, 1911.

33 See, "Undervisningen ved de tekniske skoler", *Architekten*, 14 march 1908, p. 286-288.

34 See, the programme, "Kunstakademiets bygningstekniske skole", *Architekten*, 15 August 1908, p. 514-515.

35 "Om byggeriet paa landet", *Architekten*, 5 september 1908, p. 550-554.

36 C. Jacobsen was a founding member of the society, 9 May 1885, and a member of its executive committee until 1888. In the literature dedicated to the brewer and patrons of arts, see Kristof Glamann, *Øl og Marmor*, Copenhagen, 1995.

37 *Forskønnelsen*, 1925 , p. 25; V. Malling, Rund… op.cit, 1960, p. 9-10. Those years see the reinforcement of the national liberal movement as well as important changes in Copenhagen's administration which however remained under the tutelage of the Magistrat named by the King. The municipal council had been formed in 1840 as an elected assembly under limited franchise, See, Jensen, S. & Smidt, C.M., *Rammerne sprænges*, Copenhague, 1982, p. 55-78.

cult to establish a direct link between this committee, closely related to the political changes of the 1840s, and the organisation formed 40 years later. In 1885, several events contributed toward creating a favourable ground for such an organisation. The options opened after Christiansborg Palace had burnt down, while encroachments on the King's Gardens were being debated. The last remains of the north west old fortifications and especially the Kastellet became also a matter of discussion. In the spring of 1885, a municipal commission was set up to decide upon the location for the new Town Hall, together with the architect's project.[38] The preparation for the Nordic Exhibition in 1888 also acted as a catalyst for a wealth of initiatives pledging to engage in the aesthetic improvement of the city that would host a great many visitors.[39] A vast, lavishly ornamented project was design. One of the promoters of the 1888 event, Philip Schou who was State councillor and director of the Royal Manufacture of Porcelain, was seating in the FHF together with other prominent figures of Danish industry.[40] The structures of the exhibition were to be ephemeral, as in most national and international exhibits in the second half of nineteenth century. However, the choice of location, the layout and general organisation of the temporary 'city' partly interacted with the city's remodelling in the aftermath of the dismantling of the fortifications. Ambitions, visions or interests linked to the development of the Vesterbro district could be brought forward, as well as other projects for the inner city.

In spite of a good start, which brought the society no less than 800 members, its public activities were marginal. A closer analysis would probably reveal tensions between a nineteenth-century philanthropic approach looking at urban space in artistic and moral terms, and a larger social and political vision. During its general assembly in 1888, for instance, the chairman of FHF, Fritz Hartmann insisted on calling to realise monumental and ornamental schemes, such as the fountain inaugurated in 1894 on Amagertorv, and restraining from intervention in domains pertaining to municipal authorities.[41] Yet, the lukewarm reception the fountain received was a clear sign of the exhaustion of a patrician conception of aesthetics and beautification that merely sought to replicate, also in a much milder form, the past lustre of monarchic cities.[42]

The 'Art of the Street'

In 1902, *Architekten* opened its columns to the society, noting a new departure under the guidance of architect Fritz Koch (1857-1905). Almost extinct by the turn of the century, with a membership of fewer than three hundred, and contemplating its own dissolution, FHF proved capable of renewing its vision of the city and planning new activities. Within a few years, the society enjoyed a definite renewal, its membership reaching the one thousand mark in 1908.[43] Under the chairmanship of decorator and painter Jens Møller-Jensen, FHF had gradually shifted its interest toward new aspects of the urban scene.[44] New types of actions testified to a growing attention toward the built environment, and this "patrician" society also began discussing broader urban topics.[45] FHF supported or initiated a number of projects, which were

38 Idem, p. 295; V. Malling, *Rund... op.cit.*, 1960, p. 12.

39 Den Nordiske Industri-, Landbrug- og Kunstudstilling; The 1888 exhibition largely transcended the nordic realms with the participation of Germany , England , France , Italy, Austria, Russia and Japan.

40 Especially G. A. Hagemann (1842-1916), then heading the consortium of sugar industries and town councillor, see *Forskønnelsen*, 1925, p. 47. P. Schou was chairman of Industriforeningen, since 1883.

41 *Forskønnelsen*, 1925, p. 28.

42 A caricature drawing by A. Schmidt shows agitation and wild disorder on the square and turns this monument escalated by policeman trying to expelled from the top facetious citizens into ridicule. see, J. Møller, *Borger i Klunketidens* København, 2000, p. 151. The fountain was later to be protected by fences.

43 See, *Forskønnelsen*, 1915, p. 63.

44 The chairmen were successively: The lawyer, Fritz Hartmann: 1885-1902; Martin Nyrop, architect: 1896-1902 was specially in charge of artistic questions when F. Hartmann was in charge of the administrative part. Fritz Koch, architect, 1903-1905; Jens Møller-Jensen, decorator and painter: 1906-1909; the merchant Christian Holm, 1910 –1911; Thorvald Jørgensen, architect: 1912-1919; see, *Forskønnelsen*, 1925 p. 25-48.

45 For a short account of the activities of this society see, "Foreningen til Hovedstadens Forskonnelse 1885-1915", *Forskonnelsen*, udgivet af Foreningen til Hovedstadens Forskonnelse, V Aargang, Copenhagen, MDCDXV, pp. 23-26.

displayed at Charlottenborg and aroused marked interest in the press. The landscaped project along Langelinie was particularly praised. Models presenting a new layout for Kongens Nytorv and Nyhaven were also much discussed.

On the contrary, the campaign for the colouring (some said "Italianise") of the frontages of buildings surrounding Graadbrødretorv failed to arouse enthusiasm, at least within the professional milieu of architects. Though with some reserves as to the meaning of the action and with a certain degree of condescension, *Architekten* hailed the association, which "appeals directly to the inhabitants".[46] Earlier, Schiødte had contested the effect of the Graadbrødretorv's red facades.[47] When Jens Møller-Jensen launched a new campaign, this time for colouring the buildings bordering Nyhaven, a chorus of protests arouse. *Politiken* echoed the petition by some forty renowned architects and artists of repute, which disapproved the plan led by the FHF as vulgar.[48] After a lively debate, much reported on the press, the project was carried out with less emphasis on the colouring aspect of the operation intended to clean and maintain the buildings' frontages. On this occasion, *Architekten* supported Jens Møller's initiative, without restriction: colours are of little importance as they can always be discussed and changed; what does matter is the move aiming at heightening awareness about the quality of old architecture that contributes to keep in check destructive speculative pressure in the city centre.[49] Directly addressing the preservation of ancient buildings, these campaigns surely drew attention on the city's architectonic quality. Such were also the windows' floral decoration competitions with emphasis on "picturesque bay windows" that *Politiken* sponsored in 1907.[50]

Campaigns of façade cleaning and painting were coalescing with other initiatives concerned with the appearance of the streets, including the "kunstgade" (art of the street). Protests against advertising on billboards close to historic buildings and monuments; survey of ancient street signs and traditional doors; incentives for the maintenance of public squares and for the artistic design of kiosks and street lamps are among the various efforts made for the public space. Such initiatives, widely reported in the Danish press, could also aim at invigorating the commercial life of a district, or at supplementing the action of communal authorities. This bears comparison with the "mouvement pour l'art de la rue" launched in Belgium and Switzerland under the umbrella of "l'Art public" at the turn of the century.

FHF still followed the tradition of landlord citizenship in a burgher city: taking responsibility for the beautification of the town and for stimulating 'good taste'. In the city should be embedded an ethos of culture combining the space of public walking for leisure and social intercourse as well as the space of commercial activities. It is in this perspective that the society often joined forces with Den Danske Turistforening (Danish Society for Tourism) founded in 1888 on the occasion of the Nordic Exhibition.[51]

At the society's general assembly in 1907, Casper Leuning Borch (1853-1910) (he became a member of the society's board in 1908) was invited to make a speech on the scope of SHF's activities.[52] Before attempting to suggest a course of action, architect Borch pointed to very idea of *Hovedstads forskønnelse* in the following way. Time had come for the burghers to reflect upon the consequences of the sweeping wave of industrialisation. Negative aspects were not to be evaded —for instance the "ugly and gloomy district" of Gammelholm or some workers districts that should ideally be razed to the ground. The society should therefore strive for a "harmonious city" that would also be better off economically. Borch admitted that this could easily be shown as far as tourism is concerned, but with more difficulties otherwise. It is a complex and hazardous task to assess the wealth that can be generated from the aesthetic quality of a city generally. However, the increased involvement of en-

46 *Architekten*, , 13 February 1903.

47 Schiødte, *Gamle... op.cit*, Haefte II, p. 63.

48 See, "Fra Forskønnelsesforeningens store møde i aftes", *Politiken*, 30 January 1908.

49 *Architekten*, 22 August 1908, p. 524-525.

50 One may note that during the same years such floral competitions were actively encouraged by the Art Public movement in Belgium.

51 On this society, see Hans Joakim Schultz, *Dansk turisme i 100 år 1888-1988*, 1988, esp.p. 11-49.

52 See, "Forskønnelsesforeningens Møde, Architekt Leuning-Borchs Foredrag", *Architekten*, 24 January.1907, p. 195-200.

lightened businessmen in schemes to improve urban development could be seen as an evidence of this trend. In contrast, a number of low-grade housing projects and spoiled sites by "wild urbanisation" (among which are the lakes' area) are given to illustrate the evils of ruthless mercantile projects. In short, Borch recommended to extend the society's activities toward the protection of valuable buildings and sites (especially in the suburbs) and the control of the quality of urban development projects. Thus, FHF should be concerned with urban questions, such as the elaboration of Copenhagen's by-law (Bygningslov) and make itself heard by State's administrations and municipal authorities. Borch prompted FHF to develop itself beyond beautification's schemes and embark on a broader debate, encompassing the future of both the core city and the surrounding districts.

A Platform for the Professional Movement

At that time, FHF decided to help founding *Foreningen til gamle Bygningers Bevaring* and to collaborate to its action in favour of the protection of the built heritage. Both societies stressed their converging interests in "creating new values" that would secure architectural production, which later could deserve conservation".[53]

For lack of a systematic prosoprographic study of FHF's membership, one can only note the strong presence of leading architects together with painters and sculptors at the turn of the century. We can assume that they contributed through their expertise and experiences in opening up the society up to the wider dimensions of the urban scene. In the meantime, their affiliation to the society was likely to broaden their prospect in term of commissions for the building of villas and the like, particularly at a time of weakened building activities.

The following table lists ten architects, members of the board of FHF between 1900 and 1914, in their order of entry on the board, and with the duration of their tenure:

Martin Nyrop, 1895-1905
Hans J. Holm, 1885-1907
A. O. Leffland, 1892-1906
Fritz Koch, 1902-1905
Magdahl-Nielsen, 1902-1909
Gotfred Tvede, 1906-1912
Casper Leuning-Borch, 1908-1910
Ulrik Plesner, 1911-1918
Kristoffer Varming, 1913-1921
Thorvald Jørgensen, 1911-1919.

Their names give a clear indication of the interplay of aesthetic influences that FHF represented during those years, and the platform the society became for professionals to exchange and develop views on urban questions. The society gathered some of the major actors involved in the making of the highlights of the city's built environment at that time, and as such participated in the shaping of cultural values that influenced the making of the urban form. To invite FHF in sitting the jury of the 1909 Competition was to recognise the place of the society in the realm of urban planning, alongside the two main professional organisations of engineers and architects. This paved the way for FHFs self-assertion in urban affairs. In January 1911, the first issue of the journal *Forskønnelse* announced that the society was committed itself to be a public forum for discussing the "city aspect" and supporting urban schemes that could improve it.[54] In the following issues a number of articles reported on the ongoing plans of development city, the forthcoming *Bygningslov* for Copenhagen, and the 'Garden Cities', among other town planning topics. We already mentioned the publication of the book *København, som den er og som den burde vaere*, from which we chose the contribution of V. Lorenzen, and characterised the work as the society's manifesto in the 1914. The book also included a long article by Egil fischer, which bears comparison with a framework for town planning regulations. As a whole, this work is a Danish version of Civic Art planning whereby town planning and conservation of the 'heritage' are considered in a comprehensive manner. By 1914 it could be said that FHF had much contributed to include the 'safeguarding of the city' within planning debates.

53 "Gamle Huse", *Berlinske*, 24 may 1907.

54 *Forskønnelsen*, n° 1, 1911, p. 1.

2.2 Østifternes historisk-topografiske Selskab

In contrast to FHF, the Østifternes historisk-topografiske Selskab (The Society for the historic Topography of the Danish Islands) (ØHTS) founded in 1898, was an association closely linked to official institution, namely the National Museum. Along with the organisation of archives, libraries, and royal collections the Oldnordisk Museum was merged into the Nationalmuseum in January 1892. In the new institution, two departments were set up: the 1st department inherited the collections of the Oldnordisk Museum, i.e. the prehistoric and ethnographic collections and the antiquities; the 2nd department was in charge of the collections from the Middle-Age and the Renaissance's periods, together with the conservation of topographical archives. In many ways the 2nd department was a new extension of the museum institution, in as much as its focus was the modern times, and also with respect to the personality of Sophus Müller (1846-1934), who was in charge of the prehistoric collections. In the year 1878, Müller had become an assistant to J. J. A. Worsaae, (1821-1885), the prominent archaeologist who was head of the Oldnordisk Museum in 1865-1885. Müller developed his career as a curator and eminent archaeologist and eventually became Worsaae's heir in scientific matters. When S. Müller was appointed director of the National Museum's 1st department in 1892, he was a powerful figure dominating the fields of prehistory and archaeology. He campaigned actively for a centralised national administration, regretting that the Museum's collections had been split in two bodies of supervision.[55] After the death of both the director and the first assistant of the 2nd department in 1896, William Mollerup (1846-1917) was appointed head of the division; he was a historian and teacher at the Officers' School, and had been employed at the National Museum in 1893.

The above caveats point to the context in which the ØHTS was launched in January 1898 at the initiative of W. Mollerup, who became the society's chairman.[56] With the general aim of fostering knowledge of Danish history, topography and monuments, the society also sought to draw attention to the riches held by the national and county archives, and by the new division of the National Museum, all of which were regarded as important national assets. The scope of the new society was, however, from the outset limited to the Danish Islands, since the Jydske historisk-topografiske Selskab had been covering mainland Jutland since 1865. Considering the desire to strengthen the 2nd department's position on the one hand, and the need not to encroach on the field of the senior society of Jutland on the other, it is thus hardly surprising that Zealand and especially Copenhagen became the focus of the studies to be published by the new society's organ, *Arkiv og Museum.* The outline the society gave of its activities in the year 1908 clearly indicates the intention it had to specialise in the history and topography of Copenhagen, as the "centre of the Danish Islands".[57]

Like many similar learned associations at that time, the society retained a highly institutional and scholarly character, with a large number of history professors, curators and archivists. Though it cannot be characterised as a professional body according to its statutes, which aimed at increase general awareness of the riches of the collections on Danish history and the importance of their conservation, the society was essentially geared to the promotion of 'cultural history' and to the survey cum preservation of historical artefacts. After a peak of 371 members in 1900, the ØHTS lost its dynamic with a continuous decline in subscriptions and resources, in spite of state grants.[58] Eventually it ceased activity in 1916, when professor Camille Nyrop quit the presidency and the committee chose not to be re-elected.[59]

55 Biographical notice in *Dansk biografisk leksikon*, Vol. 10, 1982, p. 177-181.

56 In 1898, the 2nd Department's direction was enlarged to the coins and medals collection; See, H.Ramussen, *Dansk museums historie – de kultur-historiske muser*, Copenhagen, 1979. See also Mollerup's biographical notice in *Dansk biografisk leksikon*, vol. 9, 1982, p. 623-625.

57 *Arkiv og Museum*, vol. 3, 1905-1908, p. 583.

58 The membership, which was mainly from Copenhagen, in 1905 was 310, 283 in 1909, and 246 in 1912, see, *Arkiv og Museum*, vol. 1,2, 3, 4, 5, 1899-1915.

59 The three members of the committee were Camille Nyrop, Christian Axel Jensen and S.L. Tuxen.

Conservation – A field of Competition?

During the 1900s and the 1910s, there appeared a growing number of associations with their own publications, dedicated to both national and local history, especially in Copenhagen. The ØHTS noticed this development, perceived as an "increased competition" in its own field. Around 1906, the association's committee was considering changing the character of the journal: a larger format with many illustrations and a stronger focus on the history of the capital. Moreover, the editors acknowledged not having still fulfilled their aim of publishing a specialised journal on Copenhagen's history. Yet, funds were not secured for that purpose. Thus, the new publication *Historiske Meddelelser om København* that came out in 1907 at the initiative of the municipality, with the city hall's archivist Villads Christensen as editor, was seen by the ØTHS as a clear contest in contention for the same field of activities.[60] Furthermore, the Dansk historisk Fællesforening was founded two years later, which aimed at fostering collaboration between societies with historical interests and institutions such as record offices, libraries and museums; it started its own journal, *Fortid og Nutid*, in 1914. Another voluntary organisation, the Historisk Samfund for København Amt, more broadly based than the rather academic societies we have mentioned, launched a journal devoted to the history and folklore of Copenhagen County in 1910. By the First World War, new associations were doing much of the work initially envisaged by the ØHTS, which was to develop scholarly studies on cultural and topographic history as well as to receive interest and support from educated people for the development of national institutions.

The journal *Arkiv og Museum* devoted a number of studies to the history of civilian buildings and reported on publications, events and discussions in relation to the town's history. By systematically reviewing the literature, which is classified under two main entries, cultural history and topography, the journal reflects a growing production of what can be labelled as urban history. It also highlights the concern for the destruction and conversely for the protection and the restoration of the historical heritage. For instance, Aage L. Mathiesen and Christian Axel Jensen carried out a long study on the mansion Bremerholm Admiralsgaard, which was destroyed in 1899, and concluded their report by calling for swift and strong action to protect remaining timber-framed buildings.[61] A study was devoted to the so-called Nybørs building. (See Plate 12 /D&E). At the same time, *Arkiv og Museum* reported on the endeavours of the National Museum's 2nd department to survey valuable historic buildings doomed to destruction and collect parts of them upon demolition. Yet, the small staff of the Museum's department could not keep pace with the rapid reconstruction of some inner districts of Copenhagen, especially Gammelmønt and Gråbrødretorv.

The journal praised the collaboration of architects and students at the Academy's School of Architecture with historians to secure the inventory of Copenhagen's historical fabric. Archaeological documentation was also a significant field for the museum. The then assistant M. Mackeprang was in charge of the most notorious excavation site under the ruins of Christiansborg Palace.[62] The contribution of amateur talents could also be of high value. The most exemplary study of this kind was the work of a schoolmaster, H. N. Rosenkjær (1851-1907), who received little institutional support in his lifetime. In the absence of a legal framework for archaeological sites, he attended the demolition of buildings and followed public works so as to survey and draw all that briefly came to light during excavations. His topographical observations of the town has remained until recently the most important documentation archaeologists could rely on. Holger Ramsing (1868-1946), a military engineer who had been in charge of works for the new ring of fortifications around Copenhagen, had also became a self-styled archaeologist with a passion for historic topography. He followed up Rosenkjær's work and developed extensive research.[63] Working both on archive material and on excavations, his studies include a seminal

60 *Arkiv og Museum*, vol. 3, 1905-1908, p. 443.

61 *Arkiv og Museum*, vol. 1, 1899-1902, p. 191-218.

62 The castle drawn by C.F. Hansen at the beginning of the 19th century burnt down in 1884. The construction of the new Christiansborg with the design of T. Jørgensen took place in 1907-1916. The archeological excavation were then undertaken, especially with the hope of finding traces from the fortress of Absalon.

63 *Weilbach*, Vol. 11, p. 595-596.

report on the evolution of Copenhagen's parcelling in the Middle Ages, though he also fell prey to a tendency to extrapolate in the hope of reconstructing a global image of the medieval Copenhagen.[64]

2.3 Foreningen til Gamle Bygningers Bevaring

Foreningen til Gamle Bygningers Bevaring (The Society for the Preservation of Old Buildings) (FGBB) was formed in the second half of 1907 to heighten public awareness of the fate of buildings of historical value all over Denmark, and to contribute to the establishment of a legal framework for their conservation. The law of 1861, Kirkessynloven, had been designed for the protection of ecclesiastic buildings and offered little to safeguard civil constructions. The FGBB has already been the subject of scholarly studies on the general framework of conservation in Denmark, and we shall focus on the early years of the society in relation to the urban development of the capital city only.[65]

The initiative to create the FGBB came in the aftermath of demolition campaigns that had destroyed remarkable historic buildings both in the provinces and in Copenhagen. These had became a bone of contention, as we mentioned earlier. The new society appears to have been the result of joint efforts by the Academy of Fine Arts and the National Museum. Among its founding members there were mostly curators such as W. Mollerup, art historians such as Fr. Beckett (1868-1943), and a strong group of leading architects such as M. Borch, H. Kampmann, M. Nyrop and H. B. Stork. Vilhelm Lorenzen became the secretary of the society and the editor of its bulletin, *Meddelelser fra Foreningen til Gamle Bygningers Bevaring.* Till 1947 Lorenzen acted as a mouthpiece of the FGBB, working tirelessly to convince his fellow Danish citizens of the historical and aesthetic quality of their architectural and urban heritage.

Lorenzen, who had taken his master in history in 1901, had been appointed chairman of a commission set up by the Ministry of Agriculture to improve the design of small rural housing. He had also worked with M. Nyrop in the committee that was set up by the Academy in 1906 to steer up action in order to help upgrade the average quality of buildings and to combat rampant ugliness.[66] He was soon to become a prolific writer on architecture and urban history, and to be associated with the founding of numerous organisations involved in architectural and urban questions. One of these was the Landsforening for Bedre Byggeskik (The National Association for Better Architectural Design) formed in 1915 with the aim of improving the design of ordinary houses and promoting a "homely" builder culture in line with what had been presented at the 1909 National Exhibition in Aarhus. He was also to become a member of the Inspection Commission for Historical Buildings set up in 1918 after the passing of the Bygningsfredningsloven (The Ancient Buildings Conservation Act). His activities illustrate the intimate links between the movement for conservation and town planning in the pre-war years. In 1921, Lorenzen took part in the foundation of the Dansk Byplanlaboratorium (The Danish Town Planning Laboratory).[67]

In its beginning, the FGBB displayed a strong commitment to the Grundtvigian type of approach of national culture an to a modern, scientific conception of conservation. An already informed public that was more and more resentful of a ruthless demolition process probably encouraged the society's founders. Nonetheless, they had to overcome differences and concealed tension between various points of views on preservation issues. For instance, one may assume that the architects from the Academy's had a so-called 'internalist' approach toward the conservation of ancient buildings, while the curators of the National Museum had an 'externalist' approach of architectural artefacts.[68] Since the beginning of the century, there

64 See K. Gabriesen, "Københavns arkæologi og den historiske topografi. Tolkninger fra 1760 til i dag", *Historiske Meddelelser om København,* 1999, p. 9-35 & "At dekonstruere Ramsing", p. 38-58.

65 For the study of the framework of conservation in Denmark, see Michael Ottosen, Bygningsfredningsloven... op.cit. p. 30-36.

66 See, "Byggeriet paa landet", *Architekten,* 4 August 1906, p. 495.

67 On the career of V. Lorenzen, Arne Gaardmand, *Dansk Byplanlægning 1938-1992,* Copenhagen, 1993, pp. 310-11; *Arkitekten,* Vol. LXIII, n°24, 1961, p. 446-447; *Dansk biografisk Leksikon,* 1981, Vol. 9, p. 130-131; *Arkitekten,* n°24, 1961.

68 According to Lorenzen, the Society was initially a joint endeavor of Mollerup and Storck. However, Ottesen drew

had been a lively debate on the conditions applying to proper restoration work, in *Architekten* in particular. In 1901, the journal published a letter by Ferdinand Boberg (1860-1946) to the Swedish Academy requesting proper guidelines for restoration work.[69] The same publication reported a lecture given by W. D. Caroë that sketched out guidelines by striking a balance between the Ruskinian preservationist ethos and a revised post- Viollet-le-Duc 'constructivist-historicist' model still pervading on most of working sites in Northern Europe.[70]

In the year 1905, the Academy's council campaigned vigorously for the enforcement of a legislation to preserve buildings of 'aesthetic value', which were left outside the Church Ministry's narrow jurisdiction; it voted a resolution to that effect addressed to this very ministry.[71] In November 1906, the Akademisk Architektforeningen formed a Committee to draft guidelines which could support a move for a bill in relation to the protection of ancient buildings, and P.V. Jensen Klint, A. Møller, U. Plesner and V.J. Mørk-Hansen signed an appeal to this effect on 10 January 1907, which was published in *Architekten*.[72] During these years, the journal brought forward the topic of conservation to its readership, stressing the respect of all aspects of the built heritage and emphasising the notion of authenticity. This discussion, common to all Europe, has also to be read in terms of a fast developing professional expertise.[73] It thus seems that the tension above mentioned between an 'internalist' attitude, mainly interested in grasping the aesthetic and stylistic cohesion of the 'work of art', and the 'externalist' approach, mainly pursuing an archivist and scientific interest, had steadily decreased, or rather been transcended by a professional outlook that could compose a scientific discourse on conservation. Points of contention could become points of discussion, and this process could sustain a movement for conservation embracing various approaches.

'Old Buildings as 'Radiating Epitomes'

F. Beckett made this gradual process quite explicit two years after the founding of the FGBB in the columns of the weekly *Illustreret Tidende* . While paying due respect to Storck as one of the highest-ranking architects, Beckett invited the master to withdraw from active restoration in favour of a young generation of professional historians who were able to distinguish between the different layers accreted over a building.[74] Personalities, such as Lorenzen, were therefore probably instrumental in the coalescence of the different strands of the conservation movement. Peter Johansen, a prominent member of the Academy who was conversant with urban problematic, seems to have also played an important role in paving the way for such convergence. As already mentioned, Johansen was also active in the FHF and, at one time, a staunch supporter of Andreas Clemmensen's project to 'reconstruct' the square of the Church Sct. Nicholas, as we have seen in the previous chapter. It is interesting here to notice that Johansen was not elected to the FGBB's board, while remaining an active member.[75]

The launch of the Society numbering a hundred of subscribers and the inaugural speech of M. Nyrop, "illuminating even though poorly worded", was widely reported in the press.[76] According to *Berlingske*, Johansen denounced in a "lively and impassioned" manner

attention to the fact that Lorenzen did not mention the latter Mollerup any more. See Ottosen, *Bygningsfredningsloven... op.cit.* p. 34; a preparatory committee, involving Storck, Johansen and Mollerup had been set up between 27 April and 23 May 1907. It appears that Johansen could be an ideal mediator on the conservation question.

69 "Restauring-spogsmaalet i Sverrig", *Architekten*, 15 March 1901, p. 153-155.

70 "Engelsk kritik over Tyske Mindesmaerkers vedligeholdelse", *Architekten*, 22 May 1903, p. 364-366.

71 "Staten and Bygningskunsten", *Architekten*, 15 July 1905, p. 409-412.

72 *Architekten*, 19 January 1907, p.163.

73 In the French context for instance this is not by chance that one of the biggest contributions to scientific conservation had been offered by the "chartist" historian Jules Etienne – Joseph Quicherat (1814-1882) with a career running parallel to the one of Viollet le Duc.

74 See F.Beckett, "Til Professor Herman Baagøe Storck' 70 aars Fødselsdag" (18 February 1909), in *Illustreret Tidende*, 28 February 1909, p. 272.

75 See *Meddelelser fra Foreningen til Gamle Bygningers Bevaring*, 1909 (2), p. 80.

76 *Politiken*, 24 May 1907. Nyrop's intervention was also reported in other newspapers.

the threats to the park of Frederiksberg Palace, the Efterslægten, the house of the Asiatic Company and even the fortifications of Christianshavn. The paper reported that the society's objectives were to foster aesthetic awareness and mobilise citizens, not to substitute itself for the responsibility of the State.[77] *Social-Demokraten* gave also a favourable account of the inaugural meeting, insisting on the fact that ancient buildings should not be treated as a "dead museum".[78] The general attitude was that the Society should, through newspapers, publications and lectures, act as a keen and watchful opponent of vandalism, while realistically concentrating its as yet limited forces on unquestionable cases.[79] The right of the community to its heritage was particularly insisted on "at a time of rising social requirements".[80] The complementary goals of the new society and the FHF were underlined by the then chairman of the later organisation, painter Møller-Jensen, pointing to the central role of conservation in the process of forging new values.

With a 700-strong membership by 1909 and a board of 27, including leading architects, art historians and academics, the FGBB both channelled and stirred within the opinion what has been a diffuse interest for conservation in Denmark. In 1908, Lorenzen felt confident to assert that striving for "progress" could not indefinitely be used as an excuse to play down other social and cultural requirements. Old buildings, long dismissed as "insignificant factors in the life of modern man", could now be rediscovered as "radiating" epitomes of the past[81] — no doubt a link with past generations, a testimony in the shape of a cultural heritage and a precious capital of more than merely utilitarian value. As a result, the ongoing conflict between conservation and speculation should be assessed on more balanced terms, preserving the "public right" to its heritage over private ownership when necessary. However, the FGBB was well aware that the emerging values of conservation were confronted within Copenhagen to the worst examples of vandalism. In 1908, the Society expressed strong reservations about a proposed project concerning the Royal Library on Slotsholmen. Moreover, it was even more difficult for the conservationist standpoint to prevail when confronted with private interests. Despite the strong mobilisation from the National Museum, the Academy, the FHF and the FGBB, all rising in defence of Efterslægten's building —a building of uncontroversial architectural quality situated on one main street of the "old city" —the movement for conservation proved powerless. It was even worse for the Municipal Council, which also failed to efficiently defend the mansion.[82] On the occasion, the FGBB insisted on the notion of the irreplaceable uniqueness of a product of human intelligence to justify the urgent necessity for a general inventory and adapted legislation.[83]

Towards a Legislation

In 1909, the journal of the Society, *Meddelelser fra Foreningen til Gamle Bygningers Bevaring,* published a thoughtful comparative study on conservation laws in various countries. In this article, Lorenzen alluded to the issue of overlapping values enshrined in inherited buildings.[84] He remarked that while the modern concept of "historic value" was on the rise, it was still often subservient to the "work of art" concept — a concept that blurred the historical dimension of the built heritage. Tracing back the modern interest in the ancient "art of building" (bygninskunst) to the vigorous stand of talented authors as Victor Hugo and John Ruskin against 'vandalism' in the nineteenth century, Lorenzen distinguished among three types of intervention that made their ways to reinforce the modern conservation ethos: the royal ordinances and gov-

77 "De Gamle huse", *Berlingske,* 24 May 1907.

78 *Social-Demokraten,* 25 May 1907.

79 *Berlingske,* op.cit.

80 *Politiken,* op.cit.

81 V. Lorenzen, "Fortids Bygninger og Nutids Mennesker", in *Meddelelser fra Foreningen til Gamle Bygningers Bevaring,* 1908, (1), p. 5-13, p. 6.

82 V. Lorenzen, "Hvad kan Staten gøre for at bevare gammel dansk Bygningskunst?", in *Meddelelser fra Foreningen til Gamle Bygningers Bevaring,* 1910, (3), p. 2-10.

83 Idem, p. 5.

84 Riegl's booklet had been published and Lorenzen who collected a large amount of literature on conservation subjects was very likely informed about this work even if he did no refer to it. See Alois Riegl, *Der Moderne Denkmalkultus: Sein Wesen und seine Entstehung,* Vienna, 1903. See, V. Lorenzen, "Lovgivningen og Bevaringen af gamle bygninger udenfor Danmark", in *Meddelelser fra Foreningen til Gamle Bygningers Bevaring,* 1909, (2), p. 3-14.

ernment memorandums protecting public buildings, which were almost compulsory everywhere; the municipal edicts enforcing protection on a particular city, with excellent results for Hildesheim and Nuremberg in Germany as well as for some cities in England and Italy; finally, though less frequently, comprehensive laws protecting public and private buildings equally.

The author drew attention to the fact that the right of property had been difficult to curtail where strong parliamentarian regimes prevailed, in contrast to countries – that one may call countries under colonial domination or influence- where powerful regulations had been enacted, placing "national artistic and historic values" over landowners' liberties. In this regard, Lorenzen mentioned Turkey, Egypt, Tunisia, Bulgaria, Romania, India and Greece. In parallel, he quoted Britain's Ancient Monuments Protection Act of 1882 as the weakest legislation, precisely "where individual liberties are the strongest". By linking the development of measures for conservation to the decline of liberalism that prevailed in the nineteenth century, Lorenzen argued that preservation should go in hand with the extension of public control on urban space through land covenants and compulsory purchase rights. French law is referred to as a chief example for its comprehensive aspect and its innovative system of listing. Italy is hailed for its systematic procedure of registering buildings. Prussia and Saxony are praised for having extended their recent measures to urban and rural sites alike. If Lorenzen deplored the virtual standstill of Danish conservation after the pioneering 1861 Church Inspection Act, he concluded that no ready-made models —certainly not those of Europe's Latin countries— could be transferred to Denmark, with its highly idiosyncratic social relations, legal customs and way of 'consensus building'.

By the time of the 1909 Competition, the FGBB had succeeded in bringing together notably different approaches toward the historical built environment, and managed to organise a sizeable lobby for conservation capable of putting pressure on the institutions. Personalities such as Lorenzen and Johansen, though hailing from different traditions, successfully joined forces: the academic and professional approach to historic buildings on the one hand, and the scientific and archaeological expertise on the other hand, not forgetting however a wider and more diffuse but very lively Grundtvigian tradition based on the feeling of a place's cultural continuity. The notable development in Denmark of "historic topography" as an independent discipline may also account for the successful attempt at fusing these distinct orientations to generate a modern conservation movement that was able to lay, over a period of a few years, the bases of the law on Bygningsfredning (The Preservation of (ancient) Buildings) that was passed in 1918, one year after the law on Naturfredning (The Conservation of Nature).

CONCLUSION

In the first part of this book it has been attempted to record the 1909 event, with special emphasis on the professional milieus that were involved in the Competition. The group-biography, which brought together all the participants, presents a synthetic image of the 'town planner' in early twentieth century, a figure that had been crossed with different professional backgrounds. To architects, engineers, landscape gardeners, and surveyors the competition was a significant step in the development of the careers generally. The competition proved to be of particular importance for German surveyors, who were then trying to enter the field of planning and to support their claims by gaining international recognition. It is also apparent that the Danish competitors built their careers in close relationship with their respective associations, Dansk Akademisk Architektforeningen and Dansk Ingeniørforeningen, which asserted their role as representatives of professional bodies in Denmark at the turn of the century. There is therefore to be observed a strong relationship between the building-up of a professional milieu for architects and civil engineers, and the almost simultaneous expansion of town planning as a new occupational field.

The competition was little remembered at later town planning congresses and exhibitions. In spite of this fact, the development of professional town planning in Northern Europe and the policy of the jury caused the Copenhagen competition to be a powerful catalyst for a majority of contributors, whatever their professional background and nationality, of which a sizeable group enjoyed successful careers in planning in the civil service or in private agencies during the inter-war period.

The second part of this study has been concerned with town plan design, with the analysis of the entries' documents. Bound together by the terms of the problem set by the programme of the Competition, the entries form together a repertory of various orientations. While perfectly reflecting the contemporary search for a rational ordering of productive activities and circulation networks, as well as concern for the improvement of housing conditions, they also reveal a strong consideration given to the existing built and non-built environment. The orientation of the award winner's entries brings testimony of this fact, as do the very character of some of the then most noticed entries, such as Alfred Raavad or Egil Fischer's. We suggest putting this process of design that focused on the inherited character of the place under the umbrella of Civic Art. However, this was by no means the only tendency to find expression in the competition. Moreover, Civic Art was rather heterogeneous in its approach to 'the historicity of the place'. The 'conservationists' tended to privilege heritage as a continuous process, one to built on, while the 'preservationists', more concerned with the formal protection of the built and natural environment, acknowledged the possible bifurcation in the making of the modern urban fabric. Obviously most of the entries lay in-between theses ideal-types.

The third part of this essay has looked at the relationships between extension planning and the emergence of the notion of 'old city'. The competition did not specifically include the question of the city core, but numerous competitors took up the issue. This led us to look more closely at the relationships established between the planning movement and an increasingly efficient network of associations dedicated to the survey, the study, and the protection of the 'historic centre'. City-dwellers' representations of urban space seem to have evolved rapidly during those years and the term 'old city' took manifold meanings. The 'old city' could be made of picturesque relics. But it could also be perceived as a crucible where to renew monumental fervour and as a commitment to the tradition of embellishment. It could be a place of antiquarian interest, and alternatively a field for scientific archaeological research. It was also a place to design a 'city-district' modelled after London's business centre. Though active restoration work did take place, it remained relatively limited. But a myriad of initiatives contributed to the continuous process whereby images of the city were created. Through an analysis of the professional movement, we have found many evidence of a close relationship between conservation and town-planning concerns. Denmark can be rightly compared to countries such as Belgium, Switzerland, Austria and parts of Italy where interest in spatial compromise, allowing for some safeguarding of the city core, infused planning concern among municipal authorities, civic organisations and professionals as well[1] .

Nowadays issues are also a perspective to this book. We do look at the past with questions of the present. There are a number of issues, which we have had in mind, such as: the destiny of the city as a spatially limited entity in the twenty-first century; planning at a low ebb in Europe; uncertainties about the very notion of town or city, when other notions such as 'blanket urbanisation' or 'metropolitan regions' are to the fore. Do "cities" exist today as anything but residual spaces restricted to historic centres, and as receptacles of surviving cultural urban signifiers?

Historic centres do indeed combine the distinctive qualities whereby the city retains some of its seduction. In the last two decades of the twentieth-century, the institutional framework that has allowed heritage to become more and more pervasive has been constantly strengthened. However, such a process is not without ambiguity, as witnessed by a variety of circumventing practices, among which 'facadism'. Recommended by a few in 1900, this technique has extended, because of appropriate buildings techniques and increased profitability.[2] The trend toward an all-encompassing heritage policy, including a few decades old artefacts, has led to the reduction in the average age of the conserved buildings and landscapes and destabilised the existing framework of conservation up to the point of a potential dead end.[3] While urban and architectural forms tend to be diluted, the trend whereby almost anything is considered heritage-worthy implies a fragile present and portends a shaky relationship with the past. This renders the results of decades of urban conservation ambiguous, at a time when 'post-modern' design seems to be blurring the split between the party of 'continuity' and that of 'rupture' with the advent of the 'collage city'.[4]

The treatises of the late nineteenth century carried the promise to 'build the town'. This is precisely what had been attempted, at a time when contemporaries perceived the tell-tale signs of the dissolution of the town, as a threat to both a political entity led by citizen "burghers" and to a physical entity. Among the most obvious signs of such transformations to be reminded of were the loss of spatial boundaries, the increasing importance of traffic areas over public space and the havoc wrought in ancient city centres by urban development schemes. This was accompanied by the proliferation of 'architectural styles' type of buildings when, according to Cornelius Gürlitt's point of view, building was more and more an 'advertising' activity.[5]

After a quarter of century of de-industrialisation,

1 This is also true with the Nordic countries as explained in Chapter I. Per O. Hallman's action in favour of 'Gamla Stan' provides an interesting example, cf. Gösta Selling, *Hur Ombyggnad till omvårdnad 1840-1940*, Uppsala, 1973.

2 Pierre Pinon, "Les origines du façadisme", *Monumental*, N° 14, 1996, p. 9-15. Also, Peter Larkham, *Conservation and the city*, London, 1996, p. 242-245.

3 The listing of "modern" buildings could have a deleterious effect in regard to the maintenance of the earlier "historic" fabric. It has been suggested to radically separate the institutional and financial system of preservation of pre-industrial buildings from the one dealing with later buildings. For a discussion of the great many "perversions" of cultural heritage, see Françoise Choay, *L'Allégorie du patrimoine*, Paris, 1992, p. 158-186.

4 According to Marcel Roncayolo, Town Planning has oscillated since it's beginning between two polarities favouring "continuity" and "rupture" respectively. Both positions have had strong ideological and political underpinnings. However, recession in Europe has played down this former antagonism. See Bernard Lamizer & Pascal Sanson (dir.), *Les langages de la ville*, Marseille, 1997, p. 27-29.

5 "Bâtir devient de plus en plus une réclame" in Cornelius Gürlitt, *Conservation du Coeur d'anciennes villes*, Traduction d'une conférence de M. Gürlitt à Salzbourg, *suivie de La conservation du Coeur de la ville de Bruxelles de C. Buls*, Brussels, 1912, p. 9.

and debate over the 'legibility of the city', there has been a reversal of context at the beginning of the twenty-first century, as the population of cities, at least in Europe, has stopped growing and tends to stagnate, even if the reduction in household size and new culture of 'inhabiting' may involve further sprawl. Even though, the growth of the city may not be the inescapable future it once seemed to be.

But does the city still matter, confronted with generalised ubiquity and with the vanishing of its counterpoint, the countryside? Some of the anxiety about the blurring of limits between town and open land, and about 'urban chaos' might mostly reflect our inability to think in complex sets of spatial forms. Discontinuous and heterogeneous urban fabrics, which are characterised by constant transformation, mixed fluxes, and conflicting forms, may have a puzzling effect preventing us from perceiving the "emerging city".[6] But it could be equally argued that the post-modern 'collage' might only reflect an aestheticizing effect showing up to deflect the questioning of the logic of urban sprawl and the pursuit of the "old vain dream of bigness".[7]

In this sense, the choice of the urban form has been presented as a major debate for citizenship. In view of the limits of functional planning, the appeals to rebuild a discipline of city forms can be seen as a precondition, and the urban project as a step to contain what may be interpreted as a "generalised disaster".[8] Researches on the 'compactness' of the city, urban forms and sustainability, the rediscovery of streets as complex multifunctional spatial entities, projects aiming at enhancing town's entrances are but a few of the new fields opened during the last decade.[9] This movement invites us to explore more attentively not only past urban forms, but also abandoned alternatives, various disciplines and professional traditions, and the diversity of cultural models of a city, all of which were our former 'horizon of expectations'.

We could also consider the enlarging rift that has occurred between two interpretations of town planning: planning understood as a locus of exchange and a field of practices based on experiences derived from different professional backgrounds; and planning seen as a developing autonomous, scientific field. Both conceptions, however, were little differentiated around 1900. The first interpretation of town planning was linked to the development of municipalism, and its scale of intervention was much confined to municipal limits Accordingly, competitions represented a 'symbolic contract' reflecting the state of the civic process, which allowed freedom of exercise through design and its drawing projection techniques cum practice as a key communicative device. The second conception was correlated to the enlargement of state-control over the national territory, and to the reinforcement of an autonomous, comprehensive domain of urban expertise based on the development of formal rationality. Town planning could be understood as regional planning by 1910. The process of differentiation developed as decades went by, marked by the abrasive effect of the First World War over most of Europe's institutions and societies. Design became an ancillary, subservient technique to a more abstract variant of town planning infused by the general post war process of rationalisation.

The 1909 Competition illustrates the strong relationship between the very idea of competition and the attempts by the municipal authorities of the time to present an intelligible figure of the urban form—a great city still perceived as a global entity, a territorial unit to be spatially, socially, and culturally identified and recognised as the product of modern citizenship. Our analysis has shown how a 'school of design' such as Civic Art could be sustained by the professionalizing process among various groups of 'form givers' with strong concerns about the civic and cultural repre-

6 See Yves Chalas, *L'invention de la ville*, Paris, 2000, p. 130-131.

7 See Charles Mulford Robinson, *Modern Civic Art and the City made beautiful*, New York & London, 1904, p. III.

8 David Mangin and Philippe Panerai have suggested principles, which are based in urban morphology, to support the formulation of urban projects in relation to what is identified as the "theoretical crisis of the urban form": *Projet Urbain*, Paris, 1999, p. 8.

9 Advantages of the 'compact city' are discussed in Gert de Roo and Donald Miller, *Compact cities and sustainable urban development, A critical assessment of policies and plans from an international perspective*, Aldershot, 2000. The street has been analysed as a case study inviting other work on the "economy of the urban form", cf. Jean -Louis Gourdon, *La rue – Essai sur l'économie de la forme urbaine*, Paris, 2001.

sentation that could be given to a swiftly expanding industrial port city.[10] In 1900, there were no 'planners' as such, but a wealth of professions both competing and joining forces to present a vision of the city. In this civic endeavour, they combined the creative practice of their own field with the rational method of space-ordering pertaining to the respective professions. Early town planning allowed the technical expertise of municipal engineering departments to interplay with the free run of professionalism through the mechanism of competitions. A clear booster to the development of town planning as a specific field, competitions were devised to encourage the formulation of comprehensive alternatives to what had been widely identified by 1880-1900 as the growing unmanageability of the city.

A number of authors have recently underlined an apparent paradox: the overwhelming process of suburbanisation unfolding in Europe's capital cities combines with a relative paucity of comprehensive analyses on the historical process out of which proceeded this form of built environment, the suburb.[11] This book is not directly concerned with the materiality of this built environment; it rather tries to present a sample of the different conceptions that had been formulated in Denmark in relation to extension planning in the early twentieth century. Our probe of the Copenhagen entries has shown, but for a minority of projects, that the peripheries were generally not thought of as tabula rasa, but regarded in relation to a space-time framework encompassing 'the historicity of places'. Freeing itself from a strict allegiance to the Fine-Arts classical tradition, the new method of design was understood as a means of revealing potentialities and qualities infused through different layers of time into both the inherited built fabric and the landscape. It was also informed by 'historical topography', which had developed by cutting across various professions, as a significant scientific and cultural interest by the 1890s. The movement for the study of the domestic building art was also in this regard a decisive impulse. In our view, the notion of 'historicity of place' in Civic Art design should not be interpreted as a residual aesthetic, nor as the simple derived function of a National Romantic style of architecture. Nor should it be reduced to a kind of social stabiliser in time of "trial of progress" and to cultural conservatism.[12] On the contrary, it seems it was a deliberate, methodical kind of approach to extension planning. It follows that to consider a culturally oriented type of planning as progressively cornered by a more socially-responsible and less local space-obsessed discipline not only misses numerous elements of continuity observable in the inter-war period, but also underestimates the ties between practical concerns at the heart of Civic Art and the search for formal design solutions favouring urban continuity – after all, as perfectly expressed in Karl Strinz's writings, lowering the cost of implementation was one of the main concerns of this 'adaptive' school. This brings out the efforts made by professionals to sustain a basic condition of planning, being its capacity for self-perpetuation, at a time when the institutional framework of planning was still weak.

What, however, was to be the destiny of Civic Art? It is beyond the scope of this study to comment on how some forms have prevailed over others. The change in urban land-use patterns and social relations, innovations in the construction industry, trends in the housing market, evolution in the scope of state intervention, etc., all this has played a part in shaping the constraints on which planners have tried to devise their strategies. One might nevertheless stress that the success and the relative permanence of cultural models of

10 On professionals as form givers, see Paul Meadows, "Cities and professionals", in J. R. Blau, Mark La Gory, John S. Pipkin, *Professionals and Urban Form*, Albany, 1983, p.15-48.

11 J.W.R. Whitehand and C.M.H. Carr have remarked this in: *Twenty-century suburbs, A Morphological Approach*, New York & London, 2001, p. VII. The conceptual and terminological confusion about the on going process of urbanisation is discussed by André Corboz, in "La description: entre lecture et écriture" in A. Corboz, *Le territoire comme palimpseste et autres essais*, Paris, 2001, p. 254-255.

12 See, Anne Rasmussen, "Le progrès en procès" and "Critique du progrès, crise de la science: débats et représentations au tournant du siècle" and Daniel Becquemont, "Herbert Spencer: progrès et décadence", *Mil neuf cent, Revue d'histoire intellectuelle*, n°14, 1996, p. 5-14, 89-113, 69-88. Our conclusion concerning urban design bears some similarity with the analysis of Barbara Miller Lane with regard to 'Romantic architecture' in the Nordic countries during the same period of time, in *National Romanticism and Modern Architecture in Germany and the Scandinavian Countries*, Cambridge, 2000.

town plans closely depended on institutional recognition, and on how easily professions could work with. The eighteenth-century tradition of embellishment has had enduring posterity, ultimately finding expression in manifold neo-classical schools of design. The 'Garden City' model gained lasting worldwide acceptance, though the green suburbs that were actually built had little to do with Howard's proposal. However, with the support of a powerful social movement, the 'Garden City' remained an appealing concept for the design of low-density housing. Both models proved able to renew as well as to perpetuate their emblematic power, as did Otto Wagner's ever-growing Großstadt, a likely archetype of the compact Modern City. Civic Art design presents nothing of the sort, or any model easy to codify and replicate. This probably explains why plans belonging to that school have long remained part of a misty territory. At the risk of oversimplifying, we shall try to sum up here the main features, innovative aspects as well as weaknesses of Civic Art design.

Civic Art design understood cities as accumulated forms out-living their original functions. The dynamism of planning should be self-generated, and consequently the strength of design was before all to bring out a 'conciliatory' and adaptive layout. Conservation came only second, as a potential result of conciliatory measures, the aim of which was to produce a cohesive integrated urban structure.[13]

A peculiar method ensues from this perspective, which provides for a flow of diversity, incorporating as it does the findings of sitology and the inheritance of artificial man-made constraints, such as networks and plot structures. The design of town plans is grounded in local conditions; it is always contextual and therefore fundamentally site-dependant. Such town plans can be best described as expressing a form of 'vertical continuity'.[14] By keeping close to the existing streetscape and housing blocks, the town-plan design maintains a high level of density, thereby producing a homogenous volumetric urban shape. The process of growth of the periphery implies that the 'old centre' retains a generative function. This can be referred to as 'horizontal continuity'.

Thirdly, both types of continuity entrenched in the design practice allow for a degree of mixed functional and social space. Designers were consequently wary of the rough specialisation and spatial segmentation of residence patterns to be found in early planning. They could search for zoning procedures, but in a way looking for detailed arrangement and overlapping or blurring the various zones.

Fourthly, as abundantly illustrated in this study, Civic Art town plans present a high quality of treatment of public open space that is systematically separated from the circulatory space. As a result, squares and public buildings attached to it are Civic Art's true representational space.

The seductive power of this method of design was especially appealing for the municipalities of 'enlightened citizens' and professional groups in the making, looking for a clear break with the Absolutist era and its aesthetic criteria. The more active supporters of the 'social city' were at liberty to adjust their programme to some of these characters, as demonstrated later by Aage Bjerre's effort to adjust some remarkable features of "Urania" to his planning.

The tailored town plans to the individuality of cities, as a balance of innovation and conservation concerns, were thought to be instrumental in resisting what was perceived by many contemporaries as the rapid erosion of urban space. These attributes contributed to the sweeping triumph of Civic Art design in a great many competitions. This process should be considered also in the perspective of the post 1848s years. Halted for some decades in a large part of Europe, the Civic process was revived by the end of the nineteenth century.[15] The town plans competitions then resumed as civic exercises where debates about the work of both the municipalities and professionals enlarged the sphere of the 'Civic city', which en-

13 The social survey assembled pragmatic knowledge and non-systematic components. However, the importance of preliminary surveys prior to the formulation of competition programmes has been emphasised by Camillo Sitte and other planners.

14 Such plans are frequently characterised as 'organic'. Yet, this analytic view seems wide off the mark, as it fails to identify the components of the design method and the distinction between the naturalistic handling of the environment and the juridical-societal empirical knowledge.

15 On this aspect, see Heidede Becker, *Geschichte der Architektur und Städtebauwettbewerbe*, Stuttgart, Berlin, Köln, 1992, esp. p. 99-115.

tailed also the representations of the 'burgher city'. This sphere opened to the emerging 'social city' striving for a balance between middle class aspirations and working class demand for housing. A 'third contender' came in the form of the 'old city'. Its representation and interpretation had still to be adjusted to transmit some sense of continuity and allow for integration into the Great City.

Nonetheless limitations are also apparent. For instance Civic Art design did not resolve the tension between conservation and preservation. As a matter of fact, both 'historicity' and 'heritage' were left open to free interpretation. Selected parts of the historical fabric could be made emblematic of preservation concerns, as with 'Wayland Smed' and 'Anno 77', but they could also be transformed as sources of inspiration, as with 'Urania'. City wide conservation did not give clear guidance as to the scope of alteration allowed, this applying both to the periphery and to the 'old city'.

Furthermore a strong area of tension was perceptible in architecture. Powerful three-dimensional devices, for instance the 'green nucleus' and the 'turbine plazas' worked out by Sitte and his followers, had to be translated in architectonic vocabulary. The design of squares and streetscapes had to be 'regionalized' and 'historicized' in the process of their adoption in various parts of Northern and Eastern Europe by way of competitions. We have looked at how formal choices could oscillate between 'historicism' and 'traditionalism', and a self-acknowledged 'transitional architecture'.

'Historicism' appears as a powerful 'statement of atonement', an ostensible reward paid to past generations by the destructive power of industrial modernity. This symbolic practice was frequently adopted in city centres, as illustrated by the treatment of 'Ny Børsen'. Yet, 'historicist architecture', while tenable for limited schemes, unfailingly contradicted the programme applying to contemporaneous buildings, thereby losing the picturesque character aimed at. 'Traditionalism', represented in Denmark by a wealth of imaginative master builders, engineers and architects, was a very attractive option, for instance in 'Kobenhavn Vaaben 1296'. This trend also permeates 'Anno 77', Fischer or Ahlmann's entry. But in the long run, this alternative suffered from its strong reliance on qualified craftsmanship, a fact that had already sealed the fate of the Arts and Crafts movement in English architecture.

Even more enduring difficulties are to be mentioned. The position of Civic Art does not seem to have gained any stronghold in institutional bodies, especially educational ones. The professional milieus failed also to display full commitment. This can be observed in Denmark despite the strong impulse given by first rank personalities like Martin Nyrop, Hack Kampmann, or P. V. Jensen Klint among others. The status of surveyors in planning at that time has been much discussed in this book. The relation of engineers to Civic Art was significant, as illustrated in the case of Swedish engineers, but still circumstantial. It seems that architects were before all interested in 'distinction' to gain ground within the circles of the Academy of Fine Arts, as evidenced by the careers of most of the actors of the Fri Architektforening, and the subsequent triumph of neo-classicism. Civic Art's key actors could have been the master builders, working in close partnership with municipal authorities. The guilds tradition was still alive in Denmark at the turn of the century. But without a renewed institutional alternative, the temptation was great of looking for ultimate recognition within the Academy. Civic Art did provide for a creative framework in design practice, but it proved unable to organise its reproductive functions within the prevailing institutions.

Notwithstanding these limitations, Civic Art much contributed to interpret and transmit the image of a dense, complex, diversified, and rich urban milieu through competitions and town planning exhibitions. Due to a strong development of cultural and topographical history, Denmark was receptive to this current, which the Competition celebrated. Combined with the fact that the country was not involved in World War I, this may help to explain the pervading influence of this school of design over the years, even if this was reoriented to shape Denmark's very own version of neo-classicism and functionalism[16]. Moreo-

16 In relation to this evolution, see the semantic adjustment made by Vilhelm Lorenzen when he constrasts the 'nordic' and 'classicist' architectural styles: "Nordisk og Klassisk", *Architekten*, n°22, 23, 25, 1914. For an in depth account of the debate within the functionalist movement in Denmark, see Arne Gaardmand, *Dansk Byplanlægning, 1938-1992*, Copenhagen, 1993.

ver, the Competition had a more direct impact and lasting effect. In Copenhagen, much of what today makes for the attractive character of one of the capitals of Nordic Europe, such as Christianshavn's fortifications or the Kastellet was under the threat of partial or total destruction at the beginning of the twenty century. As a whole, the 1909 entries suggested a landscaped conservation of the edges of Christians IV's city. Such an impressive hallmark of reconciliation of forms in time revealed to both citizens and municipal authorities the possibility of preserving the heritage of the city-core while simultaneously allowing for an expansion of the capital. The first large-scale conservation measures that were to be taken in 1918 concerned Christianshavn's fortifications.

Sources

I Archives

Bonn, Stadtarchiv

Personal Akten betr. Karl Strinz : PA 1957/ 2080 / D.

Copenhagen, Stadsarkivet

Ejendomsdirektorat – Hovedjournalsager – Sag EJ 1150 /1925 –.

kassette nr. 1; kassette nr. 2; kassette nr. 3; kassette nr. 4.

Stadsingeniørens Direktorat, Byplankontoret / Alm. Adm./ BP-sager, 1918-1984, sag 977: Bebyggelsesplan af 1909 om Københavns ydre Distrikter.

Stadsingeniørens Direktorat, Byplankontoret / Alm. Adm./ Register til BP-sager, 1918-1984.

Stadsingeniørens Direktorat, Byplankontoret / Alm. Adm./ Register til Journal A1 – 1918-1931.

Stadsingeniørens Direktorat, Byplankontoret / Alm. Adm./ Journal A1 – 1918-1931/ 1, 2, 3.

Stadsingeniørens Direktorat, Byplankontoret / Alm. Adm./ BP-sagsoversigt, 1918-1984.

Stadsarkitektens Journal 1908 / Journal 1909 /Journal 1910.

Stadsarkitektens Direktorat, Journal A, 1937-1949.

Kort- og Tegningssamlingen / IV-C. 1908-1909 /- 67; 68; 69; 70; 71; 72; 73; 74.

Kort- og Tegningssamlingen / IV-C. 1908-1909 /- Gengivelser af Konkurrenceprojekter vedrørende Københavns ydre Distrikter, 1909.

Konkurrenceprojekter vedrørende Københavns ydre distrikter/ J.nr. 625/1909.

København – de indlemmede distrikter – byplanmæssig udvikling 1901-1941; udgivet af stadsingeniørens direktorat, 252 sider i 1/4 format, 207 illustrationer, deponeres i Stadsarkivet 15/9-74.

Privat arkiver, Arkitekt Vilh. Kleins Papirer, P2-7, Reg. 40.

Copenhagen, Landsarkivet for Sjælland, Lolland-Faster & Bornholm

Foreningen til Hovedstadens forskønnelse (FHF).

FHF / generelle sager G:13: Byggeloven, m.m.

FHF / generelle sager G:14: Byplanlægning, 1917—40 ; Naturfredning 1910-39.

FHF/ bestyrelsens forhandlingsprotokol, 1906-12.

FHF / behandlede sager pk. nr. 11: ydre Distrikters bebyggelse 1907-1910.

FHF / behandlede sager, pk.nr. 16: Bymuseet, Rådhus samlingerne 1910-34.

FHF / behandlede sager, pk.nr. 20: Nobel og Rasmussens Forslag til Regulering ; Christianshavns vold, 1910-17.

FHF / behandlede sager, pk. nr. 27: det gamle Banegårdsterræn, Bebyggelsen af, 1909-17.

Copenhagen, Rigsarkivet

Ministeriet kirke og undervisnings væsenet /06: Kommissionen af 6.2.1905 ang. Ordningen af undervisningen i de for arkitekter, bygmestre og håndværkerne nødvendige tekniske discipliner m.m.

Privatarkiv, Ambt, Charles, nr. 5023.

Privatarkiv, Martin Nyrop, nr. 1447.

Privat arkiv, Vilhelm Marstrand, nr. 8002.

Copenhagen, Kommunens Bygge- og Teknikforvaltning, Plandirektorat

Papers of Karl A. Ottesen, Konkurrencen om de indlemmede distrikter 1908-1909, 4 pakker.

Copenhagen, Kunstakademiets Bibliotek, Architektur-Samlinger

Drawings of Brummer, Carl; Fischer, Egil; Schiødte, Erik; Schroeder, Rolf.

Wetzlar, Historisches Archiv
Bericht über den Wettbewerb zur Erlangung eines Bebauungsplanes für die Stadt Wetzlar und Niederschrift der Beschlüsse des Preisgerichts, 21 Märtz 1925.
Erläuterungen zu der Ausschreibung des Bebauungsplanes der Stadt Wetzlar, April 1924.
8 Pläne des entwurfes von Karl Strinz.

II Periodicals consulted

With the list below are given the years and, in some occasions only, the particular months in brackets, that is 1 for January, 2 for February, etc., which have been under systematic probe for the periodical concerned. References of articles from these periodicals are to be found in the notes.

Danish Newspapers
Berlingske politiske og Avertissementstidende: 1908 (1), 1909 (3, 4, 5, 6).
København: 1909 (5, 6).
Illusteret Tidende: [1898, 1899, 1900, 1905, 1907-1910.
Politiken: 1907-1909, 1914.
Social-Demokraten: 1900 (1, 2, 3), 1905 (1, 2, 3, 4, 5, 6), 1907 (5), 1909, 1910.

Danish Journals
Absalon, 1909-1910.
Arkitekt-Foreningens Tidskrift: 1908-1909.
Arkitekten-Tidsskrift for Bygningsvæsen: 1898-1901.
Architekten, Meddelelser fra Akademisk Architektforening: 1898-1901; 1902-1923.
Dansk Byplanlaboratorium, Meddelelser udsendt af, 1922-1926.
Den Tekniske Forenings Tidsskrift: 1888.
Fra Arkiv og Museum: 1899-1915.
Før og Nu, Historisk, Topografisk Tidsskrift: 1915-1916.
Førskønnelsen-Illustreret Tidsskrift udgivet af Foreningen til Hovedstadens Forskønnelse: 1911-1916, 1923-1925.
Gartner-Tidende: 1907-1915.
Historiske Meddelelser om København: 1907- 2001.
Ingeniøren- Udgivet af Dansk Ingeniørforening: 1898-1910, 1912, 1923.
Københavns Borgerrepræsentanters Forhandlinger: 1909-1910.
Maanedsskrift for Sundhedspleje: 1908-1909, 1917-1919.
Meddelelser fra Foreningen til gamle Bygningers Bevaring: 1908-1922.
Stads- og Havneingeniørforeningens Maanedsmeddelelser: 1910-1921; 1922-1923.
Tekninger af Ældre Nordisk Architektur: 1884-1913.
Tidsskrift for Industri: 1908-1909.

Other European Journals
Arkitektur och Dekorativ Konst: 1901-1914.
Art Public, (L'): 1907-1912.
La Construction Moderne: 1906-1909.
Le Bâtiment: 1907-1909.
The Builder:1908-1909.
The Town Planning Review: 1910.
Deutsche Bauzeitung: 1908-1910.
Der Städtebau: 1904-1905, 1907-1910.
Gartenstadt – Mitteilungen der Deutschen Gartenstadgesellschaft: 1910-1912.
Journal des géomètres- experts français: 1923.
Schweizerische Bauzeitung: 1908-1909.
Zeitschrift für Vermessungswesen: 1904-1943.
Verbands-Zeitschrift – Preussicher Landmesservereine in den Provinzen Schlesien und Posen und des Vereins der Vermessungsbeamten der Preussischen Landwirtschatlichen Verwaltung: 1908-1909.

III Books and Articles

ABENDROTH, Alfred, *Der Landmesser im Städtbau*, Berlin, Paul Parey, 1909.
ABERCROMBIE, Patrick, "International contributions to the study of town Planning and the city Organisation", *Town Planning Review*, N°2, Vol IV, 1913, p. 98-99.
AMBT, Charles, "Om Planer til Byers Udvidelse og Bebyggelse", *Den Tekniske Forenings Tidsskrift*, 1888-1889, p. 81-90.

Asmussen, Otto (red.), *København, som den er og som den burde være*. Udgivet af Foreningen til Hovedstadens Forskønnelse, Copenhagen, 1914.

Baumeister, Reinhard, *Stadt-Erweiterungen in technischer, baupolizeilicher und wirtschaftlicher Beziehung*, Berlin, Ernst & Korn, 1876.

Beckett, Francis, *Københavns Raadhus, opført, 1893-1905*, Copenhagen, August Bang Boghandels Forlag, 1908.

Bernoulli, Hans (red.), *Städtebau – Ausstellung Bern 1914, Spezialkatog* (herausgegeben vom Schweizerischen Städteverband), Zürich, Aschmann & Scheller, 1914.

Brix, Joseph, Genzmer, Felix, *Hochbahgesellschaft, Grundplan für die Bebauung von Gross-Berlin.Mit einem ersten Preise ausgeseichnet*, Berlin, 1911.

Breidahl, Axel og Kjerulf, Axel, *Københavnerliv-gemt og glemt i alvor og skaemt 1883-1912*, København A.G.F. Forlag, 1938.

Buls, Carl, *L'esthétique des villes*, Bruxelles, Bruylant-Christophe & Cie, 1893.

Christensen, Villads, *København i Kristian den Ottendes og den syvendes Tid 1840-1857*, Copenhagen, 1912.

Christensen, V., "Københavns Magistrat 1840-1919", *Historiske Meddelelser om København*, Vol 8 (1.rk.), 1921-1922, p. 36-45

Clerget, Pierre, "L'urbanisme, étude historique, géographique et économique", *Bulletin de la Société neuchateloise de géographie*, 1910, p. 213-231.

Commission du Vieux Paris, *Procès Verbaux*, Paris, Imprimerie Municipale, 1899-1909.

Dansk ingeniørforening gennem 50 aar 1892-1942, Udgivet af D.I.F, København, Det berlinske bogtrykkeri, 1942.

Deutschen Städte-Ausstellung Dresden 1903 (Amtlicher katalog der), Dresden, Verlag und Druck von Wilhelm Baensch, 1903.

Eberstadt, Rudolf, Mörhing, Bruno, Petersen, Richard, *Gross Berlin:ein programm für die Planung der neuzeitlichen Grossstadt*, Berlin, 1910.

Engelstoft, Poul og Jul. Wulff, *Danmarks kommunale forvaltning*, Copenhagen, Selskabet Vort Samfund, 1929.

Faßbender, Eugen, *Erläuterungen zum Entwurfe eines General-Regulirungsplanes über das gesammte Gemeindegebiet von Wien*, Wien, 1893.

Faßbender, E., *Ein Volksring für Wien, Ein Vorschlag siner Vaterstadt*, Wien, Lechner, 1898.

Faßbender, E. *Grundzüge der modernen Städtebaukunde*, Leipzig und Wien, Deuticke, 1912.

Fischer, Egil, "Byplanlægningens Love", in Asmussen, otto. (red.), *København, som den er og som den burde være*. Udgivet af Foreningen til Hovedstadens Forskønnelse, Copenhagen, 1914, p. 43-77.

Fournier, Emile, *Paris démoli*, Paris, Éd. Arly, 1855.

Friis-Møller, Kai, *Det skønne København*, Copenhagen, V. Pios Boghandel, 1917.

Geddes, Patrick, *Cities in Evolution:an Introduction to the Town Planning Movement and to the Study of Civics*, London, Williams and Norgate, 1915.

Geddes, P., *City Development, A report to the Carnegie Dunfermline Trust*, Shannon, Irish University Press, 1973.(First ed.1904).

Giovannoni, Gustavo, "Vecchie città ed Edilizia Nuova", *Nuova Antologia,* Fascicolo 995, 1913, p. 449-472.

Giovannoni, G., "Il "diradamento" edilizio dei vecchi centri-il quartiere della rinascenza in Roma", *Nuova Antalogia*, Fascicolo 997, 1 Iuglio 1913, p. 53-76.

Gnudtzmann, Alb & lind, Helmer, *Stor-København, skildringer og billeder af byen og dens liv i vore dage*, 2 volumes, Copenhagen / Christiana, Gyldendalske boghandel Nordisk forlag, 1907.

Goecke, Theodor, "Allgemeine Städtebau-Ausstellung, Berlin 1910", *Der Städtebau*, 7/8 Heft, 1910, p. 73-92.

Gürlitt, Cornelius, *Conservation du Coeur d'anciennes villes, Traduction d'une conference de M.Gürlitt à Salzbourg, suivie de La conservation du Coeur de la ville de Bruxelles de C. Buls*, Bruxelles, Ed. Tekhne, 1912.

Hallman, P.O. "Principerna fôr anläggandet eller utvidgandet af en stad eller stadsdel", in *Förhandlingarna vid Nordiska Teknikermötet i Stockholm 15-19 Juni 1897*, Stockholm, 1898, p. 170-174.

Hansen, Heinrich, *Historiske Meddelelser om Københavns Bygningsvæsen og dets Personale*, Copenhagen, 1931

Hegemann, Werner, *Der Städtebau nach den Ergebnessen der Allgemeinen städtebau- ausstellung in Berlin nebst einen Anhang die internationale Städtebau- Ausstellung in Düsseldorf*, 2 vol., Berlin: E. Wasmuth, 1911-1913.

HEGEMANN, W. & PEETS, Elbert, *The American Vitruvius:an Architects' Handbook of Civic Art*, New York, Architecture Book Publ.Co., 1922.

HENRICI, Karl, *Beiträge zur praktischen Ästhetik im Städte Bau – eiene samlung vom Vorträgen und Aufsätzen.* München, Verlag V. Georg D.W.Callwey, 1904.

HENRICI, K., *Preisgekrönter Konkurrenz-entwurg zu der Stadterweiterung*, München, L. Merner, 1893.

HOFFSTEDT, W., *Förhandlingarna vid Nordiska Tekniker-mötet i Stockholm den 15-19 Juni 1897*, Stockholm, Central –Tryckeriet, 1898.

HOLSØE, Poul, "Fra Kjøbenhavnske torve og Gader", *Gads danske Magasin*, 1910-1911, p. 281-289.

INDENRIGSMINISTERIETS SANERINGSUDVALG, *Betaenkning*, Copenhagen, A/S J.H. Schultz Bogtrykkeri, 1938.

INTERNATIONAL CITIES AND TOWN PLANNING EXHIBITION. *Jubilee Exhibition Gothenburg Sweden 1923*, Göteborg, 1923.

Internationale Hygiene Ausstellung, Dresden 1911- Vorsitzende und Mitglieder der wissenschaftlichen Gruppen, n.d., n.ed.

JANSEN, Herman, *Vorschlag zu einem Grundplan für Groß-Berlin*, München, 1910.

JERPERSEN, R., (red), *Biografiske oplysninger angaaende den polytekniske Læreanstlats kandidater 1829-1929*, Copenhagen, Dansk Ingeniørforening, 1930.

KLINT P.V.J., *Bygmester Skolen*, Copenhagen, Gyldendal, 1911.

LARSEN Alfred, SCHIØDTE Erik, *Gamle Kjøbenhavnske Huse og Gaarde*, Copenhagen, Foreningen Fremtiden, 4 Vol., 1894-97.

LILIENBERGER, Albert, "Législation urbaine en Suède", in *Où en est l'urbanisme en France et à l'ètranger, Société française des urbanistes*, Paris, Librairie de l'Enseignement technique, Léon Eyrolles Éditeur, 1923, p. 124-129.

LIISBERG, Bering, *København i gamle dage og Livet i Kobenhavn*, Copenhagen, H. Hagerups Forlag, 1901

LORENZEN Wilhem, "Lovgivningen og Bevaringen af gamle bygninger udenfor Danmark", in *Meddelelser fra Foreningen til GamleBygningers Bevaring*, 1909, (2), p. 3-14.

LORENZEN W., "Om bevaring af gammel bygningskunst" in ASMUSSEN, OTTO. (red.), *København, som den er og som den burde være.* Udgivet af Foreningen til Hovedstadens Forskønnelse, Copenhagen, 1914, p. 117-128.

LYAUTEY, Hubert "Comment on sauve l'art d'un pays, Conférence donnée à l'Université des Annales le 10 decembre 1926", in *Paroles d'Actions: Madagascar, Sud Oranais, Oran Maroc (1900-1926)*, Paris, A.Colin, 1927, p. 444-457.

MARSTRAND, Jacob, *Tilbageblik gennem et langt Liv*, Copenhagen 1928.

MARTIN, Camille et BERNOULLI, Hans, *L'urbanisme en Suisse*, Neuchatel, Ed. Delachaux et Niestlé S.A., 1929

MØLLER, H.C.V., "København Havn", in D.Bruun & al. *Danmark Land og Folk-Historisk-topografisk, Statistic Haandbog.* Vol 4, Copenhagen & Christania, 1922.

NOVI, Cajus Th., *Copenhagen old and new from an architectural point of view, A lecture delivered to the international visits association*, Copenhagen, J. Cohens Printing House, 1912

NYROP, C., *Bidrag til Dansk Haandværkerundervisnings Historie ved Det Tekniske Selskabs halvhundredeaarige Jubileum den 18. September 1893*, Copenhagen, Nielsen & Lydiche, 1893.

PETERSEN, A. G. V.(red.), *Beretning om Den Tekniske og Hygiejniske Kongress i Kjøbenhavn den 24.-27. Juni 1903*, Copenhagen, Jørgensen & Co, 1904.

POËTE Marcel & BONNIER, Louis *Commission d'Extension de Paris, Aperçu historique et considerations techniques preliminaires*, Paris, Chaix, 1913.

PREMIER CONGRÈS INTERNATIONAL D'ASSAINISSEMENT ET DE SALUBRITÉ DE L'HABITATION, Paris, 1-8 novembre 1904, Paris,Jules Rousset, 1905.

PREMIER CONGRÈS INTERNATIONAL ET EXPOSITION COMPARÉE DES VILLES, Bruxelles, Union internationale des villes, 1913.

PROCHAZCA, Ladislas " Sur la prétendue opposition des exigences de l'hygiène moderne avec la sauvegarde du caractère historique des villes" in *Premier Congrès International d'Assainissement et de Salubrité de l'Habitation*, Paris, Jules Rousset, 1905, p. 108-112.

RIEGL, Alois, *Der Moderne Denkmalkultus:Sein Wesen und seine Entstehung*, Vienna, W. Braumuller, 1903.

ROBINSON, Charles Mulford, *Modern Civic Art or the City Made Beautiful*, New York and London, G. P. Putnanm's Sons, 1903.

RUSKIN, John, *The seven lamps of architecture*, New York, Dover Publications, Inc, 1989 (first pub.1880).

RAAVAD, Alfred J., *En bog om dansk byplanlægning, For embedsmænd under stat og by, folkerepræsentanter, ingeniører og arkitekter samt skattydende borgere (gående, ridende og kørende; sejlende og flyvende)*, Copenhagen, Arkitektforening,1929

SCHOU, Charles I., *Om Bybygningskunst indledningsforedrag til bybygnings studier*, Copenhagen, P. Haase & Søns Forlag, 1923.

SCHUMACHER, Fritz, *Wie das Kunstwerk Hamburg nach dem grossen Brande erstand*, Hamburg, Hans Cristians Verlag, 1969 (first pub.1917).

SITTE, Camillo, *Der Städte-bau nach seinen künstlerischen Grundsätzen*, Wien, Verlag von Karl Graeser, 1922, (First ed.,1889).

SOCIÉTÉ FRANÇAISE DES URBANISTES, *Où en est l'urbanisme en France et à l'étranger?* Paris, Eyrolles, 1923.

STATUTS DE LA SOCIÉTÉ D'ART PUBLIC, Genève, Imp. La Tribune de Genève, 1908.

STÜBBEN, Joseph, *Der Städtebau*, Darmstadt, Bergsträsser, 1890

SUNDBÄRG, Fredrik, "Om stadsplaner med särskild hänsyn till svenska förhaallanden", *Ord och Bild*, 1897, p. 145-160 & 193-213.

SØRENSEN, J. et C.F.V. BOOCK, "L'organisation du cadastre en Danemark et son développement depuis le moyen-âge jusqu'en 1910 – & le cadastre de Copenhague", in *Congrès national et international de géomètres – Bruxelles 1910; comptes-rendus et rapports*, Bruxelles, Imp. Feron, 1911, p. 230-247.

THOMSON, Charles, *Les conditions de travail en Danemark, Rapport adressé au ministre des affaires étrangères*, Paris/Nancy, Berger-Levrault et cie, ed., 1891.

TROISIÈME CONGRÈS INTERNATIONAL DE L'ART PUBLIC, Liège, 15-21 September, Bruxelles, 1905.

UNWIN, Raymond, *Town Planning in practice, an introduction to the art of designing cities and suburbs*, London, Adelphi terrace, 1911, (First ed.1909).

WAAGENSEN, H., Kort over Kjøbenhavn – Kjøbenhavns lokale kommunikationer, Copenhagen, 1886, (reprint 1975).

WAGNER, Otto, *Die Groszstadtt. Eine Studie über Diese*, Wien, Verlag Schroll, 1911.

WEYL, DR.Th., *Die Assanierung von København,* Leipzig, Von Whil. Engelmann, 1921.

REFERENCES

AAKJÆR, Svend, LEBECH, Mogens og NORN, Otto, *København før og nu*, 5 volumes, Copenhagen, Alfred G. Hassings Forlag, 1949.

ABU-LUGHOD, Janet, *Rabat, Urban Apartheid in Morocco,* Princeton, Princeton University Press, 1980.

AHLSTAND, Janb Torsten, ERICSSON, Anne-Marie, ERNSTELL, Micael, HOVSTADIUS, Barbro, KARLSSON, Eva-Lena, KNUTSSON, Johan, LINE, Björn, NOLIN, Catharina, NORDIN, Svante, NYSTRÖM, Bengt, RAUSING, Birgit, *Konsten 1890-1915,* Lund, Signums Svenska Konsthistoria, Bokoförlaget Signum, 2001.

AHNLUND, Mats & BRUNNSTRÖM, Lasse, "The Company Town in Scandinavia" in GARNER, John S., (ed.) *The Company Town, Architecture and Society in the Early Industrial Age,* New York, Oxford, Oxford University Press, 1992.

ALGREEN-USSING, Gregers, BEK, Lise, FRANSEN, Steen Bo, HANSEN, Jens Schjerup, *Urban Space and Urban Conservation Aesthetic Problem,* Analecta Romana Instituti Danici suppl. XXVII, Rome, L'Erma di Bretschneider, 2000.

ALGREEN-USSING, Gregers, "Surveying architectural values in the environment in Denmark", *Interplan,* N° 9, 1991.

ALSTRUP, Inge, LA VOUR, Lisa (red.), *Byplanuddannelsen i Danmark 1930-til 1997.* Copenhagen, Dansk Byplanlaboratorium, Byplanhistoriske Noter, 38, 1997.

ANDERSEN, Kirste, *De første år : Byplanhistorisk Udvalg 1982-1999.* Copenhagen, Dansk Byplanlaboratorium, 1999.

ANDERSSON, Lilian, *Mellem byråkrati och laissez faire – en studie av Camillo sittes og Patrick Geddes stadsplaneringsstrategier,* Göteborg, Acta Universitatis Gothoburgensis, 1989.

ARNOLD, Dana (ed.), *The Metropolis and its Image – Constructing Identities for London, c. 1750-1950,* London, Blackwell, 1999.

ARTARIA, Paul & Hans SCHMIDT (Hrsg.), *Aus dem Skitzzenbuch eines Architekten,* Basel, B.Wepf, 1943.

BANIK-SCHWEITZER, Renate, "Zugleich ist auch bei der Stadterweiterung die Regulierung der innern Stadt im Auge zu behalten. Wiener Alstadt und Ringstraße im Tertiärisierungsprozeß des 19. Jahrhunderts" in FELH, Gerhard & RODRIGUEZ – LORES, Juan, *Stadt-Umbau, Die planmäßige Erneuerung europäischer*

Großstädte zwischen Wiener Kongreß und Weimarer Republik, Basel, Birkhäuser, 1995, p. 127-147.

Becker, Heidede, *Geschichte der Architektur- und Städtebauwettbewerbe*, Stuttgart / Berlin /Köln, Verlag W. Kohlhammer Gmbh & Deutscher Gemeindeverlag, 1992.

Bek, Lise o.a. (red), *Syn for rum – om byens og landskabets æstetik.* Aarhus, Aarhus Universitet Forlag, 1993.

Beller, Steven, *Rethinking Vienna 1900*, New York, Oxford, Berghahn Books, 2001.

Berdoulay, Vincent & soubeyran, Olivier, *L'écologie urbaine-aux fondements des enjeux actuels*, Paris, Éd. La découverte, 2002.

Bidstrup, Knud, *Ebenezers disciple – fra dansk byplanlægnings pionertid*, Copenhagen, Dansk Byplanlaboratorium, 1971.

Bjur, H, *Stadsplanering Kring 1900 med exempel från Göteborg och Albert Lilienbergs verksamhet*, Göteborg, Chalmers Teknika Högskola, 1984.

Blasen, Svend og Jensen, Hans Ejner, *Landmåling og landmålere – Danmarks økonomiske opmåling*, Copenhagen, Den danske Landinspektørforening, 1975.

Blau, Eve & Platzer, Monica, *L'idée de la grande ville, l'architecture moderne d'Europe centrale, 1890-1937*, Munich, Prestel, 2000

Blau, Judith R, La Gory, Mark, Pipkin, John, *Professionnals and Urban Form*, Albany, State University of New York, 1983.

Bolenz, Eckhard, *Vom Baubeamten zum Freiberuflichen Architekten, Technische Berufe im Bauwesen (Preußen/Deutschland, 1799-1931)*, Frankfurt am Main, Bern, New York, Paris, 1991.

Bollerey, F, Fehl,G, Hartmann (Hrsg.), *Im Grünen wohnen-im Blauen planen, Ein Lesebuch zur Gartenstadt mit Beiträgen und Zeitdokumenten*, Hamburg, Hans Christians Verlag, 1990.

Bramsen, B.(red.), *København før og nu – og aldrig*, 11 volumes, Copenhagen, Forlaget Palle Fogtdal A/S, 1987-1990.

Breitling, Peter, "The role of the competition in the genesis of urban planning :Germany and Austria in the nineteenth century", in A. Sutcliffe (ed.), *The Rise of Modern Urban Planning 1800-1914*, London, Mansell, 1980.

Briggs, Asa, "The Philosophy of Conservation", *Journal of the Royal Society of Arts*, October 1975, p. 685-695.

Bro, Henning, "Frederiksberg-storbykommunen i hovedstaden", *Historiske Meddelelser om København*, 2001, p.161-181.

Broadbent, Geoffrey, *Emerging concepts in urban space design*, London/ NewYork, Van Nostrand Reinhold, 1990.

Brulhart, Armand, *Guillaume Henri Dufour, Génie civil et urbanisme à Genève au XIXe siècle*, Lausanne, Payot, 1987.

Buhl, Hans & Jørgen Fink (red.), *Made in Denmark? Nye studier i dansk teknologihistorie*, Århus, Forlaget Klim, 1994.

Byskabsanalyse – ydre Nørrebro, Report issued by København Kommune, Overborgmesterens Afdeling, Plan- og Ejendomsdirektoratet, Copenhagen, 1997.

Burrage, Michael and Torstendahl, Rolf, *Professions in Theory and History, Rethinking the Study of the Professions*, London, Sage Publications, 1990.

Calabi, Donatella, *Marcel Poëte et le Paris des années vingt, aux origines de "l'histoire des villes"*, Paris, L'Harmattan, 1997.

Caldenby, Claes, Lindvall, J., Wang, W. (ed.), *20th-Century Architecture Sweden*, Munich / New York, Prestel, 1998.

Carter, Harold, *The study of urban geography*, London, Arnold, 1995.

Castex, Jean, Depaule, Jean Charles, Panerai, Philippe *Formes urbaines :de l'ilot à la barre*, Paris, Dunod, 1980.

Centre de recherche sur la rénovation urbaine, Institut d'Architecture de l'Université de Genève, Préface by André Corboz, *1896-2001, Projet d'urbanisme pour Genève*, Geneva, Georg editeur, 2003.

Chalas, Yves, *L'invention de la ville*, Paris, Anthropos, 2000.

Choay, Françoise, *La règle et le modèle, sur la théorie de l'architecture et de l'urbanisme*, Paris, Seuil,1980.

Choay, F., *L'Allégorie du patrimoine*, Paris, Seuil, 1992.

Christensen, Dan Ch., *Det Moderne Projekt, Teknik & Kultur i Danmark-Norge 1750-1814-1850*, Copenhagen, Gyldendal, 1996.

Christiansen, Jørgen Hegner, *Bygningsbevaring – en kommenteret bibliografi.* Copenhagen, Bygningsteknisk Studiearkiv, 1982.

Cohen, Jean louis, Lortie, André, *Des fortifs au périf, Paris, les seuils de la ville*, Paris, Picard & Editions du Pavillon de l'Arsenal, 1991.

Collins, George R., Crasemann, Christiane Collins, *Camillo Sitte and the Birth of Modern City Planning*, London Phaidon Press, 1965.

Corboz, André, *Le territoire comme palimpseste et autres essais,* (Presenté par Sebastien Marot), Paris, Les éditions de l'imprimeur, 2001.

Cramer-petersen, Lars, "Brønshøj sogn, indlemmelsen af nordvest", *Historiske Meddelelelser om København*, 2001, p. 107-115.

Crouch, Christopher, *Design Culture in Liverpool 1880-1914: the Origins of the Liverpool School of Architecture*, Liverpol, Liverpool University Press, 2002.

Dahlmann Olsen, Nina, "Den fri architektforening ", *Architectura* –10, 1988, p. 84-132.

Dahlmann Olsen, Nina, *Arkitekten Ivar Bentsens unge år 1900-1920*, Copenhagen, Foreningen til gamle Bygningers Bevaring, 1992.

Damsgård, Ole, Johansen, Jens, *Byplan bøger i 77 år. Udgivelser fra Dansk Byplanlaboratorium 1921-1998*, Copenhagen, Dansk Byplanlaboratoriums skriftserie, nr. 46, February 1999.

De kulturhistoriske bevaringsinteresser – nyere tid. Report issued by Fortidsminderådet, Copenhagen, 1981.

Degn, Ole, *Urbanisering og industrialisering – en forskningsoversigt*, Copenhagen, Akademisk Forlag, 1978.

Degn, O., "Oversigt- fra topografi og begivenheder til erhversliv og sociale forhold – dansk byhistorier 1967-1992", *Fortid og Nutid*, 1993.

Delafons, John, *A Policy History of the Built Heritage 1882-1996*, London, Spon, 1997.

Deland, Mats, *The Social City, Middle-way approaches to housing and suburban governmentality in southern Stockholm 1900-1945*, Stockholm, Novum Grafiska, 2001.

Depaule, Jean Charles, Demorgon, Marcelle, *Analyse Urbaine*, Marseille, Éd. Parenthèses, 1999.

Dethier, Jean, Guiheux, Alain, *La ville, art et architecture en Europe, 1870-1993*, Paris, Editions du Centre Pompidou, 1994.

Dirckinck-Holmfeld, Kim, Langkilde, H.E. et al. *Arkitekten 100 år*, Copenhagen, Arkitektens Forlag, 1998.

Dufournet, Paul, *Architecture, Urbanisme, Paysage, L'apport des modèles antique dans l'occident moderne. Continuité, rupture, retour-* Extrait des actes du Colloque consacré à l'influence de la Grèce et de Rome sur l'Occident moderne, Paris, Ecole Normale Supérieure, 14,15, 19 decembre 1975, Paris, Les Belles Lettres (Académie d'Architecture), 1977.

Dybdal, Lars, *Byplan og boligmiljø efter 1800*, Copenhagen, Gyldendal, 1973.

Dybdahl, Vagn, *Det nye samfund på vej*, 1871-1913; Vol5, Copenhagen, Gyldendal/Nordisk Forlag A/S, 1979.

Eaton, Ruth, *The Spirit of Copenhagen*, Copenhagen, P.J. Schmidt A/S, 1996.

Elliot, James, *The City in Maps – urban mapping to 1900*, London, British Library, 1987.

Epron, Jean Pierre, *Comprendre l'éclectisme*, Paris, Éd. Norma, 1997.

Etting, Vivian et al., *De kulturhistoriske interesser i lanskabet*, Copenhagen, Miljø- og Energiministeriet & Skov-og Naturstyrelsen, 1996.

Faludi, Andreas, Van der Valk, Arnold, *Rule and Order: Dutch Planning Doctrine in the Twentieth Century*, Dordrecht, Kluwer, 1994.

Federspiel, Søren, "1.maj, Fælledparken og borgmester Jensen" in *Historiske Meddelelser om København*, 1990, p.100-141.

Felh, Gerhard, *Kleinstadt, Steildach, Volksgemeinschaft, Zum "reaktionären Modernismus" in Bau und Stadtbaukunst*, Wiesbaden/ Braunschweig, Fridr. Vieweg, 1995.

Felh, Gerhard, Rodriguez –Lores, Juan, *Stadt-Umbau, Die planmäßige Erneuerung europäischer Großstädte zwischen Wiener Kongreß und Weimarer Republik*, Basel, Birkhäuser, 1995.

Finsen, Helge, *Arkitekten Ulrik Plesner*, Copenhagen, Arkitektens forlag, 1951

Fischler, Raphaël, "Toward a genealogy of planning: zoning and the Welfare State", *Planning Perspectives*, Vol. 13 (4), 1998, p. 389-410.

Flyberg, Bent, *Rationality and Power – Democracy in Practice*, Chicago – London, The University of Chicago Press, 1998.

FORCHHAMMER, Olaf (red.), *København – De indlemmede Distrikter byplanmæssig Udvikling 1901-1941*, Copenhagen, Stadsingeniørens Direktorat, 1942.

FORCHHAMMER, Olaf (red.), *København fra Bispetid til Borgertid- Byplanmæssig Udvikling til 1840*, Udgivet af Stadsingeniorens Direktorat, Copenhagen, J.H. Schultz Forlag, 1947.

FREUND, Julien, *Etude sur Max Weber*, Paris, Droz, 1990.

FUNDER, Lise, *Arkitekten Martin Nyrop, København*, Copenhagen, Foreningen til gamle Bygningers Bevaring, 1979.

GAARDMAND, Arne, *Dansk byplanlaegning 1938-1992*, Copenhagen, Arkitektens Forlag, 1993.

GABRIELSEN, Karsten, "Kobenhavns arkeologi og den historiske topografi-tolkninger fra 1760 til i dag", *Historiske Meddelelser om København*, 1999, p. 9-35.

GABRIELSEN, K., "At Dekonstruere Ramsing", *Historiske Meddelelser om København*, 1999, p. 38-58.

GANAU, Joan, "Town Planning and Conservationist policies in the Historic City Centre of Barcelona, 1860-1930", *Planning History*, Vol.19, (2/3), 1997, p. 23-31.

GARNER, John S. (ed.), *The company town- Architecture and society in the early industrial age*, New York – Oxford: Oxford University Press, 1992.

GEJL, Ib (red.) *Århus, byens historie, 1870-1945*, Vol.3, Århus, Århus byhistoriske Udvalg, 1998.

GIEDON, Siegfried, *Space, Time and Architecture*, Cambridge Mass., Harvard University Press, 1959.

GLAHN, Henrik Egede (red.), *Foreningen af 3.December 1892-Festskrift i anledning af 100-aarsdagen.*, Copenhagen, Kunstakademiets Forlag Arkitektskolen og Arkitektens Forlag, 1992.

GLAMANN, Kristof, *Øl og Marmor, Carl Jacobsen på Ny Carlsberg*, Copenhagen, Gyldendal, 1995.

GOODMAN, David & COLIN Chant (ed.), *European Cities and Technology – Industrial to post-industrial City*, London, Routledge. 1999

GOURDON, Jean Louis, *La rue, essaie sur l'économie de la forme urbaine*, Paris, L'Aube,2001.

GRANGE, Daniel J., POULOT, Dominique (dir.), *L'esprit des lieux, le patrimone et la cite*, Grenoble, Presses Universitaires de Grenoble, 1997

HABRAKEN, N. J., *The structure of the ordinary: form and control in the built environment*, Cambridge Mass., MIT Press, 1998.

HALL, Peter, *Cities in civilizations, Culture, Innovation, and Urban Order*, London, Phoenix Giant, 1999.

HALL, P., *Cities of Tomorrow, An Intellectual History of Urban Planning and Design in the Twentieth Century*, London, Basil Blackwell, 1988.

HALL, Thomas "Planning history: recent developments in the Nordic countries, with special reference to Sweden", *Planning Perspectives*, Vol. 9. (2), 1994,, p.153-179.

HALL, T. (ed.), *Planning and Urban Growth in the Nordic Countries*. London / New York, E&FN Spon, 1991.

HALL, T., *Planning Europe's Capital Cities, Aspects of Nineteenth-Century Urban Development*, London, E& FN Spon, 1997.

HARNOW, Henrik, *Den danske ingeniørs historie 1850-1920*, Aarhus, Systime A/S, 1998

HARTMANN, Kristiana, "Städtebau um 1900, Romantische Visionen oder pragmatische Aspekte", in MECKSEPER, Cord, and SIEBENMORGEN, Harald (eds), (*Die Alte Stadt: Denkmal oder Lebensraum? Die Sicht der mittelalterlichen Stadtarchitektur in 19. und 20. Jahrhundert*, Göttingen, Kleine Vandenhoeck-Reihe, 1985, p. 90-113.

HARTMANN, Sys, VILLADSEN, Villads, *Danmarks Arkitektur, Byens huse, Byens Plan*, Copenhagen, Gyldendal, 1979.

HIETALA, Marjatta, "La diffusion des innovations, Helsinki 1875-1917", *Genèses* 10, Juanary 1993, p. 74-89.

HILSTED, Finn, *1885-1985 – Forenigen til Hovedstadens forskønnelse*, Copenhagen, Nyt Nordisk Forlag – Arnold Busck, 1985.

HOLM, Axel, JOHANSEN, Kjeld, *København 1840-1940, Det Københavnske Bysamfund og Kommunens Økonomi*, Copenhagen, Nyt Nordisk Forlag –Arnold Busk, 1941.

HUMLUM, Johannes, *Landsplanlægning i Danmark*, Copenhagen, Gyldendalds Uglebøger, 1961

HYLDTOFT, Ole, "From fortified Town to Modern Metropolis. Copenhagen 1840-1914", in Hammarström, Ingrid og Thomas Hall (Red.) *Growth and Transformation of the Modern City*. Stockholm, 1979.

HYLDTOFT, Ole, *Københavns Industrialisering 1840-1914*, Aarhus, Systime Forlag A/S, 1984

HYLDTOFT, O., *Danmark okonomiske historie, 1840-1910*, Aarhus, Systime Forlag A/S 1999.

JANSEN, Henrik M., RIIS, Thomas, STRØMSTADT, Poul *A select bibliography of Danish works on the history of towns,1979-1982,* Odense, Dansk Komite for Byhistorie, 1983

JANSEN, H. M., *A select bibliography of Danish works on the history of towns published 1960-1976*, Odense, Dansk Komite for Byhistorie, 1977.

JAUSLIN, Manfred, "Hans Bernoulli", in RUCKI, Isabelle und Dorothee HUBER (Hrsg.), *Architektenlexikon der Schweiz 19./20. Jahrhundert*, Basel – Boston – Berlin, Birkhäuser Verlag, 1998, p. 51-53.

JEHLE-SCHULTE STRATHAUS, Ulrike, STEGMANN, Markus, *Hans Bernoulli- aus den skizzenbüchern, Architekturmuseum Basel*, Basel-Boston-Berlin, Birkäuser Verlag, 1996.

JENSEN, Sigurd, SMIDT, Claus M., *Rammerne sprænges-Københavns historie*, Vol. 4, Copenhagen, Gyldendalske boghandel, 1982.

JENSEN, S., *Under fælles ansvar – Københavns historie*, Vol. 5, Copenhagen, Gyldendalske boghandel, 1981

JENSEN, Hannelene Toft (red.), *Byatlas København – bevaringsværdier I byer og bygninger*, Copenhagen, Skov- og Naturstyrelsen, kontoret for bybevaring, 1996.

JENSEN, Sven Allan & Svend JENSEN, "Byplanlægningens institutioner", i CHRISTIANSEN, Ole mfl., *De gode hensigter – en mosaik om byplanlægning*. Copenhagen, Dansk Byplanlaboratoriums Skriftserie, nr. 31, 1984, p. 34-39.

JOKILEHTO, Jukka, *A History of Architectural Conservation*, Oxford, Butterworth & Heinemann., 1998.

JÜRGEN, Paul, "Der Wiederaufbau der historischen Städte in Deutschland nach dem Zweiten Weltkrieg" in MECKSEPER, Cord, SIEBENMORGEN, Harald (Hrsg.), *Die alte Stadt: Denkmal oder Lebensraum? Die Sicht der mittelalterlichen Stadtarchitektur im 19. und 20. Jahrhundert*, Göttingen, Vandenhoeck & Ruprecht, 1985, p. 114-156.

JØRGENSEN, Caspar, KNUDSEN, Tim, MØLLER, Anders, "Charles Ambt og gadeplanlægningen i Vestervold kvarter", in *Historiske Meddelelser om Copenhagen*, 1989, p. 85-107.

JØRGENSEN, C., *Aspekter af citydannelsen i København : En analyse af samspillet mellem funktionsskift og kommercielle bygninger i det indre København ca. 1870-1911*. Utrykt specialeafhandling i historie ved Københavns Universitet, 1986.

JØRGENSEN, C. "Affolkning og citydannelse i det indre København 1855-1985", *Fabrik og bolig*, nr. 2, 1987, s. 3-17.

KAIN, Roger (ed.), *Planning for conservation*, London, Mansell, 1981.

KAIN, Roger J. P., BAIGENT, Elisabeth, *The Cadastral Map in the Service of the State. A History of Property Mapping*, Chicago /London, The University of Chicago Press, 1984.

KARNAU, Oliver, *Hermann Josef Stübben – Städtebau 1876-1930*. Braunschweig/ Wiesbaden, Fr. Vieweg & Sohn Verlag, 1996.

KARSPERSEN, Lars Bo, *Associationalism-some reflections on the Danish society*, paper given at the ECPR Joint Session, Torino, March 2002.

KARSTEN, Gabrielsen, "København archæologi og den historisk topografi, Tolkninger fra 1760 til i dag", i *Historisk Meddelelser om København*, 1999, p. 9-35.

KERN, Stephen, *The Culture of Time and Space 1880-1918,* London,Weidenfeld and Nicolson, 1983.

KILDEGAARD, Bjarne (red.), *Drømmen om det 20. århundrede*. Copenhagen, Nationalmuseet, 1998.

KING, Anthony D., "Town planning a note on the origins and use of the term", *Planning History Bulletin*, Vol. 4 (2), 1982, p.15-16.

KIRKEBY, Inge Mette, "Interessen for det historiske hus", *Nordisk Arkitekturforskning*, (4), 1995, p. 103-118.

KJÆRSDAM, Finn, *Fysisk planlægning og anvendt videnskab*. Stockholm, Nordplan & Aalborg, Aalborg Universitetsforlag, 1985.

KNUDSEN, Tim, "Paradigmer og professionskampe i den tidlige danske byplanlægning", *Fabrik og Bolig*, (1), 1988, p. 3-21.

KNUDSEN, T., Historieløse planlæggere, *Byplan* 5-6, 1988, p.166-169.

KNUDSEN, T., *Storbyen støbes – København mellem kaos og byplan 1840-1917*. Copenhagen, Akademisk Forlag, 1988.

KNUDSEN, T., "International influence and professional rivalry in early Danish planning", *Planning Perspectives*, Vol. 3 (3), 1988, p. 297-310.

KNUDSEN, T, *København stadsingeniørinstitution 1858-1950,* Institut for Samfundsfag og forvaltning, i Københavns Universitet, Forsikningsrapport 1985/5.

KNUDSEN, T., *Mod del planlagte København; Kampen for planlægningen 1840-1917*, Licenciatafhandling, Copenhagen University, 1985.

KONTER, Erich, " Verheißungen einer Weltstadcity, Vorschläge zum Umbau "Alt-Berlins" in den preisgekrönten Entwürfen des Wettewerbs Groß-Berlin von 1910", in FELH, Gerhard & RODRIGUEZ –LORES, Juan, *Stadt-Umbau, Die planmäßige Erneuerung europäischer Großstädte zwischen Wiener Kongreß und Weimarer Republik*, Basel, Birkhäuser Verlag, 1995, p. 249-272.

KOPP, Anatole, BOUCHER, Fréderique, PAULY, Danielle, *L'architecture de la Reconstruction en France, 1945-1953,* Paris, Éditions du Moniteur, 1982.

KOSELLECK, Reinhart, *Futures Past, On the Semantics of Historical Time*, Cambridge Mass./ London, The MIT Press,1985.

KRAGELUND, Minna, "Martin Nyrop-vor mest dansksindede arkitekt", in KRAGELUND, Minna, *Det gode haandværk. Traaden i dansk tradition*, Hovedland, 2001.

KRISTENSEN, Johansen, *Dansk ingeniørforening gennem 50 aar, 1892-1942*, Copenhagen, Dansk Ingeniørforening, 1942.

LA COUR, Lisa, NETTERMANN, Christa, *Mallings Samling – en avisudklipsamling om byplanlægning*, Copenhagen, Danmarks Biblioteksskole – Specialeopgave, 1980.

LADD, Brian K., *Urban Planning and Civic Order in Germany, 1860-1914*, Cambridge Mass., Harvard University Press, 1990.

LADD, B. K., "Urban aesthetics and the discovery of the urban fabric in the turn of the century Germany", *Planning Perspectives*, Vol. 2 (3), 1987, p. 270-286.

LAMIZET, Bernard, SANSON Pascal, *Les langages de la ville*, Marseille, Editions Parenthèses, 1997.

LAMY, Yvon (dir.), *L'alchimie du patrimoine, discours et politiques*, Talence, Editions de la Maison des Sciences de l'Homme d'Aquitaine, 1996.

LANGBERG, Harald, *Uden for voldene Københavns udbygning 1852-1952*, Copenhagen, Den almindelige Brandforsikring, 1952.

LANZA, Elena Cogato, MARTI, Paul, "Braillard und Bernoulli als Stadtebauer", *Werk, Bauen & Wohnen* (5), May1995, p. 60-65.

LARKHAM, Peter J., *Conservation and the City*, London / New York, Routledge, 1996.

LARSON, Magali Sarfati, "The formation of professions", in TORSTENDAHL, Rolf and BURRAGE, Michael, *The formation of professions, knowledge, state, and strategy*, London, Sage, 1990, p. 24-50.

LARSON, M. S., "Emblem and Exception: The Historical Definition of the Architect's Professional Role", in BLAU, Judith R, LA GORY, Mark, PIPKIN, John's, *Professionnals and Urban Form*, Albany, State University of New York, 1983, p. 49-86.

LAURIDSEN, John T., "Byhistorien – en genre i spændetrøje eller under faglig fornyelse?", *Historie*, (1) 1999, p. 89-106.

LAURIDSEN, John T., MOGENSEN, Margit (red.), *København – porten til Europa. En antologi.* Copenhagen, Det kongelige Bibliotek, Rigsarkivet og Tøjhusmuseet. 1996

LEBECH, Mogens, *Københavnske projekter – det København som aldrig blev*, Copenhagen, Stig Vendelkærs Forlag, 1973.

LICHTENBERGER, Elisabeth, *Vienna, Bridge between cultures*, London and New York, Belhaven Press, 1993.

LINDE-LAURSEN, Anders, *Hugo Matthiessens kulturhistorie, belysninger og baggrunde*, Højbjerg, Forlaget Hikuin, 1989.

LIPSTAD, Hélène, "Architectural Publications, Competitions, and Exhibitions", in Eve BLAU and Edward KAUFMAN (ed.), *Architecture and its image, Four Centuries of Architectural Representation*, Montreal-Centre Canadien d'Architecture, Cambridge Massachusetts, The MIT Press, 1989.

LOWENTHAL, David, *The Past is a Foreign Country*, Cambridge, Cambridge University Press, 1985.

LORENZEN, Vilhelm, *Drømmen om den ideale By*, Copenhagen, Rosenkilde og Bagger, 1947.

LORTIE, André, "Dessins de villes et destins de plans", in *Quels desseins pour les villes, de quelques objets de planification pour l'urbanisme de l'entre-deux-guerres*, dossiers T.T.S, Ministères de l'Equipement, du Logement et des Transports, n°20/21, Octobre 1992, pp 285-293.

LOYER, François, *Paris XIXe siecle, l'immeuble et la rue,* Paris, Éd. Hazan, 1994.

LUQUE, Jose, "Architecture and Town Planning :Uninterrupted Dialogue; The birth of the two first urban planning tradition" in *Planning History*, Vol 24, n°2 &3, 2002, p. 35-42.

LÜTZEN, Karin, *Byen tæmmes,Kernefamilie, sociale reformer og velgørenhed i 1800-tallets København*, Copenhagen, Hans Reitzels forlag, 1998.

Lyhne, Vagn, Nielsen, Kristian Berg (red.), *Tankebygninger, Arkitektur og Kunsthåndværk, 1851-1914*, Århus, Klim, 1994.

Madsen, Hans Helge, *Chicago – København: Alfred Råvads univers*, Copenhagen, Gyldendal, 1990.

Mangin, David, Panerai, Philippe, *Projet Urbain*, Marseille, Éditions Parenthèses, 1999.

Malling, Vilhelm C., *København i søgelyset, – noget af et puslepil – Foreningen til Hovedstadens Forskønnelse 1885-1960*, Copenhagen, 1960.

Malling, V.C., *Rundt i Byen-Lidt stof til efter tanke*, Copenhagen, Tutein & Koch, 1959.

Malling, V.C., *Nogle byplanproblemer*, Vol. 2, Copenhagen, Dansk Byplanlaboratorium, 1951.

Marcus, Aage (red.), *Det kongelige akademi for de skønne kunster 1904-1954 – med en kort udsigt over akademiets historie 1754-1904*, Copenhagen, Gyldendal, 1954.

Martens, Mina, "Buls", *Biographie Nationale*, publiée par l'Académie Royale des Sciences, des Lettres et des Beaux Arts de Belgique, supplément T.II (Fasc. I), Bruxelles, Emile Bruylant, 1958.

Meckseper, Cord, Siebenmorgen, Harald (Hrsg.), *Die alte Stadt: Denkmal oder Lebensraum? Die Sicht der mittelalterlichen Stadtarchitektur im 19. und 20. Jahrhundert*, Göttingen, Vandenhoeck & Ruprecht, 1985.

Meller, Hélène, *Patrick Geddes: Social Evolutionist and City Planner*, London, Routledge, 1990.

Mellerup, Einer, *Det gamle København på vrangen*, Copenhagen, Fremads fokusbøger, 1964.

Millech, Knud, Fisker, Kay, *Danske arkitekturstrømninger 1850-1950.* Copenhagen, udgivet af Østifternes Kreditforening, 1951.

Miller Lane, Barbara, *National Romanticism and Modern Architecture in Germany and the Scandinavian Countries*, Cambridge, Cambridge University Press, 2000.

Mollik, Kurt, Reining, Hermann, Wurzer, Rudolf, *Planung und Verwirklichung der Wiener Ringstrassenzone*, Wiesbaden, Franz Steiner Verlag GMBH, 1980.

Mogensen, Margit, *Eventyrets tid – Danmarks deltagelse i Verdensudstillingerne 1851-1900*, Copenhagen, Landbohistorisk Selskab, 1993.

Muller, John, "From survey to strategy: twentieth century developments in western planning method", in *Planning Perspectives*, Vol. 7 (2), 1992, p. 125-155.

Møller, A. M., Dethlefsen, H., Johansen, H. C., *Dansk søfarts historie*, Vol. 5, *Sejlag damp, 1870-1920*, Copenhagen, Gyldendal, 1998.

Møller, Poul, *Københavns bystyre gennem 300 år, II-1858-1940*, Copenhagen, udgivet af Københavns Borgerrepræsentation, 1967.

Møller, Jan, *Borger i klunketidens København- på Frederik 7.s og Christian 9.s tid*, København, Forlaget Sesam, 2000.

Mørup, Finn Jensen (red.), *Nye vilkår, nye opgaver, Dansk Byplanlaboratorium 1971-1981*, Copenhagen, Dansk Byplanlaboratorium, 1981.

Nationalmuseet (Udgivet af), *Historiske Huse i det gamle København – Fortegnelser over bevaringsvaerdige aeldre bygninger i Bispestad og Ny København*, 1972.

Nägelin-Gschwind, Karl, *Hans Bernoulli – Architekt und Städtebauer* (Preface von Mario Botta), Basel - Boston- Berlin, Birkhäuser Verlag, 1993.

Nielsen, Vagn Rud, *Byplanlægning og ældre bydele. Foreningen til gamle bygningers bevaring.* Copenhagen, Vilh. Priors Kgl. Hofboghandel, 1951.

Nissen, Nis, *Københavns bybygning 1500-1856, visioner planer forfald*, Copenhagen, Arkitektens Forlag, 1989.

Nørlund, Poul (red.), *Bygningsfredning gennem 25 Aar*, Copenhagen, G.E.C. Gads Forlag, 1943.

Nørregaard-Nielsen, Hans Edvard, *Ny Carlsbergfondet 1902-2002*, Copenhagen, Gyldendal, 2002.

Opmaalinger – Foreningen af 3. december 1892. *Festskrift i anledning af 100-årsdagen*, Copenhagen, Kunstakademiets Forlag, Arkitektskolen og Arkitektens Forlag, 1992

Ottosen, Michael, *Dansk Bygningsrestaurerings historie – en indføring*, Arkitektskolen i Aarhus, Arkitektskolens skriftserie, n.1., 1984.

Ottosen, M., *Bygningsfredningsloven – historie og princip*, Aarhus, Archipress, 1984.

Panerai, Philippe, Depaule, Jean-Charles, Demorgon, Marcelle, *Analyse urbaine*, Marseille, Éditions Parenthèses, 1999.

Paulsson, Thomas, *Den glöma staden, Svensk stadsplanering under 1900-talets början med särskild hänsyn til Stockholm*, Stockholm, Stockholms kommunalförvaltning, 1959.

PETERSEN, Anne Marie Steen, *Som i et stof – en forskning om Grundtvigskirken og dens bygmester*, Copenhagen, Gyldendal, 1997.

PETERSEN, Vibeke and CHRISTENSEN, Inga, "Stuktidens vindskibelighed. Sanering for de fattige –boliger for de fine", *Historiske Meddelelser om København*, 1982, p. 136-171.

PICCINATO, Giorgio, *Städtebau in Deutschland 1871-1914. Genese einer wissenschaftliche Disziplin*, Brunschweig / Wiesbaden, Fr. Vieweg & Sohn Verlag, 1983.

PIGAFETTA, Giorgio & ABBONDANDOLO, Ilaria, *Architecture traditionaliste, Les théories et les oeuvres*, Sprimont, Pierre Mardaga, 1997.

PINON, Pierre, "Les origines du façadisme", *Monumental*, N°14, septembre 1996, p. 9-15.

POMIAN, Krzysztof, *L'ordre du temps*, Paris Gallimard, 1984.

PORFYRIOU, Heleni "Artistic Urban Design and Cultural Myths:The Garden City Idea in Nordic Countries, 1900-1925", *Planning Perspectives*, Vol. 7 (3), 1992, p. 263-301.

PORFYRIOU, H., "Lo spazio publico come luogo civile", *Arredo Urbano* 1989, n°32, p. 106-119.

POULOT, Dominique, "Le patrimoine universel :un modèle culturel Français", *Revue d'Histoire Moderne et Contemporaine*, Vol.34, 1992, p. 29-55.

PRICE, Nicholas Stanley, TALLEY Jr., M.Kirby, VACCARO, Alessandra Melucco (ed.), *Readings in Conservation. Historical and Philosophical Issues in the Conservation of Cultural Heritage*, Los Angeles, The Getty Conservation Institute, 1996.

PROUDFOOT, Peter R., "The symbolism of the crystal in the planning and geometry of the design for Canberra", *Planning Perspectives*, Vol. 11 (3) 1996, p. 225-257.

RÅDBERG, Johan, *Doktrin och Täthet i svenskt stadsbyggande 1875-1975*, Stockholm, Byggforskningsrådet, 1988.

RAFFESTIN, Claude *Pour une géographie du pouvoir*, Paris, Édition Litec, 1980.

RASMUSSEN, Anne, "Le progrès en procès", "Critique du progrès, crise de la science: débats et représentations du tournant du siècle", *Mil neuf cnet – Revue d'histoire intellectuelle*, Vol. 14, 1996, p. 5-14, 89-113.

RASMUSSEN, Steen Eiler, *København – et bysamfunds særpræg og udvikling gennem tiderne*, Copenhagen, G.E.C. Gads Forlag, 1994.

RECHT, Roland, *Penser le patrimoine*, Paris, Hazan, 1999.

REEH, Henrik, *Storbyens ornamenter : Siegfried Krakauer og den moderne bykultur*, Odense, Odense Universitetsforlag, 1991.

REEH, H., *Urbane dimension: tretten variationer over den moderne bykultur*, Odense, Syddansk Universitetsforlag, 2002.

REPS, John W., *Canberra 1912: Plans and Planners of the Australian Capital Competition*, Melbourne, Melbourne University Press, 1997.

RICHMOND, Peter, *Marketing Modernisms: The Architecture and Influence of Charles Reilly*, Liverpool, Liverpool University Press, 2001.

RIIS, Thomas, Jann M.Witt (Hrsg.), *A tale of two Cities, Berlin – Kopenhagen 1650-1930*, Odense, Odense University Press, 1997.

RODRIGUEZ- LORES, J., "Stadt-Umbau und Elendsviertel, zur grundrentenbildung in der innerstadt", in FELH, Gerhard & RODRIGUEZ –LORES, Juan, *Stadt-Umbau, Die planmäßige Erneuerung europäischer Großstädte zwischen Wiener Kongreß und Weimarer Republik*, Basel, Birkhäuser, 1995.

RONCAYOLO, Marcel, *Lecture de villes, formes et temps*, Marseille, Editions Parenthèses, 2002.

SAGARRA, Eda, *A social history of Germany, 1648-1914*, London, Methuen, 1977.

SAUNIER, Pierre-Yves, "Changing the City: urban international information and the Lyon municipality, 1900-1940", *Planning Perspectives*, Vol. 14 (1), 1999, p. 19-48.

SCHORSKE, Carl E, *Fin-de-siècle Vienna, Politics and Culture*, Cambridge, Cambridge University Press, 1981.

SCHMID, Werner, *Hans Bernoulli – Städtebauer, Politiker, Weltbürger*, Schaffhausen, Verlag Peter Meili, 1974.

SELLING, GÖSTA, *Hur Gamla stan överlevde, Från ombyggnad till omvårdnad 1840-1940*, Stockholms, Stockholms Stadsmuseum, 1973.

SESTOFT, Jørgen, "Industriens arkitektur og historicismen", *Fabrik og Bolig*, nr. 2, 1979, p. 3-12.

SESTOFT, J. & J CHRISTIANSEN, Jørgen Hegner, *Guide til Dansk Arkitektur 1, år 1000-1960*, Copenhagen, Arkitektens forlag, 1995.

SKALL, Egil, "Københavns Rådhus 75 år", *Historiske Meddelelser om København*, 1980, p. 28-58.

SMETS, Marcel, *Charles Buls, Les principes de l'art urbain*, Liège, Éditeur Pierre Mardaga, 1995.

Smidt, Claus M. & Anne Mette Nayberg, *Det blev på papiret – københavnske arkitekturprojekter gennem fire århundreder, katalog af udstillingen afholdes af Selskabet af arkitekturhistorie*, Copenhagen, Selskabet af Arkitekturhistorie, 1996.

Sonne, Wolfgang, *Hauptstadtplanungen 1900-1914. Die Repräsentation des Staates in der Stadt*, Dissertation ETH Nr. 14098, Den Eidgenössischen Technischen Hochschule Zürich, 2001.

Sonne, W., "Ideen für die Großstaddt: Der Wettbewerb Groß-Berlin 1910", in Scheer, Thorsten, Kleihues, Josef Paul, Kahlfeldt, Paul, *Stadt der Architektur. Architectur der Stadt, Berlin 1900-2000*, Berlin, Nicolai, 2000, p. p. 67-77.

Schultz, Hans Joakim, *Dansk Turisme i 100 år 1888-1988*, Copenhagen, Danmarks turistråd, 1988.

Strathaus, Jehle-Schulte, Stegmann, Ulrike und Markus, *Aus den Skizzenbüchern*, Basel-Boston- Berlin, Birkhäuser Verlag, 1996.

Sutcliffe, Anthony, *Towards the Planned City, Germany, Britain, The United States and France, 1780-1914*, Oxford, Basil Blackwell, 1981.

Sutcliffe, A. (ed.), *The Rise of Modern Urban Planning 1800-1914*, London, Mansell, 1980.

Svendler Nielsen, Hans Peter, "Bedre Byggeskik", *Erhvervshistorisk årbog 1979 – meddelelser fra Erhvervsarkivet*, Århus, 1979, vol. 29, p. 98-126.

Sommer, Anne-Louise, *Arkitektur & design – Politikens bog om kunstforståelse*, Copenhagen, Politikens Forlag A/S, 1995.

Szambien, Werner, "Les concours de l'an II", in Jacques, Annie, Mouilleseaux, Jean-Pierre (dir.), *Les architectes de la liberté 1789*-1799 (Catalogue de l'exposition), Paris, École nationale supérieure des Beaux-arts, 1989, p. 181-202.

Søllinge, J.D., & Thomsen, N., *De Danske Aviser, 1634-1898*, Vol. 2: *1848-1917*, Odense, Odense Universitetsforlag, 1989.

Sørensen, Esben Munk (red.), *Ejendomsændringer i det 20. Århundrede*, Copenhagen, Den danske Landinspektørforening, 2000.

Tapié, Victor, *Baroque et classicisme*, Paris, Le Livre de Poche, 1980.

Tarr, Joel and Dupuy, Gabriel, *Technology and the rise of the networked city in Europe and America*, Philadelphia, Temple University Press, 1988.

Thernstrom, Stephan and Sennett, Richard, *Nineteenth-Century Cities-Essays in New Urban History*, New haven / London, Yale University Press, 1969.

Tofte, Ulla, "Anlæggelsen af Ryvangskvarteret i København", *Fabrik og Bolig*, n°1, 1999, p. 3-21.

Torres i Capell, Manuel, Llobet i Bach, Josep, and Puig i Castells, Jaume, *Inicis de la urbanistica municipal de Barcelona: mostra dels fons municipals de plans i projectes d'urbanisme, 1750-1930*, Barcelona: Ajuntament de Barcelona, Corporacio Metropolitana de Barcelona, 1986.

Torres i capell, Manuel de, "Barcelona: planning problems and practices in the Jaussely era, 1900-1930", *Planning Perspectives*, Vol. 7 (2), 1992, p. 211-233.

Torstendahl, Rolf and Burrage, Michael, *The formation of professions, knowledge, state, and strategy*, London, Sage Pub., 1990.

Tschudi-Madsen, Stephan, *Restoration and Anti-Restoration, A study in English Restoration Philosophy*, Oslo-Bergen-Tromsø, Universitetsforlaget, 1976.

Tung, Anthony M., *Preserving the World's Great Cities, The Destruction and Renewal of the Historic Metropolis*, New York, Clarkson Potter Publishers, 2001.

Tyrwhitt, Jacqueline (ed.), *Patrick Geddes in India*, London, Lund Humphries, 1947.

Vacher, Hélène, "Byplaner og kulturelle modeller den internationale konkurrence I 1908 om Kobenhavn efter indlemmelserne", *Historiske Meddeleser om Kobenhavn*, 2001, p. 61-81.

Vacher, H., *Projection coloniale et ville rationalisée-le rôle de l'espace colonial dans la constitution de l'urbanisme en France, 1900-1931*, Aalborg, Aalborg University Printing House, vol. 33, 2001.

Vacher, H., "Henri Prost: the colonial experience", *Nordic Journal of Architectural Research*, vol. 9, n. 3, 1996, p. 67-80.

Vacher, H., "Building the Modern City – Planners and Planning Expertise at the École spéciale des travaux publics" (1898-1939)", *Planning Perspectives*, Vol. 17 (1), 2002, p. 41-60.

Vacher, H., "L'enseignement technique et l'émergence du génie civil au Denmark au XIXe siècle", in Efmertová, Marcela (ed.), *50 Let Fakulty Elektrotechnické CVUT*, Prague, Nakladatelstvi Libri, 2003, p. 48-71.

Varming, Kristofer, Lorenzen, Vilhelm, *Dansk Arkitektur gennem 20 Aar 1892-1912*, Copenhagen, Erslev & Hasselbach, 1912.

Vibæk, Jens, "Debatten om Københavns 3. hovedbanegård", *Historiske Meddelelser om København*, 1989, p. 136-169.

Voltaire, "Des embellissements de Paris", *Oeuvres*, Vol. 30, Paris, Stoupe Imprimeur, 1792.

Vernez Moudon, Anne, "The origins and development of the International Seminar on Urban Form", *Urban Morphology* (1), 1997, p. 3-10.

Wagner, Michael F., *Det Polytechniske gennembrud-romantikkens teknologiske Konstruktion 1780-1850*, Århus, Århus Universitetsforlag,1999.

Ward, Stephen V., *Planning the twentieth-century city:the advanced capitalist world*, London, John Wiley & Sons, 2002.

Weber, Klaus K., "Hans Bernoulli in Berlin (1902-1912)", *Archithèse* (6), November/Dezember, 1981, p. 10-12.

Weil, Marc, *La transition urbaine ou le passage de la ville pedestre à la ville motorisée*, Sprimont, Mardaga, 1999.

Wetterberg, Ola, *Monument och miljö. Perspektiv på det tidiga 1900-talets byggnadsvärd i Sverige*. Göteborg, Chalmers Tekniska Högskola, 1992.

Whitehand, J. W. R., Carr, C. M. H, *Twentieth-Century Suburbs. A Morphological Approach*, London, Routledge, 2001.

Wieczorek, Daniel, *Camillo Sitte et les débuts de l'urbanisme moderne*, Bruxelles, Éd. Mardaga, 1981.

Wiehmann Matthiessen, Christian, *Atlas over Danmark, Vol. 3 – Danske byers vækst*, Copenhagen, Det Kongelige Danske Geografiske Selskab, 1985.

Wilson, William H. *The City Beautiful movement*, Baltimore & London, The Johns Hopkins University Press, 1989.

Winding, Ole et al. (red.), *Arkitektskolernes byplanuddannelse, 1930-1997*, Dansk Byplanlaboratorium, Byplanhistoriske Noter 37, Copenhagen, 1997.

Wurzer, Rudolf, "Franz, Camillo und Siegfried Sitte, Ein langer Weg von der Architektur zur Stadtplanung", *Berichte zur Raumforschung und Raumplanung*, (33), 1989, p. 9-34.

Zucconi, Guido, *La Città Contesa, Dagli ingegneri sanitari agli urbanisti (1885-1942)*, Milano, Jaca Book spa, 1989, p. 123-128.

Zucconi, G., "Le destin de la Rome antique au début du siècle", in Lamy, Yvon (ed.), *L'Alchimie du patrimoine, discours et politiques*, Talence, Éditions de la Maison des Sciences de l'Homme d'Aquitaine, 1996.

Zucconi, G., *Camillo Sitte e i suoi interpreti*, Milano, Franco Angeli, 1992.